advanced

JAVA
networking

SECOND EDITION

JUL 0 9 2001

ISBN 0-13-084466-7

90000

9 780130 844668

advanced JAVA networking

SECOND EDITION

DICK STEFLIK

PRASHANT SRIDHARAN

Prentice Hall PTR
Upper Saddle River, NJ 07458
www.phptr.com

Library of Congress Cataloging-in-Publication Data

```
Steflik, Dick
     Advanced Java networking/Dick Steflik, Prashant Sridharan.—2nd ed.
     p. cm.
     First ed. by Prashant Sridharan.
     ISBN 0-13-084466-7 (pbk.)
       1. Java (Computer program language) I. Sridharan, Prashant. II.
     Sridharan, Prashant.
     Advanced java networking. III. Title.

QA76.73.J38 S83 2000
650'.0285'52762—dc21
```
                                                                    00-025838

Editorial/production supervision: *BooksCraft, Inc., Indianapolis, IN*
Cover design director: *Jerry Votta*
Cover designer: *Anthony Gemmellaro*
Manufacturing manager: *Alexis R. Heydt*
Marketing manager: *Kate Hargett*
Acquisitions editor: *Mark Taub*
Editorial assistant: *Michael Fredette*
Project coordinator: *Anne Trowbridge*

© 1997, 2000 by Prentice Hall PTR
Prentice-Hall, Inc.
Upper Saddle River, NJ 07458

Prentice Hall books are widely used by corporations and government agencies for training, marketing, and resale.

The publisher offers discounts on this book when ordered in bulk quantities.
For more information, contact:
Corporate Sales Department
Phone: 800-382-3419   Fax: 201-236-7141
E-mail: corpsales@prenhall.com

Or write:
Prentice Hall PTR
Corporate Sales Department
One Lake Street
Upper Saddle River, NJ 07458

All product names mentioned herein are the trademarks of their respective owners.

Printed in the United States of America

10 9 8 7 6 5 4 3 2 1

ISBN: 0-13-084466-7

Prentice-Hall International (UK) Limited, *London*
Prentice-Hall of Australia Pty. Limited, *Sydney*
Prentice-Hall Canada Inc., *Toronto*
Prentice-Hall Hispanoamericana, S.A., *Mexico*
Prentice-Hall of India Private Limited, *New Delhi*
Prentice-Hall of Japan, Inc., *Tokyo*
Pearson Education Asia Pte. Ltd.
Editora Prentice-Hall do Brasil, Ltda., *Rio de Janeiro*

For my Dad,
and all of my other heroes

Contents

Introduction

By now you've seen all the hype, read all the books, and discovered all the wonders of Java. But most of us still use C++ or C to create our hard-core applications, saving Java for our Web pages or leaving it to HTML jocks to fiddle with. Doing so denies us the opportunity to use a programming language that makes interfacing with a computer infinitely easier, with less frustration and faster results.

Java is much more than "Dancing Dukes" or a programming language for Web pages. It is a strong alternative to the masochistic programming of the past, in which countless months were spent debugging compared to the mere days it took to code the initial concept. Java allows us to spend more time in the conceptual phase of software design, thinking up new and creative ways to bring the vast knowledge of the Internet and its many users to our desktop.

Today, our information, and its steady flow, is garnered from the Internet and the millions of fellow computer users around the world. Up until now, you've no doubt designed programs to interface with that knowledge using C or C++. Java will change all of that. In addition to its ability to create adorable and functional user interfaces quickly and easily is Java's ability to easily connect to the Internet. Java is, after all, the Internet Language.

What This Book Is All About

Advanced Java Networking is designed to present you with a myriad of alternatives to connect your applications to the Internet. It is neither a programming reference nor a marketing brochure. We'll leave that to the geeks and marketeers to battle out. Instead, we wanted to explore each alternative without marketing bias or engineering snobbery.

One part of the engineering community will tell you that sockets are the only true way to communicate information over a network. Another segment will say that Java-only applications relying on Remote Method Invocation (RMI) will solve all your communication problems. Then, of course, there is the Common Object Request Broker Architecture (CORBA) camp. We'll discuss these alternatives, and we will also explore aspects of server-side programming in which we use a Web server as a mechanism to generate dynamic Web pages that can be connected to databases (and just about anything else). We present an honest account of each alternative and guidelines for choosing what's best for your business or programming needs. In addition to the hundreds of lines of sample code we supply to help you start from scratch with Java communication, we place an additional emphasis on migration of your existing desktop-centric applications to an Internet-ready world.

Who Should Read This Book

This book is not for beginning programmers nor is it an introductory Java text. We assume that you have a strong object-oriented programming background, preferably in Java. You should have a strong grasp of such Java fundamentals as how to create a class, how to compile and execute programs on your native system, and how to deploy Java applications. Furthermore, you should understand a good deal of the terminology of the object-oriented world.

How to Read This Book

We've conceived this book in parts, with each part further divided in chapters. Each part addresses one aspect of Internet programming, be it Java Fundamentals; Core Networking such as RMI, CORBA, or Java Database Connectivity (JDBC); Advanced Networking like Beans and Web Servers; general Java Networking information, including a special chapter on Internet security that addresses simple Applet Security restrictions; or more complex subjects such as Directory Services and JNDI. We have also included a short chapter that is an introduction to TCP/IP and how the Internet works. I have found this invaluable as the very first thing that we cover in the Internet Programming course I teach.

Finally, we want to show you that Java programming is much more than an animation floating by a Web page or interactive Internet content. Java is a language that can hold its own in the world of desktop applications and the examples in the book typically are written as applications rather than as applets. We make no effort to contain our enthusiasm for Java and certainly don't apologize for our delight in working with it. We hope that you will come to love this language as much as we have.

Conventions

We use the monospaced Courier font to denote source code and type out our code listings. If you see a Courier word within a sentence (for example "Java `Vectors` are cool"), it is the name of a class or object. We are also firm believers in the step-by-step approach to code samples. Therefore, we have generally shown the entire code listing and the additions from the previous instance of it. The changes are in Courier Bold. For example, the first time we show a code snippet, it looks like this:

```
public class Dick
{
}
```

And when we make an addition it is bolded:

```
public class Dick
{
    String loves = "Bobbie";
}
```

Also, when we show a command prompt, the part you type is also bolded:

```
%prompt% dir c:\games
```

There are sidebars throughout this book that highlight certain parts of the text, as follows.

- *Tip*s inform you of a special or unique way to accomplish something in Java networking.

- *Alert*s tell you of any bugs or "gotchas" that you should be aware of while programming your applications.

- *Note*s simply point out any information that might be useful to you in your network programming endeavors.

Fixes and Updates

We would also like to take a moment to apologize in advance for any errors. This book has been a total blast to write, and we might have gotten caught up in our own excitement here and there. In any event, we hope you have fun reading about and exploring the Java networked world!

The CD-ROM that accompanies this book (see "About the CD-ROM," at the back of the book for details regarding the CD-ROM) contains several of the applications that we have developed in this book. Additionally, a special Web page has been created. To access that Web page, please load the file named index.html, found in the root directory of the CD-ROM, into your browser. Click on the PH-PTR logo, which will take you to:

```
http://www.phptr.com
```

To err is human, and the authors of this book are as human as can be. Despite testing every example thoroughly, both from an installation and compilation perspective, problems can occur. If we find a problem with any of the programming examples in this book, we will post a fix as soon as possible on our Web site.

Thanks a Million!

About the time that Prashant Sridharan wrote the first edition of this book, I started teaching an undergraduate course titled (innocently enough) Internet Programming (CS-328). My personal goals for the course were that it would be Java based and that it would cover TCP/IP, sockets programming, the use of databases, and distributed object programming. In 1997, there were textbooks on networking and textbooks on Java, but there were no textbooks on networking using Java. I found Prashant's book in the trade book section of our local bookstore. Topically, it was almost a perfect fit for the course outline that I had developed. CS-328 began in the fall of 1997, with Prashant's book as its text. The course has been immensely popular and has been offered to a full house of juniors and seniors every semester since.

Writing the second edition of this book has been a balancing act that has been frustrating at times; rewarding in the support of colleagues, friends, and family; and—to see one's efforts in print—quite satisfying. I had never had the slightest desire to tackle the task of authoring a book, especially a technology-based book. As an adjunct faculty member in the Computer Science Department in the T. J. Watson School of Engineering and Applied Science at Binghamton University (State University of New York) for the last 25 years, I have taught many different programming courses and used texts by many authors, from many sources. I found that, after using the same textbook for several semesters, I would have collected a list of corrections and suggestions for improvements and updates in order to keep the course material current.

After four semesters (two years—a long time in the life of Java) with the first edition, I decided that the material in the book was getting a little stale. After all, Java had progressed to JDK 1.1.7 and the examples in the book were still JDK 1.0. Many of the predictions made about the course that Java would take had not materialized. The book cried out for a second edition. Like any good instructor, I phoned the publisher and eventually was put in touch with Mark Taub. I asked Mark when the second edition would be out and was told that he wished that he could tell me: Prashant no longer worked for Sun and had taken a new job at Microsoft (now there's a defection for you) and didn't have the time required for a second edition. Mark then did something I never expected and asked innocently, "You seem to know what the book needs and you've been using it for quite a while, would you be interested in tackling the second edition?"

After much soul searching and discussion with my wife and my associates in academia, Les Lander, Margaret Iwobi, and Eileene Head, I called Mark back. I told Mark that despite *my* doubts, my associates thought that it would be a good opportunity for growth (and what else did I have to do with my time?). Conveniently, they seemed to forget that I work fulltime as an Advisory Programmer at Lockheed Martin Federal Systems, Owego, New York, where I am also the site Webmaster.

It has been a busy 10 months since my first contact with Mark. I've really had fun doing this and am really grateful to Mark and Prentice Hall for giving me the opportunity to investigate and write about Java Networking (one of my favorite topics). I'm grateful, too, for the help Anne Trowbridge of Prentice Hall gave me with the CD-ROM that accompanies the book.

There are a number of people that I must credit for their help with getting this book to market. First and foremost is my wife, Bobbie, to whom I have been married for 32 years. She has patiently supported me through more projects than I care to count.

I owe special thanks to associates at Lockheed Martin: first to my manager Mary-Lou Marcotte for letting me divvy up last year's vacation in the strange way that I did to complete the writing. MaryLou, It's hard adjusting to a normal schedule again.

Scott Rush, our site electronic security guru helped me with the chapter on Java security.

My very special thanks go to Noah Ternullo. Noah is both a work associate and one our graduate students at the university. CS-328 is an undergraduate course; however, because it is an Internet-based course, it attracts a lot of graduate students. Graduate students wanting to take CS-328 must register for Independent Study, successfully complete the course, and do an additional research project in a mutually agreed upon topic in Java networking. They present their project (along with a paper) to the class at the end of the semester. At the time Noah was a graduate student in my class, Sun had just announced JINI, and he decided that that was what he wanted to research. The night that Noah did the class presentation, he and a friend dragged three PCs into the classroom from their cars and set everything up. One machine was running Linux; another, NT; and the third, W95. The presentation was not only a great demonstration of Java portability, but a really good demonstration of JINI. I was so impressed that I invited Noah to write the chapter on JINI. I hope that his contribution to this text will help him fulfill his dreams for entering a doctoral program.

Special thanks also go to my course assistant for CS-328, Edwin Chiu. Edwin has been with me through five semesters and has now earned his bachelor's degree and is currently applying to graduate schools. Edwin tackled the conversion of the Internet Appointment Calendar from Joe to the Visibroker Orb.

Additional thanks go to Peter DeAngelis of Lockheed Martin for coming to our aid when it looked like Visibroker had gotten the best of us and to Elaine Murray for her review of the general information part of the CORBA chapter.

Last, but not least I owe a real debt to the production team from BooksCraft: Don MacLaren, Bill Hartman, and Sara Black. Without Don gently reminding me of production schedules we wouldn't be at this point.

Finally, let us not forget Prashant Sridharan. I owe Prashant the greatest thanks both for writing an excellent first edition and then for changing jobs so that I could write the second edition. Much of what Prashant wrote in the first edition is still included, still applicable.

We, Prashant and I, both had a lot of fun bringing this book to you. We hope that you'll find it as useful as we found it fun.

Chapter 1

Advanced Java

▼ BASIC JAVA

▼ JAVA I/O ROUTINES

▼ INTRODUCTION TO THREADING IN JAVA

▼ OBJECT SERIALIZATION

▼ PERFORMANCE

▼ A FIRST LOOK AT JAVA NETWORKING IN ACTION

Our tour of Java networking begins with a simple and quick tutorial on several of the advanced features of the Java programming language. From there, we dive straight into the application programming interfaces (APIs) associated with connecting Java objects across disparate machines and networks. Each of these APIs has both strengths and weaknesses, and we certainly highlight the strengths while exposing the weaknesses. Finally, we describe the tools necessary to provide a safe environment for your Java applications, without sacrificing the power of the language itself. Our discussion begins here, with the fastest object-oriented tutorial this side of the Mississippi.

Basic Java

When beginners first take to C++, their primal screams can be heard for miles. Often, emergency crews are dispatched immediately to prevent the serious injuries that are typically endured when beginners are first confronted with the dreaded *pointer->. Enough to make a grown man cry, C++ is a powerful yet incredibly difficult language.

Enter Java. Java is object-oriented, modular, elegant, and—in the hands of a master—quite poetic! Java code can be beautiful and powerful, fun and exciting, and, most importantly, incredibly useful!

This chapter focuses on some of the advanced concepts you need to grasp in order to support your further endeavors using Java. Throughout the discussion, you will see sample code that highlights some of Java's inherently object-oriented features:

1

encapsulation and information hiding, modularity, inheritance, and elegance. We intend this chapter to provide you with a base of terminology, not a comprehensive Java language tutorial. Beginners should be forewarned: This book assumes you know the language.

Much of what is discussed in this chapter is the fundamental design aspects of an object-oriented language. For seasoned programmers, the urge to skip this chapter will be strong. However, many of the advanced features of Java, as well as the architectural decisions that must be made for a Java networked application, are based on the fundamental concepts we describe in this chapter and are of great importance to both veteran and rookie networking programmers alike.

Object-Oriented Design Using Java

In Java, you declare classes as a collection of operations performed on a set of data. Because data cannot be passed by reference (Java is a pointer-free language—let the cheering begin!), Java classes are needed to contain data so that it can be modified within other classes.

Classes vs. Interfaces. The prevailing assumption about Java is that you are unable to separate implementations from interfaces. However, this assumption is false. Java provides an interface component that is similar to its class counterpart except that it is not permitted to have member functions. Indeed, other objects that will implement its method and variable definitions, as illustrated in the following snippet, must reuse this interface.

```
public interface MyAdvancedJavaInterface
{
    public abstract void methodOne();
    void methodTwo();
}

public class MyAdvancedJavaClass implements MyAdvancedJavaInterface
{
    MyAdvancedJavaClass()
    {
    }

    public void methodOne()
    {
        . . .
    }

    public void methodTwo()
    {
        . . .
    }
}
```

All member functions declared within interfaces are, by default, public and abstract. This means that they are available for public consumption and must be implemented in a class before they can be used. Furthermore, interfaces do not have constructors and must be extended before they can be used.

Data Members. Good object-oriented style dictates that all data members of a class should be declared private, hidden from any operations other than those included in the class itself. But, any experienced object-oriented (OO) programmer will tell you in no uncertain terms that this is often stupid and inane for small classes. Because structs are not available in Java, you can group data into one container by using a class. Whether you subscribe to the artificially enforced private-data-member scheme of C++ or the language-enforced scheme of Smalltalk is entirely up to you. Java, however, assumes that data members are public unless otherwise instructed, as the following snippet suggests.

```
public class MyAdvancedJavaClass
{
    public int numItems;
    private int itemArray[];
};
```

Methods. Another important component of the Java class is the operation, or method. Methods allow outside classes to perform operations on the data contained in your class. By forcing other classes to utilize your data through the classes, you enforce implementation hiding. It doesn't matter to other classes that your collection of data is an array, for as far as those classes are concerned, it could be a Vector. Somewhere down the line, you could change the implementation to a HashTable if efficiency becomes a concern. The bottom line is that the classes that use your methods don't care, and don't need to know, so long as the method signature (the method name and its accompanying parameters) remains the same. The following code shows how a method can be introduced within a class.

```
public class MyAdvancedJavaClass
{
    public int numItems;
    private int itemArray[];

    public void addItem(int item )
    {
        itemArray[numItems] = item;

        numItems++;
    };
};
```

Constructors. But, there is one small problem with this example. The data is never initialized! This is where the notion of constructors comes in. Constructors set up a class for use. Classes don't need to specify a constructor; indeed a constructor is, by default, simply a function call to nothing. In this case, however, our class must call a constructor because our data needs to be initialized before it can be used.

In Java, everything is inherited from the superclass Object. All Objects must be initialized, or allocated, before they are used. For example, the declaration

```
public int numItems;
```

specifies an integer value. The int is a primitive type, but just like an Object, and therefore int needs to be initialized. We can do so in the declaration itself

```
public int numItems = 0;
```

or we can use the constructor and initialize the array as well

```
public class MyAdvancedJavaClass
{
    public int numItems;
    private int itemArray[];

    MyAdvancedJavaClass()
    {
        numItems = 0;
        itemArray = new int[10];
    }

    public void addItem(int item)
    {
        itemArray[numItems] = item;
        numItems++;
    };
};
```

Keep in mind that initializing a variable at its declaration affords little flexibility for any classes or methods that subsequently will use your object. A constructor can be modified easily to accept incoming data as well, enabling you to modify your object depending on the context of its use:

```
public class MyAdvancedJavaClass
{
    public int numItems;
    private int itemArray[];

    MyAdvancedJavaClass(int initialValue, int arrayLength)
    {
        numItems = initialValue;
        itemArray = new int[arrayLength];
    }

    public void addItem(int item)
    {
        itemArray[numItems] = item;
```

```
        numItems++;
    };
};
```

An object is allowed to have several constructors, so long as no two constructors have the same method signature (parameter list):

```java
public class MyAdvancedJavaClass
{
    public int numItems;
    private int itemArray[];

    MyAdvancedJavaClass()
    {
        numItems = 0;
        itemArray = new int[10];
    }

    MyAdvancedJavaClass(int initialValue, int arrayLength)
    {
        numItems = initialValue;
        itemArray = new int[arrayLength];
    }

    public void addItem(int item)
    {
        itemArray[numItems] = item;
        numItems++;
    };
};
```

Sometimes, confusion may arise when there are several constructors that all do the same thing, but with different sets of data. In Java, constructors are allowed to call themselves, eliminate duplicate code, and enable you to consolidate all your constructor code in one place:

```java
MyAdvancedJavaClass()
{
/*  Instead of...
    numItems = 0;
    itemArray = new int[10];
*/
    // call the more specific constructor
    this(0, 10);
}

MyAdvancedJavaClass(int initialValue, int arrayLength)
{
    numItems = initialValue;
    itemArray = new int[arrayLength];
}
```

Constructors are powerful tools. They enable you to create classes and use them dynamically without any significant hard-coding. As we will see, good constructor design is essential to an object-oriented architecture that works.

Creating and Initializing an Object.

We mentioned earlier that all Java classes inherit from the Object superclass. The constructor for an Object is invoked using the new operation. This initialization operation is used at object creation and is not used again during the object's lifecycle. One example of an object being initialized is the array initialization in our sample class. The new operation first allocates memory for the object and then invokes the object's constructor.

Because we created two kinds of constructors, our sample class can be invoked in one of two ways:

```
myAdvancedJavaInstance1 = new MyAdvancedJavaClass();
myAdvancedJavaInstance2 = new MyAdvancedJavaClass(10, 100);
```

The first instance of our class is initialized to the default values 0 and 10. When we invoked the new operation on this instance, the new operation set the values appropriately, and created a new instance of Array within the class instance. The second instance of our class set numItems to 10 and created a 100-item Array.

As you can see, this kind of dynamic class creation is very flexible. We could just as easily create another instance of our class with entirely different (or the same) initial values. This is one of the basic principles of object-oriented design espoused by languages such as Java.

Each instance of the object maintains a similar-looking but entirely different set of variables. Changing the values in one instance does not result in a change in the values of the variables of the other instances. Remember, an instance of a class is like your BMW 328i convertible. As the analogy in Figure 1-1 illustrates, it looks as cool as every other BMW 328i, but just because you modify yours to remove the annoying electronic inhibition of speed, that doesn't mean every other Beemer also will be changed!

Applying Good Object-Oriented Design Skills

Maybe you're tired of driving your minivan because your husband (or wife) makes you! What you really want is a BMW Z3 roadster. So, you drive your behemoth Toyota van down to the nearest BMW dealer and trade it in for the Z3. Now, because you have a different car, does that mean you have to learn how to drive all over again? This is obviously not the case (unless you just traded in a Volvo, in which case you have to learn to drive to begin with). That's because the world, yes the same world that brought you Elvis and Hillary Clinton, is inherently object-oriented.

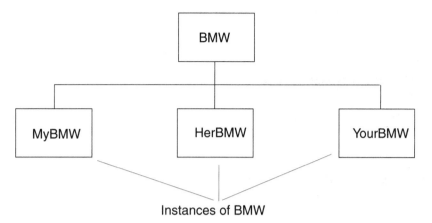

Instances of BMW

Figure 1–1 Just as customizing your BMW makes it different from other BMWs, modifying variables in one instance doesn't change them in all instances.

Inheritance. Your Z3, and every other car on the road, is a car, pure and simple. All cars have accelerators, brakes, steering wheels, and, even though you don't use them in a Beemer, turn signals. If we take this analogy further, we can say that every car inherits from the same "base class," as illustrated in Figure 1-2.

A base class is a special kind of object that forms the foundation for other classes. In Java, a base class is usually inherited later on. Think of derived classes as "kinds of" base classes. In other words, "a BMW Z3 is a kind of car." With that in mind, we create the following class structure:

```
public class Car
{
}
```

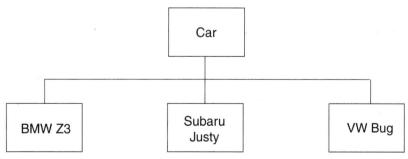

Figure 1–2 In any object-oriented environment, classes inherit the characteristics of their base classes.

```
public class BMWZ3 extends Car
{
}
```

The extends keyword tells the BMWZ3 class to utilize the properties, values, and behavior of the Car base class. But there is one small problem. Can you ever drive a generic "car"? No, because there is no such thing. There are always kinds of cars, but never a specific thing that is known simply as a car. Java gives us the notion of an "abstract base class."

An abstract base class is, quite simply, a class that must be inherited from. It can never be used as a stand-alone class. In Java, the abstract keyword gives a class this unique property.

```
public abstract class Car
{
    int topSpeed;
}
public class BMWZ3 extends Car
{
}
```

In this situation, the Car class can never be instantiated or used as is. It must be inherited. When the BMWZ3 class inherits from Car, it also obtains all the variables and methods within the Car class. So, our BMWZ3 class gets to use top-Speed as if it were its own member variable.

Somewhere in your code you might want to check what type of variable you are using. Java provides the instanceof keyword to enable you to inquire as to what the abstract base class of an object is. For example, the following two code snippets would return the value true:

```
BMWZ3 bmwVariable;
FordTaurus fordVariable;

if(bmwVariable instanceof Car) . . .

if (fordVariable instanceof Object) . . .
```

whereas the following code snippet would return the value false.

```
if(bmwVariable instanceof PandaBear)
```

Notice that Java's inheritance model is quite simple. In C++, objects are allowed to inherit from one or more abstract base classes and can be made to inherit the implementation of those interfaces as well. Java, as a matter of simplicity, does not allow this, nor does it plan to at any time in the future. There are ways to get around multiple implementation inheritance, but they do not really involve inheritance at all. The bottom line is that if you need to use multiple implementation inheritance, you probably won't want to use Java.

Code Reuse. Let's say that you are putting together your son's bicycle on Christmas morning. The instructions call for you to use a Phillips-head screwdriver. You take the screwdriver out of the toolbox, use it, and put it back. A few minutes later, you need the screwdriver again. Surely you would use the same screwdriver, not go to the hardware store and buy a new one!

Likewise, code reuse is of vital importance to the programmer on a tight schedule. You will need to streamline your code so that you can distribute commonly used tasks to specific modules. For example, many of the online demonstrations we provide with this book include animation examples. Rather than recreate the animation routines, we reused the same set of animation tools we developed beforehand. Because we coded the animators with reuse in mind, we were able to take advantage of a strong interface design and an effective inheritance scheme.

OOP—Strong, Efficient, and Effective

Whew! Whether this is your first foray using the Java language or your 101st, all of your design begins in this one place. There are three steps to creating an object that you can use time and again:

1. Strong interface design
2. Efficient class implementation
3. Effective inheritance

With the fundamentals of object-oriented programming under your belt, you are ready to explore the simplicity with which you can create programs in Java that handle input and output. The Java I/O routines are not only easy, but extremely powerful. Bringing your C++ I/O to Java will result in as little functional loss as migrating object-oriented design techniques to Java from C++.

Java I/O Routines

Java provides several tools for the input and output of data, ranging from the Abstract Window Toolkit (AWT) or the Swing Components to the core System functions of Java classes. The AWT is exactly what it says it is: a set of components for designing windows and graphical user interfaces that uses the peer components of the underlying operating system for their implementation. The Swing Components do the same thing, but rather than using the peer components of the host operation system, all the components are 100% pure Java components and can take on the look and feel of the components of the host operating system or have their own "custom" look and feel. The core System classes are built-in routines for gathering and disseminating information from Java objects.

This section highlights some of the input and output routines provided by the core Java capabilities as well as the Swing Components and Abstract Window

Toolkit. As we delve further into the realm of networked programming, we will discover that much of what drives our decisions on a networked architecture will be that which is detailed in this section. Because input and output are the most important actions a computer program performs, we must develop a strong understanding of the I/O capabilities and limitations of Java.

Streams

Imagine your grandfather fishing in a stream. He knows that as long as he stays there, he's going to get a bite. Somewhere, somehow, sometime a fish is going to come down that stream, and your grandfather is going to get it.

Just as your grandfather is the consumer of fish, your applications are either consumers or providers of data. In Java, all input and output routines are handled through streams. An input stream is simply a flow of data, just as your grandfather's stream is a flow of fish. You can write your application to fish for data out of your input stream and eventually to produce data as well. When your application spits out information, it does so through a stream. This time, your application is the producer, and the consumer is another application or device down the line.

Java provides several different kinds of streams, each designed to handle a different kind of data. The standard input and output streams form the basis for all the others. InputStream and OutputStream are both available for you to use as is, or you can derive more complicated stream schemes from them. In order to create the other kinds of Java streams, first you must create and define the basic streams.

Perhaps the most-used stream formats are the DataInputStream and the DataOutputStream. Both of these streams enable you to read or write primitive data types, giving you the flexibility within your application to control the results of your application's execution. Without this kind of functionality, you would have to write specific bytes rather than reading specific data.

File buffers are a method commonly used to increase performance in an input/output scheme. BufferedInputStreams and BufferedOutputStreams read in chunks of data (the size of which you can define) at a time. When you read from or write to the buffered streams, you are actually playing with the buffer, not the actual data in the stream. Occasionally, you must flush the buffers to make sure that all the data in the buffer is completely read from or written to the file system.

Sometimes you will want to exchange information with another application using a stream. In this case, you can set up a pipe. A pipe is a two-way stream, sort of. The input end of a pipe in one application is directly connected to the output end of the same pipe on another application. If you write to the input of the pipe, you will read the same exact data at the pipe's output end. As you can see in Figure 1-3, this is a pretty nifty way to promote interapplication communication.

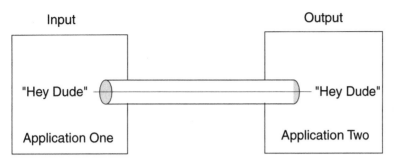

Figure 1-3 Pipes enable interaction between two or more applications.

Last, you will eventually want to fiddle with files on your local file system. The FileInputStream and FileOutputStream enable you to open, read, and write files as we will show you in a moment. Remember that Java has strict restrictions on applet security, so most file streams can be manipulated only by applications. For more information, consult Chapter 13, "Java and Security."

The Java Core System

In Java, applications are allowed to write to the standard output devices on a machine. If you use a Web browser such as Netscape, the standard output to which Java writes is the "Java Console" mentioned in one of Navigator's windows. If you write a Java application (i.e., a stand-alone applet), the standard output device is the command line from which you execute the program.

The System Class. One of the classes Java includes in every applet or application, whether you specify that it do so or not, is the System class. The System class provides support for input/output (I/O) using the Java console; you are to provide the ability to write to the console, read from the console, and write errors to the user. The Java console is provided in two ways, one for browsers and one for applications. In the browser environment the console is a separate browser window that has controls for scrolling and clearing. For applications run from the operating system (OS) command line, the console is the text interface you see and suffers the same problems as the text base OS environment (lack of scrolling backwards). The Java console is really intended to provide the same level of user interactivity as the C++ cin, cout, and cerr objects. The names of the standard Java streams are in, out, and err; these names can be changed using the System classes setIn, setOut, and setErr methods. Changing the names of these streams can only be done by the SecurityManager.

Input Using the System Class. Input in the System class is actually handled by the InputStream class contained in the Java I/O routines. System.in is an object of type InputStream that is created, maintained, and initialized by the System class. In other words, it's yours for the taking; you don't have to do a thing to use it.

The InputStream class assumes that you will be reading from the standard input stream (the keyboard you are sitting at). A stream is a sequence of characters retrieved from somewhere. The standard input stream is the location that your operating system uses to get data from you. Because streams are defined as characters from a source, it is entirely conceivable that a stream could be a file, a modem, a microphone, or even a connection to another process running on your computer or another computer. As a matter of fact, Java treats files and other peripherals as streams. This abstraction of a stream simplifies I/O programming by reducing all I/O to a stream.

So, how do you get input from the user? Simply use the System class's input stream to get the information you require. The input stream is an object with several methods to facilitate data input. For example, there are primitive, yet useful, routines to get characters and strings, to read integers and other numbers, and even to get a stream of unfiltered and untranslated bytes. Deciding which routine to use is simply a matter of which kind of data you wish to read. In our example, we will read and write strings:

```
public class InputOutputTest()
{
    String str;     //private data

    public void getInput(){
        // read a string from the Java console keyboard (sysin)
        str = System.in.getln();
    }
}
```

Output Using the System Class. As with input, output is handled through streams. How can output be a stream if a stream is a sequence of characters from a source? Well, the source is your application, and the stream is routed to a device known as the standard output. The standard output is usually your monitor, but it could be other things as well. Most notably, the standard output is set to be the Java console when an applet runs within Netscape Navigator. When you run the following example from within an applet, watch your Java console for the output. If you run it from within an application, the output should show up on the command line.

```
public class InputOutputTest(){
    String str;       // class data

    public void getInput(){
        // read a string from the keyboard
        str = System.in.getln();
```

```
    }
    public void drawOutput(){
        // write a string to the console screen
        System.out.println(str);
    }
}
```

Files

The stream classes would be pretty useless if you couldn't manipulate files as well. There are several security mechanisms defined in the security model used by Java-capable browsers for running applets. These mechanisms prevent unguarded file access and will be discussed in more depth in Chapter 13, "Java and Security." But for now, simply assume that as long as you are not writing an applet, you will be able to manipulate files. In the purest sense, standard input and output are files. As such, they are sometimes subject to the same applet security restrictions, so be forewarned.

The Basics. When reading and writing to and from files, there are three steps that must be followed:

1. Open the file for reading or writing.

2. Read or write from the file.

3. Close the file.

It is important to do each step. Failing to open a file will, obviously, prevent you from reading. But perhaps not as intuitively, you must still close the file or you may wreck your file system. Every application is allowed a certain number of file descriptors (handles) that maintain the status of a file. If you run out of available file descriptors, you will no longer be able to open any other files. The following snippet uses the FileReader class to read the contents of a file specified on the command line and the PrintWriter class to write it to the Java console:

```
import java.io.*;
public class ShowFile{
  public static void main(String args[]){
  try{
    FileReader fin = new FileReader(args[0]);
    PrintWriter consoleOut = new PrintWriter(System.out, true);
    char c[] = new char[512];
    int count = 0;
    while ((count = fin.read(c)) != -1)
      consoleOut.write(c,0,count);
    consoleOut.flush();
    consoleOut.close();
    fin.close();
```

```
   }
   catch(FileNotFoundException e){
      System.out.println(e.toString());
   }
   catch(IOException e) {
      System.out.println(e.toString());
   }
}
```

When opening a file, you have three options. You can open the file for reading so you can extract data from it, but you will be prevented from writing to the file unless you close it and open it for writing. You can open it for writing, but you will be prevented from reading from it. Finally, you can append to a file, which is similar to writing except that it preserves any data already in the file.

Taking Files One Step Further. So what do files have to do with networked computing? Well, the diagram in Figure 1-4 offers a graphical representation of input and output streams. Remember that streams are merely interfaces to collections of data. What if that data is located on a network connection rather than in a flat file or a keyboard?

The standard interface to a network in the computer world is a socket. A socket is a connection between processes across a network. The processes can be located on the same physical machine, the same Local Area Network, or even across the world on different LANs. The three basic steps still apply:

1. Open a connection to the remote process.

2. Read or write data.

3. Close the connection.

Again, as with file manipulation, you can use the InputStream and OutputStream objects to interface to the socket. In fact, sockets are nothing but files in the purest

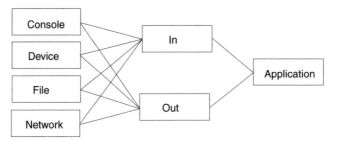

Figure 1–4 With Java, your input or output need not reside on the same physical machine on which your application is running.

sense. The advantage to this file-centric hierarchy is perhaps not as obvious as it should be. In the end, all three forms of input sources are completely interchangeable. You should not write your applications to be specific to a specific kind of file. In an object-oriented design, the objects you create should simply know that they will have to read or write data down the line.

The Abstract Window Toolkit and Swing Classes

The AWT is a half-baked attempt to create a user interface toolbox for programmers. Because all the various classes, containers, and widgets in the toolkit are capable of being used both in the applets embedded in Web pages and in the stand-alone applications on your desktop, it is a powerfully extensible tool. At the heart of this kind of flexibility is the idea that the toolkit is an abstraction—in other words, a layer on top of your current windowing system. This abstraction is more understandable if you know the background behind it. When Sun was courting its early customers, Netscape insisted that the Java Virtual Machine (JVM) included in its browser must create widgets that had the exact look and feel of the host operating system's widgets. Since "Swing" wasn't yet a gleam in its father's eye, the only way to accomplish this was to use the peer components of the host operating system. Thus we can truly say that the AWT is an abstraction of the windowing system of the operating system.

Your current windowing system may be anything from X11/Motif to Windows 95's own window system. In any event, the AWT ensures that native calls are made to these windowing systems in order to allow applications to run on top of the desktop. For applets within a Web page, the browser manufacturer essentially creates a windowing system that renders the AWT's widgets within itself.

The end result of all this is that eventually a native call is made for each action taken by the AWT. Your applications need not be aware of this, for Java's platform independence ensures that, no matter the platform on which you execute bytecodes, the results will be identical.

One of the problems with this approach to user interface (UI) implementation is that when making a UI that must be rendered the same way on all the platforms it is to be targeted to, small differences in the way that components are rendered on each of the targeted systems may cause the overall effect to have problems. For instance, a UI having several closely aligned text fields may look good on Windows platforms but appear overlayed on UNIX machines.

One of the major complaints about the AWT by people used to building user interfaces for enterprise applications was that it had a relatively small set of widgets and low functionality. AWT provided only slightly more functionality than the widgets provided in HTML's forms controls. In early 1997 the work on JDK

1.1 incorporated a number of new pieces including Netscape Corporation's Internet Foundation Classes (IFC), components from IBM's Taligent Division, and Lighthouse Design. The first release of Swing 1.0 in early 1998 contained almost 250 classes and 80 interfaces. The art of user interface creation had been raised to a new level and was now able to go head to head with platform-specific development tools.

The Java 1.2 platform provides a set of components (Swing) that eliminate this problem by eliminating the use of peer components. The Swing components are pure Java and will render reliably on all host platforms. With Swing the native look and feel of Windows, Motif, or Mac widgets are options from a predefined list of look and feels that are extensible by the user.

Input Alternatives. The AWT and Swing contain widgets designed to elicit response from the user. From simple text areas to more complex dialog boxes, each one is designed to funnel information from the user's keyboard to your application. Most of them are very easy to use and program, so we'll leave it to the several Java books on the market to provide you with a reference and a basic list and explanation of the elements that are included.

Remember that input in a windowing system is not limited to typing words on the screen. Every push button, checkbox, or scroll bar event is a form of input that you may or may not choose to deal with. Every AWT class has some way or another of checking the status of its input mechanism. For example, your scroll bar will be able to tell you if it has been moved. You may choose then to take some action, or let the AWT do it for you. There is no need to implement scrolling text for a scroll bar when the AWT is fully capable of doing it.

Output Alternatives. Obviously, the easiest way to display output with the AWT is to display something graphically. The AWT supports simple graphics routines for drawing, as well as for the usual suite of labels, multimedia, and widget manipulation. Output is significantly easier using the AWT. Without the toolkit, you would have to manage not only what to do with the input you receive, but also how to display your response.

I/O in Short

Input and output are at the heart of every program you create. No matter what the objective of your application, somehow you will need either to get a response from the user, to display a response, or maybe even both. To take things one step farther, your input or output need not reside on the same physical machine as that on which your application is running. Indeed, that is the very subject of this book. By stretching your applications to fit a networked model, you will be able to take full advantage of the input and output schemes offered to you by Java.

When your applications receive several inputs, they will often get inundated with processing. To alleviate this, Java provides a full suite of threading utilities, which we discuss in the next section. Threads allow your applications to execute steps in parallel. So, when your application receives two different inputs simultaneously, you can use threads to simultaneously resolve them and produce output.

Introduction to Threading in Java

Multithreaded (MT) programs are the current rage in computer science. Books upon books upon books have been written that describe the benefits of threading, the threading features inherent in various operating systems, and the various forms of threaded architectures.

So, what on earth are threads? How can you use them in your programs? Will threading continue to work in those applications that run native on operating systems that do not support threading? What does it mean to be MT-safe, and how do you design an MT-safe program?

The entire realm of multithreaded and multitasked programming transcends the scope of this book. We will confer that knowledge of the topic that is directly related to the ideas of networked programming and, in cases where more research may be warranted, direct you to the appropriate resources.

What Are Threads?

Let's say you're sitting in your living room watching another Washington Redskins victory. You get bored watching the massacre of the Dallas Cowboys, and you decide that you would like to see the 49ers game in progress. In the good old days, you would have to actually switch channels and choose between one or the other. But, these days, televisions have Picture-in-Picture (PIP) capability. By pressing the PIP button on your trusty remote control, you can watch the Redskins demolish the Cowboys on a little box in the corner of the TV while watching the 49ers on the rest of the screen.

This is a prime example of multithreaded programming. The little screen and the big screen share resources (in this case, the area of the full television screen), but they are not able to affect one another. In the areas in which the two games collide, one screen gives way to another.

Threads in Your Computer. In the computer world, multithreaded applications exist similarly to those in the television world. They share the same area, in our case the television screen, in reality the physical process in which the application resides and is permitted to execute. Multithreaded applications are able to execute independent pieces of code simultaneously. Each of these independently executing pieces of code is known as a thread.

Threads are implemented differently by different operating systems. In Solaris, for example, threads are defined and maintained in the user environment. The operating system maintains responsibility over the process, regardless of what the process decides to do with itself. In a sense, the operating system treats the process as an object. The OS only cares about the interface to the process, or how it starts up, shuts down, begins execution, and performs similar operations. It has no feelings whatsoever about how the process handles information.

In fact, this is the fundamental concept of threads. Threads exist as a user-created and user-managed aspect of a program. The operating system could care less if there are multiple threads in the executable or if it is single threaded. Furthermore, the operating system will not help you resolve conflicts. All it cares about is the integrity of the process, not about what goes on inside it.

Handling Conflicts. Let's say you have a couple of threads prancing along merrily within your application. Suddenly, they both access the same piece of data at the same time. This results in what is known as concurrent access. Concurrent access errors occur as a result of poor thread management on the part of the main application.

Access errors occur in everyday life, too. Let's say you've scheduled an appointment from eleven in the morning to one in the afternoon. Carelessly, you forgot your all-important staff meeting at twelve-thirty. Obviously, you can't be in two places at once! The end result is that you've placed yourself in two meetings. The threads within our applications similarly have accessed identical data at the same time.

When creating a thread, the first thing you must determine is what data that thread will touch. You then have to fence off that data so that only one possible thread can ever touch it at any given moment. In Solaris, this is done with a concept called mutual exclusion. A mutual exclusion lock placed around your data ensures that it will never be permitted to enter a concurrent access situation.

Imagine a relay team of four people competing at the upcoming Olympics. The first runner on the relay team is given a baton that must be passed to a teammate before that teammate is allowed to run. If the teammate runs without the baton, she is disqualified. However, if the baton is passed properly, the runner can continue until she arrives at the finish line or must pass the baton to another teammate.

Likewise, different threads can obtain the lock around the data so long as the lock is available. If the lock is unavailable, the thread must wait, effectively suspending itself, until the lock is available. There are specific settings to allow threads to continue without waiting, but these settings are beyond the scope of this book. If one thread grabs a lock but never lets go, then it will have deadlocked the entire application. When your methods obtain a thread, make sure that they give it up somehow. Otherwise, the rest of your application will wait for a lock that will never come free.

For more information on threads, consult the excellent Sun Microsystems title, *Threads Primer* by Bill Lewis and Daniel J. Berg.

Threading in Java

Creating and debugging threads in Java is considerably simpler than doing so in C++. Deadlocks in Java are much easier to prevent, and a ton more intuitive. But multithreaded applications in Java are not as robust or as powerful as their C++ counterparts. In short, there are tradeoffs to threading in Java, for it is not an all-encompassing answer to the multithreading question.

What threads in Java do is provide you, the application programmer, with a consistent interface to the threads of the underlying host environment. Anything that may be "quirky" in the threads of the hosting operating system will still be there. This consistency of API is important as our target environment is any platform that there is a JVM written for, and the consistency helps make our code more portable and reusable.

Java treats threads as user-level entities as well. A Java applet or application runs within a process space defined in the Java Virtual Machine. The JVM allocates processes and the resources for each process and allows the applet or application to define how that process space is used. Java programs that implement threads must do so using the Thread class or a derivative thereof.

The Thread Class. Java's language hierarchy, which includes the likes of Strings, Integers, and so on, also contains a powerful, yet incredibly simple Thread object that you can implement within your programs. The Thread class provides all the functionality necessary for you to create fully multithreaded and MT-safe applications using the Java language.

NOTE: Two approaches to spawning threads in Java are worth noting, as outlined in the following sections. Many of our networking examples later on will make heavy use of one or the other method. As always, there are tradeoffs and benefits for each architectural decision you make.

Using the Entire Class As a Thread. The first method we could employ involves spawning threads in which an entire class can reside. For example, we spawn a thread and then create a runnable class and attach it to the thread. Now the entire class exists within the thread and the stream of execution for that class is maintained by the thread. If the thread is destroyed, the stream of execution is likewise destroyed.

The biggest advantage to this method is that the class need not know anything about how it is to be implemented. Take a look at the following example:

```
public class Animator extends Panel implements Runnable
{
    Animator() { ... }
    public void run() { ... }
}
public class AnimatorManager
{
    Animator animations[];
    Thread animationThreads[];

    AnimatorManager() { ... }
    public void createAnimation(
        Animator anim
    )
    {
        // first spawn a thread for the class
        // now let the thread continue...
    }
}
```

The AnimatorManager class is responsible for creating a series of Animator objects, spawning a thread for the object to execute in and shutting down, suspending, resuming, or inquiring about the status of the thread. Note how the Animator does not know or care whether it will be in a thread of execution or in an entire process. It is a runnable class, meaning that whatever is contained within the run function will be executed if the parent process or thread allows.

The object is created normally, and our AnimatorManager assumes that the object is already created. The Thread is created, but the object is passed to it as a parameter. The corresponding constructor in the Thread class knows that the runnable object will reside solely within its thread of control.

```
public class AnimatorManager
{
    Animator animations[];
    Thread animationThreads[];

    AnimatorManager() { ... }
    public void createAnimation(
        Animator anim
    )
```

```
    {
        // first spawn a thread for the class
        animationThreads[currentThreadCount] = new Thread(anim);

        // now let the thread continue...
        animationThreads[currentThreadCount].start();
    }
}
```

NOTE: Remember that Java is inherently object-oriented, so this kind of thread creation is quite within the reach of the language. There is no funny business going on here. A thread is created and an object is told to live within it. It is actually quite intuitive in an object-oriented sense. The next method hearkens back to the days of structured programming.

Inheriting from the Thread Class. The second way to implement threads is to create a class that inherits from the Thread class. In the first method, we created an object that was a free-standing object in its own right. In this case, we will create an object that is a Thread object from the beginning. In essence, the JVM treats both methods as similar and reasonable means to spawning threaded objects, and both are acceptable from a style perspective.

Inheriting from the Thread class is actually quite simple. Instead of extending from Panel or Applet, your class simply extends from Thread. In your init method or constructor, you must initialize the thread as well. Obviously, your class must be aware that it is running in a thread.

The thread code for a class that inherits from Thread is in the Run method. As in a class that implements Runnable, inheriting from Thread automatically enables you to implement the `run` method. Any code you want to manage the thread should be placed there. If you need to make the thread sleep or suspend, that's where you should place it.

The difference, however, between extending Thread and implementing Runnable is that when you inherit from Thread, your entire class is a thread. The thread must be started and stopped from within the class, unlike the other method in which the thread controls are outside the class itself (see Figure 1-5).

Take a look at the following example, and notice how the constructor calls the `start` method or the thread:

```
public class Animator extends Thread
{
    Animator()
    {
```

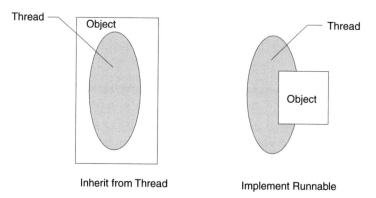

Inherit from Thread   Implement Runnable

Figure 1–5 Thread controls are accessed from differ-ent locations depending on the method chosen.

```
        start();
    }
    public void run() { ... }
}
```

As you can see, the class is clearly a threaded class. What happens if you want to use the class's methodology without using threads? You'll have to create a new class that doesn't use threads, or you'll have to revert to the first method. Implementing Runnable and placing your thread controls outside the target class is the preferred way of using threads, but inheriting from threads can be particularly useful for highly modular code in which you want to package an entire object that does not rely on anything else.

Thread Controls. A thread has several control methods that affect its behavior. Simply starting and stopping a thread's execution are but two of the many tools available to you to manipulate how programs execute. For example, on several occasions, you will want to pause a thread's execution, and eventually resume it.

The Thread class offers us a rich set of methods for controlling threads:

1. `start`
2. `stop`
3. `suspend` (deprecated in JDK 1.2)
4. `resume` (deprecated in JDK 1.2)
5. `sleep`
6. `destroy`
7. `yield`
8. `join`

9. `run`

10. `isAlive`

The `start` method does exactly what it says. It tells the thread that it may begin execution of all the steps contained in the `run` method. The `run` method itself may call any of the preceding thread controls, but obviously you will want to restart the thread somewhere if the `run` method decides to suspend it!

The `stop` routine terminates the thread and prevents the `run` method from executing any further steps. It does not, however, shut down any subthreads that it may have created. You must be careful and make sure that every thread you create eventually either terminates on its own or is terminated by its parent. Otherwise, you could very well have several threads executing and consuming resources long after the applet or application has terminated.

The `suspend` and `resume` routines are pretty self-explanatory. When `suspend` is called, the thread ceases execution of its `run` method until `resume` is called somewhere down the line. If your parent thread needs to inquire about the current running status of a thread, it may call the `isAlive` method and find out if the thread is stopped. Obviously, if the thread isn't stopped, and it isn't running, it must be suspended. Note, in JDK 1.2 `suspend` and `resume` are deprecated due to problems with deadlock situation occurring. When a thread has locked a system resource and is then suspended, other threads cannot access the resource until the `suspend` is resumed. If the thread that is supposed to do the `resume` first tries to lock the resource, a deadlock occurs.

The `join` method causes the currently executing thread to wait until it has stopped; the current thread then blocks until:

1. The currently executing thread is interrupted.

2. The currently executing thread is terminated.

3. The specified timeout has expired; if a time is not specified, the thread will wait indefinitely.

Last, the `sleep` method tells the thread to pause for a given number of milliseconds. It is particularly useful for the clock because we want it to "tick" every second.

The state diagram in Figure 1-6 should make clear the thread timing you need to be aware of. Remember that, before anything can be done to a thread, you must call `start` on it. Once you are finished with the thread of execution, you must call `stop`.

Synchronized Methods. Conflict handling within Java is implemented using method synchronization. If you have data that could potentially deadlock between two threads, then you must declare the functions in which the data is

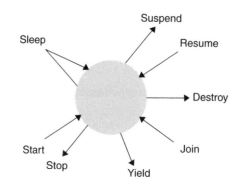

Figure 1–6 The control methods
that affect a thread's behavior.

modified as synchronized. Java prevents multiple threads from entering the synchronized methods and thereby eliminates the possibility of deadlock.

Creating a synchronized method is actually quite easy. It is simply a matter of declaring that the function will be synchronized in the method signature, as can be seen in the following snippet.

```
public class ThreadClass
{
    int data;
    ...
    public void synchronized addToData(
        int addend
    )
    {
        data += addend;
    }
    ...
}
```

There are a couple of important caveats to synchronized functions. Because multiple threads may require entry to a synchronized function, it is better to keep any function that is declared as synchronized short and sweet. When one thread enters a synchronized function, keeping its time spent in the function to a minimum will keep your programs running smoothly. After all, the idea behind threading is to get your programs to execute steps in parallel, not to spawn threads that end up waiting forever for each other to finish with the data.

yield( ), wait( ), and notify( ). In an application with multiple threads, often you will have many threads competing with one another for resources. One way to allocate those resources effectively is to set the relative priorities of each thread.

We will discuss that in a moment, but right now let's discuss some of the specific steps you can take within the thread itself. Remember that when threads execute, they all share the same process space in which the application resides. Like a bunch of kids forced to share a toy, the threads compete and vie for control of the process. Like any good parent, however, you have several tools at your disposal to make sure the threads cooperate.

Sometimes you will want to control entry into a function and label the function as synchronized. Even though the function is long, you want to yield control of the function pretty early on. You can call the `notify` method to tell the parent thread that you are finished with the synchronized lock.

In order to make a thread stand by for a `notify` message, you must add the `wait` method to the thread's execution routines. The `notify` method is called somewhere in an executing thread. Once `notify` is called, any thread awaiting execution on a `wait` call automatically proceeds.

Another way to give up the process space in which a thread runs is to call the `yield` routine specifically. When `yield` is called within a thread, the thread gives up any scheduling priority, process space, or claim to its current turn in the sharing cycle.

Thread Priorities

TIP: A more elegant, yet more confusing, way to control threads is by setting their priority. Obviously, when you set a thread to have a high priority, it gets first crack at any processing time and resources. You should be careful and judicious in setting thread priorities. Even with the best of intentions, you could very well defeat the purpose of using threads to begin with should you set every thread at a high priority.

In Java, threads may have one of three priorities: minimum, normal, and maximum. You may set the priority using the `setPriority` method of the Thread class and retrieve the priority of any thread by using the `getPriority` method, like so:

```
Thread threadOne;
Thread threadTwo;
Thread threadThree;

threadOne.setPriority(Thread.MIN_PRIORITY);
threadTwo.setPriority(Thread.NORM_PRIORITY);
threadThree.setPriority(Thread.MAX_PRIORITY);
```

Because threads are a powerful and underused aspect of most Java programs, thread scheduling and prioritizing is a flexible and equally powerful way to control how your applications behave and execute.

Daemon Threads. There are two kinds of threads. So far we have discussed application threads, which are tied to the process and directly contribute to the running of the application. Daemon threads, on the other hand, are used for background tasks that happen every so often within a thread's execution. Normally, an application will run until all the threads have finished their execution. However, if the only remaining threads are daemon threads, the application will exit anyway.

Java itself has several daemon threads running in the background of every application. Java's garbage collection is controlled by daemon threads known in computer science parlance as reaper threads, or threads that run through an application looking for dead weight. In the garbage collection thread's case, the dead weight happens to be unused but allocated memory.

If your application needs to set up a daemon thread, simply call the `setDaemon` method of the thread, as shown in the following snippet. The application in which the thread resides will know to ignore that thread if it needs to execute, and program execution will continue normally.

```
Thread t = new Thread(myClass);
t.setDaemon(true);
```

Thread Summary

Threads are one way in which you can affect the behavior of an object. Serialization is another. Serialization allows you to store your objects as strings. When we use threads, we do so to change how it behaves when it is running. Serialization does not allow us to preserve that runtime behavior, only the class's static behavior and characteristics. Whenever you reconstruct a serialized class, only your class will be reconstituted correctly, not any of the threads. Therefore, it is important that your threads be as object-oriented as possible so that they can store their state when necessary.

Object Serialization

Serialization is a concept that enables you to store and retrieve objects, as well as to send full-fledged objects "over the wire" to other applications. The reason serialization is of such vital importance to Java should be clear: without it, distributed applications would not be able to send objects to each other. That means that only simple types such as `int` and `char` would be allowed in parameter signatures, and complex objects would be limited in what they could do. It's sort of like saying you would have to talk like a 3-year-old whenever you spoke with your boss. You want to have a complex conversation, but you are limited in what you can say.

What Is Serialization?

Without some form of object storage, Java objects can only be transient. There would be no way to maintain a persistent state in an object from one invocation to another. However, serialization can be used for more purposes than maintaining persistence. The RMI system uses object serialization to convert objects to a form that can be sent over a communication mechanism.

When an object is serialized, it is converted to a stream of characters. Those characters can be sent over the wire to another location. Parameters passed in remote objects are automatically translated into serialized representation. Once an object is serialized, it can be safely sent via a communication method to a remote location.

The serialization routines have been incorporated into the standard Java Object class with several routines to facilitate the writing and reading of a secured representation. There are several security concerns that you must be aware of, and we will discuss those in a moment. Without object serialization, Java could never truly be an effective Internet language.

Handling Object Relationships

An important consideration of the object serialization facilities is that the entire process is executed in a manner transparent to any APIs or user intervention. In other words, you need not write any code to utilize serialization routines. When writing an object, the serialization routines must be sure to do so in a manner that allows full reconstruction of the object at a later time. Not only must the class structure be saved, but the values of each member of the structure must be saved as well. If you had a class with the following representation:

```
public class CuteBrownBear
{
    Color eyeColor;
    float heightInches;
    float weightPounds;
}
```

It must be saved so that the values of eyeColor, heightInches, and weightPounds are preserved and can be restored once the reading functions are invoked. Sometimes, however, things can become complicated when objects begin to refer to one another. For example, the following class contains CuteBrownBear as well as several other toy objects that we must save as well:

```
public class ToyBox
{
    CuteBrownBear bearArray[5];
    ActionFigure actionFigureArray[5];
}
```

The serialization routines must not only serialize the ToyBox object, but the Cute-BrownBear objects and ActionFigure objects as well. To handle this kind of situation, the serialization routines traverse the objects it is asked to write or read. As it traverses an object representation, it serializes any new objects automatically. If, down the line, it finds another object of a type already serialized, it merely modifies the earlier serialized representation to refer to the new instance. In this manner, serialized objects are compact and efficient without much duplicated code.

For example, when we need to serialize the ToyBox object, the serialization routines first serialize CuteBrownBear in array position one. Array positions two through five are not serialized on their own; rather the original serialized representation is modified to point to their locations and values. So, the final serialized object has one reference to the CuteBrownBear object, plus five sets of data values.

The Output Streams

Serialization output is handled through the ObjectOutputStream. Serialization calls refer to the `writeObject` method contained within the stream, passing it the instance of the object to be serialized. The stream first checks to see whether another instance of the same object type has been previously serialized. If it has, the routines handle it as we discussed in the previous section, merely placing the new values alongside the representation. If, however, the object has yet to be serialized, the routines create a new serialized representation and place the values next to it.

Most serialization is handled transparently. But an object may at any time begin to handle its own serialization by reimplementing the `writeObject` method. The `writeObject` method is part of every Object class and can be overridden on command. If you need a finer grained serialized representation, or would like to include some kind of encryption or other technique between serialization endpoints, this is where and how you do it.

As an example, let us instantiate a CuteBrownBear object and serialize it:

```
// create the streams here . . .
FileOutputStream fileOut = new FileOutputStream("filename");
ObjectOutputStream objectOut = new ObjectOutputStream(fileOut);

// instantiate the new bear object
CuteBrownBear bear = new CuteBrownBear();

// serialize the bear
objectOut.writeObject(bear);
```

Handling Object Webs

An object web is a complex relationship between two or more objects in which objects refer to other objects that may eventually refer back to it. If you were to serialize such an object representation, you could potentially be caught in an infinite loop. Let's say we had a system of roads between three cities, Seattle, Washington, DC, and San Francisco. We want to take an end-of-summer road trip and visit each city. The only instruction the auto association gave us was "if you hit one of these three roads, follow it until it ends."

Following that logic, we would start at San Francisco, go to Seattle, visit the Redskins, come back to the Golden Gate, and go to Seattle, and so on (see Figure 1-7).

Likewise, if we were to serialize San Francisco, then Seattle, followed by Washington, DC, and keep following the path back to San Francisco, we would end up following the same loop an infinite number of times. This lattice arrangement ensures that a simple tree-based algorithm will not suffice. Java's object serialization routine accounts for this kind of structure in the same manner that it handles multiple objects of the same type in the same stream.

Because of these object webs, any serialization must take into account those objects that have already been serialized. So, in addition to the serialization methods, Java's object serialization routines also keep track of the object's serialized state. Moreover, Java also keeps track of whether object types have been serialized as well. In so doing, it can keep track of the data contained in the object, not the entire object itself.

Reading Objects

Reading objects is a matter of taking the serialized representation and reversing the process that created them in the first place. Remember to handle your deserialization in the same order as your serialization, traversing any trees in a similar fashion. The objective is to reconstruct the original object.

The deserialization routines are handled with a corresponding ObjectInputStream and the `readObject` method contained therein.

Once again, to obtain control over serialization routines for your object, you need to override and reimplement the `writeObject` and `readObject` routines.

Figure 1-7 An example of serialization in which you need to store objects that are linked by a circuitous route.

Security and Fingerprinting

Sometimes objects can be serialized surreptitiously by other objects linked in by your application. If your object does things that you would prefer to keep private and unknown to the world, then you need to disable your objects. Serialization can be disabled for an object by adding the private transient tag to the class definition:

```
private transient class CuteBrownBear
{
    . . .
}
```

Or the object itself can override the serialization routines and return a NoAccess Exception. The NoAccessException tells any object that attempts to serialize your implementation that it may not do so. Furthermore, it gives a sufficient debugging warning to any applications that may reuse your object.

```
public class CuteBrownBear
{
    . . . the rest of the CuteBrownBear class goes here . . .
    public void writeObject(. . .) throws NoAccessException
    {
    }
    public void readObject(. . .) throws NoAccessException
    {
    }
}
```

Serialization Overview

Java automatically handles its own object serialization for you. However, if you are so inclined, you may reimplement the serialization routines within your own objects. We have presented you with several serialization concerns in this chapter. If you are going to handle the serialization for a given object, make sure you conform to the various restrictions we have given you. If your objects do not handle their serialization properly, your entire object system may not be serializable.

Yet another issue of importance to Java programmers is performance. While serialization ensures that our objects can be saved and restored, performance issues strike at the very limitations of the language. The greatest programmers in the world can build the applications seen only in science fiction, but they are prevented from doing so by limitations in their hardware and the speed with which their software can be run.

Performance

Performance issues are the primary reason why most major corporations have not yet begun wholesale revisions of their existing computer systems to use the Java language. Although many of these issues are real and Java has yet to become the perfect language in all respects, it is not necessarily true that performance is a major show-stopper. Often, the perception is not reality.

Performance Issues

When we speak of performance in Java, we are actually speaking of two very different problems. The first is the download performance of an applet. Today, your hard-core applets will often contain upwards of 20 to 30 classes. Incorporate a mechanism such as Java IDL or Java RMI, and the communication infrastructure may add up to 100 different classes of its own. In order for the applet to run, each of those classes must be downloaded in order to be used.

The second major issue behind performance is runtime performance. For both applets and applications, the speed with which Java computes is pretty slow. Compared to comparable statistics for similar applications written in C++, Java does not measure up. There are several initiatives and technologies becoming available that may render that issue moot.

Download Performance. For applet writers, download performance is the single most important hurdle to overcome. While most programmers can create truly artistic programs that can accomplish a wide variety of things, they often meet a brick wall when their customer tries to download them within a browser. In order to study the download performance of an applet, we must first discuss how an applet is downloaded to begin with.

Java incorporates an object called the class loader. The class loader locates the class to be downloaded, goes about fetching it, and recognizes any other dependent objects and downloads those as well. The browser does the actual downloading and the class loader merely tells it what to do. When the browser downloads an object, it first establishes the connection to be used (see Figure 1-8). Once the connection is made, the object is checked to make sure that it has not been downloaded previously. If it has been downloaded before, it is not downloaded, and the

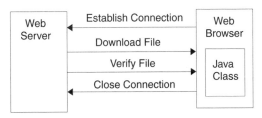

Figure 1-8 Download performance is measured by the time it takes to perform the steps involved.

connection is closed. If the class has not been downloaded before, it is down-loaded, and then the connection is closed.

So, the time it takes to download an object is determined by four factors as illustrated in Figure 1-8:

1. Time to open a connection.

2. Time to verify a file.

3. Time to download the file.

4. Time to close the connection.

And most importantly, the same four steps are applied to every single class in your entire object system. No matter what you do, you will have to spend the time to download the files. There's no getting around that part because you need those files to run your applet. However, the time spent establishing and closing connections is a waste because you are essentially doing the same thing to the same location each time.

The brilliant engineers behind Java recognized this problem and created the Java Archive. It enables you to gather all of your files, stick them in one large archive file, and let everything get downloaded in one fell swoop. This means that there need only be one open connection, one download, and one closure for the entire system of object files.

Using Java Archives is a rather simple process. You must first use the jar utility, which UNIX users will find quite similar to their tar program, to archive your files. This is not unlike "zipping" a bunch of files into one. Once completed, you simply specify the archive in the applet tag in your HTML code:

```
<applet archive="archivename.jar"
        codebase="../classes/"
        code="PrashantIsCool.class">

    . . . HTML text here . . .

</applet>
```

Java Archives greatly improve the download performance of your applets. Without something like them, applets would be restricted to small, compact programs that accomplish little more than animating a dancing duke. The trick is that the browser has to support archives. Currently, Netscape Navigator and Internet Explorer support ZIP files, and both plan to support the jar standard once it is completed.

Runtime Performance. Runtime performance is a different beast altogether. Where download performance was a relatively simple issue to resolve, runtime performance requires a significant investment in compiler technology. Thankfully, the Java engineers are ahead of the curve on this as well. They have put together a specification for a Just In Time (JIT) compiler.

Remember that Java is an interpreted language. This means that the code you develop is only halfway compiled into bytecodes. The bytecodes are then translated by your local virtual machine into native code. Finally, that native code is run on your machine. When an application executes, the bytecodes are washed through the virtual machine, and the result is then executed on your platform. This ensures platform independence because the bytecodes are translated by the virtual machine into native code as indicated by the flow diagram in Figure 1-9.

Today, non-Java applications are always compiled for the native machine, meaning that you are locked into the platform for which you bought the software but can bypass the virtual machine altogether (see Figure 1-10).

When Java came out with its promise of platform independence, people rejoiced because they no longer had to develop for every computer under the sun. However, the enthusiasm was tempered by the fact that Java was an interpreted language, meaning that the extra steps involved in translating Java code into native code made applications significantly slower. Furthermore, the bytecodes generated by the Java compiler were created with platform independence in mind. This meant that in order to preserve an adequate middle ground, Java bytecodes were

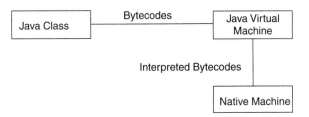

Figure 1-9 Performance of Java using a virtual machine.

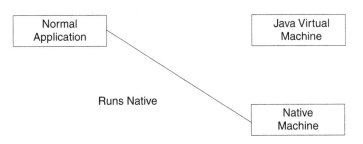

Figure 1-10 Performance of native, non-Java code.

arranged so that no platform necessarily got an advantage when it came time to translate into native code. The end result was that not only did it take a bit more time to interpret the code, but also that the code was interpreted from a platform-independent state caused the resulting native code to execute more slowly.

The JIT compiler solves most of these issues by enabling you to generate native code from your interpreted bytecode. The native code then performs exactly as it would have performed had the program been originally programmed in a native language.

As you can see from Figure 1-11, the JIT exists as part of the virtual machine, and JIT compilation happens automatically if the compiler is installed. Some virtual machines will allow you to turn off JIT compilation, but that should be necessary in only rare cases. Currently, several vendors including Sun, Microsoft, and Symantec are offering JIT compilers that either can be purchased as add-ons to a native virtual machine or are bundled as part of their own virtual machine.

Summary of Performance Issues

Performance is an issue of vital importance to Java programmers. Because of Java's promise as a platform-independent language, several architectural decisions were made to create the language. However, some of these decisions have contributed to Java's faults. Many of these issues have been addressed, namely download and runtime performance. Further deficiencies in the Java language will be corrected as time goes on if Java is to achieve its potential. Ultimately, the growth in applications using the language will uncover these faults as well as the corrections to them.

With several of the major benefits of the Java language under our belt, we can turn to finally developing a networked application. Our networked applications will use many of the techniques we have discussed thus far, as well as several more we will introduce along the way. Congratulations! Your first foray into Java networking is about to begin.

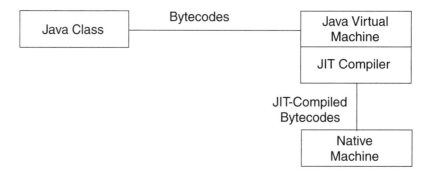

Figure 1-11 Performance of Java using a JIT compiler.

A First Look at Java Networking in Action

So far you have learned the three basic things you need to know in order to write networked applications in Java:

- Object-oriented design
- Input and output fundamentals
- Threading

A good object-oriented design will allow you great flexibility in creating clients and servers. You can extend the functionality of a well-designed class very easily. You can either alter the nuances of the class's architecture in order to facilitate the kind of communication you desire or publish your class to the "world" so that it can be used as it was intended to be used.

Solid input and output fundamentals enable your classes to process data quickly and efficiently. With a strong I/O functionality, your classes can accept, manipulate, and return data without much hassle. And once again, you can publish your class to the "world," specifying exactly which data you will accept and streamlining the processing power of your objects.

Effective threading principles will enable your class to produce fast turnaround times on object requests (those methods invoked upon your object), make good use of system resources, and begin to create an entire collection of objects that work together without affecting system performance. Figure 1-12 illustrates how a server can effectively handle information by spawning threads to process that information.

Good networked applications have three things in common:

- Useful interface definitions
- Pragmatic data definitions
- Efficient processing of data

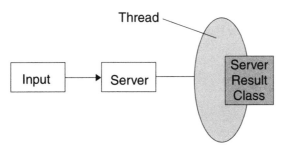

Figure 1-12 Threading can prevent servers from being bogged down.

Hopefully, the treatment of these three topics in this chapter so far has provided you with a means to satisfy the criteria set forth earlier and publish networked Java objects that take full advantage of the language.

Pulling It All Together

Throughout this book, we will reimplement the following featured application. Our Internet Calendar Manager is a simple tool designed to enable you to schedule appointments over a network. Because of Java's platform independence, you will be able to run this application on both your Windows laptop as well as your SPARC station. Because the data is held in a central repository with the Internet used as the communication mechanism between the two, it will not matter where you run the application because—no matter what—you will be manipulating the exact same data.

Road Map for Success. Your first task is to outline a clear object-oriented strategy to complete your project. For example, the Internet Calendar Manager was designed with modularity as its most crucial element. We wanted to be able to remove and replace certain parts of the program as often as we needed to without affecting the rest of the application. With that in mind, we created the class structure as shown in Figure 1-13.

As you can see, changing a component in the Scheduler does not at all affect the Calendar portion of the application. Each module is entirely separate from the other. This is an example of code reuse and modularity. Furthermore, the Network module keeps our network interaction limited to one module. All initialization, data exchange, and remote invocations take place only from within the module itself.

Furthermore, we recognized a series of objects that we would require throughout the application. Most of these are not specific to the implementation of any

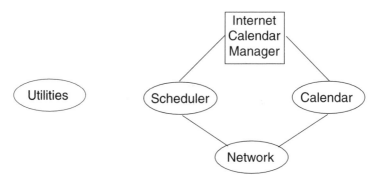

Figure 1-13 The class structure of our Internet Calendar Manager was created with modularity in mind.

module; rather, they are helper objects that deal with wide ranging things from multimedia (sounds and pictures) to animation. These objects were placed in the Utilities module so that they could be used as needed.

Project Planning. Once the project is divided as we did in the previous section, we must define the interfaces with which objects would talk to one another. In particular, the modularity of the Network component enabled us to redo it for each section without in any way affecting the rest of the application. In fact, the entire Network module wasn't even completed until two weeks before press time. The rest of the application was finished and working, talking to the Network module, but was never communicating with any remote objects.

User Interface. The Internet Calendar Manager we created is a stand-alone Java application. We made it so for ease of use. An applet version of the same application will reside on the Web site for this book. In any event, the UI components are the same. A series of buttons along the top of the application control which of the two tasks you can do: add an appointment or delete an appointment.

Pressing the Scheduler button takes you to the Add an Appointment section. There, you can specify the reason for the appointment and the time for which you would like to schedule it. Pressing the Schedule button sends the appointment to the Network module, which, in turn, talks to the server and places the appointment in the data repository.

The Calendar button takes you to the Calendar application. The Calendar application allows you to view a list of all the appointments scheduled, and the reasons and times for them. You may also delete appointments from within this application.

The content of the card layout is dependent on which button you press, as shown in Figure 1-14.

Finally, the exit button gracefully terminates the connection, telling the Network module that it wants to exit.

Network Modules. The Network module will be changed from chapter to chapter to reflect the new form of network communication. However, the APIs will remain the same. The Network module provides an abstracted layer above the network communication mechanism of choice. In so doing, we can provide a series of four methods that are of importance to the user, while keeping the network hidden from the rest of the application:

```
public class NetworkModule
{
    public void scheduleAppointment(
        String reason,
```

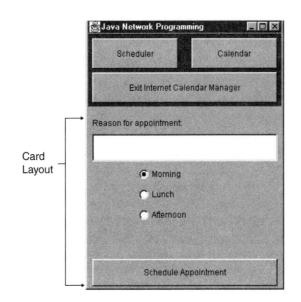

Figure 1-14 The main GUI for our featured application.

```
        int time);
    public Vector getAppointments();

    public void initNetwork();

    public void shutdownNetwork();
}
```

As far as the rest of this application is concerned, the Network module will accept information and do something with it over the network. Precisely what that something is is of no concern to the application itself.

Servers. The Network module would be useless without a server for it to talk to. Every server implements the same exact routines, regardless of whether it is a Java Database Connectivity (JDBC) server, a Remote Method Invocation (RMI) server, or an Interface Definition Language (IDL) server. In fact, the server itself is interchangeable, enabling us to choose on the fly to which one we want to talk. Simply run the proper application to take advantage of the communication mechanism of your choice.

```
public interface InternetCalendarServer
{
    void scheduleAppointment();

    void getAppointments();
}
```

The interface definition in this snippet does not take into account any kind of data structure in which to store an appointment. The server code implements both of the foregoing methods, as well as establishes and defines the following data structure:

```
public interface InternetCalendar Server
{
    Appointment Type
    {
        String reason;
        int time;
    }

    void scheduleAppointment(
        AppointmentType appointment
    );

    AppointmentType[] getAppointments();
}
```

Keep in mind that the interface definitions shown are pseudo-code only. As we will see later, server definition varies widely between each communication alternative. In Java IDL we will see how an entire language is available with which to define servers. In Java RMI we can create servers using Java itself.

NOTE: In an effort to show you how easy and fun network programming can be with Java, we have devised a simple application that we will redo every chapter. In one chapter we will use sockets, in another CORBA. Eventually, you will have six different applications that do the same thing. With the six applications, you can compare ease-of-use and performance, as well as figure out what all the hubbub is about network programming. The next four chapters will explore the basic alternatives available to network programmers intent on using the Java language.

Summary

Wow! Not only have we learned the nuances of the Java programming language, but we've also delved into the wide world of threads, explored some of the important performance issues we need to deal with, and seen how easy it is to save and restore our creations. These are great tools to have as we begin our journey through the realm of interprocess communication, networked programming, and distributed design.

Chapter 2

TCP/IP
Fundamentals

▼   IN THE BEGINNING...
▼   IP ADDRESSES
▼   PROTOCOLS

In the Beginning...

At the very heart of Java networking (and most other internetworking) is TCP/IP
(Transmission Control Protocol and Internet Protocol). TCP/IP is a protocol suite
(i.e., a set of rules for exchanging information) that sits between an application
and a network that enables an application (object) on one node of a network to
pass information back and forth to another application (object) residing on
another node of the network. The approach used by TCP/IP to do this is to
arrange the protocol into layers of subprotocols that each have their own specific
function(s) that, when used together, provide a rich functionality and an orderly
approach to data communications.

In many ways TCP/IP is very similar to other software-based protocols (i.e., protocols that are "on the wire" protocols like Ethernet, NETBIOS, NETBUI, SNA).
The major difference is the way that TCP/IP was developed: Rather than being a
protocol based on one manufacturer's view of networking and its relation to corporate profitability, TCP/IP developed out of the idea of "Open Systems." Open
Systems are systems whose specifications are developed "out in the open" rather
than behind closed doors; as long as a software developer implements the specification faithfully, the developed system is an Open System.

The Protocol Stack

One of the things that often confuses programmers who are new to the Internet
and TCP/IP is the idea of a TCP/IP stack or a protocol stack. The confusion

comes from the term "stack"; programmers automatically think of a stack as in the stack data structure. With relation to TCP/IP, the term stack simply means that a number of protocols are stacked one on top of the other in a manner that allows information from one level to be passed from one layer to the next with each layer encapsulating the information it receives from the previous layer. Moving information down the stack is analogous to sending, and moving data up the stack is analogous to receiving.

The OSI Stack

In the early 1980s the International Standards Organization (ISO) set out on a path to develop a set of standards that would ensure interconnectability and interoperability of disparate computer systems. This effort started and took place mainly in Europe; at the same time, in the United States, teams of technologists from industry, government, and the universities were busily exchanging ideas on how to arrive at the same goals as ISO (i.e., interconnectability and interoperability). In 1983 the protocol suite that has come to be known as TCP/IP was named as the U.S. Department of Defense Standard and was eventually required on all U.S. government computer systems.

Through the ISO work, the Open Systems Interconnection (OSI) reference model, referred to as the OSI stack, shown in Table 2-1, was developed. Today the OSI protocol stack remains primarily a European thing; even though the TCP/IP protocol stack is in wider use than the OSI stack, the OSI reference model (even in the United States) remains the ideal for modeling communication systems.

Table 2-2 shows a comparison of the seven-layer OSI protocol stack vs. the TCP/IP four-layer stack. Note that TCP/IP abstracts the top three layers of the OSI stack (application, presentation, and session) into a single application layer. The bottom two layers of the OSI stack (link and physical) are abstracted into a single link layer. In the OSI model, application logic is handled in the application layer; anything related to presentation (data conversions [ASCII-EBCDIC, ASCII-UNICODE]) in the presentation layer; and threading, multiprogramming, and

Table 2–1 The OSI Reference Model

Application	TELNET, FTP, SMTP, HTTP
Presentation	Byte-order, ASCII-UNICODE, COM-CORBA
Session	Login session, RPC call, ORB/RMI invocation
Transport	End-to-end communication (with possible ack)
Network	Host-to-host communication (one hop in a path)
Link	Network adapter card device driver
Physical	Ethernet, ISDN, PPP, T3, CATV

Table 2-2 OSI Reference Model and the TCP/IP Model

	OSI Model	TCP/IP	
7	Application	Application	4
6	Presentation		
5	Session		
4	Transport	Transport	3
3	Network	Network	2
2	Link	Link	1
1	Physical		

managing client sessions on the server in the session layer. In TCP/IP all these activities are performed in the application layer without requiring individual protocol layers for each of the OSI layers. This abstraction on the part of TCP/IP makes for lighter weight and more agile applications. The abstraction of the bottom two layers of the OSI model is a "makes sense" abstraction as the physical layer represents the Network Interconnection Card (NIC) and the link layer is the driver software that controls the NIC. These layers are inseparable (i.e., one isn't of much use without the other).

Not long ago, OSI, TCP, and UDP were competing network standards; today, TCP combined with UDP-based IP pretty much stands alone (as TCP/IP) as the primary Internet protocol. The Internet Protocol (IP) code maintains routing tables to make sure each IP packet gets to the next hop in a route toward its destination. Note that one UDP datagram or one TCP segment may be broken into many IP packets. Each IP packet may take a different route from the source to the destination, and the packets may arrive in a different order than they were sent. UDP sends the received packets upward toward the application code as soon as they arrive. TCP collects the IP packets and assembles a TCP segment before sending it upward, so the application receives pieces of data in the same order it was sent.

One of the more pronounced differences between the OSI model and the TCP/IP model is in the area of error-handling philosophy. The OSI approach is to require error checking to be done for each hop (node to node) a packet makes through the network. This means that for each hop a packet will be error-checked in the network layer (routers usually only consist of the link and network layers). If a packet makes 10 hops in getting from point a to point b, the error checking involved will occupy a significant percentage of the overall transmission time. The TCP/IP approach is to do error-checking only at the end points; since the whole idea is to move data reliably from point a to point b, the error-checking is done only once making for much less overhead and faster end-to-end communications.

The TCP/IP Stack

The TCP/IP stack consists of four layers:

Application   This layer is made up of protocols designed for specific applications. Many TCP/IP protocol suites come with a number of client applications that implement some of the common and widely used protocols like FTP, POP, TELNET. These protocols consist typically of a set of commands to be issued by the client (instructions to the server to do something) and a set of command responses (that are passed back to the client).

Information from this layer moves down the stack. In this respect the protocol actually functions as a queue (i.e., information moves down the stack, from one layer to the next, to send and up the stack to receive). Each protocol layer will wrap its own header or header/trailer information around whatever it receives from the previous layer. At the application layer most protocols are ASCII text based and have a command structure made up of keywords and string-based parametric data (check out the command-based protocols for FTP and POP3).

Transport   This layer provides the application with a highly reliable data transmission medium (a connection is made between two host computers and data transfers between the two are sized, acknowledged for receipt, check-summed, and timed).

Network   This layer is primarily responsible for moving the packets created in the transport layer through the network and eventually to their final destination. The workhorse of this layer is the Internet Protocol.

Link   This layer is responsible for translating the IP packets received from IP into the on-the-wire protocol (Ethernet, Token Ring, …) and consists of the user's Network Interconnection Card and software drivers required to control the NIC.

Note: Some authors break the layer into two layers—one for the hardware interconnect and one for the driver software.

This resembles (at least conceptually) the model shown in Figure 2-1.

Information starting out in a program running in the application layer is moved down the stack to the transport layer. In the transport layer the information is broken up into a series of smaller, easier-to-handle chunks for transmission. Each chunk of data is encapsulated with a TCP header containing sequencing and error-detection information and moved down the stack to the network (IP) layer.

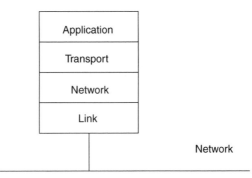

Figure 2-1 The TCP/IP protocol stack.

In the network layer each packet is further encapsulated by appending a header containing network routing information to the beginning of the packet. The network layer in turn passes each packet to the link layer, where it is converted to the actual "on-the-wire" protocol (Ethernet, Token-Ring, …) for transmission across the network.

On its way to its final destination, a packet usually will pass through one or more routers. Routers are fairly specialized devices and don't always function with a complete TCP/IP stack. A router is the network implementation of a multiplexer; i.e., one input can be distributed to one-of-n possible outputs. To do this, the router will have multiple NICs. The main purpose of a router is to move packets around the network; to do this, all it really needs to provide are the network and link layers. As a packet comes into the router it is received by the NIC and passed up the stack to the network layer. IP checks the routing information and passes the packet back down the stack to the correct NIC in the link layer and back out onto the network.

Upon reaching its final destination the packet is again received by the NIC, the NIC strips off the on-the-wire protocol information (leaving an IP packet) and passes the resulting information up the stack to the network layer. IP then removes the routing information (leaving a TCP packet) and passes it up the stack to the transport layer. TCP checks the packet for errors, removes the TCP header, and rebuilds the original application data by accumulating the packets and reassembling the original data (using the sequence numbers in the TCP header). Once the data has been reconstructed it is passed back up the stack to the application layer, where it is acted upon. This entire process is illustrated in Figure 2-2.

Now that we understand the general flow of information through a TCP/IP-based network let us look at the stack in a little more detail. We've already said the transport layer consists of two protocols—TCP and UDP—but the suite consists of

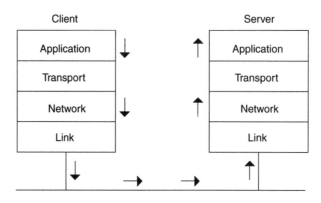

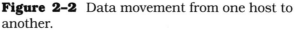

Figure 2-2 Data movement from one host to another.

many other protocols. Figure 2-3 shows the other protocols that make up the suite (application protocols are indicated at the top of the figure as plain text but are shown only as a sample and not a complete set).

Also note that there are two common versions of IP, version 4 (32-bit addressing) and version 6 (64-bit addressing) and that protocols that use IP also come in both version 4 and version 6 flavors. This being noted, the following is a brief description of what each of the protocols is used for.

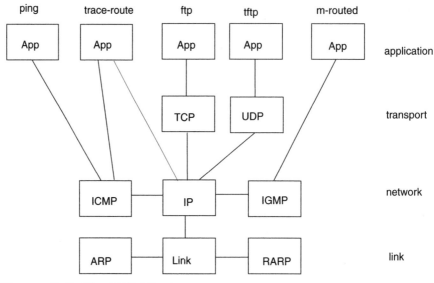

Figure 2-3 The TCP/IP suite.

TCP   *Transmission Control Protocol*. TCP can be thought of as the part of the suite that makes IP a reliable tool. It guarantees that data reaches its intended destination and is received correctly and received in a timely manner. TCP is relatively application-oriented in that using its socket facilities provides applications with a bidirectional byte stream between two hosts located at application endpoints.

A connection-oriented service is best for applications that require characters to be received in the same order in which they were sent, such as keystrokes typed from a terminal or bytes in an ASCII file transfer. Usually, the connection is kept open for a long time relative to the length of time to set up the connection (a "hand-shake" of three IP packets).

Connection-oriented protocols, such as TCP, send an acknowledgment when the data is received, and they retransmit data automatically if an acknowledgment is not received before the time-out period has expired. Each acknowledgment packet tells the receiving side how much buffer space is available at the other end. This enables both endpoints to transmit a "window" of data, perhaps several 8K packets, before stopping to wait for an acknowledgment from the other end. When the acknowledgment is received, the window size is updated from the packet header. This enables TCP to throttle data transfer when one side is running low on buffer space and to increase data transfer when the other side has plenty of room to receive data.

UDP   *User Datagram Protocol*. UDP is connectionless and acts more like a broadcast medium. Datagrams sent by UDP are not guaranteed to reach their destination. UDP is designed for speed, not reliability.

IP   *Internet Protocol*. The workhorse of the TCP/IP suite, IP takes care of the actual moving of datagrams from point a to point b. This is done by way of IP's datagram infrastructure. UDP is an application interface to IP.

ICMP   *Internet Control Message Protocol*. ICMP handles TCP/IP internally generated error messages and control messages between routers and host computers. Not used for application layer errors.

IGMP   *Internet Group Management Protocol*. IGMP is used for multicasting and will not be discussed in this text.

ARP   *Address Resolution Protocol*. ARP maps IP addresses to hardware addresses (every NIC has a manufacturer provided unique address) for broadcast style wire protocols (Ethernet, Token-Ring) but is not used by point-to-point wire protocols (SLIP, PPP).

RARP   *Reverse Address Resolution Protocol*. RARP maps hardware addresses to IP addresses. RARP is used typically to allow the Bootstrap Protocol (BOOTP) to aid a diskless workstation (X-Station) to discover its IP address so that its boot image can be retrieved.

Datagrams. Now that we've used the term "datagram" quite freely, it's best to explain what it is. Basically it's the unit information used in the IP layer. To understand this better, refer to Figure 2-4. At the physical level of a network (which isn't addressed by TCP/IP), the transmission medium is usually a piece of wire, fiber optic cable, microwaves, or some other exotic transmission medium. At this level, information travels along as a serial bit stream where the basic unit of information is a **bit**. As the bits leave the transmission medium and move into the link layer, the unit of information is called a **frame**. As the frame moves up the stack and the link layer's header and trailer information is removed, the unit of information becomes a **datagram**. IP removes its header from the datagram and passes the result to TCP as a **segment.** TCP collects the segments together until it has all that it is expecting and passes it up the stack to the application as a **message**. This whole process of receiving data can be thought of as a collecting together of all the pieces.

IP Addresses

Now here are a few words about IP addresses. First, they are called IP addresses because they are used by the IP (network) layer to route IP datagrams around the Internet.

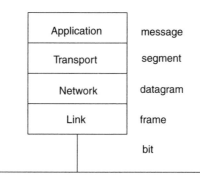

Figure 2-4 Units of information for the TCP/IP stack.

Figure 2-5 shows the five classes of IP addresses and how they are structured from a numbering standpoint. Classes A, B, and C are reserved for private networks and have the following address spaces:

Class A	0.0.0.0	127.255.255.255
Class B	128.0.0.0	191.255.255.255
Class C	192.0.0.0	223.255.255.255
Class D	224.0.0.0	239.255.255.255
Class E	240.0.0.0	247.255.255.255

Protocols

When a foreign dignitary arrives at the White House, certain protocols are observed. These describe who is introduced and when and with what fanfare. The President is always introduced last and makes his or her entrance to the tune of "Hail to the Chief." A protocol ensures that certain formalities are observed when information is exchanged across networks. This includes the format of the message, the content of the message, and the type of connection used to send the message. There are several kinds of protocols, ranging from the time-tested TCP/IP or UDP to the newer Internet Inter-ORB Protocol.

Some of the application level protocols and applications we will be examining in more depth in the chapters that follow are mentioned here.

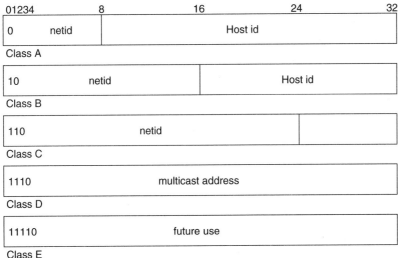

Figure 2-5 IP address classes.

DNS

Something that we haven't discussed yet that is used in every Internet transaction is the Domain Name System (DNS) and its protocol. The DNS is something that we all become aware of pretty early on in our use of the Internet but never really understand. I never thought about it until I was teaching an Internet Programming class one semester and was explaining the TCP/IP stack and layered protocols. One of the students asked, "How does IP get the dotted decimal version of the dotted word IP that we specify to our applications (FTP, TELNET)?"

The DNS is a distributed database used for translating dotted word notation (*www.myhome.com*) for IP addresses into the dotted decimal version (128.226.183.11). No single server keeps track of all IP addresses; the address space is distributed somewhat regionally and arranged in a hierarchy. DNS is commonly used as follows: Suppose we want to FTP a file from a remote server. Our FTP client builds a request packet and sends it down the stack to TCP, which adds its header and pushes the segment down to IP. IP adds an IP header, but before it can it must resolve the remote host's dotted word address to dotted decimal. This is done by IP sending a datagram request (UDP is used for speed) to the nearest DNS server. If that server can't resolve it, the request is sent up the DNS hierarchy to the next server. This is done until the address is resolved and returned to IP where it is translated into a 32-bit number and added to the IP header.

Many companies and universities that have large intranets for their campuses run their own DNS servers for performance reasons. On an intranet, most host-to-host communications are between hosts on that same intranet; they do not need to go out to the Internet to use a DNS server. It makes sense to keep a local copy of the nearest Internet DNS server locally. For private networks (not connected to the Internet), it makes sense to run a single DNS server containing only the addresses on the private network.

HTTP

HyperText Transfer Protocol (HTTP) is a TCP/IP application layer protocol that provides the connectivity between the client and server for the "killer app" of the century. HTTP is based relatively closely on an older protocol called Gopher. Gopher provided a text-based client and server that enabled the retrieval of information from large collections of research data maintained on mainly university computer systems. When HyperText Markup Language (HTML) was developed for the Mosaic browser and the Gopher protocol was modified to handle the transmission of graphics combined with text, the whole face of computing changed. This combination made the Internet easy to use for nontechnical users. HTTP enabled the development of the World Wide Web. Java is the next step to advance distributed computing in an object-oriented direction. HTTP is discussed in Chapter 7, "Web Servers, Server-Side Java, and More." It is important to remember that HTTP is entirely based on TCP sockets.

CORBA and IIOP

The Internet Inter-ORB Protocol (IIOP) is an open Internet protocol for communication between objects residing on a network. IIOP enables network objects to invoke one another using an industry standard messaging system (CORBA). Without IIOP, objects on the client end would not be able to talk to objects on the server end without first synchronizing their languages. IIOP standardizes the means clients and servers use to exchange information. It also enables clients and servers developed using different application programming languages (C, C++, Java) to interact with one another. As we will see later in this chapter, the format of the messages sent between clients and servers is of the utmost importance. In our daily lives, we even require a standard message format. If I were to start transposing my nouns and verbs (such as "were if I transposing to start my nouns and verbs"), then no one would understand me. Similarly, IIOP enables objects implemented in different languages to understand one another. When CORBA first came out, its underlying protocol was based on UDP to optimize performance. As CORBA has matured, IIOP has switched over to TCP sockets.

RMI

Remote Method Invocation (RMI) is another TCP sockets-based protocol scheme for the implementation of network objects. The general idea of RMI is that every network object consists of a client piece and a server piece. Wouldn't it be nice if this object could be treated (from an application's standpoint) just like any local object. RMI provides an infrastructure that does just that. The main complaint about RMI comes from the fact that the protocol is not openly developed or published. Because of the complaints over this, Sun Microsystems has agreed to base client/server communications on IIOP in some future release of RMI. The current implementation uses Java serialization APIs and TCP sockets to provide the underlying communications infrastructure.

JINI

JINI, rather than being strictly a protocol, is a technology not for client/server applications but for the interconnection of JINI-enabled devices into impromptu networks. An example of this would be that I go out and buy an XYZ JINI-enabled color printer. When I take it home and plug it into my whole house Ethernet, the printer automatically registers itself and its drivers with the network. I turn on my JINI-enabled workstation and get into my favorite word processor and ask to print in color (at this point my workstation only knows about my black and white printer). The print function calls out to the network "is there a color printer out there?" The network responds and transparently downloads the driver for the color printer so that the word processor can send data to the printer. Just think, I didn't have to install the drivers (or even find them); the printer had its own drivers built in and made them available to the network.

Summary

There we have the two-penny tour of TCP/IP and how it works. In the following chapters we will investigate a number of protocols and network-based client/ server strategies. Keep in mind, however, that all these mechanisms are based on TCP/IP sockets technology.

Chapter 3

Java Sockets
and URLs

Sockets and Interprocess Communication

At the heart of everything we discuss in this book is the notion of interprocess communication (IPC). In this chapter, we will look at some examples using Java mechanisms for interprocess communication. IPC is a fancy way of saying "two or more Java programs talking with each other." Usually the programs execute on different computers, but sometimes they may execute on the same host.

Introduction to IPC

When you call Charles Schwab to check on your stock portfolio, you dial a telephone number. Once connected, you press some telephone buttons to request various services and press other buttons to send parameters, such as the numeric codes for stock symbols in which you are interested. You may think of your account as an object with different methods that you can invoke to purchase or to sell stocks, to get current quotes, to get your current position in a stock, or to request a wire transfer to a Swiss bank. You are a *client* and the other end is a *server*, providing the services (methods) you request.

Of course, the server also provides services to many other clients. You can be a client of other servers, such as when you order a pizza with a push button telephone. Sometimes a server can be a client as well. A medical records query server may have to send a request to two or three hospitals to gather the information you

53

request for a patient. Thus your server becomes a client of the hospital servers it queries on your behalf.

All these situations are examples of interprocess communication. Each client and each server reside in different processes. Sometimes you, the individual, are the client; other times it is a computer. Sometimes the server is an application that listens in on what you type on your telephone pad and processes the information; other times it will be a program, perhaps written in Java as we will do later in this chapter. IPC is how our applications communicate, but it also refers to the mechanism we use. This chapter explores the fundamentals of IPC using something called a socket.

Sockets. The communication construct underneath all this communication is more than likely a **socket**. Each program reads from and writes to a socket in much the same way that you open, read, write to, and close a file. Essentially, there are two types of sockets:

- One is analogous to a telephone (a connection-oriented service, e.g., Transmission Control Protocol)

- One is analogous to a mailbox (a connectionless "datagram" service, e.g., User Datagram Protocol)

An important difference between TCP connection sockets and UDP datagram sockets is that TCP makes sure that everything you send gets to the intended destination; UDP, on the other hand, does not. Much like mailing a letter, it is up to you, the sender, to check that the recipient received it. The difference between the two protocols is very similar to comparing the differences between using the phone to talk to friends and writing them letters.

When we call a friend using a telephone, we know at all times the status of the communication. If the phone rings busy, we know that we have to try later; if someone answers the phone, we have made a connection and are initiating the message transfer; if the person that answered the phone is the right person, we talk to them thereby transferring whatever information we intended to deliver.

Had we written a letter, we know that we would have initiated an information transfer after we dropped it off at the mailbox. This is where our knowledge of the transfer, in most cases, ends. If we get a letter back and it starts out with "Thanks for your letter," we know that our letter was received. If we never again hear from the person, there is some doubt that they ever received our letter.

Sometimes when you use the postal service, your letter becomes "lost in the mail." When the letter absolutely, positively has to be there, you may need a more reliable form of postage. Similarly, your choice between using a datagram or a connection socket is easily determined by the nature of your application. If all your data fits in an 8K datagram and you do not need to know if it was received at the other end, then a UDP datagram is fine. Mailing party invitations is one example where UDP is more appropriate than TCP. If the length of service warrants the expense of establishing a connection (three handshake packets), or it is necessary that all the packets be received in the same order as they were sent, such as transferring a file that is more than 8K bytes long, then a TCP socket must be used. Likewise, if we were to mail our important package using something like Federal Express, we would be able to track the package and know when it arrives at its destination.

Here is another way to look at this. Suppose we have a server that is somewhere on the network but we don't know where. To communicate with this type of server, we must first announce our presence, listen for an answer, and then carry on the conversation in lockstep where first one end sends then listens while the other end listens then talks. This is like a student walking into the reserve room of a college library and, upon not seeing the librarian right away, saying, "Is there anyone here?" and then listening for a response.

"Good afternoon, I'll be with you in a moment."

"I'd like the book Prof. Steflik put on reserve for CS-341."

"Here it is. Please leave your Student ID card."

We announced our presence and started listening. The server was listening, heard us, replied with an implied go ahead, and returned to listening. We heard the server's response, announced what we wanted, and returned to listening. The server (librarian) heard our request, retrieved the information (the book), and delivered it. This back and forth type of communication is known as half duplex, where only one endpoint talks at a time; contrast this with full duplex, where both endpoints can talk and listen at the same time.

NOTE: A socket is sometimes called a "pipe" because there are two ends (or points as we occasionally refer to them) to the communication. Messages can be sent from either end. The difference, as we will soon see, between a client and a server socket is that client sockets must know beforehand that information is coming, whereas server sockets can simply wait for information to come to them. It's sort of like the difference between being recruited for a job and actively seeking one.

In this chapter, we will write an online ordering application, using TCP, and a broadcast communication application, using UDP. These applications will use the following classes from the *java.net* package, as illustrated in Table 3-1.

Table 3–1 Java.net.* Types and Their Corresponding Protocol

Mechanism	Description
Socket	TCP endpoint (a "telephone")
ServerSocket	TCP endpoint (a "receptionist")
DatagramSocket	UDP endpoint (a "mailbox")
DatagramPacket	UDP packet (a "letter")
URL	Uniform Resource Locator (an "address")
URLConnection	An active connection to an Internet object (e.g., a CGI-bin script, a DayTime service)

What Are Sockets? At the root of all TCP and UDP communications is a virtual device called a socket or a port; the terms are pretty much interchangeable. Sockets are a visualization mechanism for a software buffering scheme that is implemented deep in the bowels of the transport layer of the TCP/IP stack. The term "socket" actually comes from the old-fashioned telephone switchboard that Lily Tomlin's character Ernestine, the telephone operator, uses. The concept is pretty similar: Each socket in the switchboard represents a person or service that an incoming call can be routed to; when an incoming call is answered, the operator connects it to the appropriate socket, thereby completing the connection between the client (the caller) and the server (person being called). In the telephone switchboard each socket represented a specific person or service; in TCP/IP certain sockets are dedicated to specific agreed-upon services.

If we were to look at the packet level, we would see that a socket is really identified by a 16-bit number thereby giving us about 65,000 possible sockets. The first 1024 sockets are dedicated to specific agreed-upon services and are therefore called well-known ports. For each of the services provided on the well-known ports, there is a corresponding protocol that defines the manner in which clients and servers using that port should communicate. The protocols themselves are arrived at through a process known as the RFC process. Table 3-2 lists some of the more common TCP/IP services, their "well-known" ports, and their respective RFCs. Every Internet standard starts out as a "Request for Comment" or RFC. Through an interactive process an RFC, if "worthy," will be refined and developed by the Internet community into a standard.

Exploring Some of the Standard Protocols. When starting to understand sockets programming, it's always best to start out by examining the "trivial" protocols first and then move on to the more complex and finally to our own, application-specific protocols. The trivial protocols are a subset of Internet protocols that are simple, straightforward, and easy to implement.

Table 3–2 Some Well-Known Port Services

Port	Protocol	RFC
13	DayTime	RFC 867
7	Echo	RFC 862
25	SMTP (e-mail)	RFC 821 (SMTP) RFC 1869 (Extnd SMTP) RFC 822 (Mail Format) RFC 1521 (MIME)
110	Post Office Protocol	RFC 1725
20	File Transfer Protocol (data)	RFC 959
80	Hypertext Transfer Protocol	RFC 2616

Daytime. The Daytime service is usually provided on TCP and UDP port 13. Assuming that we have the address of a host that is running the Daytime service, the operation is straightforward. Using TCP the client connects to the Daytime port (13) on the remote host; the remote host accepts the connection, returns its current date and time, and closes the connection. This can be easily demonstrated using the Windows 95 Telnet client. Open up the Telnet client and click on Connect and the Remote System. Enter in the address of your host that provides the Daytime service, select the Daytime port, and click Connect. Notice that a date/timestamp is displayed in the client area and that a small dialog box indicates that the connection to the host has been lost.

This example is trivial but illustrates two things: First, the Windows Telnet client can be used to explore standard TCP-based protocols (we'll see this later with other protocols. Second, we really did demonstrate how the client end of the protocol works; the client makes a connection to the server, the server sends the timestamp and closes the connection, and, finally, the client receives the timestamp. To implement our own client, understanding what the client needs to do makes the task quite simple. A high-level design is

> Create a socket
> Create an input stream and tie it to the socket
> Read the data from the input stream and display the result

To create a socket, define a variable for the socket class and initialize it using the class constructor:

```
Socket s = Socket("localhost", 7);
```

"localhost" is the name assigned to address 127.0.0.1 in your hostsfile; address 127.0.0.1 is known traditionally as your machine's "loop back port," and lets your machine talk to itself. The line above creates a socket named "s" and connects it to port 7 on your loop back port. To connect to the Daytime service on any other host, just replace localhost with a string containing the dotted decimal name or IP address of whatever host you want to connect to.

This single instruction will create the socket object and attempt to connect it to the specified host. Because this has a possibility of failing (throwing an exception—a connection may not be established), we need to code it in a try/catch construct.

```java
import java.io.*;
import java.net.*;
public class DayTimeClient{
    public static final port = 13;
    public static void main(String args[])
    {
        Socket s = null;
        String timestamp;
        try
        {
            // create the socket to the remote host
            s = new Socket(args[0], port);
            // create an input stream and tie it to the socket
            InputStream in = s.getInputStream();
            BufferedReader in =
                new BufferedReader(new InputStreamReader(in));
            // tell user they are connected
            System.out.println("Connected to : " +
                s.getInetAddress() + "on port " + s.getPort()) ;
            while (true) {
                // read the timestamp
                timestamp = in.readLine();
                if (timestamp == null) {
                    System.out.println("Server closed connection");
                    break;
                }
                System.out.println("Daytime : " + timestamp);
            }
        }
        catch (IOException e) { System.out.println(e);}
        finally
        {
            // force the connection closed in case it's open
            try
            { if (s != null)  s.close(); }
            catch (IOException e2)
            { }
        }
    }
}
```

The code follows our high-level design pretty closely. We first create a socket and then create a stream and tie the two together. Notice that all I/O is done in a try construct so that all I/O problems (socket or stream) are automatically caught as exceptions. In fact, especially notice that the finally clause of the main try/catch/ finally uses a nested try to catch the fact that if the connection is already closed so that we can terminate the program gracefully in the null catch statement.

Now that we've mastered the most trivial of the protocols, let's move on to something a little more complicated.

Echo. "Well-known port" 7 on most hosts provides a service called echo. Echo is pretty much a diagnostic service and works as follows (see RFC 862 on the companion CDROM for a fuller description):

1. The client connects to the server on port 7 and proceeds to send data.

2. The server returns everything it receives to the client. This may be done on a character-by-character basis or a line-by-line basis depending on the implementation of the server.

Let's start out our examination of echo by first writing a non-sockets-based version of Echo just to get a feel for what it is that we want to do.

```
public class EchoTest
{
    public static void main (String args[])
    {
        BufferedReader in = new BufferedReader
                            New InputStreamReader(System.in));
        String line;
        while(true)
        {
            line="";
            try
            {
                line = in.readLine();
            }
            catch (IOException e)
            {
                System.err.println(e.getMessage());
            }
        System.out.println(line);
        }
    }
}
```

The program is quite simple and straightforward. First, we define an input stream and connect it to the standard input keyboard (System.in); then we define a string for our only program variable, which will hold the string we read from the keyboard and print on the Java console. Finally, we put the read and write in a do forever loop. Remember, in Java it is not only considered good form to provide try/catch constructs when doing I/O it is necessaary.

You can execute the program that we created by doing the following, and get similar results:

```
%prompt% javac EchoTest.java
%prompt% java EchoTest
abc                   input...
abc                        ...output
def                   input...
def                        ...output
xyz                   input...
xyz                        ...output
^C
%prompt%
```

Moving EchoTest to Sockets. Taking another step toward proficiency using Java sockets, we modify our echo program to do the following:

1. Read a line from the keyboard.

2. Write it to a socket connected to TCP port 7.

3. Read the reply from the socket connection.

4. Print the line from the socket to the screen.

A socket object is created as follows:

```
Socket s = Socket("localhost", 7);
```

The two arguments to the `Socket` constructor are *hostname* and *port number*. We use "localhost" to keep it simple. The hostname is passed as a `string` variable, typically from the command line and the port number as an `int`.

Here is a simple TCP client written in Java. First, we must create the `EchoClient` class and import all the Java libraries that we will use in our program.

```
import java.io.*;
import java.net.*;

public class EchoClient
{
}
```

Now, we must create a function in which we will place a loop similar to the one we created with our Java-only client. This loop must have two objects on which to act—the BufferedReader from the socket from which it will get data and the Print-Stream from the socket to which it will write data. We assumed this was standard input and standard output for our Java-only client, but we will not make that assumption here:

```
import java.io.*;
import java.net.*;
public class EchoClient
{
    public static void echoclient(BufferedReader  in;
                                  PrintStream out)
                                  throws IOException

    {
    }
}
```

Now, we must get an input stream for the keyboard. For this we'll use another BufferedReader tied to System.in. We will also add the loop here. The loop will first get input from the keyboard using the stream we just created. Then it will write that data directly to the socket.

```
import java.io.*;
import java.net.*;
public class EchoClient
{
    public static void echoclient(BufferedReader  in;
                                  PrintStream out)
                                  throws IOException

    {
      kybd = new BufferedReader(
                             new  InputStreamReader(System.in);
      String line;
      while(true)
      {
         line="";
         // read keyboard and write to the socket
         try
         {
            line = kybd.readLine();
            out.println( line );
         }
         catch (IOException e)
         {
            System.err.println(e.getMessage());
         }
      }
    }
}
```

To finish up, we now read the activity on the socket and stick it on the screen by writing to the Java console using the System object.

```
public class EchoClient
{
```

```
public static void echoclient(BufferedReader in,
                              PrintStream out)
                      Throws IOException
{
    // make a stream for the keyboard
    BufferedReader kybd = new BufferedReader(
                          new InputStreamReader(
                              System.in));
    String line;    //for reading into
    while(true)
    {
        line="";
        // read keyboard and write to TCP socket
        try
        {
            line = kybd.readLine();
            out.println( line );
        }
        catch (IOException e)
        {
            System.err.println(e.getMessage());
        }
        // read TCP socket and write to java console
        try
        {
            line = sin.readLine();
            System.out.println(line);
        }
        catch (IOException e)
        {
            System.err.println(e.getMessage());
        }
    }
}
```

Finally, we can create our main application. In our main application, we will create the socket first and then get a BufferedReader and a PrintStream based on it. This enables us to read and write to the socket easily, as well as pass it on to the function we created earlier. Once we are finished, we must close the connection to the socket.

 As we will discuss later, too many open connections are a system liability. If a connection is not in use, but is still open, other applications may not be able to connect to the port to which you are connected.

```java
import java.io.*;
import java.net.*;
public class EchoClient
{
    public static void echoclient(BufferedReader in,
                                  PrintStream    out)
                                  throws IOException
    {
        // make a stream for reading the keyboard
        BufferedReader kybd = new BufferedReader(
                                new InputStreamReader(
                                    System.in));
        String line;
        while(true)
        {
            line="";
            // read keyboard and write to TCP socket
            try
            {
                line = kybd.readLine();
                out.println(line);
            }
            catch(IOException e)
            {
                System.err.println(e.getMessage());
            }
            // read TCP socket and write to console
            try
            {
                line = in.readLine();
                System.out.println(line);
            }
            catch(IOException e)
            {
                System.err.println(e.getMessage());
            }
        }
    }
    public static void main(String[] args )
    {
        Socket s = null;
        try
        {
            // Create a socket to communicate with "echo"
            // on the specified host
            s = new Socket(args[0], 7);
```

```java
        // Create streams for reading and writing
        // lines of text from and to this socket.
        BufferedReader in = new BufferedReader(
                        new InputStreamReader(
                        s.getInputStream()));
        PrintStream out = new(
                        PrintStream(s.getOutputStream());
        // Tell the user that we've connected
        System.out.println("Connected to " +
                        s.getInetAddress() + ":" + s.getPort());
        echoclient(in, out);
    }
    catch (IOException e)
    {
        System.err.println(e);
    }

    // Always be sure the socket gets closed
    finally
    {
        try
        {
            if(s != null)  s.close();
        }
        catch (IOException exc)
        { ; /* terminate gracefully */}
    }
}
}
```

When we execute our program, we send a message to the Echo socket, read whatever information comes back on the socket, and then print it. Because the echo socket merely takes whatever input it gets and bounces it right back to the port, what we get in return on the socket is exactly what we sent. The output is displayed next. If you need to connect to another host, substitute its name for localhost.

```
%prompt% java EchoClient localhost
Connected to localhost/127.0.0.1:7
abc         request...
abc             ...reply
xyz         request...
xyz             ...reply
^C
```

This service (and most others) can be tested using the Telnet client that is available as an application with most TCP/IP stacks. In this case, the Telnet program acts in the same manner as our client, sending information to the port and reading whatever it gets back.

```
%prompt% telnet localhost 7
Trying 127.0.0.1...
Connected to localhost.
Escape character is '^]'.
abc           request...
abc                ...reply
^C
xyz           request...
xyz                ...reply
^]     control-right-bracket
telnet> quit
Connection closed.
```

URL and URL Connection

Before we leave the topic of using sockets to connect existing Internet servers, let's look at using some of the more common and popular services provided on the Internet. We need to examine a couple of other members of *java.net*: URL and URL Connection.

A Uniform Resource Locator (URL) is a string that identifies a resource on the Internet. RFC 1738 gives an in-depth description of everything you would ever want to know about URLs. Table 3-3 is a brief description of the various things that make up a URL.

Table 3–3 Makeup of a URL

Protocol	An identifier (usually an acronym) that specifies the protocol to use to access the resource
Host name	The name of the host or domain where the resource is located (*www.binghamton.edu*, localhost)
Port number	The TCP/IP port number that the service is being provided on
Filename	Path- and filename of resource
Reference	#anchorname

The URL class gives us the ability to construct URL objects and a number of "getter" methods that let us extract the various parts of a URL. From a networking standpoint, the methods of getContent(), openConnection(), and openStream() provide us with some very useful tools that we can use to interface with a number of protocol servers.

To retrieve a file from a Web server, all we really need to know is its URL:

```
Class GetURL
{
   try
   {
```

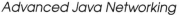

```
String host = "watson2.cs.binghamton.edu";
String file = "~steflik/index.html";
String line;
BufferedReader in;
URL  u = new URL("http://"+host+"/"+file);
Object content = u.getContent();
System.out.println("class: " + content.getClass());
System.out.println("content: " + content.toString());
In = new BufferedReader
           (new InputStreamReader(u.openStream()));
while ((line = in.readLine() != null)
{
  System.out.println(line);
}
}
catch (MalformedURLException e) { e.printStackTrace();}
catch (IOException e) {e.printStackTrace();}
}
```

All we had to do was create a URL object and then use the openStream() method to create an InputStream and eventually a BufferedReader that we can use to retrieve the file. At this point all that is needed is a loop to read the lines out of the file.

This technique can be exploited for doing things like populating selection lists in an applet-based shopping cart application with data from a set of pricing files kept on the Web server. This technique can also be used to run scripts stored on a Web server.

Summary of Sockets

We have shown you what, in the most basic sense, sockets are and how they are used in Java to build client applications that communicate, using well-defined protocols with standards-based (developed using the RFC process) servers. The subsequent sections in this chapter build on this material and show you how to create an entire client/server system using only sockets. The rest of this book showcases several other Java communication technologies that use sockets as their underlying mechanism to transfer data across networks. In the large of it, applications use protocols to direct the way they talk to one another and protocols use sockets as their network interface.

Client/Server Methodology

In the previous section we developed client applications for servers that already exist. This isn't the way that we would necessarily approach developing a sockets-based client/server application. In the next few pages we will examine a client/server application for an Internet-based pizza ordering/delivery service that will be made up of a client (that pizza lovers around the community can install on the home computers to order a pizza), a server (running at the store), and a protocol that directs the information exchange between the client and the server.

Suppose that you are at home with your cronies watching the Super Bowl, and, as luck would have it, the Washington Redskins are playing. As invariably happens, you've run out of nachos and dip before half time, so you decide to replenish the nutrition supply by ordering a pizza. Today, when you want to order that pizza, you pick up the phone and call your favorite pizzaria to request a delivery.

A few years ago, a small start-up company in the Silicon Valley called the Santa Cruz Operation (SCO) developed an Internet pizza-ordering application. By today's standards, it was quite low-tech, based solely on HTML forms and requiring someone to read the information manually on the other end via e-mail. The nifty thing about this Internet Pizza Hut was the idea that you could simply use your computer to communicate with a faraway place and get a pizza. In this sense, SCO was pretty well ahead of the game—they were among the first to genuinely use the Internet, not the corporate intranet, to conduct business with remote users.

In this section, we will develop our own pizza client/server system as an ultra-hip high-tech alternative to the telephone and publish it to the world. This time, however, we will use Java and implement our `PizzaServer` using sockets.

The Pizza Order Protocol (TPOP)

To design the protocol we need to examine what information must be passed from the client to the server and vice versa. If the user interface for our client application is as shown in Figure 3-1 we can readily see that to constitute an order we need to send the name, address, phone number, pizza size (small, medium, or large) , and which topping (Veggies, Meat, or California) is to be added to a standard cheese pizza.

The protocol that is required to place an order is pretty simple, as shown in Table 3-4.

Let us further decide that, since we're in this early part of design, all data exchanged between the client and the server is to be as plain old text strings (in the true tradition of the Internet), each of which is to be delimited by the " | " character.

The next decision we need to make is which component we will develop first: the client or the server. If we choose to develop the client first, we won't be able to test it until we develop the server and then end up with the possibility of having to use two untested pieces of software to test each other. Realizing the possible disaster that can occur if this avenue is followed, let's think about developing the server first. If the server is running, we can always test it using our Telnet client. To do this, all we do is start up our Telnet client, connect to port 8205 of the server,

Figure 3-1 A sample GUI for the PizzaTool.

Table 3-4 TPOP

Client	Server
	Start server listening on port 8205
Connect to port 8205 of the server	
	Accept the connection and spawn a thread to handle the connection data
Send the order information and then wait for the price to display	
	Receive the order, print it out, calculate the price, return price to client application, and break the connection
Display the price	

type in the data separated by " | " characters, and press Enter. The server will process the data, send back the price information, and, close the connection. This approach helps set us up for success rather than failure.

The TPOP Server

Server Methodology

For every client there must somewhere be a server. In an attempt to make server creation as simple as possible, Java provides a Server Socket class as part of *java.net*. Server Sockets, once created, listen on their assigned port for client connection requests. As requests are received, they are queued up in the Server Socket. The Server Socket accepts the connection request; as part of this acceptance the Server Socket creates a new socket, connects it to the client, and disconnects the connection on the Server Socket port, leaving it open for more connection requests. The client and server now talk back and forth on the new socket connection, and the server listens for connection requests on the Server Socket.

This all sounds pretty simple, but we haven't mentioned anything about threads yet. One of the basic ideas of client/server methodology is that one server should service as many clients as possible. To do this there must be something in the recipe that provides parallelism. That something is threads. The Thread class provides Java with a consistent, operating system neutral way of using the threading capabilities of the host operating system.

Java threads, sockets, and AWT components are similar in that the classes provided are really interfaces to the threads, sockets, and GUI widgets supplied by the operating system that is hosting the Java virtual machine. This means that if you are on Windows, you are really interacting with the TCP/IP protocol stack provided by *winsock.dll*; if you are on a UNIX platform, you are most likely using Berkley sockets. If you are on a Sun Solaris, you are using the threading provided by the Solaris operating system. If you are on Windows 98 using AWT widgets, you are really using the widgets provided by Windows. Used this way by Java, these components are known as peer components or objects. The adding of the Swing components to Java 1.1 starts to get away from this by providing 100% Java GUI components.

A typical TCP application opens a "well-known" port to receive connection requests, and then it spawns a child process or a separate thread of execution to perform the requested service. This ensures that the server is always ready for more invocations. A single-threaded server must poll the sockets constantly. When it detects activity, it must spawn a new process to handle the incoming request. Our multithreaded server can simply wait for information on a socket and spawn a thread to handle incoming requests.

The `PizzaServer` that we will implement will hang on port 8205 and wait for information. When the client sends its bar-delimited request, the server will spawn a thread to handle the request. The thread reads the information, processes it, and sends a reply.

Setting Up the Server

We must create the `PizzaServer` object itself. The `PizzaServer` is a stand-alone Java application with its own application main (on the accompanying CD, two versions of the server are provided—one with a GUI interface and one without). We must also create a `PizzaThread` that inherits from the Java `Thread` class. This threaded object will be created every time we detect activity on the port. As we discussed in our Chapter 1 section on threads, it is one of two ways we could have implemented the server object. We leave the other threaded version as an exercise to the reader.

```java
import java.net.*;
import java.io.*;
import java.lang.*;
import java.util.*;
public class PizzaServer
{
    public static void main(String args[])
    {
    }

    // threaded pizza!
    class PizzaThread extends Thread
    {
    }
```

Initializing the Server Socket

Inside the main program, we must create a `ServerSocket`. The `ServerSocket` is a Java type whose sole purpose is to enable you to wait on a socket for activity. Initialize it by specifying the port on which you want to wait.

```java
import java.net.*;
import java.io.*;
import java.lang.*;
import java.util.*;
public class PizzaServer
{
    public static void main(String args[])
    {
      // initialize the network connection
      try
      {
        ServerSocket serverSocket = new ServerSocket(8205);
      }
      catch(Exception exc)
      {
        System.out.println("Error! - " + exc.toString());
      }
    }
}
// threaded pizza!
```

```
class PizzaThread extends Thread
{
}
```

Creating the Thread

The `PizzaThread` object will accept one variable, the `incoming` socket from which it gathers information. We need to specify this here because the main server program has already grabbed hold of the socket, and we don't want to do so twice. We merely pass the socket obtained by the main program on to the thread. We will also implement the `run` method for the thread.

```
import java.net.*;
import java.io.*;
import java.lang.*;
import java.util.*;
public class PizzaServer
{
    public static void main(
        String args[]
    )
    {
        // initialize the network connection
        try
        {
            ServerSocket serverSocket = new ServerSocket(8205);
        }
        catch(Exception exc)
        {
            System.out.println("Error! - " + exc.toString());
        }
    }
}

// threaded pizza!
class PizzaThread extends Thread
{
    // the socket we are writing to
    Socket incoming;

    PizzaThread(    Socket incoming )
    {
        this.incoming = incoming;
    }

    // run method implemented by Thread class
    public void run()
    {
    }
}
```

Detecting Information and Starting the Thread

Now, we must wait on the thread until activity occurs. Once we detect some semblance of information coming across the socket, we must spawn a thread automatically and let the thread get and process the information. Our main program merely delegates activity to others.

```java
import java.net.*;
import java.io.*;
import java.lang.*;
import java.util.*;
public class PizzaServer
{
    public static void main(String args[])
    {
        // initialize the network connection
        try
        {
            ServerSocket serverSocket = new ServerSocket(8205);

            // now sit in an infinite loop until we get something
            while(true)
            {
                // accept the message
                Socket incoming = serverSocket.accept();

                // spawn a thread to handle the request
                PizzaThread pt = new PizzaThread(incoming);
                pt.start();
            }
        }
        catch(Exception exc)
        {
            System.out.println("Error! - " + exc.toString());
        }
    }
}

// threaded pizza!
class PizzaThread extends Thread
{
    // the socket we are writing to
    Socket incoming;

    PizzaThread(Socket incoming)
    {
        this.incoming = incoming;
    }
    // run method implemented by Thread class
    public void run()
```

```
    {
    }
}
```

Notice also how we must call the `start` method explicitly on the thread. As we discussed in the Threads section of Chapter 1, if a class inherits from the Java `Thread` class, the thread must be started from outside the class.

Gathering Information

Once the thread is running, it needs to go to the socket and get information. To do so, we must obtain input and output streams to read and write to/from the socket. Remember that the socket is merely a construct. In order to get information from it, it must be abstracted into an input/output mechanism. We will then be able to read and write to the socket. As we will discuss in our client section, the data we are going to receive is in a bar-delimited format. We must use a `StringTokenizer` object to extract the information from the message.

```java
import java.net.*;
import java.io.*;
import java.lang.*;
import java.util.*;
public class PizzaServer
{
    public static void main(String args[])
    {
        // initialize the network connection
        try
        {
            ServerSocket serverSocket = new ServerSocket(8205);

            // now sit in an infinite loop until
            // we get something
            while(true)
            {
                // accept the message
                Socket incoming = serverSocket.accept();

                // spawn a thread to handle the request
                PizzaThread pt = new PizzaThread(incoming);
                pt.start();
            }
        }
        catch(Exception exc)
        {
            System.out.println("Error! - " + exc.toString());
        }
    }
}
```

```java
// threaded pizza!
class PizzaThread extends Thread
{
    // the socket we are writing to
    Socket incoming;

    PizzaThread(Socket incoming)
    {
        this.incoming = incoming;
    }

    // run method implemented by Thread class
    public void run()
    {
        try
        {
            // get input from socket
            DataInputStream in =
                new DataInputStream(incoming.getInputStream());

            // get output to socket
            PrintStream out =
                new PrintStream(incoming.getOutputStream());

            // now get input from the server until it closes the
            // connection
            boolean finished = false;
            while(!finished)
            {
                String newOrder = in.readLine();

                // convert to a readable format
                try
                {
                    StringTokenizer stk =
                        new StringTokenizer(newOrder, "|");
                    String name = stk.nextToken();
                    String address = stk.nextToken();
                    String phone = stk.nextToken();
                    int size =
                        Integer.valueOf(stk.nextToken()).intValue();
                    int toppings =
                        Integer.valueOf(stk.nextToken()).intValue();

                    // no exception was thrown so calculate total
                    int total = (size * 5) + (toppings * 1);

                    // send the result back to the client
                    out.println("$" + total + ".00");

                    // put our result on the screen
                    System.out.println("pizza for " + name +
                        " was " + totalString);
```

```
            }
            catch(NoSuchElementException exc)
            {
                finished = true;
            }
        }
    }
    catch(Exception exc)
    {
        System.out.println("Error! - " + exc.toString());
    }
    // close the connection
    try
    {
        incoming.close();
    }
    catch(Exception exc)
    {
        System.out.println("Error! - " + exc.toString());
    }
}
}
```

Note in particular the two lines we actually use for reading information from the socket and sending information back:

```
String newOrder = in.readLine();
// send the result back to the client
out.println("$" + total + ".00");
```

These two lines have the same syntax as they would if they were reading and writing a file. In fact, as we discussed in Chapter 1's input/output section, to the programmer a socket is nothing more than a file. We are able to use streams, read and write information, and save sockets just as we would files. This is an important concept to grasp because the security restrictions that apply to sockets also apply to files. We will discuss security in greater detail in Chapter 13, "Java and Security."

The TPOP Client

Clients are the end user interface to an application and end up being responsible mainly for collecting user input and sending it to the server. Servers are the recipients of that information. Think of a client approaching your restaurant with a pocket full of money and you the owner, as the server, gladly accepting that money for your product and services. In this section we begin our discussion of client/server programming by developing an application that transmits information across a network connection to another program.

Developing Clients for Servers

The PizzaTool we are about to create is a stand-alone Java application and will have a fancy GUI interface that you can design yourself. Our GUI code's framework looks something like this:

```java
import java.awt.*;
import java.net.*;
import java.io.*;
public class PizzaTool extends Frame
{
    // AWT Components
    . . . skip these for now . . .

    PizzaTool()
    {
        // initialize the application frame

        // create the GUIs
    }
    public boolean action(
            Event evt,
            Object obj
    )
    {
        if(evt.target == sendButton)
        {
        }
        return true;
    }
    public static void main(
      String args[]
    )
    {
        PizzaTool pizza = new PizzaTool();
        pizza.show();
    }
}
```

When displayed, our pizza tool GUI will look something like the one shown in Figure 3-1.

We need to modify this working client to send its information over the network to the other end. To do so, we must create a socket in our application's constructor and initialize it as we did earlier. We will use port number 8205 in this application.

```java
import java.awt.*;
import java.net.*;
import java.io.*;
```

> **NOTE:** As will be our practice throughout this book, we show you the completed GUI rather than showing the code development process for it. There are several GUI builders on the market, and we hope you will choose one to assist you. If you are a neophyte at Java, we recommend using a text editor and Sun's JDK (Java Development Kit) until you become proficient at Java. GUI builders like Visual Café, J++, and JBuilder are great tools and can really increase productivity; the problem is that they really hide a lot (especially in building the user interface) from you. In some cases, the code produced by the GUI builders is not necessarily good code, but it is code that will work.

```
public class PizzaTool extends Frame
                    implements ActionListener
{
    // AWT Components
    . . . skip these for now . . .

    // network components
    Socket socket;
    DataInputStream inStream;
    PrintStream outStream;

    PizzaTool()
    {
        // initialize the application frame

        // create the GUIs

        // define Exit button handler

        // define Reset button handle
    }
    public void actionPerformed(ActionEvent e)
    {
        // handle the Submit button here, build and send the order
    }
    public static void main(String args[])
    {
        // use the constructor to build the GUI
        PizzaTool pizza = new PizzaTool();
        // show the GUI and wait for an Action Event
        pizza.show();
    }
}
```

Inside the `actionPerformed` method, we need to send the information we gather from our GUI back to the server. The server then makes a calculation and sends us the total for the order. First, we must send information across the socket using the `outStream` variable we derived from the socket. Then, just as we did earlier, we

must turn around and read information from the same socket using the `inStream` variable.

```java
import java.awt.*;
import java.net.*;
import java.io.*;
public class PizzaTool extends Frame
                      implements ActionListener
{
    // AWT Components
    . . . skip these for now . . .
    // network components
    Socket socket;
    DataInputStream inStream;
    PrintStream outStream;
    PizzaTool()
    {
        // initialize the application frame
        // create the GUIs
        // define Exit button handler
        // define Reset button handler
        resetButton = new Button("Reset Order");
        resetButton.setBounds(160,270,140,60);
        add(resetButton);
        resetButton.addActionListener(
            new ActionListener()
            {
                public void actionPerformed(ActionEvent e)
                {
                    instructionField.setText("Select Pizza");
                    nameField.setText("");
                    addressField.setText("");
                    phoneField.setText("");
                }
            }
        );
    }
    public void actionPerformed(ActionEvent e)
    {
        // handle the Submit button here, build and send the order
        // create the socket and attach input and output streams
        try
        { // open the socket to the remote host
            socket = new Socket("localhost", 8205);
            in = new BufferedReader(
```

```
                new InputStreamReader(socket.getInputStream()));
        outStream = new PrintStream(socket.getOutputStream());
    }
    catch (Exception e)
    {
        System.out.println(IO Exception: " + e.toString());
    }
    // Send the order to the server
    instructionField.setText("Sending order");
    try
    {
        outStream.println(
                nameField.getText() + "|" +
                addressField.getText() + "|" +
                phoneField.getText() + "|" +
                size + "|" +
                toppings);
    }
    catch (Exception e)
    {
        System.out.println("Error: " + e.toString());
    }
    // read the price from the server
    String totalString = new String();
    try
    {
        totalString = inStream.readLine();
    }
    catch (Exception e)
    {
        System.out.println("Error: " + e.toString());
    }
}
public static void main(String args[])
{
    // use the constructor to build the GUI
    PizzaTool pizza = new PizzaTool();
    // show the GUI and wait for an Action Event
    pizza.show();
}
}
```

Please check out the bold, italicized text that defined the Reset button and its event handler. This looks a little strange but really isn't; what you are looking at is an anonymous inner class being used as the event handler. With the new event model that came about with JDK 1.1 came some improved event handling. Using an anonymous inner class, the event handler can be kept right with the code (this aids maintainability) and eliminates the need for large if/then/else structures for decoding what caused the event. This makes the code run considerably faster.

Notice also how we send information to the server. We have created our own protocol and message format to use to send the three important customer fields, as well as the kind of pizza ordered, directly to the pizza server. The format is delimited by the bar sign (" | ") and, as we will see in a moment, is interpreted on the server end.

```
outStream.println(
    nameField.getText() + "|" +
    addressField.getText() + "|" +
    phoneField.getText() + "|" +
    size + "|" +
    toppings);
```

Once complete, our application then is able to publish the information it received from the server.

NOTE: In order to conserve paper (save some trees), we have not shown you the entire code listing for both the GUI and the network portion of our application. As always, a full, working version of this application can be found on the CD-ROM that accompanies this book.

Socket programming is at the heart of everything we discuss in this book. Every communication technology involved with computers uses sockets in some fashion. Often, having control over the format and length of messages between clients and servers is of great importance. We could just as easily have created our pizza application using a mechanism found in other parts of this book. However, by using sockets, we had full control over how the communication (protocol) is implemented.

Clients and Servers in Short

So far we have implemented an application for which we know what is on both ends. This form of point-to-point communication is one way to create a networked application. We created a message, located the destination for the message, and shipped it off. While reliable, point-to-point communication is important, we also want to be able to form a message and broadcast it. In so doing, anyone anywhere can grab the message and act on it. This form of broadcast communication can also be accomplished using Java sockets and is discussed in the next section.

UDP Client

We have spoken so far about TCP communication, which we have mentioned is a point-to-point, reliable protocol. Well, what makes an unreliable protocol? An unreliable protocol is one in which you send a chunk of information, and if it gets lost along the way, nobody really minds. TCP provides an infrastructure that ensures a communication is sent and arrives safely. Another protocol, User Datagram Protocol (UDP), is a "spit in the wind" protocol. One day, you wake up, spit into the wind, and hope it will land somewhere. Likewise, with datagrams you can easily form a message, send it, and hope it gets to the other end. There are no guarantees that it will ever arrive, so be careful when choosing to use a UDP socket over a TCP-based socket for your application.

Datagrams

In the last chapter, we referred to datagrams as letters that we send to a mailbox. In fact, a datagram is a chunk of memory, not unlike a letter—a chunk of paper into which we put information and send off to a mailbox. Just as with the U.S. Postal Service, there is absolutely no guarantee that the letter will ever arrive at its destination.

Here's a sample "receive buffer" datagram:

```
DatagramPacket packet = new DatagramPacket(buf, 256);
```

You must give the constructor the name of a byte or character array to receive the data and the length of the buffer in bytes or characters. You get data as follows:

```
socket.receive(packet);
```

where socket is created as follows:

```
socket = new DatagramSocket();
```

The `DatagramSocket` class is an endpoint (mailbox) for UDP communication. Like the `Socket` class (which uses TCP), there is no need for a programmer to specify the transport-level protocol to use.

After a datagram is received, you can find out where it came from as follows:

```
address = packet.getAddress();
port = packet.getPort();
```

and you can return a reply as follows:

```
packet = new DatagramPacket(buf, buf.length, address, port);
socket.send(packet);
```

This datagram will go out the same UDP port (akin to a "mailbox"), to the other process-receiving datagrams on that UDP port number. A UDP server can specify its service port number in its constructor, in this case port number 31543.

```
socket = new DatagramSocket(31543);
```

> **NOTE:** Datagrams are sort of like that old "I Love Lucy" episode in which Lucy and Ethel go to work in a candy factory. As they stand in front of a conveyor belt, little candies begin to flow out. Lucy and Ethel are able to wrap and package the candies as they come out. Soon, their boss speeds up the belt, and the candies begin to flow out really fast; Lucy and Ethel are unable to keep up. Similarly, datagrams happen along the port and are picked up by receiver programs that happen to be listening. Unlike Lucy and Ethel, however, if you miss one, nothing bad will happen.

Creating a UDP Sender

To pay homage to Lucy and Ethel in our own bizarre, twisted way, let's create a cookie factory! In our factory, we will be able to build chocolate chip cookies and specify the number of chips we want in each one. Then we will send them along the conveyor belt to be packaged and shipped off to some Java engineer turned writer who is in desperate need of a Scooby Snack.

Real-world implementations of broadcast communication include stock tickers that constantly publish stock quotes for NASDAQ or the New York Stock Exchange. By simply plugging your receiver into the port, you can grab that information and do something with it (like displaying it as a ticker tape message across the bottom of your screen). Modifying our sample program to similarly broadcast and grab information is quite simple.

To begin our sender program, we must create a Java application for our `Cookie-Bakery`. The application will have a simple GUI in which you can specify the number of chips in the cookie using a slider and then simply press a button to send the cookie to the conveyor belt.

The GUI framework looks like this:

```java
import java.awt.*;
import java.net.*;

public class CookieBakery extends Frame
{
    // AWT components

    CookieBakery() //constructor
    {
      // initialize the application frame
      // build the GUI and event handlers

      sendButton = new Button("Send Cookie");
      sendButton.setBounds(10,270,290,60);
      add(sendButton);
      sendButton.addActionListener(
```

```java
new ActionListener()
{
  public void actionPerformed(ActionEvent e)
  {
      // determine the number of chips
      int numChips = chipsScrollbar.getValue();
      String messageChips = numChips + " chips";

      // build the message and send it

            // display final result
            instructionField.setText(
                    "Sent Cookie with " +
                    numChips + " chips!");
  }
}
// all events handled by inner classes, this is required
public void actionPerformed(Event e){;}

public static void main(String args[])
{
    CookieBakery cookies = new CookieBakery();
    cookies.show();
}
}
```

The GUI itself will resemble that shown in Figure 3-2 with a slider to select the number of chips and a button to press so that you can "bake" it.

Formatting a UDP Packet. In order to send a packet to the server, we must create and format one. Packets are created using buffers and contain an array of bytes. Therefore, any string message that you wish to send must be converted to an array of bytes. We will do this in a moment. Also, we need to define and obtain

![Number of Chips slider with Bake Cookie and Exit buttons]

Figure 3-2 Sample GUI for the CookieBakery.

the Internet address of the machine on which this application runs. UDP requires it as part of its protocol.

```java
import java.awt.*;
import java.net.*;
import java.awt.event.ActionListener;
import java.awt.event.ActionEvent;
public class CookieBakery extends Frame
{
    // AWT components

    CookieBakery() //constructor
    {
        // initialize the application frame
        // build the GUI and event handlers

        sendButton = new Button("Send Cookie");
        sendButton.setBounds(10,270,290,60);
        add(sendButton);
        sendButton.addActionListener(
            new ActionListener()
            {
                public void actionPerformed(ActionEvent e)
                {
                    // determine the number of chips
                    int numChips = chipsScrollbar.getValue();
                    String messageChips = numChips + " chips";

                    // convert the chip message to byte form
                    int msgLength = messageChips.length();
                    byte[] message = new byte[msgLength];
                    message = messageChips.getBytes();

                    // send a message
                    try
                    {
                        // format the cookie into a UDP packet
                        instructionField.setText(
                                "Sending Cookie...");
                        DatagramPacket packet = new DatagramPacket(
                                message, msgLength,
                                internetAddress, 8505);

                        // send the packet to the server
                            DatagramSocket socket = new
                                                DatagramSocket();
                            socket.send(packet);
                    }
                    catch(Exception exc)
                    {
                        System.out.println("Error! - " +
                                            exc.toString());
```

```
          }
          // display final result
          instructionField.setText(
                  "Sent Cookie with " +
                      numChips + " chips!");
      }
    }
    public void actionPerformed(Event e){;}
    public static void main(String args[])
    {
        CookieBakery cookies = new CookieBakery();
        cookies.show();
    }
  }
}
```

Sending the Packet to the Server.

In order to send the cookie to the conveyor belt, we must create a DatagramSocket. Then we can send the packet we just created using the send routine.

```java
import java.awt.*;
import java.net.*;
import java.awt.event.ActionListener;
import java.awt.event.ActionEvent;
public class CookieBakery extends Frame
{
    // AWT components

    CookieBakery() //constructor
    {
      // initialize the application frame
      // build the GUI and event handlers

      sendButton = new Button("Send Cookie");
      sendButton.setBounds(10,270,290,60);
      add(sendButton);
      sendButton.addActionListener(
          new ActionListener()
          {
            public void actionPerformed(ActionEvent e)
            {
                // determine the number of chips
                int numChips = chipsScrollbar.getValue();
                String messageChips = numChips + " chips";

                // convert the chip message to byte form
                int msgLength = messageChips.length();
                byte[] message = new byte[msgLength];
                message = messageChips.getBytes();
```

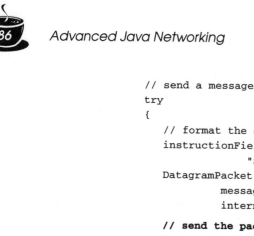

```
            // send a message
            try
            {
               // format the cookie into a UDP packet
               instructionField.setText(
                            "Sending Cookie...");
               DatagramPacket packet = new DatagramPacket(
                            message, msgLength,
                            internetAddress, 8505);

               // send the packet to the server
               DatagramSocket socket =new DatagramSocket();
               Socket.send(packet);
            }
            catch(Exception exc)
            {
               System.out.println("Error! - " +
                                    exc.toString());
            }
            // display final result
            instructionField.setText(
                            "Sent Cookie with " +
                            numChips + " chips!");
         }
      }

   public void actionPerformed(Event e){;}
   public static void main(String args[])
   {
      CookieBakery cookies = new CookieBakery();
      cookies.show();
   }
   }
}
```

Now that we have created an application that sends a message containing "xx chips" to a port, we need something on the other end to receive and decode the message into something useful. After all, we don't want to waste our delicious chocolate chip cookies!

Creating a UDP Receiver. The UDP Receiver we will create will listen in on a port and wait for cookies. When it gets one, our CookieMonster will let us know by printing a "Yummy, tastes good" message. As with our CookieBakery, the CookieMonster will listen in on port 8505, a totally random selection. To start our CookieMonster, first we must create the CookieMonster object with its own application main containing the packet that we will read and the socket from which we will get it. Note that we are importing the java.net.* package once again.

NOTE: We find throughout this book that servers, in this case a receiver, must be applications, whereas clients very easily can be applets as well. The reason is that Java's security mechanism will not allow a downloaded applet to have unlimited access to a port on the machine to which it is downloaded. Because of the Java security model, you are prevented from developing downloadable servers. This may change with the introduction of browsers that are able to change those security restrictions.

```java
import java.awt.*;
import java.net.*;
public class CookieMonster
{
    public static void main(
        String args[]
    )
    {
        // our socket
        DatagramSocket socket = null;

        // our packet
        DatagramPacket packet = null;
    }
}
```

Now we must create and initialize the packet that we will receive. Note that we have to specify a buffer into which the packet will read the message. A packet by itself is composed of four elements. The first is shown in the following code.

```java
import java.awt.*;
import java.net.*;
public class CookieMonster
{
    public static void main(
        String args[]
    )
    {
        // our socket
        DatagramSocket socket = null;

        // our packet
        DatagramPacket packet = null;

            // create a receive buffer
            byte[] buffer = new byte[1024];

            // create a packet to receive the buffer
            packet = new DatagramPacket(buffer, buffer.length);
    }
}
```

Once our packet is put together, we need to sit on a socket and wait for someone to fill it with information. We use the `DatagramSocket`'s `receive` routine to hang on a UDP port and get information. We must pass the packet to the sockets `receive` method so that the packet knows where to put the information it gets.

```java
import java.awt.*;
import java.net.*;
public class CookieMonster
{
    public static void main(
      String args[]
    )
    {
        // our socket
        DatagramSocket socket = null;

        // our packet
        DatagramPacket packet = null;

        // create a receive buffer
        byte[] buffer = new byte[1024];

        // create a packet to receive the buffer
        packet = new DatagramPacket(buffer, buffer.length);

        // now create a socket to listen in
        try
        {
            socket = new DatagramSocket(8505);
        }
        catch(Exception exc)
        {
            System.out.println("Error! - " + exc.toString());
        }

        // now sit in an infinite loop and eat cookies!
        while(true)
        {
            // sit around and wait for a new packet
            try
            {
                socket.receive(packet);
            }
            catch(Exception exc)
            {
                System.out.println("Error! - " + exc.toString());
            }
        }
    }
}
```

So now we have a cookie in our hands, and we have to somehow eat it. To do so, we must first extract the cookie from the packet by retrieving the packet's buffer.

Because we specified the buffer size when we created the packet, the `CookieMonster` waits until the buffer is filled before it returns the packet. This means that if the packets on the sending end are smaller than the packets we are reading here, we will end up with a packet, plus a little bit of the packet that comes down the pike afterwards, causing havoc in our messaging system. If our buffer is too large on the sending end, we will receive only a little bit of the message. It is important that you synchronize both the receiver and the sender so that they receive and send the same size buffer.

```java
import java.awt.*;
import java.net.*;

public class CookieMonster
{
    public static void main(
        String args[]
    )
    {
        // our socket
        DatagramSocket socket = null;

        // our packet
        DatagramPacket packet = null;

        // create a receive buffer
        byte[] buffer = new byte[1024];

        // create a packet to receive the buffer
        packet = new DatagramPacket(buffer, buffer.length);

        // now create a socket to listen in
        try
        {
            socket = new DatagramSocket(8505);
        }
        catch(Exception exc)
        {
            System.out.println("Error! - " + exc.toString());
        }

        // now sit in an infinite loop and eat cookies!
        while(true)
```

```
    {
        // sit around and wait for a new packet
        try
        {
            socket.receive(packet);
        }
        catch(Exception exc)
        {
            System.out.println("Error! - " + exc.toString());
        }
        // extract the cookie
        String cookieString = new String(buffer, 0, 0,
            packet.getLength());

        // now show what we got!
        System.out.println("Yummy!  Got a cookie with " +
            cookieString);
    }
    }
}
```

Now that we have learned how to create point-to-point and broadcast communication mechanisms, let's apply our knowledge to implement our featured application. In this real-world scenario, we must create a mechanism that enables a client to change its state and to send that information to a server to be stored and retrieved at a later date. To develop such an application, we need a point-to-point protocol because reliability is of the utmost premium. After all, we don't want to schedule an appointment and not know if it actually got on our calendar.

Featured Application

As we discussed in Chapter 1, "Advanced Java," we will reimplement the same "featured application" in this chapter and in each of the next four chapters. We hope that this gives you an insight into the advantages and disadvantages of each of the major communication alternatives that we present in this book. Our socket implementation needs to be preceded by a discussion on how we plan to implement messaging between the client and the server. Once that is complete, we can implement the client and the server to exchange information in that format.

Messaging Format

Our messaging format must incorporate the two major elements contained in our notion of an appointment—the time of the appointment and the reason for the appointment. Therefore, we will create a message format akin to the Pizza

Tool's message. In the Pizza Tool we implemented a few sections ago, we delimited our message with the bar symbol (" | "). Once again, we will use the bar symbol to separate the time and reason in our message from the client to the server.

From the server to the client, we need a slightly similar but more robust format. When the server sends information to the client, we will need to string a variable number of bar-delimited appointments together. The client can then use the `StringTokenizer` object to extract the information it needs.

But, the client cannot accept messages without asking for them first. Therefore, we need a header to the message. When we schedule an appointment (i.e., send a message from the client to the server), we precede the message by the word "store." When we merely prompt the server to send the client a message (i.e., the client sends a message to the server telling it to go ahead and reply), we precede the message with the word "retrieve."

Therefore, our message will be in one of the following two formats:

```
store|Take Fleagle to dentist|1
retrieve
```

The retrieve message prompts the server to send a message back with appointments strung together but delimited by the bar symbol.

Client

Because implementing the client for the featured application is quite similar to the Pizza Tool's client, the code we are about to produce will look remarkably similar to the code for the Pizza Tool. In order to plug our featured application socket implementation directly into the Calendar Manager, we must implement the `NetworkModule` that we declared in Chapter 1.

```
public class NetworkModule
{
    public void scheduleAppointment(String reason, int time);

    public Vector getAppointments();

    public void initNetwork();

    public void shutdownNetwork();
}
```

Specifically, we need to implement the `scheduleAppointments` and `getAppointments` methods. We will also have to create and implement a constructor to open and establish the socket connection. We will first implement the constructor. The code is basically cut and pasted directly from the Pizza Tool:

```
import java.awt.*;
import java.util.*;
```

```
import java.net.*;
import java.io.*;
public class NetworkModule
{
    // network components
    Socket socket;
    DataInputStream inStream;
    PrintStream outStream;

    NetworkModule()
    {
        try
        {
            socket = new Socket("localhost", 8205);
            inStream = new BufferedReader(
                        new InputStreamReader(
                        socket.getInputStream()));
            outStream = new
                        PrintStream(socket.getOutputStream());
        }
        catch(Exception exc)
        {
            System.out.println("Error! - " + exc.toString());
        }
    }

    public void scheduleAppointment(
                    String appointmentReason,
                    int appointmentTime)
    {
    }
    public Vector getAppointments()
    {
    }
    public void initNetwork()
    {
    }
    public void shutdownNetwork()
    {
    }
}
```

Now we must implement the `scheduleAppointment` method that goes to the server with a formatted message containing the new appointment. Notice how we put together the message so that it conforms to the messaging format we just agreed upon.

```
public void scheduleAppointment(
```

```
            String appointmentReason,
            int appointmentTime )
{
   try
   {
      outStream.println(
          "store|" +
          appointmentReason + "|" +
          appointmentTime + "|");
   }
   catch(Exception exc)
   {
      System.out.println("Error! - " + exc.toString());
   }
}
```

Once again, the `StringTokenizer` comes to our rescue as we begin to decode the server's message to us in the `getAppointments` method. In order for the server to send us a message, we must prompt it to do so. That way, a socket connection is established, and a reply can be sent along the same route. It isn't entirely necessary to do things this way, but it is the preferred and time-honored method. Once we get our string from the server, we must tokenize it, step through each field, and convert it into a `Vector`.

```
public Vector getAppointments()
{
   // the variable to store all of our appointments in
   Vector appointmentVector = new Vector();
   // the string to put our appointments in
   String appointmentString = new String();
   // now get the appointments
   try
   {
      // tell the server we want the appointments it has
      outStream.println("retrieve|");
      // now listen for all the information we get back
      appointmentString = inStream.readLine();
   }
   catch(Exception exc)
   {
      System.out.println("Error! - " + exc.toString());
   }
   // tokenize the string
   StringTokenizer stk =
           new StringTokenizer(appointmentString, "|");
   // translate into a Vector
   while(stk.hasMoreTokens())
   {
```

```
    // create a variable to stick the appointment in
    AppointmentType appointment = new AppointmentType();
    // now get the next appointment from the string
    appointment.reason = stk.nextToken();
    appointment.time =
            Integer.valueOf(stk.nextToken()).intValue();
    // put the appointment into the vector
    appointmentVector.addElement(appointment);
    }
    // return the Vector
    return appointmentVector;
}
```

Server

To implement the server, we will blatantly plagiarize code from the pizza application earlier in this chapter. Basically, we take all the server code from there, including the thread portion, and modify it for our needs. First, we need to implement the Store method. We will store our appointments in a `Vector` for simplicity's sake. The code snippet that follows is from the `Run` method of the `CalendarThread`.

NOTE: You could just as easily use some kind of serialization or even a file to keep your appointments persistent. When the server shuts down, we will lose all the appointments in our current implementation. Our server keeps data in a *transient* state, meaning that it is not maintained between executions.

```
// convert to a readable format
try
{
    StringTokenizer stk =
        new StringTokenizer(newOrder, "|");
    String operation = stk.nextToken();
    if(operation.equals("store"))
    {
        String reason = stk.nextToken();
        int time =
            Integer.valueOf(stk.nextToken()).intValue();

        // no exception was thrown so store the appointment
        AppointmentType appt = new AppointmentType();
        appt.reason = reason;
        appt.time = time;
        appointmentVector.addElement(appt);
        // put our result on the screen
        System.out.println("stored" + reason + "|" + time);
```

```
        }
}
catch(NoSuchElementException exc)
```

Now we must implement the retrieve function. The retrieve function creates a new string, delimited by the bar symbol, of course, that contains every appointment in our Vector. It then sends that information back to the client using the same socket on which it received the original message.

```
else
{
    String returnValue = new String();
    // put together a string of appointments
    for(int x = 0; x < appointmentVector.size(); x++)
    {
        AppointmentType appt  =
          (AppointmentType)appointmentVector.elementAt(x);
        returnValue += appt.reason + "|" + appt.time + "|";
    }
    // now write the appointments back to the socket
            out.println(returnValue);
}
```

Summary

Sockets are the backbone of any communication mechanism. Everything we talk about in this book from here on will use them in some way or another. For example, in the past some CORBA implementations used UDP for their socket infrastructure, eliminating complex webs of point-to-point connections. This sped up their implementation because they spent less time routing messages and more time sending them. When new objects were added to the system, UDP enabled them to be plugged in with little effort and little impact on the rest of the system. Lately, however, the onset of TCP-based IIOP has pushed almost all CORBA vendors to the more reliable protocol.

TCP is a reliable protocol system that has been used by generations of computer programmers. We all somehow, somewhere get our start in network programming by first using TCP/IP and writing to pipes and sockets. In the next chapter, we will explore Database access using Java Database Connectivity. JDBC is a technology that is basic to the concept of enterprise programming (i.e., tying our applications to our corporate databases). Although hidden from us by the API, at the very heart of JDBC are sockets. From JDBC we'll examine two examples of network object technologies. First we'll look at Java Remote Method Invocation, an all Java approach to distributed object computing. After RMI we'll look at the Java version of the grandfather of distributed object computing, CORBA. What we'll see when examining these technologies is that the abstractions of the object models entirely hides the need to do socket level programming; this is done to simplify how we program. By eliminating the need to do our own socket programming, the abstractions provided by network object models provide a simpler programming model for us to deal with.

Chapter 4

Java Database Connectivity

▼ INSIDE JDBC

▼ DATABASES AND SQL

▼ RETRIEVING INFORMATION

▼ STORING INFORMATION

▼ A JDBC VERSION OF THE FEATURED APP

Today, nearly all companies choose to store their vast quantities of information in large repositories of data. These databases are vital to the dissemination of information via the Internet. Java, as the anointed Internet language, answers the need to connect information storage to application servers using the Java Database Connectivity framework.

As we will see in these next few chapters, JDBC is a core set of APIs that enables Java applications to connect to industry standard and proprietary database management systems. Using JDBC, your applications can retrieve and store information using Structured Query Language statements as well as a database engine itself. Included in this chapter is a brief introduction to SQL and its merits.

Inside JDBC

The guidelines for creating the JDBC architecture all center on one very important characteristic—simplicity. Databases are complex beasts, and companies that rely on them generally have an army of personnel ready to administer and program them. As a result, transferring that complexity to Java via JDBC would violate the ethos of the language. Therefore, the JDBC architects developed the specification with the idea that database access would not require advanced degrees and years of training to accomplish.

Knowing full well that there are a plethora of databases in existence today, the architectural challenge for JDBC was to provide a simple front-end interface for connecting with even the most complex of databases. To the programmer, the interface to a database should be the same regardless of the kind of database to which you want to connect. Figure 4-1 shows the 50,000-foot view of our JDBC application model.

Database Drivers

In the world of distributed computing it is easier to understand databases if we think of them as devices rather than software. First of all, we usually install databases on separate machines that are network accessible, and second, we almost always access the database through a standardized driver rather than using native interfaces. If we think of our database as a device, the idea of a driver makes more sense due mainly to our preconceived ideas (and experiences) with having to install device drivers every time we want to add a new card or peripheral device to our workstation.

Standardized drivers for databases came about in much the same way that many other ad hoc standards get developed; in the case of databases, Microsoft developed Open Database Connectivity as a standard for Windows applications to connect to and use Microsoft databases. ODBC became so popular so fast that other database vendors saw the writing on the wall for proprietary APIs and databases whose interface was based on proprietary APIs that they quickly came out with ODBC drivers for their databases. This allowed anyone's database to be accessed from a Windows application in exactly the same way that a Microsoft database

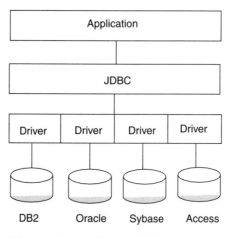

Figure 4-1 Basic JDBC application architecture.

would be accessed. ODBC was designed into Windows, and the coupling between it and Microsoft databases was extremely tight and performance-oriented. Other database vendors took a slightly different approach to ODBC; they built an ODBC interface that then translated ODBC into their native API calls. This puts an extra layer between the application and the database. This type of driver is the reason that ODBC has gotten a bad rap on some database platforms.

JDBC takes a number of approaches to database connectivity, and it is important to remember that JDBC is really a published standard interface to databases similar to ODBC. There are currently four common approaches to database connectivity each with a corresponding driver type.

Type 1 Drivers. The JDBC-ODBC bridge driver takes the simple approach of translating JDBC calls to equivalent ODBC calls and then letting ODBC do all the work. Drivers of this type require that an ODBC driver also be installed on each workstation and that some proprietary libraries (Vendor APIs) that help with the JDBC to ODBC conversion must also be installed. Although effective, these drivers provide relatively low performance due to the extra software layer(s). This driver is handy for putting together application prototypes for "early on" customer demonstrations; because you do not have to install a full blown relational database management system, this is one place where MS Access is a perfectly fine tool. There is a caveat with using MS Access databases: Always remember that an .mdb file is just that, a file (not a database management system). The ODBC driver makes .mdb files appear to be database management systems. Now here is the caveat, the ODBC drive must be able to find the .mdb file on a mapped drive (i.e., the *.mdb* file can be anywhere on your LAN that the ODBC driver [on the machine] you are using as your data server can find via a mapped drive). This means that, if the database is on a machine that only has TCP/IP connectivity, you are out of luck. This also means that, if you are a UNIX user, you are normally out of luck and must resort to using RDBMs even for prototypes. See Figure 4-2 for an architectural view of a type one driver application.

In the case of Microsoft databases like Access and SQL Server, which are designed around ODBC, the ODBC driver to database connection is direct and the only

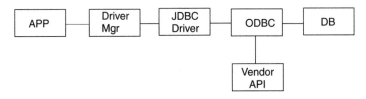

Figure 4-2 Type 1 JDBC/ODBC bridge.

extra layer involved is the conversion from JDBC to ODBC. In the case of other vendors' databases that have their own native APIs, there can be an additional conversion from ODBC to the vendor's native API.

An additional thing we need to remember when programming for the Enterprise is that, in the case of Java applets, an applet can only make a network connection back to the machine (IP address) that it was served from. This requires that our database be running on the same machine as our Web server. This could have some serious implications from the standpoint of overall performance for a busy Web site. In most cases, the best solution to this problem is to not use a type 1 driver. Instead, use another driver type and pick a three-tier architecture rather than the two-tier approach of the type 1 driver.

Type 2 Drivers. Drivers in this category typically provide a partial Java, partial native API interface to the database. Typical of this type of driver is the driver provided by IBM for its DB2 Universal Database (UDB). UDB provides a native driver in the form of the DB2 Client Enabler (CAE), which must be installed on each client machine. The CAE installs a rather elaborate set of driver software that allows access to any DB2 database to which the client machine has network connectivity. Along with the CAE comes a JDBC driver. The JDBC driver is placed in your virtual machine's CLASSPATH. Once loaded by the JDBC Driver Manager and a database connection is established your application has a fairly high-performance pipe to the database. Figure 4-3 illustrates this architecture.

DB2 (and most other modern databases) can be configured to do connection pooling at the database; this doesn't really constitute a three-tier solution, it is still a two-tier (maybe pseudo three-tier) solution.

Type 3 Drivers. Drivers of this type are usually called network protocol drivers and convert the JDBC calls into a database independent protocol that is transmitted to a middleware server that translates the network protocol into the correct native protocol for the target database. The middleware server is usually run on an independent, high-performance machine and has the ability to convert the network protocol to the required native protocols for a number of different database vendors' products. It also is the JDBC driver source for the client driver manager. The middle tier usually uses a type 1 or 2 driver for its connectivity to

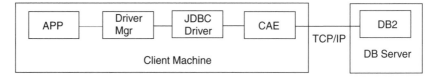

Figure 4-3 Type 2 DB2 JDBC driver.

the database. Because many databases are good places to store and retrieve information (but are poor connection managers), the middle-tier server often has the job of being a connection manager for the databases (i.e., when started up, a number of database connections are established and held open; the middleware then acts as a router, routing database transactions to already open database connections). The beauty of this is that the end user never incurs the penalty of establishing the connection (which is considerable) to the database. Figure 4-4 illustrates this architecture.

Type 4 Drivers. Last but not least is the all Java, type 4 driver (see Figure 4-5). These drivers require no special software to be installed on client machines and are typically provided by database vendors or vendors like Intersolv and Hit Software that specialize in database drivers. Solutions that use type 4 drivers are typically two-tier, but with the connection pooling that most databases currently provide we have that previously mentioned pseudo three-tier architecture. These drivers are perfect for applet-based clients as everything required by the client is self-contained in the client download from the Web server.

In the desktop world, a driver enables a particular piece of hardware to interface with the rest of the machine. Similarly, a database driver gives JDBC a means to communicate with a database. Perhaps written in some form of native code but usually written in Java itself, the database drivers available for JDBC are wide and varied, addressing several different kinds of databases.

The JDBC API is available for users as part of the JDK. The JDBCODBC bridge is supplied as part of the JDK; other drivers are available from the database vendors or driver specialty companies.

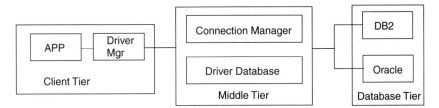

Figure 4–4 Type 3 driver.

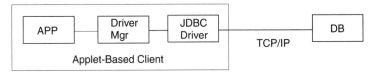

Figure 4–5 Type 4 driver.

The DriverManager Object. At the heart of JDBC lies the DriverManager. Once a driver is installed, you need to load it into your Java object by using the DriverManager. It groups drivers together so that multiple databases can be accessed from within the same Java object. It provides a common interface to a JDBC driver object without having to delve into the internals of the database itself.

The driver is responsible for creating and implementing the Connection, Statement, and ResultSet objects for the specific database, and the DriverManager then is able to acquire those object implementations for itself. In so doing, applications that are written using the DriverManager are isolated from the implementation details of databases, as well as from future enhancements and changes to the implementation itself, as you can see in Figure 4-6.

Database `Connection Interface`. The Connection object is responsible for establishing the link between the Database Management System and the Java application. By abstracting it from the `DriverManager`, the driver can isolate the database from specific parts of the implementation. It also enables the programmer to select the proper driver for the required application.

The `Connection.getConnection` method accepts a URL and enables the JDBC object to use different drivers depending on the situation, isolates applets from connection-related information, and gives the application a means by which to specify the specific database to which it should connect. The URL takes the form of `jdbc:<subprotocol>:<subname>`. The subprotocol is a kind of connectivity to the database, along the lines of ODBC, which we shall discuss in a moment. The subname depends on the subprotocol but usually allows you to configure the database that the application will look at.

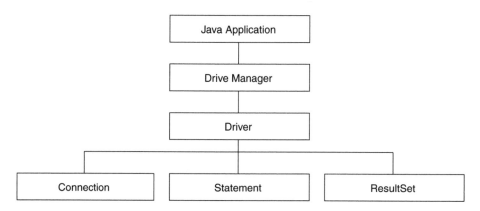

Figure 4-6 The Driver abstracts the Connection, Statement, and ResultSet objects from the application.

Database Statement Object. A Statement encapsulates a query written in Structured Query Language and enables the JDBC object to compose a series of steps to look up information in a database. Using a Connection, the Statement can be forwarded to the database and obtain a ResultSet.

ResultSet Access Control. A ResultSet is a container for a series of rows and columns acquired from a Statement call. Using the ResultSet's iterator routines, the JDBC object can step through each row in the result set. Individual column fields can be retrieved using the get methods within the ResultSet. Columns may be specified by their field name or by their index.

JDBC and ODBC. In many ways, Open Database Connectivity (ODBC) was a precursor to all that JDBC is intended to accomplish. It adequately abstracts the boring tedium of databases, and the proprietary APIs to those databases, from the application programmer; it ties many different kinds of databases together so that you only have to create one source file to access them; and it is fairly ubiquitous. Recognizing the relative acceptance of ODBC technology, JDBC offers a JDBC-to-ODBC driver free with the JDK.

With this, JDBC applications can talk to the same database access engine as non-Java applications. Furthermore, integrating JDBC into your existing business process can be done fairly easily because the bridge ensures that no additional work is required to enable Java Database Connectivity.

NOTE: Because of copyright restrictions, we are unable to supply these drivers on the CD-ROM, but you may visit the JDBC page on the JavaSoft Web site at *java.sun.com/jdbc* and get the latest information on drivers and the pointers to them.

As you can see, the JDBC application communicates with the database using the same existing OLE or COM protocol. Furthermore, any administration issues associated with the database are negligible because the existing administration strategy is still applicable. Application programmers need know only that the ODBC bridge will be used and that they should not tailor their application to it.

Installing the ODBC driver for Windows will be discussed in the next section. Because it is a Microsoft product, the process is easy, but the reliability is in doubt. Keep in mind that most mission-critical applications are run using heavy-duty, workstation-based databases. These databases are expensive and difficult to administer but they are more reliable than a Microsoft Access solution. In any event, we will show you how to write applications tailored for Microsoft because the general computing populace, and more importantly the audience of this book, will not necessarily have access to database servers like Sybase, DB2, or Oracle.

JDBC in General

Java Database Connectivity encapsulates the functionality of databases and abstracts that information from the end user or application programmer. Creating simple JDBC applications requires only minor knowledge of databases, but more complex applications may require intensive training in database administration and programming. For that reason, we have chosen several simple and fun examples to display the power of a Java solution that will more likely than not be used by mission-critical applications.

So far we have only addressed the use of JDBC on Windows-based platforms. We, as application developers and architects, shouldn't lose sight of the fact that JDBC works on any platform that supports the version 1.1 (or newer) Java Virtual Machine. This includes many UNIX platforms from IBM, Sun, and HP to name a few and mainframe computers like IBM's OS390, VM/CMS and its midrange OS/400-based computers. On all these platforms JDBC provides a consistent interface to relational databases native to these platforms. Almost all modern relational database management systems provide TCP/IP-based access to their data stores via SQL. This gives us as enterprise application developers connectivity from virtually any Java-based client to any relational database on any host platform.

Databases and SQL

Databases are storage mechanisms for vast quantities of data. An entire segment of the computer industry is devoted to database administration, perhaps hinting that databases are not only complex and difficult but also best left to professionals. Because of this level of difficulty and of our desire to get you started in linking Java to databases, we have chosen to implement a widely available, easily administered, and simply installed database. Microsoft Access can be purchased at your local software retailer. If you want to get started, it's a good place to start. From there, you can move on to more complex databases such as Oracle and Sybase.

In this section, we intend to introduce and create a simple database. In the next section, you will create a simple Java client that accesses the database and gets information from it. We suggest that further exploration into JDBC be preceded by a serious investigation into SQL (any of the currently available texts on Relational Database Management Systems will suffice; check Amazon.com for currently available texts). The Structured Query Language enables you to create powerful instructions to access databases. Once you grasp SQL, you will be able to understand the reasoning and theories behind JDBC.

Creating an Access Database

We will need to first start Microsoft Access so that we can create a database to talk to. This is an important step, but one that those who either do not have access to or who do not wish to use Microsoft's database can tailor for their own database. After starting Access:

1. Select "Database Wizard" so Access will help you create a database.

2. Select the "Blank Database" icon.

3. Name the database and then you will get a series of tabbed folders. Go to "Tables" and click on "New."

4. You will get a spreadsheet-like view in which you can enter your data.

5. Enter your data as shown in Figure 4-7 and then select "Save" to store the table to the database. Name your table PresidentialCandidate.

As you can see in Figure 4-7, we entered the important statistics from the last presidential election. The percentage is stored as a whole number, not as a decimal. This allows the application to determine how it will represent the information. We also store the electoral votes that each candidate received.

Simple SQL

Now that we've put the statistical data about the candidates into our database table, we can use Access to help us design the queries that we will need for our GUI. To do so, we need to know a little bit of SQL. This is by no means intended to

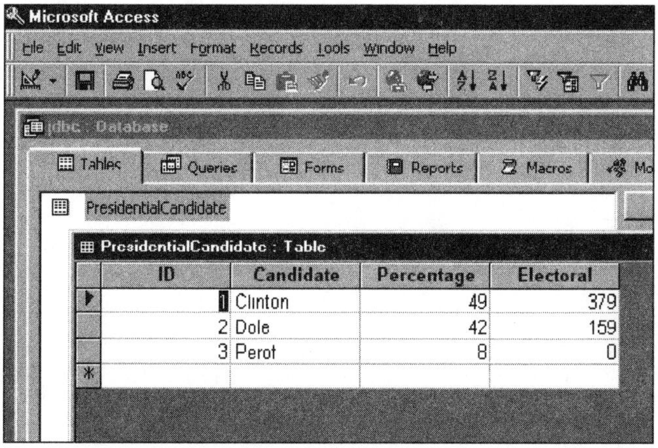

Figure 4-7 Our database entry.

be the be-all and end-all of SQL tutorials. This is a Java book, and as such we will minimize our discussion of SQL. Suffice it to say that, for a programming language that has no program control statements and is completely declarative, it is extremely powerful.

The most often used instruction in SQL is the Select statement. Select enables you to retrieve a copy of specific portions of a database table. As part of the Select statement, you must specify both the database table from which you want the information and a filter for the information (if required). So, when you Select From a table Where the parameters match your requirements, you get a result back.

```
SELECT column list FROM myTable WHERE filter
```

The Where clause of the Select statement may contain what is known as a filter. Filters are specified as conditionals and enable you to further tailor the match parameters for a database query. In a moment, we will query a database table for all the presidential candidates who received electoral votes in the 1996 election. From a field of three candidates, we will end up with two. Big party politics aside, our query will return a result based on the parameters we specify.

In theory, that result always will be a database table of its own. For example, given the following table of presidential election results and the accompanying SQL statement, we will receive a table in return (see Figure 4-8).

This table is like a local variable. It disappears from memory if we don't use it right away. Using JDBC, this results table is saved for us to retrieve the results data from an object called a ResultSet, which will go away (be garbage collected) when the object goes out of scope. We could just as easily include this SQL statement within another SQL statement and achieve predictable results. These are called subqueries and are another powerful tool of which SQL programmers can take advantage.

The beauty of SQL is its simplicity. Obviously, a language of such great importance has several nuances that database experts have long known, but it is still fairly easy to start writing SQL statements, as we will discover in this chapter.

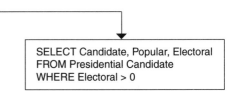

Candidate	Popular	Electoral
Clinton	49	379
Dole	41	159
Perot	8	0

```
SELECT Candidate, Popular, Electoral
FROM Presidential Candidate
WHERE Electoral > 0
```

Figure 4-8 SQL statements can be made to return entire tables.

Generating SQL. In order to create the necessary queries for our Access data, we must do the following steps. This will let us call these super queries rather than being forced to specify SQL in our Java code. There are advantages and disadvantages to this approach, which we will discuss in a moment.

1. Select the "Queries" tab in the main database view.

2. Select "New."

3. Select "Design View."

4. Immediately select "Close" in the "Show Table" view.

5. Go to the "Query" menu and select "SQL Specific" and then "Union."

Now we are presented with a little text input area in which we can enter our query. Using the limited amount of information we have just learned, we must create three queries, one for each candidate, that will retrieve the important statistics for us. We have shown the ClintonQuery in Figure 4-9, and you can see what your database will look like when all three queries are completed.

Note that we have limited the number of queries. You could just as easily create more complex queries, and if you know SQL pretty well, we encourage you to do so. Otherwise, it is probably best to get this "proof of concept" example down pat before proceeding.

Introduction to the ODBC Driver. Once the database is completed, we must make it available via the database server. To do so, we must edit the ODBC Control Panel. The ODBC Control Panel assigns our database to the driver, allowing invocations on the database to pass through the driver right into the database. Unless the database is made public to the ODBC driver, this cannot happen because the system will not know about the database's existence.

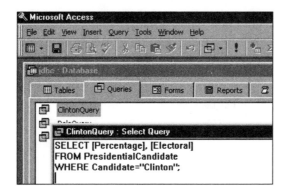

Figure 4-9 Getting statistics on Bill Clinton from the database.

To assign the database to the driver, select the driver Control Panel. The Control Panel should have been installed with Access. If it is not there, check your Microsoft Access installation instructions. Inside the Control Panel, select "MS Access 7.0" and "Select" the proper database from within the Setup dialog box (see Figure 4-10).

Once completed, the ODBC driver will be aware of the database you have created and await invocations on it. As long as the incoming queries specify the "Election-Database" database, they will be dispatched to the database and from there to our SQL queries.

Summary

ODBC is a proprietary database management protocol. It enables you to access information on databases from within Microsoft Windows. Once ODBC is set up on our machine, we can get information from the database by creating Java applications that interface to it.

One thing to make sure that you remember when using Access like this is that Access is a personal database and not a full blown relational database management system like Oracle, DB2, and SQL Server. The mdb file that Access uses as its

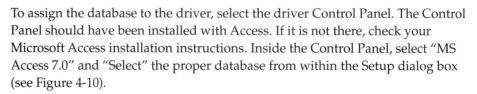

Figure 4-10 Starting the ODBC driver.

data storage element is just a file, it is the ODBC driver that makes it look and act like a database.

Retrieving Information

At first glance, you probably wonder where the "server" part for this section is. Well, we created it when we created our database! The database is the server. The beauty of JDBC clients is that they link directly with databases. In client-server terms, this is referred to as a "two-tier" model in which the client is the first tier and the database itself is the second tier. In the rest of the book we will promote the three-tier model in which clients do nothing but look good and interface with servers. The servers contain all the business logic, and the databases only store data.

In JDBC and the two-tier model, the client contains all the business logic and is responsible for contacting and accessing the database. Our JDBC client uses SQL queries to contact our Microsoft Access database. The downside to this is the complexity of the client and the scalability of the system. With potentially hundreds of clients banging on the same database, the database could get overloaded. With a three-tier model, the database is queried by only one application—the server—and the server is responsible for (and is more capable of) handling hundreds of simultaneous requests.

In any event, we will present you with a more thorough look at the advantages and disadvantages of the two- and three-tier models in Chapter 14, "Making an Architectural Decision." In this section, we show you how to go to a database and get information. In the next section, we will show you how to put information into the database.

Creating the User Interface

Our user interface should be simple and elegant. Once again, we don't want to confuse people with what we are trying to do. We will create a button for each candidate. Upon activation of the button, the client will execute SQL statements on the server and get information. Then it will display the information in the text fields provided. See Figure 4-11 for a sample GUI.

The user interface will enable us to underscore the simplicity of JDBC. We have seen how it can handle the most complex of cases, but here we once again keep our examples fun and easy.

As we proceed, we will show you how to implement the two important functions in this application. The PresidentialElection application's constructor and its corresponding action method will initialize and invoke the database, respectively.

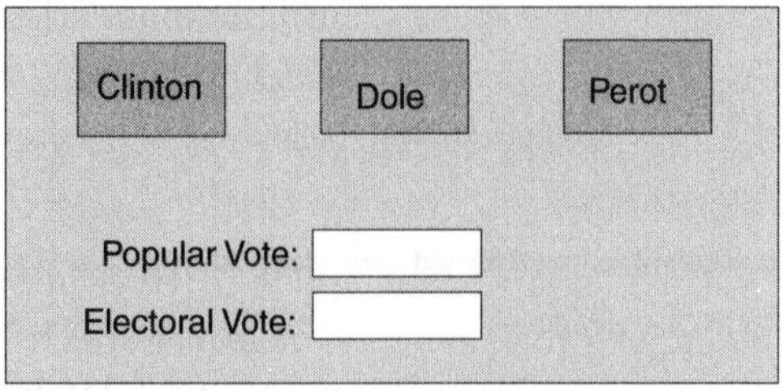

Figure 4-11 Sample GUI for the PresidentialElection application.

```
public class PresidentialElection
{
    Button clintonButton;
    Button doleButton;
    Button perotButton;

    TextField popularField;
    TextField electoralField;

    PresidentialElection()
    {
        // create the user interface here
    }
    public void actionPerformed(ActionEvent e)
    {
        String arg = e.getActionCommand();
        if(arg.equals("Clinton"))
        {
        }
        else if(arg.equals("Dole"))
        {
        }
        else if(arg.equals("Perot"))
        {
        }
    }
}
```

Database Security

Because we are writing an application, handling our own security is not a requirement. However, if we wanted to write an applet, we would need to use a SecurityManager to set our access to the host database. Because Java applets are able to connect only to their host machine, our security manager is required to make sure we have access to the database on the host machine. By setting the security manager, you can check to see if you have access to the database before a query is executed. Keep in mind that the security manager deals with security as it relates to Java. Database access security (userid and password) is handled through the instantiation of the Connection object.

Using the JDBC Driver

As we discussed earlier, we must include the JDBC driver in our application. To do so, we obtain a Connection object from `DriverManager`. The `DriverManager` takes a URL and translates it into a handle for an actual database. Then we can invoke our SQL statements on the database and retrieve information. From the `Connection` object, we can retrieve `Statement`, `PreparedStatement`, and `CallableStatement` objects to help us format our SQL queries.

As JDBC gains more acceptance, database vendors will provide drivers for Java applications to use to contact their databases. Often, there will be some overlap between these different drivers. Choosing the proper driver can be a difficult task, but JDBC enables you to create a colon-separated list of drivers through which JDBC will search for the first available driver.

Here, we will use the standard ODBC driver included with JDBC. This will enable us to connect to ODBC databases such as the Microsoft Access database we just created. As long as our ODBC driver has been set up to await this kind of query, this will succeed. We will need to load the specific class for the database "manually."

```java
import java.sql.*;

public class PresidentialElection
{
    Button clintonButton;
    Button doleButton;
    Button perotButton;

    TextField popularField;
    TextField electoralField;

    // the connection to the database
    Connection dbConnection;

    PresidentialElection()
    {
        // create the user interface here

        // create the URL representation of our database
        String url = "jdbc:odbc:PresidentialCandidate";

        // load the database driver
        Class.forName("sun.jdbc.odbc.JdbcOdbcDriver");

        // make the connection to the database
        dbConnection = DriverManager.getConnection(
            url, "username" "password");
    }
```

```
public void actionPerformed(ActionEvent 2)
{
    String arg = e.getActionCommand();
    if(arg.equals("Clinton"))
    {
    }
    else if(arg.equals("Dole"))
    {
    }
    else if(arg.equals("Perot"))
    {
    }
}
}
```

After we created the URL representation for our database, we needed to connect to the database itself. Once that is done our application is linked to the database and can make invocations at will.

Creating Queries

Now, we must fill in the actionPerformed so that we can make the query on the database. Here, we will specify the SQL query right in the executeQuery method. We could also do this by just executing the queries we created and stored in the database itself. Since we may be beginners with JDBC, I think it is more meaningful to start out showing the queries along with the code.

```
import java.sql.*;
public class PresidentialElection
{
    Button clintonButton;
    Button doleButton;
    Button perotButton;

    TextField popularField;
    TextField electoralField;

    GubernatorialElection()
    {
        // create the user interface here
        // create the URL representation of our database
        String url = "jdbc:odbc:GubernatorialCandidate";

        // load the database driver
        Class.forName("sun.jdbc.odbc.JdbcOdbcDriver");

        // make the connection to the database
        Connection connection = DriverManager.getConnection(
            url, "username" "password");
    }
```

```java
public void actionPerformed(ActionEvent e)
{
    String who = new String("");
    String arg = e.getActionCommand();
    if(arg.equals("Clinton"))    who = "Clinton";
    else if(arg.equals("Dole"))  who = "Dole";
    else if(arg.equals("Perot")) who = "Perot";
    else System.out.println("Error");
    try
    {
      Statement statement = dbConnection.createStatement();
      String s = "select percentage,electoral " +
                 "from PresidentialCandidate " +
                 "where candidate='" + who +"'";
      ResultSet result = statement.executeQuery(s);
      popularField.setText(who + " " + result.getInt(1));
      electoralField.setText(who + " " + result.getInt(2));
    }
    catch (SQLException se)
    {
        System.out.println("SQL Error: " + se.toString());
    }
  }
}
```

In place of the Select statement, we could just as easily have executed the query that we had earlier stored in the database. As already mentioned, we choose not to help improve the learning experience.

Database and SQL Overview

Once we are able to interface with the database, we should be able to put information in it. Databases are not static entities. They are ever changing, and in keeping with that trait, Java provides some pretty cool tools to get to databases and change the data stored therein.

Storing Information

JDBC also gives you a means to store information in a table. Once again, this is done using standard Structured Query Language statements. By using SQL, JDBC makes sure that its own learning curve is pretty small. JDBC gives you much flexibility in creating statements.

Let's say that suddenly we discover that Bill Clinton is really Daffy Duck! The 700,000 people who wrote in "Daffy Duck" on their ballot as their choice for President of the United States really voted for Bill Clinton. As a result, the percentage by which Bill Clinton won the 1996 election changed. We need to create a JDBC query to modify the percentage.

Creating the Connection

The first thing we must do is create the connection as we did before. We will also add a button to change the percentage of votes for Bill Clinton. We could with a slight bit more complication and effort create a more customizable change area. It could have text fields for each entry and a submit button. Using the data in the text field, we could change the data in the table. For now, however, that is more complex than is needed.

```java
public class PresidentialElection
{
    Button clintonButton;
    Button doleButton;
    Button perotButton;
    Button changeButton;
    TextField popularField;
    TextField electoralField;

    PresidentialElection()
    {
        // create the user interface here
        // create the URL representation of our database
        String url = "jdbc:odbc:PresidentialCandidate";

        // load the database driver
        Class.forName("sun.jdbc.odbc.JdbcOdbcDriver");

        // make the connection to the database
        Connection connection = DriverManager.getConnection(
            url, "username" "password");
    }
    public boolean action(
        Event evt,
        Object obj
    )
    {
        if(evt.target == clintonButton)
        {
            . . . same as before . . .
        }
        else if(evt.target == doleButton)
        {
            . . . same as before . . .
        }
        else if(evt.target == perotButton)
        {
            . . . same as before . . .
        }
```

```
        else if(evt.target == changeButton)
        {
        }
    }
}
```

We also needed to insert event-handling information for the new button. As you can see, there is no change between the connection for retrieving information and the connection here for setting the information.

Forming a Statement

The burden, in JDBC, is placed on the formation of statements. As database programmers expect, there is no need to learn anything new or confusing. Java is treated as nothing more than a container for an SQL statement. The SQL statements we create here as well as when we stored information are nothing fancy, nothing special, and no more interesting than a normal SQL statement.

In order to change the information in a database, we need to use the SQL Update statement. We must specify a column and row to change. But, instead of encapsulating the SQL statement with a regular JDBC statement, instead we will use a PreparedStatement. PreparedStatements give you the ability to insert parameters within the statement itself. The following example contains two parameters, popularvote and candidate:

```
UPDATE PresidentialCandidate
SET popularvote = ?
WHERE candidate = ?
```

The popularvote field is marked as field number one, and candidate is field number two. To set the fields, we use the set methods supplied with JDBC along with the number of the field you want to change: setInt, setString, etc. To define the fields, use the question mark.

Now we can create a PreparedStatement. Note, however, that in this chapter we are not using precreated queries. Instead, we will create the query directly from JDBC. As we discussed earlier, either approach is completely acceptable. The choice is not one of effort but rather of programming approach. If your business makes heavy use of precreated queries, obviously you will choose to invoke them from JDBC. If database interaction is not as important, then there is really no need to define queries ahead of time.

```
public class PresidentialElection
{
    Button clintonButton;
    Button doleButton;
    Button perotButton;
    Button changeButton;
```

```
TextField popularField;
TextField electoralField;

PresidentialElection()
{
    // create the user interface here
    // create the URL representation of our database
    String url = ""jdbc:odbc:PresidentialCandidate";

    // load the database driver
    Class.forName("sun.jdbc.odbc.JdbcOdbcDriver");

    // make the connection to the database
    Connection connection = DriverManager.getConnection(
        url, "username" "password");
}

public boolean actionPerformed(ActionEvent e)
{
    String arg = e.getActionCommand();
    if(arg.equals("Clinton"))
    {
        . . . same as before . . .
    }
    else if(arg.equals("Dole"))
    {
        . . . same as before . . .
    }
    else if(arg.equals("Perot"))
    {
        . . . same as before . . .
    }
    else if(arg.equals("Change"))
    {
        // create the statement
        PreparedStatement pstate =
            connection.prepareStatement(
                "UPDATE PresidentialCandidate " +
                "SET popularvote = ? " +
                "WHERE candidate = ?");

        // set the parameters for the statement
        pstate.setInt(1, 50);
        pstate.setString(2, "Clinton");

        // execute the statement
        pstate.executeUpdate();
    }
}
}
```

Now that we can create a simple system of clients that change information in a database, we can try to create a client for our featured application that will store and retrieve its information from a similar database. By creating this purely two-tier model, it can be compared to the applications we created in Chapter 3 for using sockets.

A JDBC Version of the Featured App

As we have seen in the previous sections, creating a JDBC interface to a database is fairly easy. The difficult parts involve setting up the database and installing the driver. Although we won't discuss the finer points of drivers or database administration, we will create the database as well as the interface to it.

Creating the Database

Once again, we will create the database and associated queries using Microsoft Access as shown in Figure 4-12. As before, our decision to use Access is due largely to its ubiquity and ease of use. We want you to be able to create interfaces to databases quickly and easily, and Microsoft Access provides a simple means to do so. As with all third-party products, if you require assistance with Access, contact Microsoft. In any event, if you have access to Sybase, Oracle, or another database, feel free to use it. You should not have to modify the code, but you will have to install a driver for the database you plan to use.

We will store our appointments in the database using two keys—the reason for the appointment and the time of the appointment. This conforms to the interface to the Network module. In a moment we will discuss how to map the network module to the database. For now, take a look at the Access table in Figure 4-13.

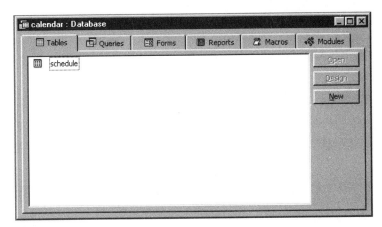

Figure 4-12 Our new database.

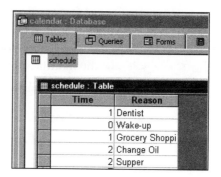

Figure 4–13 Table for our appointments.

We must create our query either within the database or within our program (NetworkModule) to get appointments to the client interface. My preference, for the purpose of this text, is to code it into the program. This isn't as efficient from the standpoint of execution performance, but it keeps everything in the NetworkModule.

```
SELECT TIME,REASON
FROM SCHEDULE
ORDER BY TIME
```

We'll use the ORDER BY clause of the SELECT statement to get our appointments for the morning, afternoon, and evening grouped together like a real appointment scheduler would.

Mapping the Network Module to Database Queries

Now we need to connect the network module to the database. Remember that a driver must be installed for the database. Without it the database access queries cannot function. Our network module's interface looks like this:

```
public class NetworkModule
{
    public void scheduleAppointment(String reason,int time);
    public Vector getAppointments();
    public void initNetwork();
    public void shutdownNetwork();
}
```

Obviously, we will map the scheduleAppointment method to a PreparedStatement query, but we will map the getAppointment method to the GetAppointments query. We will pass our constructor's code directly to the initNetwork method, and we must close our connection to the database (the shutdownNetwork method is the logical place to include that code).

Developing the Client

The majority of our client application was developed in Chapter 3, leaving us to modify the `NetworkModule`. Doing so is just as simple as before. Let's first take a look at the network module's code without the modifications. We must incorporate the JDBC classes as well as the classes for the driver.

```
import java.sql.*;

public class NetworkModule
{
    NetworkModule()
    {
    }
    public void scheduleAppointment(
                String reason, int time)
    {
    }
    public Vector getAppointments()
    {
    }
    public void initNetwork()
    {
    }
    public void shutdownNetwork()
    {
    }
}
```

Once our client is ready, we must fill in the information for each function. First, we will schedule appointments using the scheduleAppointment query that we created earlier. Essentially, the network module acts as a pass-through from the rest of the application directly to the database. Normally, we would try to incorporate some kind of middleman to handle the pass-through from our GUI to the database, but for simplicity's sake we will not develop a three-tier application here. In the future, if you desire a three-tier application, your middle-tier server would make these calls.

Establishing the Connection

First, we must create the connection to the database and link our network module to it. This ensures that we have a clear path to the database. Any errors here should be caught and thrown back. We also must make sure to load the database driver manually by specifying its entire class name.

```
import java.sql.*;

public class NetworkModule
```

```
{
    // create the connection to the database
    Connection dbConnection;

    NetworkModule()
    {
        // init the network connection to db
        initNetwork();
    }

    public void scheduleAppointment(
                    String reason, int time)
    {
    }

    public Vector getAppointments()
    {
    }

    public void initNetwork()
    {
        // load the database driver
        Class.forName("sun.jdbc.odbc.JdbcOdbcDriver");
        // create the URL representation of our database
        String url = "jdbc:odbc:Schedule";
        // make the connection to the database
        dbConnection = DriverManager.getConnection(
            url, "username" "password");
    }

    public void shutdownNetwork()
    {
    }
}
```

Making an SQL Invocation

Invoking the database is relatively straightforward and not unlike our earlier invocation of the PresidentialElection database. Here, we substitute our own invocation. The difference in this invocation, however, is that we will retrieve a complex type from the SQL query. As a result, we must translate the complex type into the Vector that is expected as a return value for the getAppointments invocation.

```
import java.sql.*;

public class NetworkModule
{
    // the connection to the database
    Connection dbConnection;

    NetworkModule()
    {
```

```java
    // init the network
    initNetwork();
}

public void scheduleAppointment(
                String reason, int time)
{
}

public Vector getAppointments()
{
    // create a vector to pass back
    Vector appointmentVector = new Vector();
    try
    {
        // create the statement
        Statement statement = dbConnection.createStatement();
        String s = "SELECT TIME, REASON " +
                    "FROM SCHEDULE " +
                    "ORDER BY TIME";
        // get the result
        ResultSet result = statement.executeQuery(s));
        // walk through the result set for the information
        while(result.next())
        {
            // create a variable to hold the appointment
            AppointmentType appointment = new AppointmentType();
            // get the next appointment from the results set
            appointment.time = result.getInt("TIME");
            appointment.reason = result.getString();
            appointmentVector.addElement(appointment);
        }
    }
    catch (SQLException e)
    {
        System.out.println("Error: " + e.toString());
    }
}

public void initNetwork()
{
    // load the database driver
    Class.forName("sun.jdbc.odbc.JdbcOdbcDriver");
    // create the URL representation of our database
    String url = "jdbc:odbc:Schedule";
    // make the connection to the database
    dbConnection = DriverManager.getConnection(
        url, "username" "password");
}
```

```
    public void shutdownNetwork()
    {
    }
}
```

Notice how the current invocation steps through the ResultSet and makes it into a Vector. When your applications need to handle more complex results from an SQL query, you will need to do much of the same.

Invoking SQL to Make a Change

Now we must implement the Java side to our setAppointment operation. Our setAppointment query assigns a new entry into the database.

```
public void scheduleAppointment(
            String reason, int time)
{
}
```

We must first take the reason and time variables and translate them into an SQL statement. Unlike our previous database modification example, here we must insert an element, not simply change an existing one. To do so, we need to use the SQL Insert statement.

```
INSERT INTO Schedule
VALUES (1, 'Meet with marketing');
```

We will once again use the PreparedStatement object to put together a statement.

```
public void scheduleAppointment(
            String reason, int time)
{
  try
  {
   Statement insertStatement = dbConnection.createStatement();
   String insert = "INSERT INTO SCHEDULE " +
                   "VALUES('" + appointmentTime + "','"
                        + appointmentReason + "')";
   insertStatement.executeUpdate(insert);
}
```

Shutting Down the Connection

In JDBC, we must close the connection to our database. This ensures that the database management system has sufficient connections for other applications to connect to it. For high-availability databases, this is quite an important characteristic. The database must be available at all times, and even though our connection disappears when the application shuts down, we must still publish an interface to the database connection that will allow us to eliminate it.

```
public void shutdownNetwork()
{
}
```

Summary

Databases are storage mechanisms designed to enable you to warehouse vast quantities of data. By linking Java applications to them, you can create programs that are instantly useful. Today, there are hundreds of applications that interface with databases using outdated, archaic applications.

In the next two chapters we will explore combining Java, JDBC, and network object technology to develop enterprise class applications.

Chapter 5

Java RMI: Remote Method Invocation

▼ DISTRIBUTED OBJECTS

▼ CLIENT

▼ SERVER

▼ CALLBACKS

▼ A JAVA RMI VERSION OF THE FEATURED APP

▼ NEW IN JDK 1.2

As we were all growing up, there was always a person (a friend, a foe, or a parent) who knew just how to push our "buttons" to get a desired reaction out of us, sometimes good and sometimes bad. The actions we were manipulated into doing were things that were built into our personalities. This idea of pushing someone else's buttons is exactly the idea behind Remote Method Invocation. Think of yourself as an action/reaction server and the things you could be manipulated into as your methods; now think of your antagonist as a client to your server. If the client sends the right messages, it can get the server to do anything that is in the server's set of known actions.

Java Remote Method Invocation is a simple, yet powerful, Java-based framework for distributed object design. Although it shares many traits with its cousin, Java IDL (Chapter 6), it has distinct advantages over IDL in several key areas, notably usability. Java RMI-based objects can be quickly deployed and managed across networks. It has several shortcomings that we will discuss later, but Java RMI is a fast and adequate introduction to Distributed Object Programming.

In this chapter, we will discuss the architectural decisions behind RMI and why they were made. We will also guide you through the process required to create a simple client/server system using the Remote Method Invocation mechanisms.

Distributed Objects

Remote Method Invocation (RMI) is similar to other distributed object technologies; it, however, enables you to create applications that communicate with one another without the overhead of CORBA. A remote method invocation is similar to Remote Procedure Call (RPC) used frequently in C/C++. Instead of creating and instantiating an object on your local machine, you create it on another machine and communicate with that object through its interface, just as if it were a local object. This gives the effect of creating a local object that we then take hold of with both hands and stretch out across the network. We then drop one end on one host (client) and the other end on another host (server); the two ends are still connected and make up a single object. Even if we replicate the client part of the object on multiple hosts, we still have only one object.

So, with the advantages of the Java language, you will be able to create distributed objects that communicate with one another. Unlike CORBA, your applications must be written in Java, but that may not be a bad thing in the end. It will be difficult to re-implement your legacy applications because they must be rewritten in Java. Yet, being able to write distributed applications without expending any real effort is highly attractive. If Java is your language of choice, then RMI may be your best communication alternative.

What Is RMI?

In the good old days of programming, all the things you wanted to do resided in one program. If you needed a file, you simply opened it. If you needed to optimize your program, you either reduced functionality or sped it up. Lately, the notion of distributed programming has taken the industry by storm. Instead of opening a file, you open another application. Instead of reducing functionality, you farm out the work to another application and keep tabs on the process by communicating with it. Figure 5-1 illustrates the differences between local and remote object invocation.

Java RMI enables you to farm out work to other Java objects residing in other processes, or in other machines altogether. Not only can you execute steps in parallel using threads, but you can also farm out work to other processes that will execute steps in parallel on a different machine!

Sure, many of the alternatives presented in this book enable you to do the same thing, but why would you want to do all that work when you can let Java—the same language you've spent so much free time learning anyway—do all the work automatically? Where CORBA flaunts its language independence, RMI makes no effort to hide the fact that you are locked into a Java-only solution.

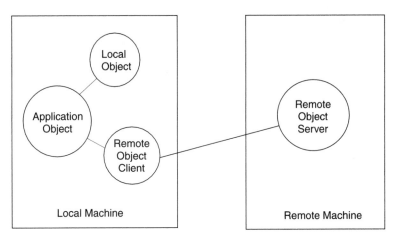

Figure 5–1 Invocations on remote objects appear the same as invocations on local objects.

How Does RMI Work?

When your client invokes your server, several layers of the RMI system come into play. The first, and most important to the programmer, is the stub/skeleton layer. The stubs are Java code that you fill in so that you can communicate with the other layers. For example, in Chapter 6, "Java IDL: Interface Definition Language," you will see how the IDL to Java compiler generates code that we will later fill in and use as the framework for a distributed application.

Likewise, the Java RMI system automatically enables you to use several helper functions. By inheriting from the RMI classes, your class implements the stubs or skeletons. To put it simply, stubs are reserved for client code that you fill in, and skeletons refer to server code.

Once the stubs and skeleton layers are completed, they pass through the other two layers in the RMI system. The first of these layers is the remote reference layer. The remote reference layer is responsible for determining the nature of the object. Does it reside on a single machine or across a network? Is the remote object the kind of object that will be instantiated and started automatically, or is it the kind of object that must be declared and initialized beforehand? The remote reference layer handles all these situations, and many more, without your intervention.

Finally, the transport layer is similar to a translator that takes your RMI code, turns it into TCP/IP (or whatever communication mechanism is used), and lets it fly over the network to the other end. Because the RMI system supports a technique called object serialization, any objects passed as parameters to a remote method, no matter how complicated, are converted into simple streams of characters that are then easily reconverted into their original object representation. The real implication of this is that only objects that are serializable can be passed as arguments. This can pose problems at times; for example, at times it would be convenient to pass a stream to a server object, but streams are not serializable, so we can't.

As you can see in Figure 5-2, a client that invokes a remote server first talks to its stub code, which, in turn, sends the message to the remote reference layer, which then passes it through the transport mechanism to the other machine. The other machine takes what it gets through the transport layer and retranslates it into the remote reference layer representation, which passes it on to the skeleton code where the request finally makes its appearance at the remote method.

Stub/Skeleton Layer. When your client begins to invoke a server on a remote machine, the API with which you, as programmer, are concerned is the stub/skeleton code. By inheriting from the appropriate RMI class, your object obtains several RMI methods that you are required to fill in.

When the invocation is actually made, the remote object (depending on how the server has been designed) could be a replicated object. A replicated object is an object that has several instances executing at the same time (possibly created by a factory process). For example, a given application may have several instances of the Java String class within its threads of execution. If the String class were a remote server object, a client that invokes it should not have to worry about its various instances. The stub/skeleton layer precludes this notion of replicated objects. When you write your application and code, the necessary tools to talk to a

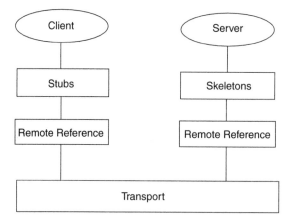

Figure 5-2 Java RMI architecture.

remote object, you need not concern yourself with the implementations on the remote side.

The stub/skeleton layer also abstracts you from the various transport mechanisms in the other layers. In short, the stub and skeleton layers both make sure that your program is platform-independent.

Remote Reference Layer. The reference layer serves two purposes. First, it handles the translation from the stub and skeleton layers into native transport calls on the hosting architecture. The early version of RMI was not as platform-independent as it purported to be. The problem lay in the Java Developer's Kit, and not in the RMI system itself. With the introduction of the next major revision of the JDK, the RMI system now functions properly. The RMI system is truly platform-independent as it, and the Java language, were meant to be.

The reference layer also is in charge of carrying out remote reference protocols. These protocols may be point-to-point communication (i.e., local object to remote object invocations). Or, the reference protocol may refer to replicated objects. The RMI system ensures that, when you invoke a remote object that happens to be replicated, all the replicated instances will hear the same message. The replication strategy is customizable, but we refer you to the RMI System Architecture section of the RMI specification.

There is a corresponding server-side reference layer that accepts the client-side instructions and retranslates them into programmer code. It ensures that the invocations are made reliably, and that the RMI system knows about any exceptions. Exceptions are thrown from this level for any problems in establishing connections, fulfilling invocation requests, or closing connections.

Basically, the reference layer is responsible for bridging the gap between programmer code and network communication. It is a go-between of data, taking what you want to do, and making sure it can be done using the network.

Transport Layer. When the first miners found gold in California, they exclaimed "Eureka!" Well, Eureka! This is where the action is. Even though you are not able to manipulate these routines yourself, it is important to understand how the transport is implemented. From here, you will understand the limitations of RMI and be able to make an architectural decision based on them.

The transport layer is responsible for setting up connections, maintaining them, alerting applications of problems, listening for connections, and shutting them down. The transport layer consists of four components: the objects, the space between local and remote address spaces, the physical socket, and the transport protocol. Figure 5-3 illustrates a simple transport model.

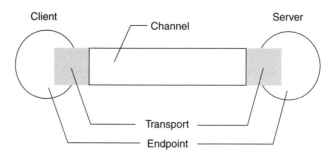

Figure 5-3 The transport layer is responsible for all connection-related functions.

The objects, or endpoints, are the beginning and end of an invocation. Between one object's transport endpoint to another's transport endpoint resides the entire communication mechanism on which RMI is based. The channel between the address spaces is in charge of upholding the connection and monitoring for signs of trouble, say the loss of an object or maybe the loss of the physical connection itself. The socket connection is basically the same kind of socket we saw in Chapter 3. As we mentioned before, sockets really are the basis for all communications in Java. Finally, the transport protocol is the language in which sockets talk to one another.

Local vs. Remote Objects

So, what are the semantic differences between local and remote objects? All along we have stressed that at the heart of the entire system is the notion that to the client programmer, everything looks exactly like normal, nonremote Java code. In fact, even Java IDL's client applications look no different than local Java code.

Java Remote Method Invocation is quite interesting in a semantic sense. Indeed, the very idea that instantiating an object that happens to be on another network is interesting in and of itself, but to add to that the caveat that the remote object exhibits all the properties of a local Java object adds a certain amount of usefulness to the whole matter.

What kinds of characteristics do Java objects exhibit? Well, most importantly, they are easy to implement. They are garbage-collected, meaning that once your program has no use for them, they are automatically dereferenced and their resources returned to the system. We discuss remote garbage collection in the next section.

Java objects are, of course, platform-independent, as are Java RMI objects. When you make a remote method invocation in a non-Java language, chances are you must learn not only the nuances of the communication mechanism of your own machine but that of the machine you are talking to as well. Imagine being a Solaris programmer who is trying to talk to a Windows 95 machine! It's hard enough to master Solaris interprocess communication without having to learn the esoteric Windows 95 communication layers as well!

Java RMI frees you from that morass, just as Java frees you from recompiling your code for multiple architectures. When you invoke a RMI method across different platforms, the RMI system adjusts its communication layers automatically; and because those layers are abstracted from you, the programmer, you never have to concern yourself with that confusing network code.

Garbage Collection. One of the biggest advantages to Java is that there are no pointers. There is no memory to deallocate, and you never have to deal with memory storage schemes. Java's platform independence mantra wouldn't allow it anyway, but if you were to develop for multiple platforms, you would need to be concerned with the nuances of memory management for each architecture, which, like mastering multiple transport layers, is a daunting task.

Java RMI is no exception to the rule. In fact, it contains a complicated garbage collection scheme based on Modula-3's Network Objects concept of object reference counters. RMI places an object reference counter into each object. Every time another object talks to the remote object, the object reference counter is incremented, and once the object no longer needs the remote object, the counter decrements.

There are many protective layers around the garbage collection algorithm that prevent premature object deallocation. Most of RMI's distributed garbage collection farms off the work to the local Java Virtual Machine's garbage collection algorithm. Thus, RMI does not reinvent the wheel, so to speak.

For example, when our local object begins a conversation with a remote object, we begin to talk through the RMI system's layers. As part of the remote reference layer, our local object creates a "network" object. On the other end, at the remote machine, the remote reference layer creates another network object that converses with the remote object. The remote virtual machine realizes that the remote object should not be deallocated and holds off garbage collection as long as the remote network object is referring to it (see Figure 5-4). Thus, the remote object is not blown away.

Back at the local machine, when we are no longer using the remote object, the remote reference layer removes all references to the local network object. Once the local Java Virtual Machine realizes that the local network object is no longer used, it garbage-collects it. As part of its finalize routine, the local network object sends a message to the remote network object through the reference layer that it should let go of its reference to the remote object. In so doing, the remote network object causes the remote Java Virtual Machine to garbage-collect the remote object.

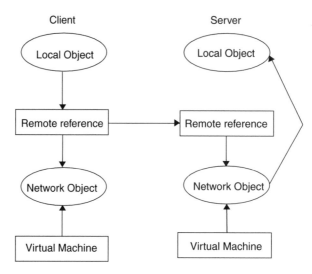

Figure 5-4 The creation of network objects during object communication prevents Java's garbage collection from interrupting the conversation.

Security. When you instantiate a local object from within a Java applet, security is not a concern. The applet security mechanism has already cleared your applet, and you are free to allocate and deallocate your objects.

However, security is very much a concern for remote objects. When you try to instantiate a remote object, you must have permission to do so. The Applet class loader that is in charge of getting every class your application requires may or may not be able to instantiate the remote object. As a result, RMI in applets is limited to invoking methods on classes that are already in existence. You are not allowed to create a remote object because the applet class loader will not let you.

Applet vs. Application

Currently, RMI servers must be created as Java applications. Servers cannot be embedded within a Web page. There are several reasons why, most notably that the applet security mechanisms prevent it; but, for the time being, the RMI system does not support applet servers. We will discuss the callback alternative as implemented in RMI in a few sections.

Dynamic Method Invocations

RMI enables you to invoke a server without knowing anything about what methods are contained within the server. It's like going into a restaurant and ordering without ever seeing the menu. If you know you're in an Italian restaurant, chances are pretty good that they offer spaghetti and meatballs. Likewise, if you know what kind of server you are talking to, you can invoke it without actually knowing anything about the methods it implements.

Overview of RMI

Java's Remote Method Invocation system is a significantly easier and lighter weight approach to distributed objects than Java IDL. Contained completely within the Java language, RMI is an extension to the language itself, whereas Java IDL is a language-independent Java implementation. RMI is simple, fast, and effective for lightweight distributed systems. As your applications become more complex, Java IDL may be your best alternative.

Nevertheless, client and server programming is quite simple with RMI. As we will see in the next two sections, creating clients in RMI is a natural extension to creating Java objects.

Client

In order to create a distributed system, one part of your objects must be a client, and the other must be a server. Sometimes servers can be clients as well, but in this section we will discuss the simplest case. RMI was designed with the idea that, with minimal effort, you will be able to create complex distributed systems with all the advantages of Java and none of the detriments of other distributed designs. In fact, with the addition of a single line in your code, you can make an object a distributed object instead of a local one.

The beauty of RMI is that even though your code gives the illusion of normal, single-process applications, it is in fact a distributed system. When you get over-loaded at work, you begin to delegate to others. Likewise, Java RMI says rather than overloading an application, why not delegate to other applications?

RMI Client Methodology

Let's say you call up Penney's and decide to order one of those fancy toaster covers from their catalog for your mother's birthday. The operator greets you and asks for your order number. Because the client is always right, you decide to amuse yourself and annoy the poor person taking your order. Instead of being cooperative and actually having an order number, you simply tell him that you want the "toaster oven cover with the purple polka dots and a portrait of Heath Shuler on the side."

Clearly amused, the operator goes to his catalog database and asks for the "toaster oven cover" with the appropriate description. What he gets in return is the order number and so he is able to process your order.

Similarly, in RMI you have to go to a catalog of objects and ask for the object by its commonly known name. Once you have the object you can continue to process your application. The steps you need to take in order to create a client are:

1.   Get the client object from the Naming Service.

2.   Process the object and ready it for invocation.

3.   Invoke the object.

RMI Remote Classes. RMI's Remote class is a standard interface that you must extend from your server in order to export functionality to an RMI client. All remote objects inherit from the Remote class, and your client needs to know what it's talking to. It's kind of like knowing the language you are going to talk before you converse with someone from another country.

Once your server inherits the remote object, it can be instantiated upon and invoked on by remote objects. In the example in this section, we are implementing a simple RMI client that will make remote method invocations to an RMI server to retrieve statistical data for a given NFL team. The StatsServer implements three functions that we will implement in our RMI servers section. We want our clients to be able to get the total running yardage, the total passing yardage, and the total number of turnovers for a team that we specify by a string. We start by including RMI in our file, and defining the client class itself.

```
package rmi.Stats1;

public class StatsClient
{
}
```

The Remote classes also implement remote versions of the standard Java exceptions. Inheriting from Java's exception mechanism, RemoteExceptions can do everything that Java exceptions can do. The only difference between the two is that remote exceptions refer to problems with remote objects rather than local Java errors.

TIP: The RemoteObject class extends the Java Object class. So, if you were to create two versions of an application—one that talks to remote objects and one that refers only to local ones—it would simply be a matter of changing the inheritance.

RMI's Naming System. As we discussed earlier, the RMI system provides a simple naming system that allows you to refer to objects as special kinds of strings, rather than as special words. In order to use a remote object, you must first retrieve it from the Registry. The Registry ensures that an object is available for use. It binds the object reference to a simple string and provides routines for accessing an object by the string under which it is stored.

In order to use the Registry, you must first start it up on some machine on your network; for our purposes this will be your local machine. The Registry clings to a predefined port (because it is not a well-known port and the stubs and skeletons hide all the protocol from you, you don't need to know; but if you're really curious it is 1099) on your machine and funnels TCP/IP messages between clients, servers, and the Registry on that port. Embedded within the code for the RMI system is this specially assigned port, enabling the RMI system to always be able to access a running Registry. The Registry is a stand-alone Java application, so starting it is pretty simple:

```
%prompt%  rmiregistry &     (on UNIX systems)
D:\ start rmiregistry       (on Windows systems (95, 98 or NT))
```

To start up the registry on some port other than the default, simply follow the command with the desired port.

```
D:\ start rmiregistry 12345
```

Getting an object from the Registry is actually pretty simple. You can get an object and begin invocations on it immediately by invoking one of the Registry's three functions for binding objects to strings, unbinding objects, and retrieving objects:

```
package java.rmi;

public class StatsClient
{
    StatsClient()
    {
        // get the remote object from the Registry
        String url = "//localhost/STATS-SERVER";
        StatsServer remoteObject = (StatsServer)Naming.lookup(url);
    }
}
```

Remote Invocations. The object that is retrieved is a remote base object. We need to transform that generic remote object into a specific StatsServer object. In geek terms this is referred to as narrowing. We can narrow our remote base object down to a StatsServer object by performing a simple cast operation, giving us access to all the functions within the StatsServer:

```
package java.rmi;

public class StatsClient
{
    StatsClient()
    {
```

```
            // get the remote object from the Registry
            Remote remoteObject = Naming.lookup("STATS-SERVER");

            // narrow the object down to a specific one
            StatsServer statsServerInterface;
            if(remoteObject instanceof StatsServer)
                statsServerInterface = (StatsServer) remoteObject
        }
}
```

Finally, we are ready to invoke methods on our remote server. Remember that we have three possible functions to choose from. Creating a user interface for the client is a trivial task and should be integrated into the application just as you normally would. Here, we invoke all three functions and return the data to the user on the standard output device:

```
package java.rmi;

public class StatsClient
{
    StatsClient()
    {
        // get the remote object from the Registry
        Remote remoteObject = Naming.lookup("STATS-SERVER");

        // narrow the object down to a specific one
        StatsServer statsServerInterface;
        if(remoteObject instanceof StatsServer)
            statsServerInterface = (StatsServer) remoteObject

        // make the invocation
        System.out.println("Total yardage is: " +
            statsServerInterface.getTotalRunningYardage("Redskins"));
    }
}
```

Catching Exceptions

So far we have done nothing in the way of error checking. In order for our client to handle every possible contingency during a remote invocation, it needs to catch any exceptions thrown by the server. During a normal remote invocation, the exceptions can be anything from user-defined exceptions within the server to standard RMI transport exceptions. In any event, you can catch either generic Java exceptions or specific RMI ones.

RMI client invocations should catch one of seven different exceptions. The RemoteException class is the parent class of all exceptions thrown by the RMI system. Other exceptions include Registry-thrown exceptions, such as AlreadyBound-Exception and NotBoundException. RMI object invocations themselves throw four kinds of exceptions:

1. `StubNotFoundException`
2. `RMISecurityException`
3. `NoSuchObjectException`
4. `UnknownHostException`

Using the standard Java methodology for adding exceptions to a program, we catch the RMI exceptions as follows:

```java
package java.rmi;

public class StatsClient
{
    StatsClient()
    {
        // get the remote object from the Registry
        try
        {
            Remote remoteObject = Naming.lookup("STATS-SERVER");
        }
        catch (java.rmi.NotBoundException exc)
        {
            System.out.println("Error in lookup() " +
                exc.toString());
        }

        // narrow the object down to a specific one
        StatsServer statsServerInterface;
        if(remoteObject instanceof StatsServer)
            statsServerInterface = (StatsServer) remoteObject

        // make the invocation
        try
        {
            System.out.println("Total yardage is: " +
                statsServerInterface.getTotalRunningYardage("Redskins"));
        }
        catch (java.rmi.RemoteException exc)
        {
            System.out.println("Error in invocation " +
                exc.toString());
        }
    }
}
```

Handling Security Constraints

Because we dynamically load classes from the file system within our client, we must set up a corresponding Java security manager within our client. The client's security manager prevents the client from abusing any privileges granted by the server. For example, our server may have unrestricted access to the local file system. In order to keep the client honest and prevent it from having the same unrestricted access to the server's host, the client security manager monitors the loading process of the remote class and sets the appropriate file access permissions, as required by the client's host machine.

In our StatsServer example, our client loads the remote StatsServer and begins invocations on it. The StatsServer could very well get its data from a local file or database. In order to do so, the StatsServer would have permission to read and/or write the local file or database. To keep our client from abusing this right, we set the security manager so that the client inherits the restrictions of its machine. If the client were in a browser, it would inherit the security restrictions set in the browser. If it were a stand-alone application (as is the case in this example), it would be given the access permissions of the stand-alone application.

Adding and setting the security manager is a simple matter of inserting a line in the client. We will discuss RMISecurityManager in the next section as we design the server for this client.

```java
package java.rmi;

public class StatsClient extends Remote
{
    StatsClient()
    {
        // set the client security manager
        try
        {
            System.setSecurityManager(new RMISecurityManager());
        }
        catch (java.rmi.RMISecurityException exc)
        {
            System.out.println("Security violation " +
                exc.toString());
        }

        // get the remote object from the Registry
        try
        {
            Remote remoteObject = Naming.lookup("STATS-SERVER");
        }
        catch (java.rmi.NotBoundException exc)
        {
            System.out.println("Error in lookup() " +
                exc.toString());
        }

        // narrow the object down to a specific one
        StatsServer statsServerInterface;
        if(remoteObject instanceof StatsServer)
```

```
            statsServerInterface = (StatsServer) remoteObject
    // make the invocation
    try
    {
        System.out.println("Total yardage is: " +
     statsServerInterface.getTotalRunningYardage("Redskins"));
    }
    catch (java.rmi.RemoteException exc)
    {
        System.out.println("Error in invocation " +
            exc.toString());
    }
    }
}
```

Client Overview

As you can see, designing a client in RMI is a pretty straightforward process. Once the client is finished, you must create a server to which to interface. We will do so in a moment, but we should keep in mind that the client portion of our client/server system changes most often. Therefore, we highly advise that you create your clients with a strong modular design. In so doing, you can build software components that are easily replaced. Furthermore, the user interface aspects of your application will most likely affect the client and should not play a part in server design.

Server

Servers enable other objects to connect to your local object as if they actually resided on the requesting machine. To the client nothing is different, but the server requires some added functionality to support TCP/IP processing and communication. Furthermore, a server needs to include all the underlying garbage collection mechanisms that enable it to behave as a normal Java object that will disappear if it is no longer used.

RMI Server Classes

In order to get the Java tools necessary to develop an RMI server, you need to make sure your classes inherit from the RemoteServer class. The RMI system provides several different versions of the RemoteServer class, but as of now RMI gives you only the UnicastRemoteObject class.

The RemoteServer class extends RemoteObject, which gives you all the functionality you had in a client. If your server will eventually be a client as well, you need not inherit the client code again. Furthermore, the RemoteObject superclass also makes sure that you have access to the entire RMI system. The RemoteServer class extends the RemoteObject to provide utility functions getClientHost and getClientPort, which enable clients to determine the proper port to open in order to talk to your server.

The extended class UnicastRemoteObject is a form of a RemoteServer. Eventually, Java RMI will give you several different versions of communication. The Unicast server has the following three characteristics:

1. The server cannot be started remotely. It must exist already and the reference lasts only for the life of the process.

2. TCP/IP is used underneath.

3. An object stream is used to pass parameters and invocations from client to server.

Once your class inherits from UnicastRemoteObject, you can create your server using the two constructors provided with the class. The first constructor forces you to create an object on the default port, and the other allows you to specify the port.

Creating a Server Interface

RMI is driven by the notion of interfaces. As you will recall, interfaces enable you to separate the method signatures you publish to the world from the way those methods are actually implemented. For example, I can tell you that your computer comes with a mouse. You will know how to use it, how to clean it, and how to feed it cheese. In other words, all mice share a common interface. If I were then to add that you were getting a laser mouse like the ones supplied with Sun SPARC stations, you would not have to make a huge shift in thinking to use the new kind of mouse. You still know how to use it, how to clean it, and how to feed it.

In our StatsServer example, we need to create a simple interface with three different methods that can be invoked on it, like so:

```
public interface StatsServer extends Remote
{
    int getTotalRunningYardage(String teamName)
        throws RemoteException;
    int getTotalPassingYardage(String teamName)
        throws RemoteException;
    int getTotalTurnovers(String teamName)
        throws RemoteException;
}
```

Implementing a Server

The interface defines the contract that you must now fulfill. In order for your client's invocation to map onto the server's actual implementation, you need to make sure that your server's methods signatures match the interface signatures exactly. Your server implementation must implement the UnicastRemoteObject class we spoke of earlier, as well as extend the StatsInterface we created:

```
import java.rmi.*;

public class StatsServerImpl extends UnicastRemoteObject
                            implements StatsServer
{
}
```

First we need to implement the constructor for the server. Because the server will be a stand-alone application (RMI does not yet support applet clients or servers), we need to make sure that all our initialization is done in that constructor. RMI requires a constructor to be present. In order for the RMI system to complete its own initialization, the constructor must be invoked and must throw a Remote-Exception in case something goes wrong. Our constructor should also call the super class's constructor:

```
import java.rmi.*;

public class StatsServerImpl extends UnicastRemoteObject
                            implements StatsServer
{
    StatsServer() throws RemoteException
    {
        // call the super class' constructor
        super();
    }
}
```

Now you need to implement the three methods we had defined interfaces for:

```
import java.rmi.*;

public class StatsServer extends UnicastRemoteObject
                        implements StatsInterface
{
    StatsServer() throws RemoteException
    {
        // call the super class' constructor
        super();
    }
    public int getTotalRunningYardage(String teamName)
            throws RemoteException
    {
        if(teamName.equals("Redskins"))
            return 432;
        else
            return 129;
```

```
    }
    // we implement the others as above . . .
}
```

As you create interfaces and methods, keep in mind that the methods themselves need not be concerned that they reside in an RMI server. In fact, the objects you create as RMI servers should be in line with the RMI philosophy. These are objects that could just as easily be local objects. The fact that they are remote should not affect the actual implementation of the methods themselves.

RMI Registry Classes

As you can see, creating an RMI server is just as easy as creating a Java object. We define our interface, implement the interface, and now we need to publish the interface to the world so that any client can access and use our StatsServer. As we mentioned earlier, the RMI Registry keeps track of objects using a simple string. In our client we retrieved an object by the name of STATS-SERVER. In order for this server to be retrieved in that instance, we need to use the same string here as well.

Typically, RMI Registry procedures are implemented in the main routine of your stand-alone application. In the future, when RMI supports applets as well, these procedures will be placed in the init method:

```java
import java.rmi.*;
public class StatsServer extends UnicastRemoteObject
                         implements StatsInterface
{
    StatsServer() throws RemoteException
    {
        // call the super class' constructor
        super();
    }
    public int getTotalRunningYardage(
        String teamName
    ) throws RemoteException
    {
        if(teamName.equals("Redskins")
            return 432;
        else
            return 129;
    }
    . . . we implement the others as above . . .
    public static void main(
        String args[]
    )
```

```
    {
        // create a local instance of our object
        StatsServerImpl statsServer = new StatsServerImpl();
        // put the local instance into the Registry
        Naming.rebind("STATS-SERVER", statsServer);
    }
}
```

RMI Server Security Constraints

As we discussed when we designed the client for this object, we need to specify a security manager. The manager we implemented in the client is the Java RMI-SecurityManager.

NOTE: The RMISecurityManager should be used when the server requires minimal security restrictions. If you require a security system to provide more robust access control, feel free to substitute your favorite security manager in its place.

In any event, the security manager should be set with the System class's setSecurityManager method. If you do not specify a security manager, then the RMI system loads only those classes specified in the Java CLASSPATH environment variable.

RMI uses the CLASSPATH as a default security manager to prevent unexpected and potentially dangerous results from RMI objects.

Adding a security manager is as simple as it was with the client. Remember that the client's security manager prevents downloaded objects from modifying the local file system. The server's security manager prevents the server from doing harm to the host machine. This kind of control is not necessarily meant to control the server itself, but to prevent any client from using the server in a malicious manner.

```
import java.rmi.*;

public class StatsServerImpl extends UnicastRemoteObject
                            implements StatsServer
{
    StatsServer() throws RemoteException
    {
```

```
        // call the super class' constructor
        super();
    }
    public int getTotalRunningYardage(String teamName)
            throws RemoteException
    {
        if(teamName.equals("Redskins")
            return 432;
        else
            return 129;
    }
    . . . we implement the others as above . . .
    public static void main(String args[])
    {
        // set the security manager
        try
        {
            System.setSecurityManager(new RMISecurityManager());
            // create a local instance of our object
            StatsServerImpl statsServer = new StatsServerImpl();

            // put the local instance into the Registry
            Naming.rebind("STATS-SERVER", statsServer);
        }
        catch (java.net.MalformedURLException me)
        {
            System.out.println("Malformed URL :" + me.toString());
        }
        catch (RemoteException re)
        {
            System.out.println("RemoteException: " + re.toString());
        }
    }
}
```

Generating Stubs and Skeletons

Once the interface is completed, you need to generate stubs and skeleton code. Stubs are sort of like backup quarterbacks. They stand in for the starter when he is not available. Sometimes the actual Java object could reside in another virtual machine. Stub code is generated to stand in for the remote class that cannot be accessed in order to provide a successful compile. The RMI system provides an RMI compiler (rmic) that takes your generated interface class and produces stub code on its behalf:

```
%prompt%  javac StatsInterface.java
%prompt%  javac StatsServer.java
%prompt%  rmic StatsServer
```

Once the stub code is compiled and linked in, your RMI application may be completed and installed in the Registry. Once the RMI application resides in the Registry, it is available for the client to invoke as we did in the previous section.

Once the stubs and skeletons are completed, you must start the RMI Registry by hand. RMI objects are not started automatically upon invocation. Therefore, because the RMI Registry is an RMI object in its own right, it must be started by hand:

```
D:\ start rmiregistry
```

Once the Registry is started, the server can be started and will be able to store itself in the Registry. If the server is available through the Registry, the client can invoke it.

```
D:\ java - Djava.security.policy=C:\advjavacd\rmi\Stats1\policy.all
  rmi.Stats1.StatsServer
```

This all looks rather complicated, so let's take it apart and look at what we are saying:

Java	We are asking the Java virtual machine to run something.
-D	Set a system property to some value. In this case set java.security.policy to whatever is in the file C:\advjavacd\rmi\Stats1\policy.all (because of the finer grained security model in Java 2.0 you must set up a security policy for RMI).
rmi.Stats1.StatsServerImpl	Since we created our client and server in a package and my classpath is set to C:\advjavacd, we must fully qualify the class we want to run.

Needless to say, if you put the *advjavacd\rmi\stats1* directory in your class path and started the server up from that directory, this could be reduced to

```
D:\ java -Djava.security.policy=policy.all rmi.Stats1.StatsServerImpl
```

Because this is a little lengthy and complicated, it is best to put it in a script or bat file (see the *R.BAT* file in the *rmi\stats1* directory on the accompanying CD).

Later on when we compare Java IDL and Java RMI, we will discover that location independence and automatic startup are vital to mission-critical applications. For now, take note of the differences as you formulate the alternative more suited for your applications.

NOTE: As you can see, creating an RMI server is not a difficult task. In fact, it is amazingly similar to Java IDL in many respects. This is not an accident. Both Java IDL and Java RMI share the same lineage within Sun Microsystems. The architects of RMI and the brains behind Java IDL both come from the same distributed object projects. As a result they have created Java-based distributed object systems that share the same characteristics.

Server Overview

So now that we can create servers in RMI, we can publish services to the rest of the world. Clients anywhere can use our servers as if they were remote objects. But, what if we wanted every client to use a different instance of the remote server? If we used our current paradigm, we would have to make sure our clients created their own server somewhere else. But, we want them to all use the same server process remotely, just use different instances of the server itself. We can accomplish this with the notion of factories. Factories enable clients to create servers on the fly, all of them contained within the factory's process. That way, if two clients are banging on the same kind of server, what one does won't affect the execution of the other.

Callbacks

When we last spoke of callbacks, we used them as a means to get around the limitation of having no servers within an applet. It enabled us to create a method that would allow a C++ object to invoke our Java applet embedded inside a Web page. While we sacrificed by not having control over the initialization or startup of the callback applet as we would have had with a CORBA server, we were satisfied that our applet would be able to act as the recipient of data.

Java RMI has similar limitations with its servers. Unfortunately, a Java RMI server cannot be embedded within a Web page, so we have to implement similar callback mechanisms inside our servers and clients.

Why Callbacks?

Let's say that clients of our StatsServers wanted to display new data as it arrived to the server. Rather than routinely pinging the server for information and creating a network backlog, we would like our client to change its on-screen state information only when the server has new information to report.

Just as we used the callback mechanism in Java IDL to support this kind of dynamic update, we will implement a server-driven event mechanism that will enable our client to passively update live information. Our solution should be scalable, meaning that it should work just as efficiently for a few clients as it should for several thousand clients. It should be easy to implement, and it should solve the problem without hassle to the client programmer.

Creating the Callback

Because our callback object essentially will be an RMI object, we need to create a new client interface. As you can see in the following code, we need to create a method that the server will invoke when it senses a change in its information.

In order to set up this client interface, we must create a new public interface file similar to the ones we created for the StatsServer itself:

```
public interface StatsCallbackInterface
{
    void statsChanged(
        String teamName,
        int passingYards,
        int rushingYards,
        int turnovers);
}
```

We also must modify the StatsServer itself so that it can register for these call-backs. Remember that we need to tell the server that it has to send us information back when it gets a change. In order to do so, we have to send it an object on which it can invoke the callback. Because our client will implement the StatsCall-backInterface object, we should pass an object of that type to the registration function:

```
// new file. . .
public interface StatsServerInterface extends Remote
{
    int getTotalRunningYardage(
        String teamName);
    int getTotalPassingYardage(
        String teamName);
    int getTotalTurnovers(
        String teamName);

    void addCallback(
        StatsCallbackInterface statsCallbackObject);
}
```

Implementing the Callback Client

Now that we have created the proper interfaces to our callback client and changed the server to use callbacks, we need to modify the client appropriately so that it will register for a callback as the first step in its own initialization phase. Remember that, whenever the server gets changed, the client makes a call to the statsChanged function, so we need to add that function to our client class. In addition, we need to make sure that the client implements the StatsCallbackInterface

interface; otherwise, it will not be able to send itself to the server and be registered for an update.

```java
package java.rmi;

public class StatsClient extends StatsCallbackInterface
{
    public void statsChanged(
        String teamName,
        int passingYards,
        int rushingYards,
        int turnovers
    )
    {
    }

    StatsClient()
    {
        . . . same as before . . .
    }
}
```

Filling in the Callback Method

Now, we need to do something with the information we receive when a callback is invoked. For now, we'll write our results to the standard output device, but keep in mind that we could just as easily have a user interface handle our display routines.

```java
package java.rmi;

public class StatsClient extends StatsCallbackInterface
{
    public void statsChanged(
        String teamName,
        int passingYards,
        int rushingYards,
        int turnovers
    )
    {
        System.out.println("Received dynamic update: ");
        System.out.println("Yards passing: " + passingYards);
        System.out.println("Yards rushing: " + rushingYards);
        System.out.println("Turnovers: " + turnovers);
    }

    StatsClient()
    {
        . . . same as before . . .
    }
}
```

Registering Callbacks

After we've completed the Callback method itself and modified all the interfaces, we need to have the client add itself to the server's callback list. The server then will be able to go down the list whenever it gets a change and invoke the statsChanged method on all of the clients. However, the server will not be aware of the client unless the client registers itself for updates.

```
package java.rmi;

public class StatsClient extends Remote
{
    public void statsChanged(
        String teamName,
        int passingYards,
        int rushingYards,
        int turnovers
    )
    {
        System.out.println("Received dynamic update: ");
        System.out.println("Yards passing: " + passingYards);
        System.out.println("Yards rushing: " + rushingYards);
        System.out.println("Turnovers: " + turnovers);
    }

    StatsClient()
    {
        // set the client security manager
        try
        {
            System.setSecurityManager(new RMISecurityManager());
        }
        catch (java.rmi.RMISecurityException exc)
        {
            System.out.println("Security violation " +
                exc.toString());
        }

        // get the remote object from the Registry
        try
        {
            Remote remoteObject = Naming.lookup("STATS-SERVER");
        }
        catch (java.rmi.NotBoundException exc)
        {
            System.out.println("Error in lookup() " +
                exc.toString());
        }

        // narrow the object down to a specific one
        StatsServer statsServerInterface;
```

```
    if(remoteObject instanceof StatsServer)
        statsServerInterface = (StatsServer) remoteObject

    // register the callback right here
    try
    {
        statsServerInterface.addCallback(this);
    }
    catch (java.rmi.RemoteException exc)
    {
        System.out.println("Error in lookup() " +
            exc.toString());
    }
    }
}
```

TIP: Note how we removed the initial invocation on the server from the previous listing. With callbacks added, we do not have to go to the server to get information, the server will come to us to give us information. Wouldn't it be nice if the BMW dealer came to you to give you a car instead of the way they do things now?

We must now modify the server to add the callback to its list. Like Santa Claus, it checks to see if everything is naughty or nice and make sure you are signed up for your gift, in this case a series of updates to the server. Our server keeps track of each callback object in a vector so that it is easy to traverse the list when the time comes to provide an update.

```
import java.rmi.*;

public class StatsServer extends UnicastRemoteObject
                        implements StatsServerInterface
{
    // the list of callback objects
    Vector callbackObjects;

    StatsServer() throws RemoteException
    {
        // call the super class' constructor
        super();
    }

    public void addCallback(
        StatsCallbackInterface statsCallbackObject
    )
    {
        // store the callback object into the vector
```

```
            callbackObjects.addElement(statsCallbackObject);
    }
    public int getTotalRunningYardage(
        String teamName
    )
    {
        if(teamName.equals("Redskins")
            return 432;
        else
            return 129;
    }
    . . . we implement the others as above . . .
    public static void main(
        String args[]
    )
    {
        // set the security manager
        try
        {
            System.setSecurityManager(new RMISecurityManager());
        }
        catch (java.rmi.RMISecurityException exc)
        {
            System.out.println("Security violation " +
                exc.toString());
        }
        // create a local instance of our object
        StatsServer statsServer = new StatsServer();
        // put the local instance into the Registry
        Naming.rebind("STATS-SERVER", statsServer);
    }
}
```

Invoking Callbacks

Note that our server in its current state does not have any methods with which it will accept changes in the information it sends back. Your servers more than likely will include a method or something similar to setPassingYards. We have created a fake setPassingYards method, which follows, that gets the team name and the passing yardage for that team as a parameter. See how we actually invoke the callbacks from within this function:

```
import java.rmi.*;
public class StatsServer extends UnicastRemoteObject
                        implements StatsServerInterface
{
```

```java
// the list of callback objects
Vector callbackObjects;

StatsServer() throws RemoteException
{
    // call the super class' constructor
    super();
}

public void addCallback(
    StatsCallbackInterface statsCallbackObject
)
{
    // store the callback object into the vector
    callbackObjects.addElement(statsCallbackObject);
}

public void setPassingYards(String teamName,int passingYards)
{
    // do everything that needs to be done to set the variable
    // internally. . .
    // now go down the vector and invoke on
    // each callback object
    for(int x = 0; x < callbackObjects.size(); x++)
    {
        // convert the vector Object to a callback object
        StatsCallbackInterface callback =
        (StatsCallbackInterface) callbackObjects.elementAt(x);

        // invoke the callback
        callback.statsChanged(teamName, passingYards,
            rushingYards, turnovers);
    }
}

public int getTotalRunningYardage(
    String teamName
)
{
    if(teamName.equals("Redskins"))
        return 432;
    else
        return 129;
}

. . . we implement the others as above . . .

public static void main(
    String args[]
)
{
    // set the security manager
```

```
try
{
    System.setSecurityManager(new RMISecurityManager());
}
catch (java.rmi.RMISecurityException exc)
{
    System.out.println("Security violation " +
        exc.toString());
}
// create a local instance of our object
StatsServer statsServer = new StatsServer();

// put the local instance into the Registry
Naming.rebind("STATS-SERVER", statsServer);
    }
}
```

Callbacks in Short

Callbacks are important tools for developers of high-availability servers. Because servers can easily be inundated with invocations from clients, the logical step is to defer those invocations until a time that is both convenient and proper. By setting up callbacks, you can engineer your server to process and accept invocations more efficiently by enabling servers to make invocations when they are ready.

With a suite of tools that enable us to create simple clients and servers to more advanced factory servers and callback servers, we can go about implementing our calendar application once again. With sockets, we were able to define our own application messaging system. Now, with Java RMI we will find that creating a server for our featured application is just as easy as creating a regular Java object.

A Java RMI Version of the Featured App

The advantage of Java-only systems is the language itself. Java's simplicity and gentle learning curve give RMI itself an appearance of simplicity. Java-centric applications do not, however, have the advantages of Java IDL, namely language independence and implementation hiding.

We will start by first rewriting the public interface for our server. After that step is complete, we can go about writing clients to talk to the interface and server that will subsequently implement the interface. The RMI system is easy, and finishing the Internet Calendar Server using it is equally so.

RMI Interface

Remember that our interface must extend the RMI system's Remote classes. As we discussed earlier, the Remote classes provide the functionality for our server interface to talk to the remote reference layer of the RMI system. Without this kind of "translator," we would never be able to receive invocations within our server. So, following the instructions we outlined earlier, we must declare our interface as follows:

```
public interface CalendarServerInterface extends Remote
{
    public void scheduleAppointment(AppointmentType appointment);

    AppointmentType[] getAppointments();
}
```

Note in the interface that the getAppointments method returns an array of AppointmentType objects. AppointmentType is a separate class that has no method defined for it and has only a default constructor. The class is used more as a data structure than as a Java class.

```
public class AppointmentType
{
    String reason;
    int time;
}
```

RMI Client

Once our interface has been defined, we can create our client and then talk to the server. Remember that we will simply reimplement the NetworkModule class so that we can have a seamless interaction with the rest of the Calendar application. After all, we are changing only this module; we never want to touch any other parts of the code.

```
public class NetworkModule
{
    public void scheduleAppointment(String reason, int time)
        { }
    public Vector getAppointments(){}
        { }
    public void initNetwork()
        { }
    public void shutdownNetwork()
        { }
}
```

Since our network connection to the server will be by way of RMI rather than our own sockets connection, we can get rid of the initNetwork and shutdownNetwork methods because they are no longer needed (we will need some of their functionality, namely the database connection and shutdown because we will be moving the database part of the application to the RMI Server).

Our client will first initialize the RMI system in its NetworkModule constructor. The constructor not only will get the RMI system, but it will also initialize the remote object variable. When we retrieve the remote object from the RMI Naming server, we will also have to narrow it down to a specific CalendarServer object.

```
public class NetworkModule
{
    CalendarServerInterface calendarObject;

    Public NetworkModule()
    {
        // install a Security Manager
        System.setSecurityManager(new RMISecurityManager());
        // first get a handle on the object
        calendarObject =
            (CalendarServerInterface)Naming.find("CALENDAR");
    }

    public void scheduleAppointment(String reason, int time)
    {
    }

    public Vector getAppointments()
    {
    }
}
```

After we have completed the constructor information, then we must fill in the rest of the methods. Once again we need to translate the array of AppointmentType variables into a Java vector. The rest of our application does not need to know how we are storing the appointments, just that they can retrieve the appointments at will.

```
package rmi.calendar;

// import Java
import java.awt.*;
import java.util.*;

// import RMI
import java.rmi.*;

public class NetworkModule
{
    CalendarServerInterface calendarObject;
    NetworkModule()
    {
        try
        {
            // first get a handle on the object
            calendarObject =
                (CalendarServerInterface) Naming.lookup("CALENDAR");
        }
        catch(Exception exc)
```

```
    {
        System.out.println("Error! - " + exc.toString());
    }
}

public void scheduleAppointment(String reason,int time)
{
    AppointmentType appointment = new AppointmentType();
    // first create the appointment
    appointment.reason = reason;
    appointment.time = time;
    try
    {
       // now send the appointment to the server
       calendarObject.scheduleAppointment(appointment);
    }
    catch (RemoteException e)
    {
        System.out.println("RemoteEcception 1: " +
                            e.toString());
    }
}

public Vector getAppointments()
{
    // the variable to store all of our appointments in
    AppointmentType appointments[] = null;
    try
    {
       // now get the appointments
       appointments = calendarObject.getAppointments();
    }
    catch(RemoteException e)
    {
        System.out.println("RemoteExceprion 2: " +
                            e.toString());
    }

    // translate into a Vector
    Vector appointmentVector = new Vector();
    for(int x = 0; x < appointments.length; x++)
        appointmentVector.addElement(appointments[x]);

    // return the Vector
    return appointmentVector;
    }
}
```

Once again, we do not have to initialize the network because the RMI system handles all the underlying mechanisms for us. RMI objects are location transparent.

We do not care where or how these objects are implemented, only that they are available for our use. The network sockets, protocols, and connections are handled for us by the RMI system; therefore, we need not concern ourselves with them.

Now we must set our security mechanism so that the client application we have created will have access to the server. Later on, our server will set its security manager so that clients cannot access the local machine on which the server is hosted. Here, we conform our security manager to that of the server so that we can have access in the first place:

```
package rmi.calendar;

// import Java
import java.awt.*;
import java.util.*;
// import RMI
import java.rmi.*;

public class NetworkModule
{
    CalendarServerInterface calendarObject;
    NetworkModule()
    {
        try
        {
            // set up the security manager
            System.setSecurityManager(
                        new RMISecurityManager());
            // first get a handle on the object
            calendarObject =
                CalendarServerInterface) Naming.lookup("CALENDAR");
        }
        catch(Exception exc)
        {
            System.out.println("Error! - " + exc.toString());
        }
    }
    public void scheduleAppointment(String reason,int time)
    {
        AppointmentType appointment = new AppointmentType();

        // first create the appointment
        appointment.reason = reason;
        appointment.time = time;
        try
        {
            // now send the appointment to the server
            calendarObject.scheduleAppointment(appointment);
        }
```

```
        catch (RemoteException e)
        {
            System.out.println("RemoteEcception 1: " +
                                e.toString());
        }
    }

    public Vector getAppointments()
    {
        // the variable to store all of our appointments in
        AppointmentType appointments[] = null;
        try
        {
            // now get the appointments
            appointments = calendarObject.getAppointments();
        }
        catch(RemoteException e)
        {
            System.out.println("RemoteExceprion 2: " +
                                e.toString());
        }

        // translate into a Vector
        Vector appointmentVector = new Vector();
        for(int x = 0; x < appointments.length; x++)
            appointmentVector.addElement(appointments[x]);

        // return the Vector
        return appointmentVector;
    }
}
```

RMI Server

The server we create will need to inherit from the interface we defined earlier. We will then implement each method in the server, starting with the constructor. The constructor will establish the object's presence on the RMI system and ready it for invocations:

```
public class CalendarServer extends UnicastRemoteObject
                            implements CalendarServerInterface
{
    CalendarServer() throws RemoteException
    {
        // call the super class' constructor
        super();
    }

    public void scheduleAppointment(
        AppointmentType appointment
    )
```

```
    {
    }
    public AppointmentType[] getAppointments()
    {
    }
}
```

We must now fill in the methods of our server so that we can process information. As with the previous implementations of the server, we will not concern our-selves with the specifics of how the data will be stored. Rather, we will leave those implementation details for later.

```
// import Java
import java.awt.*;
import java.util.*;
import java.net.*;
import java.io.*;
import java.sql.*;

// import RMI
import java.rmi.*;
import java.rmi.server.*;

public class CalendarServer extends UnicastRemoteObject
                implements CalendarServerInterface
{
    // create the database connection object
    Connection dbConnection;

    CalendarServer() throws RemoteException
    {
        super();
    }

    public void scheduleAppointment(AppointmentType appt)
    {
        try
        { int appointmentTime;
          String appointmentReason;
          appointmentTime = appt.time;
          appointmentReason = appt.reason;
          System.out.println("Inserting new appointment");
          Statement insertStatement =
                        dbConnection.createStatement();
          String insert = "INSERT INTO SCHEDULE " +
                        "VALUES('" + appointmentTime + "','"
                            + appointmentReason
                            + "')";
          System.out.println(insert);

          insertStatement.executeUpdate(insert);
```

```
      }
    catch(Exception e)
    {
      System.out.println("schedAppt  Error: " +
                        e.toString());
    }
  }

public AppointmentType[] getAppointments()
                                 throws RemoteException
{
  // the variable to store all of our appointments in
  AppointmentType[] appointments = new AppointmentType[20];
  try
  {
    Statement statement = dbConnection.createStatement();
    String s = "SELECT TIME, REASON " +
               "FROM SCHEDULE " +
               "ORDER BY TIME";
    ResultSet result = statement.executeQuery(s);
    for (int i=0 ; result.next(); i++)
    {
      // create a variable to stick the appointment in
      AppointmentType appointment = new AppointmentType();

      // now get the next appointment from the string
      appointment.time = result.getInt("TIME");
      appointment.reason = result.getString("REASON");
      appointments[i] = appointment;
    }
  }
  catch(SQLException exc)
  {
    System.out.println("NetworkModule Error 4: " +
                      exc.toString());
  }

  // return the Vector
  return appointments;
}

private void initNetwork()
{
  try
  {
    // load the database driver
    Class.forName("sun.jdbc.odbc.JdbcOdbcDriver");
    //create a URL object for the database
    String url = "jdbc:odbc:Calendar";
    // connect to the database
```

```
         dbConnection = DriverManager.getConnection(url,"","");
      }
      catch (ClassNotFoundException e)
      {
         System.out.println("initNetwork Error: " +
                            e.toString());
      }
      catch (SQLException se)
      {
         System.out.println("initNetwork SQL Error: " +
                            se.toString());
      }
   }
   private void shutdownNetwork()
   {
     try
     {
       dbConnection.close();
     }
     catch(Exception e)
     {
        System.out.println("shutdown Exception: " + e.toString());
     }
   }
}
```

Because RMI servers are Java applications, we must add a main function to our
class. The main function will not only launch the application code but also bind
our application to the Naming server under a given name. The name we used in
the client section was "CALENDAR," so that is the name under which we must
store our server:

```
// import Java
import java.awt.*;
import java.util.*;
import java.net.*;
import java.io.*;
import java.sql.*;

// import RMI
import java.rmi.*;
import java.rmi.server.*;

public class CalendarServer extends UnicastRemoteObject
              implements CalendarServerInterface
{
    // create the database connection object
    Connection dbConnection;

    CalendarServer() throws RemoteException
```

```java
{
  super();
}
public void scheduleAppointment(AppointmentType appt)
{
    try
    { int appointmentTime;
      String appointmentReason;
      appointmentTime = appt.time;
      appointmentReason = appt.reason;
      System.out.println("Inserting new appointment");
      Statement insertStatement =
                      dbConnection.createStatement();
      String insert = "INSERT INTO SCHEDULE " +
                        "VALUES('" + appointmentTime + "','"
                                   + appointmentReason
                                   + "')";
      System.out.println(insert);

      // insert the new appointment
      insertStatement.executeUpdate(insert);
    }
    catch(Exception e)
    {
      System.out.println("schedAppt  Error: " +
                      e.toString());
    }
}

public AppointmentType[] getAppointments()
                                throws RemoteException
{
  // the variable to store all of our appointments in
  AppointmentType[] appointments = new AppointmentType[20];
  try
  {
    Statement statement = dbConnection.createStatement();
    String s = "SELECT TIME, REASON " +
                "FROM SCHEDULE " +
                "ORDER BY TIME";
    ResultSet result = statement.executeQuery(s);
    for (int i=0 ; result.next(); i++)
    {
      // create a variable to stick the appointment in
      AppointmentType appointment = new AppointmentType();

      // now get the next appointment from the string
      appointment.time = result.getInt("TIME");
      appointment.reason = result.getString("REASON");
```

```java
      appointments[i] = appointment;
    }
  }
  catch(SQLException exc)
  {
    System.out.println("NetworkModule Error 4: " +
                       exc.toString());
  }
  // return the Vector
  return appointments;
}
private void initNetwork()
{
    try
    {
      // load the database driver
      Class.forName("sun.jdbc.odbc.JdbcOdbcDriver");
      //create a URL object for the database
      String url = "jdbc:odbc:Calendar";
      // connect to the database
      dbConnection = DriverManager.getConnection(url,"","");
    }
    catch (ClassNotFoundException e)
    {
       System.out.println("initNetwork Error: " +
                          e.toString());
    }
    catch (SQLException se)
    {
       System.out.println("initNetwork SQL Error: " +
                          se.toString());
    }
}
private void shutdownNetwork()
{
  try
  {
    dbConnection.close();
  }
  catch(Exception e)
  {
    System.out.println("shutdown Exception: " + e.toString());
  }
}
public static void main(String args[])
{
```

```
      try
      {
        // create the local instance of the CalendarServer
        CalendarServer svr = new CalendarServer();
        System.out.println("Got here OK");
        // put the local instance into the registry
        Naming.rebind("CALENDAR", svr);
        CalendarServerInterface csi =
            (CalendarServerInterface) Naming.lookup("CALENDAR");
        System.out.println("Server is waiting..." );
        svr.initNetwork();
      }
      catch(Exception exc)
      {
        System.out.println("Error! - " + exc.toString());
      }
    }
}
```

Now, we need to set our security manager so that we can limit the client's access to our host machine. Even though our application is rather innocuous, we don't want harmful clients to come along and maliciously wound our host machine. This is the Java security mechanism at its best:

```
// import Java
import java.awt.*;
import java.util.*;
import java.net.*;
import java.io.*;
import java.sql.*;

// import RMI
import java.rmi.*;
import java.rmi.server.*;

public class CalendarServer extends UnicastRemoteObject
                    implements CalendarServerInterface
{
    // create the database connection object
    Connection dbConnection;

    CalendarServer() throws RemoteException
    {
      super();
    }

    public void scheduleAppointment(AppointmentType appt)
    {
       try
       { int appointmentTime;
         String appointmentReason;
```

```
      appointmentTime = appt.time;
      appointmentReason = appt.reason;
      System.out.println("Inserting new appointment");
      Statement insertStatement =
                          dbConnection.createStatement();
      String insert = "INSERT INTO SCHEDULE " +
                      "VALUES('" + appointmentTime + "','"
                              + appointmentReason
                              + "')";
      System.out.println(insert);

      insertStatement.executeUpdate(insert);
    }
    catch(Exception e)
    {
      System.out.println("schedAppt  Error: " +
                      e.toString());
    }
}
public AppointmentType[] getAppointments()
                          throws RemoteException
{
  // the variable to store all of our appointments in
  AppointmentType[] appointments = new AppointmentType[20];
  try
  {
    Statement statement = dbConnection.createStatement();
    String s = "SELECT TIME, REASON " +
              "FROM SCHEDULE " +
              "ORDER BY TIME";
    ResultSet result = statement.executeQuery(s);
    for (int i=0 ; result.next(); i++)
    {
      // create a variable to stick the appointment in
      AppointmentType appointment = new AppointmentType();

      // now get the next appointment from the string
      appointment.time = result.getInt("TIME");
      appointment.reason = result.getString("REASON");
      appointments[i] = appointment;
    }
  }
  catch(SQLException exc)
  {
    System.out.println("NetworkModule Error 4: " +
                      exc.toString());
  }
  // return the Vector
```

```
      return appointments;
  }
  private void initNetwork()
  {
      // set up the database connection and load the drivers
      try
      {
        // load the database driver
        Class.forName("sun.jdbc.odbc.JdbcOdbcDriver");
        //create a URL object for the database
        String url = "jdbc:odbc:Calendar";
        // connect to the database
        dbConnection = DriverManager.getConnection(url,"","");
      }
      catch (ClassNotFoundException e)
      {
          System.out.println("initNetwork Error: " +
                            e.toString());
      }
      catch (SQLException se)
      {
          System.out.println("initNetwork SQL Error: " +
                            se.toString());
      }
  }

  private void shutdownNetwork()
  { // close the database connection
    try
    {
      dbConnection.close();
    }
    catch(Exception e)
    {
      System.out.println("shutdown Exception: " +
                        e.toString());
    }
  }
  public static void main(String args[])
  {
    try
    {
      // set the security manager
      System.setSecurityManager(new RMISecurityManager());
      // create the local instance of the CalendarServer
      CalendarServer svr = new CalendarServer();
      System.out.println("Got here OK");
      // put the local instance into the registry
```

```
        Naming.rebind("CALENDAR", svr);
        CalendarServerInterface csi =
          (CalendarServerInterface) Naming.lookup("CALENDAR");
        System.out.println("Server is waiting..." );
        svr.initNetwork();
      }
      catch(Exception exc)
      {
        System.out.println("Error! - " + exc.toString());
      }
    }
  }
}
```

We must now generate the skeleton and stub code. Remember that the RMI system provides an RMI compiler, rmic, which we can use to generate those stubs from Java class files. Unlike the idltojava compiler supplied with Java IDL, Java RMI's compiler generates its skeleton code from precompiled Java classes:

```
%prompt%   javac InternetCalendarServerInterface.java
%prompt%   javac CalendarServer.java
%prompt%   rmic CalendarServer
```

New in JDK 1.2

RMI in JDK 1.2 has two major new features—activatable objects and the ability to use a secure transport, like SSL, for RMI.

Activatable Objects

Since the introduction of RMI in JDK 1.1 the programming model included the RMI Registry; a server implementing the UnicastRemoteObject interface that could be started on some remote host. It would then register itself with the Registry and sit and wait for clients to instantiate it remotely. Clients could do this as long as the server was up and running all the time. The idea of the server having to be running all the time was a bitter pill to swallow (especially for CORBA developers who were not under this restriction). Two things have been added to JDK 1.2 to help alleviate this problem: first, the introduction of the java.rmi.activation.Activatable class and, second, the creation of an RMI daemon (rmid). The introduction of these two items enables us to write and deploy an RMI server that can be created and run on demand. The RMI daemon provides a JVM from which other JVM instances may be spawned.

The general process for doing this follows:

1. Make our client as normal.

2. Build our remote interface server by extending java.rmi.remote implemented by ActivatableImplementation.java (our server, the class to be activated).

3. Build a setup program that will register the server (but not instantiate an instance of it) with the Registry and the RMI daemon.

4. Run the setup program.

5. Use the client as normal; the daemon will start up the server as needed.

Detailed instructions, a tutorial, and sample code for doing this are provided with the JDK 1.2.n distribution and should be referred to (see *jdk1.2.1/docs/guide/rmi/ index.html*).

Custom Socket Factories

In Java 1.1 it was possible to install your own custom RMI socket factory and use other than TCP-based sockets for RMI client/server communications. Doing so gave you the ability to use your own custom sockets, but you were then stuck with using that socket type for all your RMI objects. With Java 1.2 you can, on an object-by-object basis, create and use different types of sockets within the same application.

Summary

Java RMI is a powerful alternative to sockets programming for client/server applications. RMI provides us with a tool that eliminates the tedium of low-level sockets programming and lets us focus more on the business logic of our applications than on the communications required for the client and server to pass information back and forth. In the next chapter we'll examine CORBA IDL and how we can use it to create network objects for client/server implementations.

Java IDL: Interface Definition Language

- ▼ CORBA
- ▼ THE INTERFACE DEFINITION LANGUAGE
- ▼ LANGUAGE MAPPINGS
- ▼ CORBA CLIENTS
- ▼ CORBA SERVERS
- ▼ CORBA CALLBACKS
- ▼ A JAVA IDL VERSION OF THE FEATURED APP

The Common Object Request Broker Architecture (CORBA) is an industry standard that has been around since 1991; it defines how applications can communicate with one another no matter where they are located, or what programming language they are written in. Before Java, creating CORBA-based objects was a difficult and time-consuming process. With Java, much of the pain associated with it has been limited or removed altogether. Along with Java's simplicity and elegance, the CORBA framework gives your applications the underlying machinery necessary to produce large-scale mission-critical applications that are distributed across platforms, machines, or networks.

By the end of this chapter, you will have a strong understanding of what CORBA is, how to create your own CORBA clients and servers, and why CORBA is still around after spending so many years in the ivory tower of computer science. CORBA may well be the cog that finally makes Java the true Internet programming language.

Once again, we will reimplement the Internet calendar from the previous chapters, this time using Java Interface Definition Language (IDL). Our application will use CORBA for its communication protocol rather than sockets or RMI. In so doing, we can compare the performance, reliability, and ease of development of the three.

By the end of this chapter, you should have a firm grasp of CORBA along with enough fundamentals of distributed object design to help you make informed architectural decisions on your own.

CORBA

CORBA is a standard developed by the Object Management Group, the world's largest computer consortium. It is not a product; it is not a vision; it is not vapor ware. Many companies have chosen to implement CORBA, most notably Iona Technologies and SunSoft. The CORBA community is by far the more academic of the various communities behind the other communication alternatives we cover in this book. Indeed, their academic nature is both a benefit and a detriment to the average programmer.

Like all academic projects, CORBA has become a kitchen sink standard. Everything you could possibly want is covered in the specification, if not actually implemented by the various CORBA vendors. Much of what CORBA has to offer is intended to be hidden from the programmer. The programmer APIs are not defined; rather each vendor is charged with creating its own API.

In this chapter, we refer to the ORB as an entity, not as a concrete product. Much of our code is from SunSoft's NEO product, chiefly because it is the project the authors actually work on. However, we have created objects for which we will always specify the object's definition, with the idea that any ORB can be used.

CORBA-Style Communication

Let's say that your Aunt Fran calls you from South Dakota. When she dials your number, the phone eventually rings on your side. You pick up the phone, have a conversation, hang up the phone, and terminate the connection. Your Aunt Fran is the requester, or client, and you are the called party, or server. Aunt Fran doesn't care where your phone is in your house. She doesn't care if it's a cordless phone. She doesn't care if it's a conventional phone or a cell phone. All she knows is that she dials a number, you answer, you talk, and you hang up. In other words, Aunt Fran does not care how the call is implemented; she only cares that the call goes through.

If Aunt Fran were to dial using the socket paradigm, she would have to dial the number, specify which phone to ring, specify who should answer the phone, and it would be a shot in the dark. If the call doesn't go through, she won't be told why. She'll probably wait and wait and wait for a phone to ring even though it never will.

Remember also that CORBA does not specify how something will be implemented. Aunt Fran should be just as happy using a satellite phone as she would be using a regular phone. Java is the only language you can use to create a networked object with most of the alternatives in this book. Even though Java may be the greatest thing since the fork-split English muffin, many large-scale distributed systems are still written in C++, C, or, heaven forbid, COBOL. CORBA enables you to use those legacy systems without having to rewrite everything in Java.

The CORBA Vision

As an example, let's say your beanbag has a beautiful interface. You can employ a few operations on it: you can fluff it and you can sit on it. Do you care what goes on underneath? If someone were to come by one day and replace your cloth beanbag with a vinyl beanbag, would you still know how to use it? Yes, because the interface didn't change; only the implementation did.

The beauty of CORBA is that you can create a number of interfaces that are implemented in a variety of different ways. If you want to talk to an object, you have the interface: in essence a contract that states what you will give the object and what you will get from the object in return. Because of that, objects are interchangeable so long as they share the same interfaces.

For the Internet, this means that we can deploy an object and tell people what they must do in order to use it. Later on, if we discover an enhancement to the object, we can merely swap the old inferior object with my new enhanced one, and no one will ever know or care. One of the ways we do this at Sun is with our support feedback tool. Our customers can submit problem reports for our products using a Java interface that communicates over the Internet with an object. From time to time we upgrade or fix the object, but our customers never know. To them, the interface remains the same. Figure 6-1 shows a graphical representation of how object implementations are different from their interfaces.

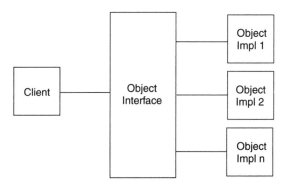

Figure 6–1 Clients only care about interfaces, not implementations.

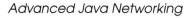

In geek terms, this is referred to as "three-tier client/server computing." The first tier is your client, whether it is a Java applet or a Windows 95 OLE client, and it communicates with the second tier. The second tier is the object you implement in CORBA using the IDL. Finally, the third tier is your data source, perhaps a database or other implement. Information is passed through the three tiers with the idea that changes may be made to any tier, and no effect will be seen on any of the other tiers. Figure 6-2 shows how the data is kept separately from the client by using object servers as the middleman.

Communication with CORBA

Similarly, when you request information from a CORBA object, you don't care how it is implemented; you only care that your request goes through and that the object responds. CORBA, the Object Request Broker (ORB), specifically, ensures that your request gets there, and if it doesn't, you will find out. Moreover, the ORB will start up a server if one isn't already running.

CORBA ensures reliability of communication. If a request does not go through, you will know about it. If a server isn't there, it will be started up, and you will be told if there is a problem. Every possible communication contingency is covered in the specification. In general, CORBA can be referred to as communications middleware.

But this kind of reliability does not come without a price. CORBA provides a ton of functionality to devise object schemes that work. CORBA programming is far from easy, but as a tradeoff you receive significant benefits for your effort.

Separation of Interface and Implementation

Just as Java objects are defined as collections of operations on some state, CORBA objects are defined similarly. Unlike Java itself and Java RMI, CORBA enables you

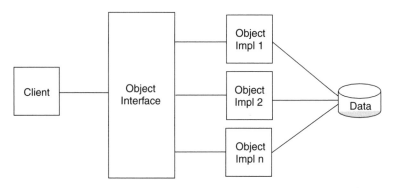

Figure 6-2 The three-tier client-server architecture consists of a client, an object, and a data source.

to define your interface definition separately from your implementation. As you can see in Figure 6-3, splitting the interface from the implementation enables you to create multiple objects from the same interface, each handling the method signatures differently. In the end, however, the greatest advantage to the split is that your interfaces are likely to remain static, while your implementations will change dramatically over time.

Software architects will spend considerable time and energy creating objects and their interfaces, leaving the implementation up to their staff. The interface implementers will code their objects in the programming language of their choice. Once the objects are finished and registered with the ORB, they are ready to be invoked. One of the few advantages to C++ over Java is this kind of separation between implementation and interface, and CORBA allows you to have the same kind of functionality.

A client that invokes on an object knows only the interface definition. The implementation of the object is of no concern to the requester, who cares only that the object request gets to the server and that a response is sent back. Theoretically, client programmers and server programmers don't need to know any of the details of each other's implementations. The interfaces are defined using the Interface Definition Language. The IDL enables us to know what methods can be invoked on an object. A typical CORBA object lifecycle requires the most time in developing the interfaces. Once you are satisfied with the interface, you move on to the implementation.

In the business world today, a great push toward Java is taking place. Because of its tremendous advantages over C++, many organizations are planning an eventual move to Java programming with the idea that several of the language's drawbacks will be addressed appropriately in subsequent revisions. If these organizations had taken a CORBA-like approach to their original software design, then the migration

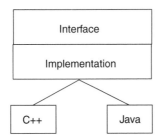

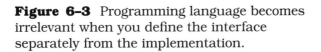

Figure 6-3 Programming language becomes irrelevant when you define the interface separately from the implementation.

would hardly be an issue. Because each CORBA object has an interface that is published and well known, changing its implementation does not involve changing the implementations of any other object that talks to it. As you can see in Figure 6-4, objects in CORBA talk to interfaces, while objects not written using CORBA talk directly to one another.

CORBA objects can be written in any language for which a language mapping is specified. Therefore, the implementation can vary between objects, but the client should not care. The language mapping is defined by the OMG, and the various vendors then choose to implement the mapping. NEO, for example, does not implement the Smalltalk mapping but has created its own Java mapping. Language mappings are discussed in detail in the next section.

Different Vendors, Different ORBs

What if you create a client that accesses your chosen ORB and another object comes along, written in another ORB, and you would like to talk to it? In the early days of CORBA, you would have to rewrite your client—no small task considering that clients are where the pretty stuff is. You'd have to redo all your pretty graphics and recompile your client for the new ORB. For that reason, ORB consumers often stayed a one-ORB shop. If their servers were created in Orbix, their clients generally were as well.

In the new CORBA world, all objects and clients speak to one another using the Internet Inter-ORB Protocol, or IIOP. IIOP (usually pronounced "eye-op") ensures that your client will be able to talk to a server written for an entirely different ORB. Note how this takes advantage of the client abstraction we spoke of earlier. Now, your clients need not know what ORB the server was written in and can simply talk to it.

Furthermore, the ORB is the only fully native portion of the entire CORBA system. The ORB is specific to the platform on which it runs. Orbix, Iona Technologies' entry into the CORBA market, runs on just about every platform imaginable because they have made the effort to port Orbix to every platform imaginable.

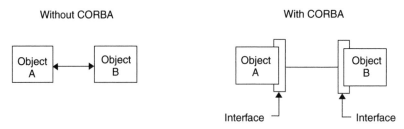

Figure 6–4 Objects talk to interfaces, not to implementations.

SunSoft's NEO, on the other hand, runs exclusively on Solaris but does so better than any other CORBA option.

NOTE: Because Orbix's ORB was written with quick portability in mind, it tends to offer less power than NEO does and also has significant problems with scalability. Again, this is a trade-off issue, and one that must be evaluated on a case-by-case basis. With the universal acceptance of IIOP, there is no reason why your CORBA objects need to be written in one ORB only.

Advantages of CORBA

CORBA is an example of Distributed Object programming. If you were to create two objects, say a Character object and a String object, you would be splitting up functionality across different objects. Your String object would instantiate several Character objects, and all would be happy in your plain vanilla object-oriented world (see Figure 6-5).

If, however, you were to take things one step farther and have your String object instantiate its Character objects on a different machine, you would be entering the distributed object world and all the insanity that revolves around it (see Figure 6-6). When instantiating objects across multiple machines, certain precautions and measures must be taken to ensure the proper routing of messages. If you

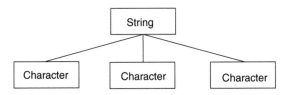

Figure 6-5 Objects are composed of other objects.

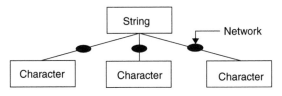

Figure 6-6 Distributed Objects allow objects to be composed of other objects residing on other networks.

were to use CORBA as your basis for creating these objects, all those situations would be addressed already.

CORBA gives you the tools you need to distribute your objects across multiple machines running on perhaps several different networks. You need only to instantiate your object before using it just as you normally would use a local object.

As mentioned already, CORBA makes a big distinction between interface and implementation. The interface is the list of methods with which you will communicate; the implementation is how those methods are created. Let's say I want to print a document that I just wrote. I know that there is a printer application checked into the same ORB I 'm checked into. I only have to know how to call the printer application (the interface). I don't care how it actually prints my file (the implementation). I do care if it prints it or not, and using an ORB gives me this advantage.

Common Object Services

When you programmed in C++, chances are you used a class library of some sort. The famous Rogue-Wave class libraries give you a great number of classes and objects that you can reuse in your code, ranging from the sublime String classes to the vastly more complex Hash Tables.

Likewise, part of the CORBA specification deals with a set of distributed class libraries known as the Common Object Services. The Common Object Services refer to specific types of objects that are beneficial to programmers in a distributed environment, including transaction objects, event service objects, relationships objects, and even lifecycle objects.

Perhaps the most useful of all the Common Object Services is the Naming Service. The Naming Service provides you with a directory-like system for storing and organizing your objects so that other programmers can access and invoke them. In Figure 6-7, we map the string "Object One" to the physical object "1," but are able to map "Object Two" to the physical object "3." The Naming Service allows

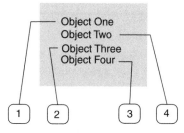

Figure 6-7 With the Object Naming Service, every string is mapped to an object.

us to also change that on the fly. In fact, the Naming Service, and all Common Object Services for that matter, are nothing more than CORBA objects. Therefore, if you can get the interface to the Naming Service, you can create a client that modifies it yourself.

TIP: Some CORBA customers even use the Naming Service as a sort of versioning system, creating a new directory in the Naming Service for each new version of their object system. If you can do it with a directory, you can do it with the Naming Service.

Object Administration

One of the biggest obstacles to distributed computing is the management of objects across multiple platforms and multiple networks. Though the CORBA specification does not specify an administration scheme, several vendors have created administration tools you can use to manage your entire system.

Tasks that run the gamut from server startup and shutdown all the way to machine-specific parameters are addressed in these tools. Often the tools are written in the same CORBA implementation that they manage, and many even have Java interfaces. Most of the tools address the issue of object registration and invocation. When an object is registered, it is stored in a location called the Interface Repository. Accessing objects from the Interface Repository is often quite difficult, has great overhead, and requires a significant knowledge of the OS. The Naming Service addresses some of these concerns by creating a user-friendly front end to objects that are stored in the Interface Repository. But in order to manipulate objects directly within the Interface Repository, you need object administration tools.

NOTE: Because the object administration tools vary widely among CORBA vendors, we will not address them in detail. The OMG, as a matter of fact, does not even specify the kinds of administration tools that are required to support an object system; that determination is left to the vendors. NEO includes a full suite of Java-based tools to manipulate your objects, and Orbix has similar tools available from the command line.

Clients and Servers and Networks, Oh My!

Client programming in CORBA is significantly easier than creating a server. Because, in the simplest sense, all you are doing is instantiating a class that just happens to be on a remote machine, it is quite intuitive as well. When you instantiate a class in CORBA, you specify not only the name of the class but the location as well. The location can be a specific machine or a specific server, but is usually determined by referencing the Naming Service.

The Naming Service contains a find method that enables you to retrieve an object by using a string name that you specify:

```
...
myFirstObject = NamingService.resolve("MyFirstObject");
myFirstObject.myFirstMethod();
...
```

Once an object is retrieved, invoking it is exactly the same as invoking a locally instantiated class. In fact, underneath the covers, a local class is instantiated. Let's say that you get an object called MyFirstCORBA from the Naming Service and invoke myFirstMethod on it. In reality, the local copy of MyFirstCORBA maps that call to a method that invokes across the ORB to the remote object, as illustrated in Figure 6-8.

Writing a server is much more complicated, and many vendors do not yet support full Java server capability. In later parts of this chapter, we will discuss full Java server capability and what it means for the future of C++ objects in CORBA. Needless to say, the ease-of-use aspects of Java help to minimize overhead and the learning curve of CORBA in general. Yet, Java is thus far not as capable of the performance numbers generated by identical C++ applications.

What CORBA Means for You

CORBA is perhaps the single most developed of all the various communication alternatives that we discuss in this book. Without much effort, you will be able to create clients that you can publish on the World Wide Web and make available to anyone who wishes to take advantage of your objects. With a significantly greater investment of time and energy, servers can be generated that take full advantage of client/server computing over the Internet. While the learning curve is greater

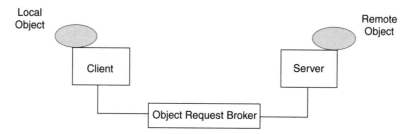

Figure 6-8 Objects invoke on remote objects via the Object Request Broker.

compared to other alternatives, the payoff is also potentially greater. Even though CORBA may be difficult for you to grasp, once you learn it you will agree that it is the best of any alternative presented in this book, or potentially available in the Java industry.

The Interface Definition Language

As we discussed in Chapter 1, "Advanced Java," one of the most important concepts of object-oriented programming is implementation hiding. In CORBA, the implementation can be any number of things, ranging from different programming approaches to different programming languages altogether. In light of this, the OMG created the Interface Definition Language to help make clear the separation between interface and implementation.

The IDL does exactly what it says: define interfaces. IDL contains no implementation details. The IDL, as the name implies, is a language in and of itself, but there are no assumptions made as to how (or if) an object will be created. Rather, the IDL specifies what the object will look like from both a client and a server perspective. IDL defines an object's attributes, parent classes, exceptions, typed events it emits, methods it supports (including input/output parameters and their data types). In this section, we will examine closely the basics of the IDL. Subsequent sections will explain how you can implement the interfaces you create here in Java. Keep in mind, however, that we choose to implement our objects in Java because this is a Java book, but you could just as easily implement your objects in any language for which a language mapping exists.

Interfaces

Interfaces are the backbone of the IDL. In an object-oriented language, you can create interfaces as well as implementations, but here we are allowed to specify only the method signatures and the variables associated with them. For example, if we were to create an interface to our television, it would look something like this:

```
interface TelevisionSet
{
    long currentChannel;
    void changeChannel(long newChannel);
    void increaseVolume();
    void decreaseVolume();
}
```

As you can see, we do not imply either that this is the 50-foot giant screen TV in our break room or the 13-inch TV in our kitchen. Rather, we mention only the common interfaces to both. It will be up to the implementer to define how his interface will behave. Note also that we have not included any kind of method for powering the set on or off. In fact, the underlying CORBA mechanisms take care of that for us. Remember that merely invoking an object instantiates its implementation and readies it for further use. Not using the object for a while has the reverse effect. After a specified time-out period, the object will shut itself down, not unlike the new Energy Saver computer monitors!

Modules

Let's say we now want to model all the appliances in our home using the IDL. The first step is to create an interface for each appliance (we've done a few in this section) and then to implement each as we see fit. After that, we need to group the appliances together in a module. A module is essentially a name space for a group of interfaces or a logical unit. It enables each interface to have a common name when referred to in code, as evidenced in the following snippet.

```
module Appliances            // a logical unit
{
    interface TelevisionSet  // a CORBA class
    {
        . . .
    }
    interface Radio
    {
        string currentBand;   // can be "am" or "fm"
        long currentStation;

        void changeBands();   // interface
        void stationUp();
        void stationDown();
    }
    . . . many more as well . . .
}
```

As you can see, modules are highly logical extensions to object-oriented interface design. In fact, the module itself could be enclosed in yet another module, allowing groups of modules to be grouped together. In order to call the Radio object's stationUp method, you would probably make a call like:

```
Appliances.Radio.stationUp();
```

Keep in mind, of course, that the syntax of this call is entirely language dependent, and that the IDL makes no assumptions whatsoever about language use. Notice that Appliances is set as the parent object for Radio, as it would be for TelevisionSet as well.

Interface Inheritance

There are several situations in which we would like our interfaces to inherit from one another. Just as we did with Java objects, we can define language-specific inheritance that is translated through the language mapping down to the implementation.

```
interface TelevisionSet
{
    . . .
}
interface EnhancedTelevision : TelevisionSet
{
    void activatePIP();
    void deactivatePIP();
}
```

In this example, EnhancedTelevision inherits from TelevisionSet, getting all of the features from our initial TelevisionSet object, as well as adding a few of its own. When you instantiate EnhancedTelevision, you get not only the features you added, but the TelevisionSet properties as well, integrated by the language mapping with the EnhancedTelevision object as if they were part of the EnhancedTelevision to begin with. Any client that uses EnhancedTelevision has no idea that it is an inherited object.

Because the IDL is an interface language, inheritance does not imply implementation inheritance. When you inherit methods from another object, you do not get the implementations that go along with that method. Remember, the IDL does not care what kinds of implementations you create for an interface. In keeping with that, IDL does not link implementations together for inherited objects. In order to enact your own implementation inheritance, you need to create within your server client code that contacts the object implementation you want to use.

Variables and Structures

When you include variables within an interface, you have to be careful. Are those variables matters of implementation (you do not want to start creating counter variables, for example) or are they a matter of interface definition (the current channel is vital for the operation of the TelevisionSet object)? In the previous examples in this section, we showed you several examples of variables including type enumerations, simple variable types, and parameter values. There are a few simple types available for use within the IDL, as you can see in Table 6-1.

But the IDL also gives you a means to create complex data types in containers known as structures. A structure is, essentially, a class with no methods. The IDL makes the distinction because some languages make the distinction. C++, for example, gives you the benefit of structures as a legacy from its C ancestry. Java, however, does not provide structures and forces you to make the more logically object-oriented choice of classes. A complex data type is, by definition, a group of

Table 6–1 Available Types Within IDL

Type	Explanation
long	Integer type ranging from –231 to 231
short	Integer type ranging from –215 to 215
float	IEEE single-precision floating point numbers
double	IEEE double-precision floating point numbers
char	Regular 8-bit quantities
boolean	TRUE or FALSE
octet	8-bit quantity guaranteed to not be changed in any way
string	A sequence of characters
any	Special type consisting of any of the above

simple data types. In the following example, AnsweringMachineMessage is a complex data type composed of a bunch of strings:

```
struct AnsweringMachineMessage
{
    string dateStamp;
    string timeStamp;

    string message;
}
```

Methods

In order to manipulate your IDL-defined servers, you need to declare methods. In the previous TelevisionSet example, we defined several methods such as changeChannel and increaseVolume. Each method may have a series of parameters, as in the case of changeChannel. These parameters may be simple types or complex types, or a special IDL-defined type called Any.

The Any type is a special type that is most often used within method declarations (although it is permissible to use them as variables as well). In C or C++, Any is mapped to a void pointer (void *), while in Java it is mapped to an Object (remember how everything in Java inherits one way or another from type Object). As in the implementation languages, you would use Any to represent an unknown (at interface design time) quantity.

Parameters may be passed in one of three ways. If you pass a parameter as an input (in) parameter, the parameter will not be sent back from the method in a modified state. Parameters passed as output (out) parameters cannot be accessed from within the method, but can be set inside the method. Finally, input/output (I/O) parameters can be sent back both modified and accessed from within the method itself.

Constructed Data Types

Besides structures, there are a few more kinds of constructed types. A union is a form of a structure, but the members of a union, unlike a structure, can vary from instance to instance. Let's say you had two cars, a BMW Z3 convertible and a Volvo station wagon. For trips to the grocery store, you would use the Volvo because the Z3 has no trunk space. But, for fun trips to the Santa Cruz beaches, you would definitely take your Z3. The kind of car you drive depends on your situation.

The last structured type supported by the IDL is the enumeration. An enumeration is similar to an array except that its contents are determined beforehand and cannot be changed. In our radio example earlier, we had a variable called current-Band. The currentBand was set using a string, but in reality it can have only two values, AM or FM. The IDL enables us to define the enumeration as follows:

```
module Appliances
{
    interface TelevisionSet
    {
        . . .
    }

    interface Radio
    {
        typedef enum _RadioBand { AM_BAND, FM_BAND } RadioBand;

        RadioBand currentBand;
        long currentStation;

        void changeBands();
        void stationUp();
        void stationDown();
    }
    . . . many more as well . . .
}
```

Exceptions

As in Java, exceptions are a great way to propagate errors back through your objects. You define exceptions using the exception keyword in the IDL. The Java Language Mapping translates those exceptions into Java exceptions that you can then use in your applications. In the following example, the exception Rotten is thrown whenever someone tries to eat an apple that happens to be rotten.

```
interface Apple
{
    exception Rotten { };

    void eatApple() throws Rotten;
}
```

Overview of the IDL

The Interface Definition Language is a powerful tool both for CORBA programming and for software architecture. Although it is primarily the foundation on which you can create CORBA objects, it can just as easily be used to define entire object systems. For this purpose alone, the IDL warrants further study. If you are a masochist and enjoy scintillating beach reading, check out the CORBA specification from the Object Management Group. If you prefer a less technical tome, Thomas Mowbray's *Essential CORBA* is, well, essential.

Now that we have learned about IDL, we can define interfaces using it. Eventually, those interfaces need to be translated into code. This is done by mapping every construct in the IDL to constructs in the language of choice. While we will only discuss C++ here, CORBA objects defined in IDL can be developed in any language so long as a language mapping exists. This is the greatest benefit to CORBA. Your language independence allows you to spend time intelligently creating interfaces and worrying about implementations later. Today Java is the hot potato; tomorrow it could be a new language altogether. By defining good interfaces, you can protect yourself from being torn in the winds of change.

Language Mappings

Because CORBA is independent of the programming language used to construct clients or servers, several language mappings are defined to enable programmers to interface with the CORBA functionality from the language of their choice. The OMG's member organizations are free to propose mappings that must then be approved by the rest of the consortium. Needless to say, getting the likes of DEC, Hewlett Packard, and Sun to agree on something small is difficult enough without having to introduce an argument like a language mapping.

Language mappings are vast, complex things that underscore the different ways of doing the same thing from within a language. The beauty of a programming language, and what keeps programmers employed, is that there are often several ways to accomplish the same thing. Indeed, one approach to a problem affects portability, while another has an impact on performance. No two approaches are the same; therefore, no one approach is ever "better" than another. It may be better in a particular context, but often that overused term "tradeoff" is bandied about to reflect why one OMG member prefers its mapping to another.

What Exactly Are Language Mappings?

A language mapping in CORBA refers to the means necessary to translate an IDL file into the programming language of choice. Currently, the OMG specifies mappings for C, C++, Smalltalk, and Java. Because of its wide acceptance and object-oriented nature, C++ is the language most often used by CORBA programmers.

Since the introduction of Java, however, the CORBA community is excited over the use of Sun's language to eliminate many of the pitfalls of the C++ mapping.

C++'s greatest problem so far is not its difficulty—that is enough of a barrier as it is—but its painful memory management requirements. In a distributed paradigm in particular, memory management becomes a significant issue. Let's say you instantiate a local String class, passing it an array of characters. In C++, you can easily define which object, the parent object or the child String object, will be responsible for deallocating that memory. If you expand the situation to instantiating a String object on a remote computer, then you begin to deal with memory on two different machines! You allocate an array on your local machine, pass that array to a String class on another machine, and end up with a quandary. Which machine's object will deallocate the memory?

Once again, Java comes to the rescue. Because it is a garbage-collected language, memory deallocation is of no concern to you. Let's say you wrote the preceding situation in Java code. Neither the remote object nor the local parent object needs to worry about memory because, once the memory is no longer used, Java automatically returns it to the system. Because of this and countless other problems with the C++ mapping, and with the use of C++ in general, the OMG is beginning to consider Java language mappings from its member consortiums.

Because the authors of this book are Sun employees, we show a definite bias toward the Sun Microsystems Java IDL language mapping. We apologize for our behavior in advance, but we believe that the Java IDL mapping designed in our own office building is much better than that of anyone else. To be fair, we recognize that some of what we have to tell you may differ from other companies' efforts, and we will make every effort to point out such nuances as they occur.

The Sun Microsystems Java Language Mapping

NOTE: The language mapping described in this section is in a state of flux. Because of the fast-moving Java and CORBA communities, Java IDL is always trying to stay in step with Javasoft and CORBA. Naturally, the language mapping may change slightly from month to month, but, in general, it remains the same overall.

Sun Microsystems bundles a program called idltojava that actually does the mapping and generates the necessary files. The Sun approach to CORBA files is to create several user-level files that are directly modified by the programmer, and several stub files that are not intended to be modified, but instead provide the mapping functionality.

Interfaces, Modules, and Methods

The mapping takes every IDL-defined module and translates it into a Java package. For example, the IDL module Appliances, as follows:

```
module Appliances
{
    . . .
}
```

becomes the following in the generated Java files:

```
package Appliances;

public class
{
    . . .
}
```

Interfaces map directly to Java classes because IDL modules are, as discussed earlier, name-scoping mechanisms. The corresponding Java name-scoping mechanism is the package. For every interface in a module (if there is a module at all, for modules are not required), a Java class is generated in the code:

```
module Appliances
{
    interface TelevisionSet
    {
    }
}
```

becomes the following:

```
package Appliances;

public class TelevisionSet
{
    . . .
}
```

As for parameters, Java maps them, as we will discuss in upcoming sections on simple and complex types. However, Java does not support pass-by-reference variables because it is a pointer-free language. There is no way in the Java language to pass a parameter that can be modified in the method and sent back to the calling function. As a result, the IDL out and inout parameters cannot be supported in Java without some special workarounds.

The Sun mapping supports the notion of holders in order to circumvent the lack of a pass-by-reference model in Java. A holder contains not only the variable itself but methods to modify that method as well. So, when a variable is passed by reference, Java passes a class instead.

Interface Inheritance

Inheritance is a difficult task to take on in the Java language mapping because IDL interfaces support direct multiple inheritance while Java classes do not. In order to make classes multiply inheritable, they must be first declared as interfaces and then implemented as classes. While it sometimes becomes counterintuitive because inherited interfaces do not follow the norm for regular interfaces, it is the only way to complete the language mapping on the inheritance subject.

For example, the following multiply inherited class:

```
module Appliances
{
    interface Speaker
    {
    }
    interface Listener
    {
    }
    interface Phone : Speaker, Listener
    {
    }
}
```

becomes the following collection of interfaces and classes in Java:

```
package Appliances;
public interface SpeakerRef
{
    . . .
}
public interface ListenerRef
{
    . . .
};
public interface PhoneRef extends Appliances.SpeakerRef,
        Appliances.ListenerRef
{
    . . .
}
public class Speaker
{
    . . .
}
```

Variables and Structures

Table 6-2 outlines each of the simple types supported by the IDL and their result-ing Java representation.

Table 6–2 IDL Types and their Java Representations

Type	Java Mapping
long	Java int
short	Java short
float	Java float
double	Java double
char	Java char
boolean	Java boolean
octet	Java byte
string	Java's language module's String class (*java.lang.String*)
any	Special type consisting of any of the above

The Sun mapping does not support unsigned types, however, because Java has no corresponding manner in which to represent an unsigned type. The Sun mapping leaves the implementation of unsigned types up to the user. When you try to interface with an unsigned type in one of your programs, you need to provide the logic that converts the negative values into their corresponding positive representation. Eventually, when Java supports unsigned types inside its *java.lang.Long* and *java.lang.Integer* objects, the Sun Java mapping will follow suit with proper unsigned support.

Constructed Data Types

IDL structures are mapped directly to a Java class consisting of each member variable as well as two constructors. One constructor is for initializing each member variable to a statically defined value, while the other can accept data upon instantiation. So, the following IDL:

```
struct PhoneNumber
{
    // xxx-xxx-xxxx format
    string areaCode;
    string prefix;
    string suffix;
};
```

becomes:

```
public class PhoneNumber
{
    public String areaCode;
    public String prefix;
    public String suffix;
}
```

IDL sequences and arrays are equally easy to map into their Java counterpart. Every sequence is mapped directly into a Java array. Every Java array consists not only of the array values but also of infrastructure to supply the length of the sequence as well. Furthermore, IDL arrays are directly related to Java arrays and, therefore, fall in suit with sequences. The extra array subscripting features provided by IDL sequences also were not originally intended to be included in IDL arrays. Because no harm can come from including the extra details in the array mapping, the decisions make sense. The end result is that if both your client and server implementations are going to be written in Java, then there is no real difference between sequences and arrays.

```
sequence <Phone> allThePhonesInMyHouse;
```

Thus, the preceding IDL declarations map to reasonably straightforward Java counterparts:

```
Phone allThePhonesInMyHouse[];
```

The Enumeration and Union constructed IDL types are much more complicated. Because Java supports neither enumerated types nor variable classes, several layers of additional Java infrastructure must be provided to implement the details of the IDL types properly.

Exceptions

Java supports an exception capability very similar to both IDL and C++. As a result, the mapping between the IDL and Java is extremely obvious. Furthermore, CORBA C++ programmers will find that the helper methods provided by Java exceptions are much more intuitive and easier to use than their C++ counterparts. In the end, the Java exception and the IDL exception are perfect partners in object-oriented error tracking.

Java and CORBA Together

Because CORBA is designed as an all-encompassing standard designed to provide answers to most, if not all, object-oriented programming questions, it does not quite fit into the Java philosophy. Java was designed as the exact antithesis to C++. Both Java and C++ are object-oriented languages; however, Java does not attempt to, nor does it, satisfy C++ and CORBA's insatiable need to be everything to all people.

But, for all their differences, Java and CORBA can be made to work well together. As we have seen in this section and we will see in the next few chapters, CORBA provides a ton of functionality. Most of it will never be required by the average programmer, and thus it can become quite a burden. Meanwhile, Java is accessible to all programmers, both beginner and highly experienced. Java actually makes CORBA manageable because CORBA provides the plumbing, while Java gives you, the programmer, a means to access the plumbing without knowing how it works. After all, you don't care how your car works, you just care that it does. Similarly, no one (outside of geeks who desperately need a little bit of sun) really cares how CORBA works.

Once you are comfortable with language mappings, it is time to move on to actually developing client/server applications using CORBA. We will use the IDL, and its corresponding Java language mapping, to develop a client and server.

CORBA Clients

Writing a CORBA client is pretty simple, if you can grasp the nuances of the language mapping. After you obtain the interface (usually by looking at the IDL) for the server you wish to contact, you have to generate Java stubs. Java stubs contain all the underlying functionality needed to make a call across a network to a server in an unknown location. Remember that your server will not be in any definite location; in fact, the beauty of the Naming Service is that the corresponding string name can point you to any object at any time.

With that in mind, the last thing you want to concern yourself with is network code. Let the ORB deal with all of that, and you can concentrate on creating a client that works for you. Your client will be mostly a User Interface. The few instances in which it needs to make a network call are usually to relay information from the UI back to the server, and to refresh information on the UI with data stored on the server. In client/server parlance, this is called a "thin client," meaning that the functionality of the client related to the server is minimal.

Designing a User Interface

Since the beginning of the "Java revolution," an enormous number of GUI builders have been released, all with cute coffee-related names that were devised by a marketer in a cold sweat. In this section, we assume that every client is a thin client, choosing to concentrate the hard work on the server side and leaving the fun, cool stuff on the client. Clients are sort of like your starving artist little sister, they're beautiful and fun, but they don't do much work.

With that in mind, we have chosen not to endorse any one GUI builder. We believe that there is no single tool out there that could possibly be all things to all people. Which GUI builder you choose is of no consequence to the rest of this chapter. Rather than step through the Java code for designing a GUI, we will let you just design the GUI as we describe in this section and then we'll move on.

Defining the Problem

One of the things that Prashant liked best about working at Sun was their incredible break rooms. Every break room has a nifty little water cooler. Now, the first time you look at it, you'll say to yourself, "Gee, big deal."

But, wait, there's more! That little water cooler also spits out warm and hot water! When you first gaze upon this marvel of technological prowess, you will be stymied and get the urge to write an applet to unveil your discovery to the world. This is precisely what we intend to do.

Typically, you will have some information that needs to be published to the outside world. In the realm of client/server computing, this is done by creating a server to publish that information. Clients are then able to access that information through the server. In our example, we want to publish information about our water cooler, and we will do so by creating a client to access that information followed by a server to provide it.

The Cooler Interface Definition

We need to model the interface definition so that it is intuitive. For example, our IDL will need three operations, one for each of hot, warm, and cold water. We need three data accessors to get the level of each kind of water. With that in mind, the interface definition would look something like the following:

```
interface Cooler
{
    int getHotWaterLevel();
    int getWarmWaterLevel();
    int getColdWaterLevel();

    int getHotWater();
    int getWarmWater();
    int getColdWater();
};
```

We will also need to track errors in invocation, just in case there is no water to get:

```
interface Cooler
{
    int getHotWaterLevel();
    int getWarmWaterLevel();
    int getColdWaterLevel();

    exception NoMoreWaterException { };

    int getHotWater() throws NoMoreWaterException;
    int getWarmWater() throws NoMoreWaterException;
    int getColdWater() throws NoMoreWaterException;
};
```

The Cooler User Interface

Our user interface will display three buttons, one each for hot, warm, and cold water. By clicking on the Hot Water button, you will diminish the level of hot water in the cooler; clicking the Warm Water button will diminish the level of warm water, and so forth. The server will store the current level of each one and make sure we don't take out water when there's none there. So, the UI for the Cooler client is pretty obvious (see Figure 6-9), and you can draw it in just about any of the GUI tools.

We should also create another client that watches the server and shows the level of all three water sources at any given moment. This way, if we stick the applet on the Web, people all over the world can see how much water we Sun employees actually drink. The Monitor client also will have a button to reset the water source whenever we feel like it (see Figure 6-10).

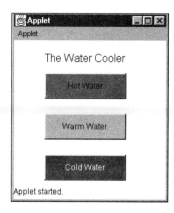

Figure 6–9 The user interface for our water cooler example is a basic three-button display.

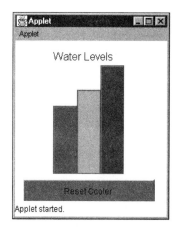

Figure 6–10 Our second client displays the level of water in our example cooler.

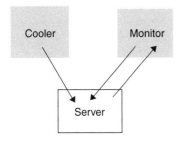

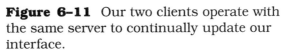

Figure 6–11 Our two clients operate with the same server to continually update our interface.

Once we are finished, we have two clients banging on the same server. One client will modify the server, the other will only do queries to the server to get information. For terminology's sake, we will call our Water Cooler applet the supplier and our Monitor applet the consumer (see Figure 6-11).

The full source code for the client is on the CD-ROM that accompanies this book, but there are two methods that we need to implement here for demonstration purposes. The Init method will initialize both clients, just as you would any normal Java applet. We also need an action method to handle button events when they arrive.

The source code we show you for Java IDL is practically pseudo CORBA code. Because we do not want to endorse any one ORB, we have decided to show you the methodology for developing CORBA applications. The featured app at the end of the chapter is implemented using Imprise's Visibroker ORB. When you attempt to execute the other examples on your own, you will need to consult the documentation for your ORB, be it NEO, Visibroker, or Orbix, to be absolutely correct in your syntax. The source code included on the CD-ROM for the cooler project is NEO code. If you think this is a problem, you are correct. The proliferation of ORBs, and the impact they could very well have over the course of the next few years, leads us to believe that someone, somewhere, needs to come up with a standard language mapping. This source code portability would ensure that everyone's CORBA implementation looked the same. After all, the IDL is the same among all of them; why can't the source code for that IDL be the same as well?

```
public void init()
{
    // do any of the UI stuff you need to do here...
}
public void actionPerformed(ActionEvent e)
{
    String arg = e.getActionCommand();
    if(arg.equals(hotWaterButton))
    {
    }
    else if(arg.equals(warmWaterButton))
    {
    }
    else if(arg.equals(coldWaterButton))
    {
    }
    return true;
}
```

Once your UI works to your satisfaction and you are able to generate events, run within a Web page, and do all of the other fun stuff that makes Java so wonderful, you are ready to move on to the next step.

Initializing the Client ORB

At this point, you need to take your client and plug it into the ORB system. The actual steps involved in doing so are pretty simple and are outlined in the next few sections. The first, and most important, step is to actually import the ORB into your files:

```
import corba.*;
```

Once the ORB is included, you can have your applet class extend the ORB:

```
public class Cooler extends CORBAApplet
{
    . . .
}
```

You then have to initialize the ORB so that your Applet is prepared to talk to the ORB itself. Because we extend the ORB to begin with, all we have to do is call the init method for the super class:

```
public void init()
{
    super.init();
}
```

Finally, your init method needs to obtain a reference to the remote object with which you would like to talk. Let's assume that we have stored the object in the Naming Service under the name "Cooler":

```
public void init()
{
    super.init();
    coolerObject = NamingService.find("Cooler");
}
```

Now that we have a reference to the object, we can communicate with the remote object just as if it were a local object. As we will see, the Java syntax looks exactly as it would were the remote object a local object.

Invoking a Remote Object. Now that we have the object and know that the server is ready to be started, we can go about the process of talking to the object itself. Up until now we have communicated only with the Naming Service in order to get the object; this will be our first invocation of the object. Note that even if the server has not been started, the ORB will allow us to talk to it. This is because the underlying CORBA mechanism makes sure the object has started and that it is ready to be invoked. Sometimes the latency between a client call and a server response is long, usually because the ORB is in the process of starting and initializing a server in order to handle the request.

```
public void actionPerformed(ActionEvent e)
{
    String arg = e.getActionCommand();
    if(arg.equals(hotWaterButton))
    {
        coolerObject.getHotWater();
    }
    else if(arg.equals(warmWaterButton))
    {
        coolerObject.getWarmWater();
    }
    else if(arg.equals(coldWaterButton))
    {
        coolerObject.getColdWater();
    }
    return true;
}
```

In this example, our invocations are pretty obviously triggered. For every button that is pressed, we will make a remote call to an object. The call will block the client until the server lets go of the invocation. If we wanted asynchronous communication rather than synchronous communication, we would need to take some steps in our IDL file to specify that a certain method should not block when invoked. For example, we could spawn a thread instead of making a direct invocation. For simplicity's sake, we have chosen not to do this. However, if your server side code is complicated and takes some time to execute, you may want to spawn threads to handle invocations for you.

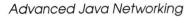

Tracking Errors. Java's exception-handling mechanisms will enable us to track and report errors when they arrive. Furthermore, the exception handlers will prevent our program from crashing in the event a server encounters a problem somewhere down the line. If this were a mission-critical application, the client side would not experience any problems should the server flake out for some reason.

In order to make the most effective use of the exception handlers, you need to declare your own exceptions in the IDL file. After doing so, your servers must throw those exceptions when necessary. This enables us to obtain a specific exception for every error rather than a generic "an error has occurred" message.

```
public void actionPerformed(ActionEvent e)
{
    String arg = e.getActionCommand();
    if(arg.equals(hotWaterButton))
    {
        try
        {
            coolerObject.getHotWater();
        }
        catch (NoMoreWaterException exc)
        {
            // error handling here. . .
        }
    }
    else if(arg.equals(warmWaterButton))
    {
        try
        {
            coolerObject.getWarmWater();
        }
        catch (NoMoreWaterException exc)
        {
            // error handling here. . .
        }
    }
    else if(arg.equals(coldWaterButton))
    {
        try
        {
            coolerObject.getColdWater();
        }
        catch (NoMoreWaterException exc)
        {
            // error handling here. . .
        }
    }
    return true;
}
```

As you can see, exception handling enables us to protect our clients from server malfunctions. It also gives us the benefit of the doubt when making invocations that could be deemed risky (i.e., invocations across multiple networks, firewalls, and so forth). It is precisely those special conditions that gives CORBA the most fits when dealing with network traffic.

Implementing the Monitor. The monitor is a client in the same way that the cooler we created previously was a client. However, the monitor client is also required to routinely obtain the levels for each kind of water so that it can display each level graphically. In order to implement this pinging effect, we need to pop a thread within which the monitor will query the server every second:

```
public class Monitor extends Applet implements Runnable
{
    Thread monitorThread = null;

    public void start()
    {
        if(monitorThread == null)
        {
            monitorThread = new Thread(this);
            monitorThread.start();
        }
    }
    public void stop()
    {
        if(monitorThread != null)
        {
            monitorThread.stop();
            monitorThread = null;
        }
    }
    public void init()
    {
        super.init();
        coolerObject = NamingService.find("Cooler");
    }
}
```

As you can see, we simply invoke and create a thread. Now we need to add the run method inside of which we will ping the server every second. While this is a very brutish approach to retrieving information at a steady rate from the server, it will have to suffice. In our section on callbacks, we will modify this client so that it obtains information from the server only when the information has changed.

```
public class Monitor extends Applet implements Runnable
{
```

```java
Thread monitorThread = null;
public void start()
{
    if(monitorThread == null)
    {
        monitorThread = new Thread(this);
        monitorThread.start();
    }
}

public void stop()
{
    if(monitorThread != null)
    {
        monitorThread.stop();
        monitorThread = null;
    }
}

public void init()
{
    super.init();
    coolerObject = NamingService.find("Cooler");
}

public void run()
{
    // prioritize the main thread
    Thread.currentThread().setPriority (
        Thread.NORM_PRIORITY - 1);

    while (kicker != null)
    {
        // get the water level
        coolerObj.getHotWaterLevel();
        coolerObj.getWarmWaterLevel();
        coolerObj.getColdWaterLevel();

        // pause the thread
        try
        {
            Thread.sleep (pause);
        }
        catch (InterruptedException e)
        {
            break;
        }
    }
}
}
```

Shutting Down Your Connection. The final step to coding your client is to release the object reference. In Java, this is not as much a concern as it is in C++, for any memory management issues are of no concern. This does not mean, however, that object references are "free" in Java. On the contrary, the ORB keeps track of each object reference out there. If multiple clients possess object references, then the server will hunt down the necessary resources, allocating and deallocating memory as it sees fit, in order to keep the server functioning smoothly. By preventing multiple unused object references from being allocated, your server can function properly and to its utmost ability.

Client Overview

In this section, we have constructed a simple client. More complex clients will follow the same model: Create the user interface first, then fill in the CORBA details. As your clients begin to get more and more complicated, your user interface and CORBA modules will begin to intersect. To make debugging and performance tuning much easier, it is highly recommended that you consider splitting your code as we did in the featured application that we described in Chapter 1 and that we will implement using IDL in a few sections.

Now that you're familiar with creating and implementing CORBA clients, let's turn the tables and see what's involved with setting up CORBA servers. In order for us to split our processing appropriately between the client and the server, the server should be the focus of all our attention. The client should do nothing more than funnel information back and forth between the user and server. You should limit the amount of processing you do in your client. Save all the hard work for your server.

CORBA Servers

One of the beauties of CORBA servers is that they are started up automatically by the Object Request Broker. When we used sockets and RMI, we had to start our servers manually, but here we simply create our server, register it with the ORB, and forget about it. Every time a client invokes the server, the server will start up (if it isn't running already), initialize itself, and ready itself for invocations. To the client, all of this happens seamlessly and with no additional work needed.

Defining an Interface and Generating Code

In the previous section, we defined our interface as follows:

```
interface Cooler
{
    int getHotWaterLevel();
    int getWarmWaterLevel();
    int getColdWaterLevel();
```

```
    exception NoMoreWaterException { };
    int getHotWater() throws NoMoreWaterException;
    int getWarmWater() throws NoMoreWaterException;
    int getColdWater() throws NoMoreWaterException;
};
```

Now we need to implement the interface. The first thing we need to do is to generate all our stub code. The stub code provides the underlying CORBA functionality to our server so that we can concentrate on developing the server logic itself. Because we generate code, we don't need to know the nuances of how CORBA works.

Java IDL includes an idltojava compiler that translates IDL code into Java code. The IDL file that we defined earlier gets six generated analogs that handle the CORBA plumbing for us. First, the Holder class is generated. As we discussed previously, a Holder allows us to pass a CORBA object as inout and out parameters to CORBA methods. We also get an Operations class that defines a simple Java interface from which the other files can inherit.

The meat of the generated server code lies in the Servant, Skeleton, and Stub code. The client uses a Skeleton to obtain a basic framework for the object to which it desires to communicate. The Skeleton is sort of like a roadmap. Using it, you can get a good idea of where you are going, but you will get no information as to the scenery along the way. A Skeleton enables the client to know what is possible, but not how that is accomplished.

Both the Skeleton and the Servant use the Stub code to handle the interaction of the Server code with the ORB itself (see Figure 6-12). While the Stub does all the work, the Skeleton and Servant are what we actually see.

As you can see from the diagram in Figure 6-12, the Stub is the foundation of the entire CORBA server. The other classes use the Stub to obtain information about how they will implement the IDL. We will see in a moment how Java RMI classes are generated after we create the server file. Java IDL works very differently. Whereas RMI works on generated classes, IDL generates code based on the IDL file. As we have noted before, interfaces defined using the IDL are inherently language independent. We could just as easily have created a C++ server as a Java server.

When we use the idltojava compiler on our *Cooler.idl* file, we get the following six classes:

1. CoolerRef
2. CoolerHolder
3. CoolerOperations
4. CoolerStub

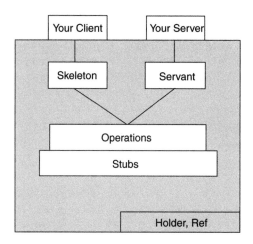

Figure 6–12 The generated components for a Java IDL server.

5. CoolerServant

6. CoolerSkeleton

As we discussed previously, each of these classes plays an integral role in how our server behaves under the CORBA umbrella. It is highly recommended that you not modify these generated files.

Creating the Server Implementation. Once we generate code, we need to create a class that will contain the routines we want to provide when a method is invoked. Unlike RMI, we create our server after we generate the underlying code functionality for it. The skeletons, stubs, and servants are, as their names imply, placeholders. We must supply the logic for our methods; it just doesn't appear out of mid-air. By convention, our server class's name contains the name of the IDL object, followed by the "Impl" descriptor. Keep in mind that we don't have to name our class CoolerImpl, but we do because that is the general CORBA convention.

The first step in creating our server is to include all the generated code:

```
import Cooler.*;
```

Once we have done that, we create a CoolerImpl class that implements the CoolerServant we generated earlier. In so doing, our Cooler server obtains the CORBA plumbing provided by the generated code.

```
import Cooler.*;

public class CoolerImpl implements CoolerServant
{
}
```

Now, we need to fill in the names of the functions we must implement in order to fulfill our contract with the IDL definition and create a constructor:

```
import Cooler.*;
public class CoolerImpl implements CoolerServant
{
    CoolerImpl()
    {
        super();
    }
    public int getHotWaterLevel()
    {
    }
    public int getWarmWaterLevel()
    {
    }
    public int getColdWaterLevel()
    {
    }
    public int getHotWater() throws NoMoreWaterException
    {
    }
    public int getWarmWater() throws NoMoreWaterException
    {
    }
    public int getColdWater()throws NoMoreWaterException
    {
    }
}
```

Finally, we need to fill in each of the functions so that they do what they are intended to do.

```
import Cooler.*;
public class CoolerImpl implements CoolerServant
{
    private int hotWaterLevel;
    private int warmWaterLevel;
    private int coldWaterLevel;

    CoolerImpl()
    {
        super();

        hotWaterLevel = 0;
        warmWaterLevel = 0;
        coldWaterLevel = 0;
    }
```

```java
public int getHotWaterLevel()
{
    return hotWaterLevel;
}
public int getWarmWaterLevel()
{
    return warmWaterLevel;
}
public int getColdWaterLevel()
{
    return coldWaterLevel;
}
public int getHotWater() throws NoMoreWaterException
{
    if(hotWaterLevel >= 10)
        hotWaterLevel -= 10;
    else
        throw new NoMoreWaterException;
}
public int getWarmWater() throws NoMoreWaterException
{
    if(warmWaterLevel >= 5)
        warmWaterLevel -= 5;
    else
        throw new NoMoreWaterException;
}
public int getColdWater()throws NoMoreWaterException
{
    if(coldWaterLevel >= 3)
        coldWaterLevel -= 3;
    else
        throw new NoMoreWaterException;
}
}
```

Die-hard CORBA veterans will attest to the charming simplicity with which this is done in Java. C++ servers contain the same steps, but can be drastically more complicated than they need to be. We have now completed the creation of our server implementation.

Creating the Server Executable. The code we created in the previous section is known as servant code. A servant is the physical process in which your server executes, and the server implementation is contained therein. A server is the set of interfaces and methods published in the IDL. The interface definition is the contract that the server fulfills and the servant executes.

That said, we must now create the server for our Cooler. The server must do three things:

1. Start itself up in a physical process.

2. Create a servant instance to reside in the process.

3. Bind itself to a name in the Naming Service.

All this is analogous to an ordinary table lamp. There are several table lamps in your home, all of which implement the same interface—namely "turn on" and "turn off." Just because they all implement the same interface doesn't mean that they all must be the same lamp. Indeed, you need many lamps; otherwise, you would trip on your shoes as you went to bed. So, once we create several different lamps, we need to put them in their designated locations and plug them into the socket. Likewise, once we create a servant, we need to put it inside a server and plug it into the ORB.

To do so, first we must create the class so that the server can begin executing in its own process space. After we create a class, we need to supply it with a main routine and link up with the ORB. If we do not link up with the ORB here, subsequent invocations that create the stubs, skeletons, and servants will be unable to work properly.

```
import Cooler.*;

public class CoolerServer
{
    // private variables
    private CORBA corba;

    public static void main(
        String argv[]
    )
    {
        // link up with the ORB
        corba = new CORBA();
    }
}
```

Next, we need to create an instance of the CoolerImpl servant class that we created in the previous section. We also need to use the CoolerRef container class to support our servant instance. Remember that clients don't want servants to talk to, they want servers. With servers, they get a sketch of the contract provided for in the IDL. With servants, they get all the legal mumbo jumbo in the contract itself. Clients don't need to know that stuff.

```
import Cooler.*;

public class CoolerServer
```

```
{
    // private variables
    private CORBA corba;
    private CoolerRef coolerRef;

    public static void main(
        String argv[]
    )
    {
        // link up with the ORB
        corba = new CORBA();

        // create the servant class
        CoolerImpl coolerImpl = new CoolerImpl();

        // create the container class
        coolerRef = CoolerSkeleton.createRef(
            corba.getORB(), coolerImpl);
    }
}
```

Finally, the server must take the CoolerRef instance and bind it to a unique name in the Naming Service.

```
import Cooler.*;

public class CoolerServer
{
    // private variables
    private CORBA corba;
    private CoolerRef coolerRef;

    public static void main(
        String argv[]
    )
    {
        // link up with the ORB
        corba = new CORBA();

        // create the servant class
        CoolerImpl coolerImpl = new CoolerImpl();

        // create the container class
        coolerRef = CoolerSkeleton.createRef(
            corba.getORB(), coolerImpl);

        // bind this server to the Naming Service
        corba.rebind("Cooler", coolerRef);
    }
}
```

Note how the name we have bound to is the same name that we referred to in the previous section on clients. After compiling all our code, we have a working server that the clients in the previous and next chapters can talk to.

Registering with the ORB. Finally, the CORBA server we have created must be placed inside the Interface Repository, the location of all objects known to the ORB. When the ORB receives an invocation from a client, it looks in the Interface Repository for the proper object and, if it is found, starts the object up and readies it for invocation. Consult your CORBA vendor's documentation on how to register an ORB with the Interface Repository. For example, in NEO, registering an ORB is as simple as typing:

```
%prompt%  make register
```

Server Overview

As we did for our client, we created a simple CORBA server that accepts invocations and passes back results. This server is, in essence, no different from the most complex CORBA servers. The steps involved in creating servers remain the same:

1. Define your object using the IDL.
2. Generate stubs and skeletons from the IDL.
3. Fill in the code.
4. Create the server container object.
5. Register the object.

In so doing, any object server you create will run efficiently, will be very reliable, and will have the flexibility to be changed often.

Sometimes, you do not want your Java IDL application to be a full-fledged server. For example, servers cannot be embedded within an applet and, therefore, cannot exist on a Web page. If you still require dynamic updates to your server, the only way to get them is to use a callback, which we'll discuss in the next section.

CORBA Callbacks

Let's say you've been pestering your Aunt Fran about the details for her latest wedding. You call her every day, and she is getting sick of it. Finally, she tells you that she will call you "only when something happens."

In essence, the two of you are setting up callbacks between one another. When Aunt Fran gets an event that you should be aware of, you will get a call. Otherwise, her phone will be silent, and she will not be bothered.

Java Callbacks

Java IDL enables your client object to send itself to a server, setting up a reference bridge to the client object. Whenever the server must tell the client something, it will make calls on the client objects it stores. In this manner, a Java IDL server can keep track of all the clients that are speaking with it and funnel information back and forth between the objects.

For example, if every member of the wedding party, not just you, were pestering Aunt Fran, she could tell them all that she will call when something happens. Aunt Fran will then be annoyed only when an event occurs. She would probably make a list of all the people she needs to call and go down the list when the time comes.

Likewise, a Java IDL server keeps track of all its clients and prevents an overload of the system. The alternative to callbacks is for each client to routinely ping the server every few seconds or so to get information. Although this methodology may work for one or two clients, when several clients start harassing the same server, the server and the network begin to get unnecessarily burdened. With callbacks, the network traffic is high only when an event occurs, and never at any other time. In geek terms, this is referred to as scalability. Callbacks are scalable because they work just as efficiently for several thousand objects as they do for only a few.

Creating a Callback

In order to use callbacks, you must create and define a callback object within your IDL file. The client that needs to set up a callback must first contact the server. In order for it to be allowed to call the server and set up a callback, the client must have access to a method defined for that purpose. Because the server is the one that will register client objects and call them back, the server must have that method as part of its suite of possible invocations.

```
interface CoolerCallback
{
    void waterLevelChanged (
      in long hotLevel,
          in long warmLevel,
          in long coldLevel);
}
interface Cooler
{
    int getHotWaterLevel();
    int getWarmWaterLevel();
    int getColdWaterLevel();

    int getHotWater();
    int getWarmWater();
    int getColdWater();

    // public method for the callback
    long registerCallback (in CoolerCallback coolerCB);
    void unregisterCallback (in long callbackID);
};
```

Notice how the registerCallback function contains a CoolerCallback object as a parameter. Your Java client will implement the CoolerCallback object. When the

Java client sends itself as the parameter for the registerCallback invocation, it is essentially telling the server, "I'm the guy that you need to call when you get a change!" The register function also returns an integer specifying the ID of the object. If the object ever wants to unsubscribe to callbacks, it can give the server its ID number and the server will remove it from its callback list.

Furthermore, the client should implement callback methods just as we did in the server section. In essence, the callback will implement server methods without server infrastructure. The end result is that your client can be invoked by a server as if it were a server, but the client need not be burdened by the overhead of being a server (see Figure 6-13).

Registering a Callback

In order for the server to invoke a callback on a client, the client must first register itself with the server as a callback object. This is done in the init function. We need to remove the code having to do with threads from our non-callback client, and instead place the following invocation in our init method. We may also remove the Run method because we need not bother with actually making invocations on the server. In addition, our client should implement the callback object:

```
public class Monitor extends CORBAApplet implements CoolerCallback
{
    public void init()
    {
        super.init();

        coolerObject = NamingService.find("Cooler");

        int callbackID = coolerObject.registerCallback(this);
    }
}
```

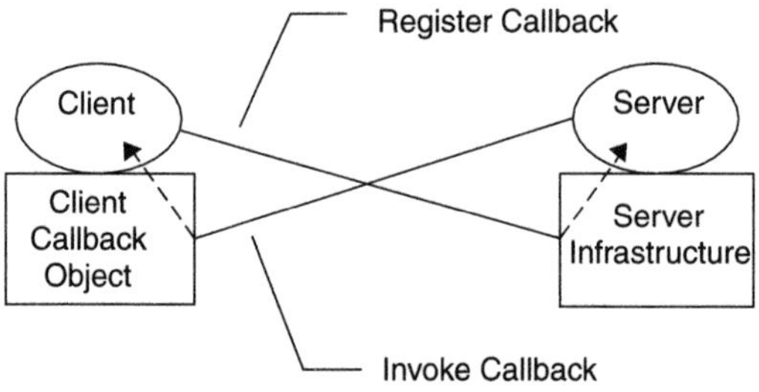

Register Callback

Client

Client
Callback
Object

Server

Server
Infrastructure

Invoke Callback

Figure 6–13 Clients must first register themselves with the server before the server will be able to call them back.

Notice how we pass the Register method a copy of our own object, as we discussed earlier. The Monitor client is now ready to be invoked by the server. Later on we will implement the actual callback function that enables us to process the data we receive.

The Java IDL server should then keep track of the client object in some kind of storage mechanism. None of this is automatic; the programmer must code it all. In the following example, we store the client object in a Vector because efficient searching is not required. We only need to call them all back sequentially. The two functions in the following code should be added to your server definition from the previous section:

```java
import Cooler.*;

public class CoolerImpl implements CoolerServant
{
    private int hotWaterLevel;
    private int warmWaterLevel;
    private int coldWaterLevel;

    // our callbacks
    private Vector callbacks;

    CoolerImpl()
    {
        super();

        hotWaterLevel = 0;
        warmWaterLevel = 0;
        coldWaterLevel = 0;

        callbacks = new Vector();
    }
    public int getHotWaterLevel()
    {
        return hotWaterLevel;
    }
    public int getWarmWaterLevel()
    {
        return warmWaterLevel;
    }
    public int getColdWaterLevel()
    {
        return coldWaterLevel;
    }
    public int getHotWater() throws NoMoreWaterException
    {
        if(hotWaterLevel >= 10)
            hotWaterLevel -= 10;
        else
```

```
            throw new NoMoreWaterException;
    }
    public int getWarmWater() throws NoMoreWaterException
    {
        if(warmWaterLevel >= 5)
            warmWaterLevel -= 5;
        else
            throw new NoMoreWaterException;
    }
    public int getColdWater()throws NoMoreWaterException
    {
        if(coldWaterLevel >= 3)
            coldWaterLevel -= 3;
        else
            throw new NoMoreWaterException;
    }
    public int registerCallback(
        CoolerCallback coolerCallback
    )
    {
        callbacks.addItem(coolerCallback);
    }
    public void unregisterCallback(
        int callbackID
    )
    {
        callbacks.removeItemAt(callbackID);
    }
}
```

Once the callback is registered, the server can continue with its execution until an event is triggered to which it must respond. When Aunt Fran suddenly discovers that her husband turns out to be the Chia Pet she dated five months before, she can go down her list of wedding people and call each of them back. In the same manner, we will be able to look at our table of callback objects and respond.

Receiving and Handling a Callback

In order to receive a callback, you need to set up a callback function. This is analogous to giving Aunt Fran your phone number. When she needs to tell you something, she will have a specific place to call you. Likewise, your callback recipients need to let the server know where to call.

When the server gets an event, it invokes a remote procedure call on the callback function, passing any parameters as necessary. Your callback function accepts and processes the data given to it by the server. Figure 6-14 offers an illustration of this process.

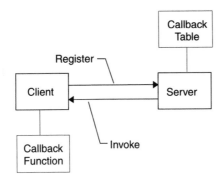
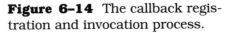

Figure 6–14 The callback registration and invocation process.

TIP: Remember that callbacks are an option to servers. Your callback recipient is acting like a server, but it is not quite a server. It cannot be instantiated on its own by a remote object. Each individual function must be set up with the callback server, and the flexibility you had with full-fledged servers is completely lost. On the other hand, your applet can receive events from a CORBA server without much overhead, it can be used within a browser, and it is easier to implement than a server.

Because our callbacks actually implement the CallbackObject interface, they automatically inherit the waterLevelChanged method. Our client should process all its data in the waterLevelChanged function:

```
public class Monitor extends CORBAApplet implements CoolerCallback
{
    public void init()
    {
        super.init();
        coolerObject = NamingService.find("Cooler");
        int callbackID = coolerObject.registerCallback(this);
    }
    public synchronized void waterLevelChanged (
            int hotLevel,
            int warmLevel,
            int coldLevel
    )
    {
        System.out.println ("received a callback!");
        . . . handle the UI stuff you need to . . .
    }
}
```

Your callback function will merely receive the water levels for all three kinds of water. You can then effect the GUI however you please. Notice how we never actually invoke a method on the server after we register. Instead, we sit back, drink our martinis (shaken, not stirred), and wait for the server to call us. As they say in Hollywood, "Hey babe, don't call me, I'll call you."

To that effect, the server will contain within it the code necessary to invoke the callback itself. Here, we have chosen to invoke on all the callbacks whenever the water level is changed in any way:

```
public int getHotWater() throws NoMoreWaterException
{
    if(hotWaterLevel >= 10)
    {
        hotWaterLevel -= 10;

        for(int x = 0; x < callbacks.size(); x++)
        {
            // get the callback object
            CoolerCallback cb =
                (CoolerCallback) callbacks.itemAt(x);

            // invoke on the callback object
            cb.waterLevelChanged(
                    hotWaterLevel,
                    warmWaterLevel,
                    coldWaterLevel);
        }
    }
    else
        throw new NoMoreWaterException;
}
```

A similar method will be employed for the getWarmWater and getColdWater functions.

Callbacks in Short. In order to process invocations from multiple clients efficiently, a server should ideally set up a mechanism with which it can control how invocations are handled. Because the server does the bulk of the work, it should get to call the shots. With callbacks, we can do what corporate management has never figured out. The people who do all the work get to make all the decisions. What a novel idea!

A Java IDL Version of the Featured App

Now that we know how to create full IDL and CORBA servers along with the clients that accompany them, let's put our talents to use. The Internet calendar manager we discussed in previous chapters is divided into two parts: the Network client module and the Calendar server with which the module will communicate. First, we will create the client and then we will create the server. But before that we need the interface definition of the server itself.

Unlike the version of this application in the first edition of this book the Calendar application has been modified to use a Microsoft Access Database to store appointment data. JDBC is used on the server to interact with the database. The loadDB method of the server is what initializes the Database.

The example that follows was made using JDK 1.3, JDBC 2.0, and the Imprise Visibroker ORB.

Server Interface

The following IDL outlines the method signatures of the remote calendar server object. The server may reside anywhere and, as we discussed earlier, can be retrieved through the Naming Service. For demonstration purposes, we'll store our calendar server in the Naming Service under the name "CalendarObject." Notice how we have enclosed our object within a module. The module will act as a holder for all of our calendar-related objects. For example, in order to access the AppointmentType object from within Java, you would have to specify Calendar-IDL.AppointmentType. As we discussed in our earlier section on language mappings, modules get translated into Java packages.

```
module CalendarIDL
{
    struct AppointmentType
    {
        string reason;
        string time;
    };

    interface Calendar
    {
        void scheduleAppointment(
        in string reason,
        in string time);

        void loadDB();

        typedef sequence <AppointmentType> AppointmentList;
        AppointmentList getAppointments();
    };
};
```

NetworkModule

As you will recall, the NetworkModule has a simple set of methods with which we can change the server. It is instantiated by the client and takes the high-level data structures given to it by the rest of the client and sends it off to the server. Our server will then process information and maintain state. We have incorporated several methods that will enable us to access the information on the server. Here is the original code for the NetworkModule. Note the addition of the import statement to include all the calendar's IDL server files. In so doing, we do not have to specify the entire package name for the calendar's files.

```java
import CalendarIDL.*;

public class NetworkModule
{
    public void scheduleAppointment(
        String reason,
        int time);

    public Vector getAppointments();
    public void initNetwork();
    public void shutdownNetwork();
    public void startCorba(org.omg.CORBA.ORB orb);
}
```

We will now implement the constructor for this object. The constructor initializes the connection to the CORBA server and sets up the remote IDL object for use by the other routines. We will keep track of the remote object with the calendarObject variable:

```java
public class NetworkModule
{
    // make a calendar object
    Calendar  calendar;

    NetworkModule()
    {
        org.omg.CORBA.ORB orb = org.omg.CORBA.ORB.init(args,null);
        calendar = CalendarHelper.bind(orb, "CalendarObject");
        calendar.loadDB();
    }

    public void scheduleAppointment(
        String reason,
        int time)
    {
    }

    public Vector getAppointments()
    {
    }
}
```

We now need to fill in the functionality of the `NetworkModule`. Because we've already initialized the remote object, we can feel free to use it and communicate with the server. In the getAppointments method, we will need to translate the array of AppointmentType objects to a Java Vector. We do this so that the rest of the application will not need to be aware of the implementation details of the server itself.

```
public class NetworkModule
{
    CORBAServer calendarObject;

    NetworkModule()
    {
      String[] args ;
      org.omg.CORBA.ORB orb = org.omg.CORBA.ORB.init(args,null);
      calendar = CalendarHelper.bind(orb, "CalendarObject");
       calendar.loadDB();
    }
    public void scheduleAppointment(
                String appointmentReason,
                String appointmentTime )
    {
      calendar.scheduleAppointment
                (appointmentReason, appointmentTime);
    }
    public Vector getAppointments()
    {
        // the variable to store all of our appointments in
        Vector appointmentVector = new Vector();
        CalendarIDL.AppointmentType[] appointment;
        if (calendar != null)
        {
            appointment = calendar.getAppointments();
            if (appointment.length != 0)
              for (int i=0; i < appointment.length; i++)
                appointmentVector.addElement(appointment[i]);
        }
        // return the Vector
        return appointmentVector;
    }
}
```

Note how we need not implement the initNetwork and shutdownNetwork methods. In Java IDL, all the underlying network functionality is handled for us automatically. CORBA objects are location transparent, meaning that we don't care where or how they are implemented. Because we use the Naming Service to get to the objects, we don't have to worry about initializing connections in our client.

The Object Request Broker handles all the networking mess for us with easy-to-use programmer APIs.

Calendar Server

As we have seen in our previous section on CORBA servers, implementing a server can be a tricky process. Now, we need to apply the language mapping and develop code for what the server interface is going to look like in Java. We've already shown you what the IDL for the server looks like, so here is the Java result for it. Note that we are including the Calendar objects by using the module name.

```java
import corba.*;
import java.util.*;
import CalendarIDL.*;

public class CalendarImpl implements CalendarServant
{
    public void scheduleAppointment(
        String reason,
        int time)
    {
    }

    public void loadDB()
    {
    }

    public AppointmentType[] getAppointments()
    {
    }
}
```

Now, we need to fill in the scheduleAppointment and getAppointments method. In scheduleAppointment, we will store our appointments transiently in a Vector. The Vector needs to be initialized in the constructor for our implementation object.

```java
import corba.*;
import java.util.*;
import CalendarIDL.*;

public class CalendarImpl implements CalendarServant
{
    public void scheduleAppointment(String reason,  int time)
    {
      try
      {
        Statement insertStatement =
            dbConnection.createStatement();

        String insert = "INSERT INTO SCHEDULE " +
            "VALUES('" + time + "','" + reason + "')";
```

```
            System.out.println(insert);
            insertStatement.executeUpdate(insert);
            dbConnection.commit();
        }
        catch(Exception e)
        {
            System.out.println("NetworkModule 3  Error: " +
                e.toString());
        }
    }
    public void loadDB()
    {
    }

    public AppointmentType[] getAppointments()
    {
    }
}
```

The loadDB method does all the database initialization:

```
import corba.*;

import java.util.*;
import CalendarIDL.*;

public class CalendarImpl implements CalendarServant
{
    public void scheduleAppointment(String reason, int time)
    {
      try
      {
          Statement insertStatement =
              dbConnection.createStatement();

          String insert = "INSERT INTO SCHEDULE " +
              "VALUES('" + time + "','" + reason + "')";
          System.out.println(insert);
          insertStatement.executeUpdate(insert);
          dbConnection.commit();
      }
      catch(Exception e)
      {
          System.out.println("NetworkModule 3  Error: " +
              e.toString());
      }
    }
    public void loadDB()
    {
      try
      {
```

```
        // load the database driver
        Class.forName("sun.jdbc.odbc.JdbcOdbcDriver");
        // connect to the database
        dbConnection =
                DriverManager.getConnection(dbPath,"","");
    }
    catch (ClassNotFoundException e)
    {
        System.out.println("NetworkModule 1 Error: " +
                e.toString());
    }
    catch (SQLException se)
    {
        System.out.println("NetworkModule 2 SQL Error: " +
                se.toString());
    }
}

public AppointmentType[] getAppointments()
{
}
}
```

Our getAppointments method will return an array of AppointmentType variables. Unlike in our sockets implementation in Chapter 3, and unlike our subsequent implementations for RMI and JDBC in chapters 4 and 5, here we do not
need to define our own AppointmentType. Because we declare it in the IDL, the
code for it automatically gets generated.

```
import corba.*;
import java.util.*;
import CalendarIDL.*;
public class CalendarImpl implements CalendarServant
{
    public void scheduleAppointment(String reason, int time)
    {
      try
      {
        Statement insertStatement =
            dbConnection.createStatement();
        String insert = "INSERT INTO SCHEDULE " +
            "VALUES('" + time + "','" + reason + "')";
        System.out.println(insert);
        insertStatement.executeUpdate(insert);
        dbConnection.commit();
      }
      catch(Exception e)
      {
```

```java
       System.out.println("NetworkModule 3  Error: " +
             e.toString());
    }
}
public void loadDB()
{
   try
   {
      // load the database driver
      Class.forName("sun.jdbc.odbc.JdbcOdbcDriver");
      // connect to the database
      dbConnection =
             DriverManager.getConnection(dbPath,"","");
   }
   catch (ClassNotFoundException e)
   {
      System.out.println("NetworkModule 1 Error: " +
             e.toString());
   }
   catch (SQLException se)
   {
      System.out.println("NetworkModule 2 SQL Error: " +
             se.toString());
   }
}
public AppointmentType[] getAppointments()
{
   Vector v = new Vector();
   int numberOfRows;
   AppointmentType[] appointment = null;

   try
   {
     // creating a scrollable Result Set
         Statement statement = dbConnection.createStatement(
            ResultSet.TYPE_SCROLL_INSENSITIVE,
            ResultSet.CONCUR_READ_ONLY);
         String s = "SELECT TIME, REASON FROM SCHEDULE" +
                     " ORDER BY TIME";
         ResultSet result = statement.executeQuery(s);

         // determine the number of rows in the Result Set
         result.last();
         numberOfRows = result.getRow();
         result.beforeFirst();
         numberOfRows =(numberOfRows > 0) ? numberOfRows: 1;
         appointment = new AppointmentType[numberOfRows];

         // corba hates null values, check very carefully for
```

```
                // any uninitialized values
                int i=0;
                while(result.next())
                {
                    if (numberOfRows > i)
                    {
                        appointment[i] = new AppointmentType();
                        String tmpOne = "", tmpTwo = "";
                        appointment[i].time = "";
                        appointment[i].reason = "";
                        if ((tmpOne = result.getString("TIME"))
                                != null )
                        appointment[i].time = tmpOne;
                        if ((tmpTwo = result.getString("REASON"))
                                != null)
                        appointment[i].reason = tmpTwo;
                        i++;
                    }
                }

                // make sure every single index of the array have
                // its time and reason initialized
                while (numberOfRows > i+1)
                {
                    appointment[i] = new AppointmentType();
                    appointment[i].time = "";
                    appointment[i].reason = "";
                    i++;
                }
            }
            catch(SQLException exc)
            {
                System.out.println("NetworkModule Error: " +
                        exc.toString());
            }

            // final check against null variables
            if (appointment != null)
                return appointment;
            else
            {
                appointment = new AppointmentType[1];
                appointment[0].time = "";
                appointment[0].reason = "";
                return appointment;
            }
        }
    }
```

We must now create a server process for the servant to exist inside. We do this just as we created the server for the Cooler example earlier in this section. Inside the application main, we will initialize CORBA and rebind to a unique name in the Naming Service, in this case "CalendarObject."

```
public class CalendarServer {
  public static void main(String[] args) {
    // Initialize the ORB.
    org.omg.CORBA.ORB orb = org.omg.CORBA.ORB.init(args, null);
    // Initialize the BOA.
    org.omg.CORBA.BOA boa =
            ((com.visigenic.vbroker.orb.ORB)orb).BOA_init();
    // Create the calendar object.
    CalendarIDL.Calendar calendar = new
        CalendarImpl("CalendarObject", "jdbc:odbc:Calendar");
    // Export the newly created object.
    boa.obj_is_ready(calendar);
    System.out.println("Calendar server is ready.");
    // Wait for incoming requests
    boa.impl_is_ready();
  }
}
```

We will then need to register the server. You will once again need to consult the documentation for the ORB vendor you have chosen to find out how to do this. Once registered, you can run your client and never again be late for an important meeting.

"Different Vendors, Different Problems"

Because one of the biggest drawbacks to CORBA is that there are several disparate vendors for JAVA IDL, the OMG created a complex protocol with which objects can communicate.

The Internet Inter-ORB Protocol, or IIOP (pronounced eye-op), is the "language" used by objects to exchange information. It is based on TCP/IP, as opposed to UDP, and forms a common base for all CORBA clients and servers to communicate.

You, the application programmer, will never see IIOP, and you will never know that IIOP is going under the covers. However, the Object Request Broker uses IIOP to funnel information to other ORBs. In so doing, a Visigenic ORB and an Iona ORB can talk the same language, so to speak, when communicating with one another.

So, IIOP addresses one major issue, the interoperability of objects written for different ORBs, with different CORBA implementations. However, one more major problem still exists.

CORBA applets often have serious download performance problems. Because an ORB must exist on every platform with a CORBA client or server, CORBA applets must include, as part of their implementation classes, the entire ORB. In so doing, a CORBA applet must download 400 or so Java classes that constitute the ORB. As we discussed in our Chapter 1 section on "Performance," 400 classes is a major data transfer as far as Java applets are concerned.

To solve this problem, the Netscape browser includes, as part of LiveConnect and as part of the Netscape *classes.zip* file, the entire Imprise Visibroker ORB. This will allow the browser to refrain from downloading the entire ORB in a CORBA applet, creating a great performance boost for CORBA applets.

However, what if the CORBA applet was written in a non-Visibroker ORB? Well, at that point, Netscape has no choice but to download the entire ORB as it would have done without the presence of Visibroker, negating any performance boost.

Even though IIOP addresses interoperability on a protocol and communication level, no CORBA vendor has yet to agree on interoperability on an object source level. As of this book's publication, many of the vendors were still negotiating on the exact contents of that so-called "Java IDL" that would then be incorporated as part of the Java Developer's Kit.

Summary

CORBA is quickly becoming an industry standard. With industry giants Sun/Netscape Alliance firmly behind the technology, it may soon make an appearance in our regular programming diet. Even though Java begins to negate some of CORBA's difficulty, CORBA is still a long way from being standard fare on everyone's desktop because of staunch competition from its Java-only brother, Java RMI.

Chapter **7**

Web Servers, Server-Side Java, and More

▼ INSIDE AN HTTP SERVER

▼ COMMON GATEWAY INTERFACE AND CGI SCRIPTS

▼ SERVLETS

▼ DYNAMIC DOCUMENTS

▼ A SERVLET VERSION OF THE FEATURED APP

▼ JAVA SERVER PAGES

▼ MULTIPURPOSE SERVERS

What if your normal Web server was capable of providing dynamic network content? If it could go out and connect to other distributed objects, using solutions from earlier in this book, it would be able to funnel information to a client without the client even once knowing of the machinery behind the scenes. So far we have discussed alternatives that have brought networked computing to the client side while creating specific client applications to accept that information. With the Java Web Server, a servlet, in essence a server-side applet, can funnel information back to a Web browser as a standard HTML file. The browser need not know anything about object design, internal machinery, or even what a servlet is.

In this chapter, we will explain the basic functionality of an HTTP server, followed by a brief tutorial on servlets and how to modify servlets to be an object server, like CORBA or RMI, at the same time. The Web servers and the servlet architecture is an exciting use of the Java language that we have come to know and love. The examples in this chapter are designed to bring that excitement and fun back to you.

Inside an HTTP Server

As we will see in a moment, Java Web Server is nothing more than an enhanced Web server product. The fact that it is written in Java does not distinguish it from

Microsoft's own BackOffice Web server or Netscape's Commerce Server. Java Web Server provides dynamic content without having to employ the cumbersome tools that we have seen thus far.

But, what is an HTTP server anyway? What does it do, and what purpose does it serve?

Web Server Architecture

At its most bare bones and most basic level, an HTTP server simply listens for client request messages on the "well-known" HTTP port (80) and returns results. The interaction between the client (browser or application) and the HTTP (Web) server is governed by the Hypertext Transfer Protocol (RFC 1945 HTTP/1.0, RFC 2616 HTTP/1.1). It does so by clinging to the predesignated HTTP port and awaiting requests. HTTP requests are typically of the form "GET filename." When presented with such a request, the HTTP server will search its document tree for the requested document and return it to the requesting client. The general public's perspective of what is going on is "they're on the Web" and haven't the faintest idea that they are participating in client/server computing.

The portion of the Web server that listens for file requests is called an HTTP daemon. A daemon, as we discussed in a Chapter 1 section on threads, is a special process whose entire role is to hang around with no distinct startup time and no distinct shutdown time. It has a specific role that it plays, in this case to fetch files and return them across a network, but does so without any special hoopla. More often than not, a Web server will handle multiple requests simultaneously (see Figure 7-1). These requests can be from the same client (browser) as in the case of the delivery of an HTML file and the graphics that are embedded in it or from multiple clients.

Once the daemon gets a request, it will go and get the file and return it to the requester. As we discussed in our chapter on sockets, this is a pipe, or two-way connection between the client and the server.

The HTTP Protocol

So far we've been using the HTTP acronym pretty freely without really understanding what it is or how it works. HTTP is a relatively straightforward client/server protocol made up of client requests and server responses. It is also "stateless" meaning that from one request and reply to the next there is no preservation of state (as in program state between the client and server).

Remember that the primary goal of an HTTP client request is to retrieve all the resources (text, formatting and layout instructions, and graphics) needed to present a Web page to the client user. Each client request requests one and only

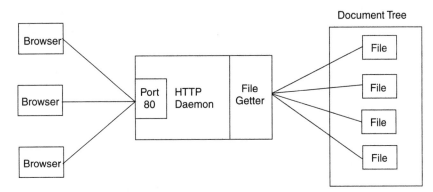

Figure 7–1 Web servers handle requests for multiple files.

one thing from the server; this means that getting everything needed by the lay-out and presentation engine in your Web browser may take many requests.

The basic HTTP request is made up of two parts: a request header and the actual data request. The request header includes information about your browser and operating environment. The actual data request is made up of a command (GET, POST, or STAT) and a Uniform Resource Locator (URL, RFC 1738, RFC 1808). HTTP URLs are a little more complicated than the simple URLs that we've seen previously in this book. An HTTP URL consists of the protocol (http, ftp, mailto, ldap), the host name, the domain name, the port the Web server is listening on (the well-known port for HTTP is port 80), the path to the resource being requested, and any parametric information that the resource might need.

Upon accepting a client connection, the Web server receives the request header and stores the client environmental information; it then receives the actual request. The server then shuts down the connection on port 80, spawns a thread, and opens another connection back to the client on a non-well-known port (>1024) to return the data on. This is done to minimize the time that port 80 is tied up and to maxi-mize its availability to receive other client requests. The same thing happens in every instance of the thread; the server searches its document tree for the requested resource (typically a file) specified in the URL. In responding to the "GET," the Web server builds a response header (server environmental information and status of the overall transaction) and sends it back to the client immediately followed by either the resource from the document tree or an error indication.

Using a Web Server

Today, we use a Web browser to get static document content. The server gets a request from the browser, finds the file it is looking for, and returns it to the calling browser. This is the way the Web works today.

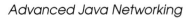

More than likely, the Web will shift to more dynamic data. Data (essentially HTML files) today is created beforehand, placed on a server, and downloaded by clients. Eventually, the Web will move to a point where the information is never created beforehand, but generated on the fly. It will facilitate small, efficient programs that create dynamic content for you and help to prevent the timely distribution of data. How many times have you gone to a Web page and found the link unattached or the file outdated? With dynamic data, you can assure that the file is generated today rather than five or six months ago.

As you can see in Figure 7-2, the shift to executable rather than static content on the Web is actually pretty easy to do. The next few sections will outline the Java answer to this particular Web server question.

Advanced Web Server Features

The Web servers of today also incorporate several advanced features such as security, performance enhancements, and administration. Security is discussed in detail in Chapter 13, "Java and Security," and, indeed, many of the Java security concerns that have cropped up over the last few years stem from concerns over the Web server itself. Will secure electronic transactions actually work over the Web? These are issues that will be dealt with by the Web server community far before they are incorporated into Java itself.

Performance enhancements are created due largely to smarter multithreaded environments, faster hardware, and more capable network connections. Often, a Web server is performance tuned by spawning a thread for every HTTP request.

Finally, network administration is an issue in and of itself, but Web network administration embodies more than that of its traditional father. Network administration deals largely with local area networks. With Web servers, the network administration issues are expanded on a wider scale, over Wide Area Networks. What happens when machines fail, or when HTTP servers get overloaded? As advances in hardware failover technology and Java Network Management are

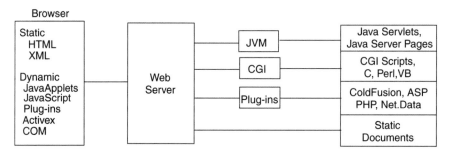

Figure 7-2 The World Wide Web moves to executable content.

unveiled, the Web administration will continue to get easier, but at the same time more complex.

HTTP Server Overview

The HTTP server is the most common means normal people use to harness the power of the Internet. But even the tried and true HTTP server is moving away from the simplicity of serving static data. The Web as a whole is moving toward executable content. Servlets give us a way to program the server side of an HTTP connection. Today, we have several alternatives ranging from Web browsers to FTP clients that allow us to plug in to the network. What's been lacking is the server-side connection to that interactive content.

Common Gateway Interface and CGI Scripts

Digging back into the history of the Internet a little bit, we find that before the Web and Web browsers and graphical content there was something called Gopher. When the primary users of the Internet were the universities and the research community a purely text-based World Wide Web existed. This web allowed users (using a Gopher client or for the real geeks a simple Telnet client) to search for and retrieve textual documents from large text-based repositories all over the world. Since the advent of the graphical Web browser and definition of HTML, Gopher has taken a back seat to HTTP, but in many universities (especially in the far East and third world) Gopher is still alive and well.

The way that Gopher allowed users to search these large text repositories was to provide the Gopher servers with a mechanism through which a user could request the server to run a program as a child process of the server. To provide a defined interface between the server and the application to be run, the Common Gateway Interface specification was developed (see *http://hoohoo.ncsa.uiuc.edu/cgi/* for the specification).

Basically CGI defines a set of environment variables made up of the environmental information contained in the request and response headers exchanged by HTTP clients and servers. As a set of system environment variables, this information is available to any application written in any programming language that is supported. Quite often these programs are written in one of the UNIX shell languages, and they became known as CGI scripts. Today, it is common to hear any program that is run by the Web server called a CGI Script or CGI Program.

CGI is a very important tool in our Web programming toolkit. Once you understand the information provided in the interface and can envision what you could use it for, it becomes apparent how your name got on so-and-so's e-mail list after you visited so-and-so's Web site. Interrogating the HTTP_USER_AGENT from our CGI program allows us to determine on a request-by-request basis the

Table 7–1 CGI Environment Variables

SERVER_SOFTWARE	Name and version of the server software
SERVER_NAME	Server's host name, DNS alias, or IP address
GATEWAT_INTERFACE	The version of CGI being used (CGI/1.1)
SERVER_PROTOCOL	Name of and revision of protocol request was received as (HTTP/1.1)
SERVER_PORT	Port number being used by the server
REQUEST_METHOD	The request method "GET", "HEAD", "POST"
PATH_INFO	The path portion of the request
PATH_TRANSLATED	Normalized version of the PATH_INFO
SCRIPT_NAME	Virtual path to the script
QUERYSTRING	Parametric information attached to the URL
REMOTE_HOST	Hostname of the requesting host
REMOTE_ADDR	IP address of REMOTE_HOST
AUTH_TYPE	Type of client authentication provided
REMOTE_USER	If server supports authentication and the script is protected, this is the username they have authenticated as
REMOTE_IDENT	Remote username from the server if it supports RFC 931
CONTENT_TYPE	Usually the MIME type of the retrieved data
CONTENT_LENGTH	Length (in octets/bytes) of the data being returned
HTTP_ACCEPT	MIME types to be accepted by the client
HTTP_USER_AGENT	Client browser name and version

browser being used by the end user and allows us to customize dynamic content to best exploit features supported by specific browsers.

Before Java Web Servers and Web servers with built-in Java support, a Java program could be run as a CGI program in a slightly roundabout way as long as there was a Java Virtual Machine available on the Web server's host machine. The way it was done was to create a short script that would load the JVM and then run the Java application on the JVM. For instance, on an NT platform that had the JVM in the system path, the script (*.bat* file) would contain the single statement:

```
"java myprog"
```

Typically, when a CGI program is run as a child process of the Web server, anything written to "sysout" is captured by the Web server and returned to the client. In Java then, to create dynamic HTML to be returned to the client, all we need to do is use the System object to write our content.

```
System.out.println("<html><head><title>My CGI</title></head>");
System;out.println("<body>. . .jdbc query results . . .</body></html>");
```

This method of running Java on the server side was crude and rude and suffered the same problem as CGI scripts written in C, C++, or scripting languages (i.e., as child processes of the Web server they are extremely wasteful of machine resources). Having to load the JVM each time the *.bat* file was executed also meant that performance was also pretty bad . . . but it did work.

The new Web servers address this with support for servlets; i.e., server-side Java applications that dynamically produce HTML, do database queries, and integrate the two.

Servlets

Until now, an HTTP server has functioned solely to provide the client with documents. The documents, usually written in HTML, perhaps with embedded Shockwave or Java functionality (in the form of applets), have been statically created days, weeks, even months before the client actually fetched it. If you want to create dynamic document content, you must use the Common Gateway Interface. CGI scripts were a hack designed to provide two-way communication via the World Wide Web. Servlets replace the need for CGI scripts and give you a much cleaner, more robust alternative.

What Is a Servlet?

Servlets are Java applications that reside on the server side of an HTTP server. More likely than not you created several Java objects designed to be used by the client. Typically, these Java objects are restricted by security constraints that challenge your ability to use files and networks on a whim. Servlets are not subject to artificial security restrictions and enable you to extend the easy nature of Java programming to the server side of an HTTP connection (see Figure 7-3).

Servlets can be used to create dynamic HTML documents. The documents generated by a servlet can contain data gleaned from other sources, including remote objects, databases, and flat files. As we will see in a later section, servlets also can be integrated with your existing RMI or IDL server. Furthermore, the investment of time required to learn servlet programming is negligible because knowing Java automatically ensures that you will "know" servlets.

So, why don't we just use RMI? Normal Java objects have well-defined public interfaces that can be used by a variety of clients, including Web pages, other applets, even CORBA servers. These Java objects are conventional objects that are instantiated every time one is needed. In the end, if you create an object, you very well could have five or six copies hanging out there being used by object requesters.

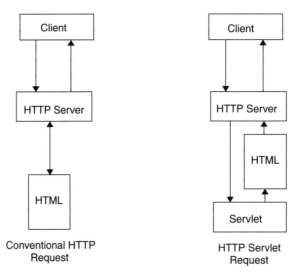

Figure 7-3 Servlets create documents on
the fly rather than getting documents that
were already there.

Servlets, on the other hand, have no defined interfaces. They are faceless Java
objects. The Java Web server simply maps a request onto a servlet, passing it the
entire URL call. The servlet then does what it is programmed to do and generates
dynamic content. Servlets cannot have an interface as we know it. Instead, all its
functionality is restricted to one function within its class hierarchy.

The Servlet API. The Servlet API maps each servlet to a specific HTTP request.
Most currently available Web servers support the Servlet API. This is done in much
the same way that the Web server supports CGI programs. In the Web server
administration, there is an option that you set to indicate that you are going to use
servlets; this will have the Web server start up the Java Virtual Machine as part of
its startup process. Elsewhere in the administrative portion will be a place where
you can identify where you wish to locate the "magic" */servlet/* directory.

The Web server is responsible for taking the mapping and invoking the proper
servlet. Servlets can be initialized, invoked, and destroyed depending on the
request. The Java Virtual Machine being run by the Web server makes sure that
the servlet carries out its instructions correctly.

Furthermore, because servlets are implemented in Java, they are platform-
independent and architecture-neutral. As with normal Java objects, servlets
require a valid Java Virtual Machine to be present on the machine on which it
runs. In addition, the servlet requires a Web server that is compliant with the
Servlet API specification.

Most Web servers have a number of "magic" directories that are used for special purposes. The magic directory "cgi-bin" can be physically located anywhere on the Web server machine (*D:\executables\perl*) but will be relocated to */cgi-bin/* by the Web server; the servlet directory is another "magic" directory, the Web server administration client will allow us to map any directory we like to */servlet/*. In addition to the "magic" directories of "cgi-bin" and "servlet," Web servers also support a feature called Additional Document Directories; this feature allows us to set up our own name to directory mappings. For instance you might find it useful to set up your own "magic" directory called */javascript/* to store all of your embeddable Java script files.

The concept of directory mapping becomes more important as we make more and more of our Web pages dynamic and our databases interactive. With more dynamically created pages on our Web sites, we need more servers. If our Web servers are also clients to our Local Area Networks or shared file systems (like the Andrew File System—AFS), we can have multiple Web servers serve our application objects from the same shared "magic" directories. This ensures that all users are getting the same versions of the objects and is part of an overall configuration management scheme.

NOTE: The servlet API is currently part of the JDK 1.2 and considered a part of Java 2.0.

Objects that want to be dynamic information providers should implement the servlet interface shown in Figure 7-4. In the diagram in Figure 7-4, those objects that provide the functionality defined in the servlet interface are capable of handling ServletRequests.

The ServletRequest object contains the entire HTTP request passed to the servlet by the Java Web Server. The ServletRequest is also capable of extracting parameters from the HTTP request itself. For example, the following URL contains four elements:

```
http://watson2.cs.binghamton.edu/servlet/steflik.html?courses
```

First, the request defines the protocol being used. Here, we use the hypertext transfer protocol. The HTTP request is fairly ubiquitous on the Web these days, but as new protocols such as the Lightweight Directory Access Protocol (LDAP) become more prevalent, this portion of the request will become more and more important.

We then see the domain name for the request. In this instance, we access the Web site *watson2.cs.binghamton.edu*, presumably to check what courses Steflik is teaching this semester. Obviously, this portion of the address varies widely from

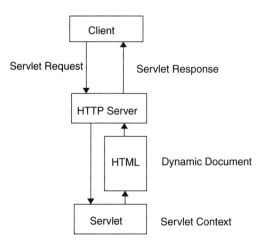

Figure 7–4 The Servlet class hierarchy gives you easy access to input and output streams for dynamic documents.

software development oriented domains like *java.sun.com* to education oriented domains like *www.binghamton.edu*.

Finally, we access the document and its parameters. The Java Web Server maps the *steflik.html* document request to a servlet, passing the parameter courses as part of the ServletRequest data structure. Keep in mind that the physical document *steflik.html* does not actually exist; it will be generated on the fly by the servlet.

Responses are sent back to the requesting client via the ServletResponse object. The Java Web Server translates the ServletResponse object into a dynamic document of some kind. We will see later how we can generate dynamic applets, but we will still pass the data back through a ServletResponse instance.

Why Not CGI Scripts? CGI scripts are language-independent. They can be written in everything from C++ to PERL to AWK. Scripts implementing the Common Gateway Interface simply pass environment variables to one another all the while generating dynamic documents. They can provide a ton of functionality, as we have seen with the explosive growth of the Web. Certainly without CGI scripts the Web could never have become a two-way form of communication that was readily accepted by the general public.

CGI scripts have two major drawbacks, however. First, they suffer from horrible performance. They are turtle slow and are not scalable. Multiple CGI requests on the same server end up creating new processes for each request. The end result is that CGI processes do not cooperate with one another as threaded applications would. Instead, they hog system resources and slow not only the scripts themselves but the HTTP server that hosts it as well.

CGI scripts are also completely platform-dependent. Although the language with which they are written can vary, they cannot be transported from a Windows machine to a Macintosh. They are written once, and used in one place.

The Java Servlet interface provides an alternative to this morass. Because they are written in Java, servlets are platform independent. They can be moved between machines with ease and without recompiling. Servlets also can take advantage of clever threading mechanisms and provide fast turnaround and efficient processing of data. One other thing about CGI is that it is easy to hang up a Web server with a script that has not been well written and tested; because servlets run as a thread of the JVM and not as a child process of the Web server, they are safer.

Servlets Overview

These days, HTTP servers are commodities to be had in much the same way as a pair of Nike Air Jordans. You can get HTTP servers from Netscape, from Microsoft, even for free via the World Wide Web. Companies whose sole product is a Web server are doomed to failure. In an effort to provide a new kind of Web server to the Web surfing public, Sun Microsystems has created the Java Web Server architecture.

Servlet-compliant Web servers generate dynamic documents through normal protocol requests. Java objects known as servlets create the dynamic documents. As we will see in the next two sections, servlets are both easy and fun to write. Without much effort, you can create a dynamic document server that will render your CGI scripting techniques of the past obsolete.

Dynamic Documents

We spoke earlier about the Java Web Server translating document requests into servlet calls that, in turn, create and pass back a document corresponding to the request. The servlet must be capable of accepting different parameters from the client and also be able to formulate a response quickly and efficiently. By using servlets, we would not have to create those documents days, weeks, perhaps even months in advance. Rather, we simply create a program that, given a set of parameters, can generate a document at the moment of the request. In so doing, we generate up-to-the-minute information without resorting to software hacks like CGI scripts.

Creating the Servlet

All servlets need to inherit from the Servlet or HTTPServlet base classes. The difference between these two classes is that the Servlet class is more generic and can be used with RMI and CORBA objects as data sources, whereas the HTTPServlet focuses on HTTP and interfacing with Web servers. The base class creates all the functionality required to map Java Web Server requests onto a physical servlet process. The servlet process is started automatically by the server if it isn't yet running. Any subsequent requests on the servlet process can either be queued until the servlet is ready to process it or transferred to another servlet where it can be started up and processed. These are administrative tasks that we will discuss in a moment.

Meanwhile, we need to implement the servlet architecture to retain a request, process data, and send documents back. Let's say we want to make a servlet that will accept a request from our favorite Web browser and echo back to us a Web page containing some of the information contained in the HTTP Request Header. This exercise is informative not only about writing our first servlet but also about what information is included in the request header and how we can extract it.

We start by creating the GetBrowserDataServlet object that extends the HTTP-Servlet base class. As we mentioned before, the HTTPServlet base class is required for all servlets and implements the underlying HTTP to servlet mechanisms.

```
public class GetBrowserDataServlet extends HTTPServlet
{
}
```

Handling Java Web Server Requests. Every object that inherits from the HTTPServlet base class must implement the service function. The service function has two parameters, an HttpServletRequest object and an HttpServletResponse object, and can throw one of two exceptions, either the ServletException or an IOException. The HttpServletRequest object gives us information about the request sent to us, particularly what kinds of parameters we are receiving. In this simplest of cases, we are not dealing with parameters, but we will in a moment. The response object enables us to set the proper stream to which we can write our dynamic document.

```
public class GetBrowserDataServlet extends HttpServlet
{
    public void doGet( HttpServletRequest rqst,
                       HttpServletResponse resp)
                       throws ServletException, IOException
    {
    }
}
```

Setting Headers and Defining Content. Once we implement the service function, we can fill in the details. We must set our response parameters first. In order for the Web server to pass back a dynamic document, we need to tell it what kind of document we are sending back. Is this a Quicktime movie or an HTML file? In browser parlance, the Content Type field of the response header specifies the type of file; this is usually the files MIME type. If you were to start Netscape or Internet Explorer and play around with the settings, you could farm off content types to different helper applications. For example, all *.mov* Quicktime files sent to a particular browser could end up starting a Quicktime Movie Player and start the animation. In much the same way, we need to specify what kind of document we are sending back by setting the content type. This is done by using the setContentType method of the HttpServletResponse object.

```
public class GetBrowserDataServlet extends HttpServlet
{
    public void doGet( HttpServletRequest rqst,
                       HttpServletResponse resp)
                       throws ServletException, IOException
    {
        // set up the response
        resp.setContentType("text/html");
    }
}
```

Creating the Document. Now, we need a standard output stream to which we can write our dynamic document. As we discussed in the first chapter, streams are wonderful things that have numerous purposes. Here we take a regular response object and obtain an output stream for it:

```
public class GetBrowserDataServlet extends HttpServlet
{
    public void doGet(HttpServletRequest rqst,
                      HttpServletResponse resp)
                      throws ServletException, IOException
    {
        // set up the response
        resp.setContentType("text/html");
        // get the dynamic document's output stream
        ServletOutputStream out = resp.getOutputStream();
    }
}
```

In order to send information back to the client, we must create an HtmlPage object that will handle much of our HTML formatting. Now, we can generate our dynamic document simply by writing HTML strings to the output stream we just defined. In effect, this sends the data we write directly back to the client browser via the Web server.

```
public class GetBrowserDataServlet extends HttpServlet
{
```

```java
public void doGet(HttpServletRequest rqst,
                  HttpServletResponse resp)
                  throws ServletException, IOException
{
    // set up the response
    resp.setContentType("text/html");

    // get the dynamic document's output stream
    ServletOutputStream out = resp.getOutputStream();

    // get the data for the HTML page
    String browserAddr = rqst.getRemoteAddr();
    String userAgent = rqst.getHeader("user-agent");
    If (userAgent == null) userAgent = "Unknown browser";
    String method = rqst.getMethod();
    String path = rqst.getServletPath();
    String server = rqst.getServerName();
    Int port = rqst.getServerPort();

    // build the HTML
    out.println("<html><head><title>Remote User Information"
              + "</title></head><body>"
              + "<p>Remote IP Address: "+ browserAddr
              + "<br>Remote Browser: " + userAgent
              + "<br>Request Method: " + method
              + "<br>Servlet: " + path
              + "<br>Server: " + server
              + "<br>HTTP Port: " + port );
    out.println("</body></html>");
}
}
```

The following is the static HTML produced by the GetBrowserDataServlet after I did a Save As in my browser. I doctored it up a little bit in my favorite text editor. The reason that I needed to doctor it up was to put in some line feed so it would be viewable. If you notice, in the code there are no carriage returns in the stream of data that goes to the output stream. The browser's layout engine receives this continuous stream of characters and formats it according to HTML layout rules; remember that carriage return characters are just one more character that has to be parsed and then discarded.

```html
<html><head><title>Remote User Information</title></head>
<body><p>Remote IP Address: 127.0.0.1
<br>Remote Browser: Mozilla/4.5 [en] (Win98; U)
<br>Request Method: GET
<br>Servlet: /servlet/GetBrowserDataServlet
<br>Server: localhost
<br>HTTP Port: 8080
</body></html>
```

Figure 7-5 `GetBrowserDataServlet` output.

This HTML, after laying out by the browser, produced the layout shown in Figure 7-5.

Now a Few Words on Servlet Testing and Deployment. Web servers are pretty amazing creatures; the people who create and nurture these software entities fill them with features that make them very useful and above all as fast as possible. We all know that our browsers use caching techniques to help performance; they will not go back to the server if a page is cached in the local store. To help servlet performance, Web servers cache servlets so that they are always readily available in memory if needed. This is a nice performance feature and, coupled with a high performance Java Virtual Machine, really helps make servlets as fast as possible. Now comes the hitch; because servlets are cached as soon as they are loaded, testing becomes complicated. As soon as we compile a new version of our servlet and want to test it, we must first copy it to the Web server's "magic" */servlet/* directory and then click on the reload button of our browser. Lo and behold, the old version of the servlet is run. To test the new version of the servlet, we must get the Web server administrator to "cycle" (turn off, then on) the Web server to clear the cache so that it will load the new version of the servlet. Doing this frequently can make a real enemy of your normally mild-mannered Web server administrator. In a production environment, we want to make sure that servlets are extensively tested before they are put into production, so that once put into production only one cycling of the Web server is necessary.

Enter the servletrunner, a piece of software that is distributed as part of Sun's Java Servlet Development Kit (JSDK). The servletrunner allows you to test servlets on your own Windows-based workstation. Servletrunner is a special-purpose Web server that you can configure and run on your own workstation. You will still have to go through the hassle of having to stop servletrunner to clear the cache to test your new version of a servlet, but that is preferable to alienating the Web administration staff.

Servlets and HTML Forms Processing. The biggest use of servlets today is in the dynamic creation of HTML-based forms and processing the data returned by a client browser to the Web server from the form. Being Java programmers, we are all familiar with building user interfaces using AWT and Swing to create applets for delivery to a Web browser. Plain old HTML provides us with a much thinner client that can be created very quickly by a servlet and sent to the client browser much more quickly than an equivalent Java applet. (I hate to say it, because I really like the stateful behavior of an applet, but having to wait for the class loader to do all of its security checks while the applet is loading really makes me dread the "Applet starting" message on the browser's message line.)

HTML's data entry widgets (tags) provide a set of data entry objects sufficient for most data entry applications. Let's review the HTML set of data entry objects.

Form Tag. To send data from a form to the Web server requires a minimum of a single <form> . . . </form> tag set. Web pages may contain multiple forms, each being logically independent of the other.

```
<form name=name method=GET/PUT action=/servlet/myservlet>. . .</form>
```

The <form> tag has no associated layout implications for the browser; its only implications are processing oriented.

The name attribute of the form can be anything we wish as long as it contains no embedded blanks and is unique to this particular form (within the current Web page).

The method attribute of the tag is used to indicate to the browser how data from the form is to be sent to the Web server. There are two possible choices: GET or POST. GET instructs the browser to use an HTTP GET or an HTTP POST request header. A GET will attach all the data from the form to the URL sent to the server (this will be available to your servlet via the getQueryString or getParameterValues method). Setting the method attribute to POST instructs the browser to send the data as part of the request header where it will be made available to the servlet either by reading the ServletInput Stream or via the get-ParameterValues method.

Depending on your choice of the GET or POST method, your servlet will have to overload the doGet or doPost method of the HTTPServlet base class. In the GetBrowserDataServlet, the execution of the servlet was kicked off by the implied HTTP Get of just requesting the servlet's URL; this is why we overloaded the doGet method in the servlet.

Input Tag. The <input> tag is a multipurpose tag and is really quite versatile. We'll look at each of the variations of the <input> tag individually.

As a Text Input or Password Field.

```
<input name=nnn type=text size=m maxlength=n value=p>
```

> name—assigns a name to the field
>
> type—provides text for a text input field password for a password field
>
> size—indicates the width (characters) of the displayed widget
>
> maxlength—indicates the maximum numbers of characters to be typed in
>
> value—provides the initial value to display in the field

Text input fields are the workhorses of the data input widgets and are used for collecting both textual and numeric data. The only differentiation between text, numeric, date, . . . , information is the context in which it is used. Enforcement of data type checking is left to the user either by including Javascript data type checking functions in the Web page or by having the data-handling servlet check the data for correctness and post error messages back to the browser as special Web pages. The general feeling is that including Javascript to do this is preferable to having the servlet do the checking as it localizes the checking to the client, places no extra processing load on the Web server, and cuts down servlet size.

Password fields are the same as text input fields except that, when typed into, the typed characters will display as * characters; when submitted, the name/value pair will contain the text as it was typed.

As a Check Box. Check boxes are little square boxes that, when clicked on, display a small check mark. If a box is already checked, clicking will remove the check mark. Check boxes are convenient for allowing a user to choose a set of options.

```
<input name=nnn type=checkbox value=p checked>
```

> name—a form unique name for the field
>
> type—must be checkbox
>
> value—a value to be sent to the server if the box is checked (A name/value
>> pair will only be sent is the box is checked when submitted.)
>
> checked—if present, indicates to display the box as initially checked

As a Radio Button. Radio buttons are a metaphor for the one-of-many kind of selection device we have on automobile radios. When you press one, it cancels out any previously selected choice.

```
<input name=nnn type=radio value=p checked>
```

> name—a form unique name for a group of radio buttons
>
> type—must be radio

value—the value associated with this button (This value will be sent to the server with the name/value pair if it is selected at submit time.)

checked—display this button as initially selected

This widget allows you to have multiple widgets with the same name. This allows grouping buttons into one of n devices. For example,

```
<input name=car type=radio value=Chevy checked>Chevrolet<br>
<input name=car type=radio value=BMW>BMW<br>
<input name=car type=radio value=Subaru>Subaru<br>
```

will display three radio buttons vertically, each followed by the car brand. If the BMW button is selected and the form is submitted, the name/value pair to be sent to the server will be car=BMW. Figure 7-6 illustrates uses of the <input> tag.

As a Submit Button. Submit buttons are the widget that initiates the transfer of data from a form to the Web server.

```
<input name=nnn type=submit value=text>
```

name—the name of this button; if not included, the default text will be "Submit Query"

type—must be submit

value—the text to be displayed on the button face and sent to the server as the value of the name/value pair when clicked on

A form may have many submit buttons all with the same name; only the name/value associated with the clicked button will be sent to the server. This gives us a convenient mechanism to use to decode which button was used as the submit button.

If a submit button has no name or value associated with it, no name/value pair will be sent to the server. A submit action will take place.

As a Reset Button. Reset buttons are used to clear all the data that has been set in a form. The reset action happens locally to the browser and sends nothing back to the server.

Figure 7-6 Sample radio buttons and checkboxes.

```
<input type=reset value=text>
```

type—must be reset

value—the text to be displayed on the button face

As a Hidden Field. Hidden fields are nondisplayable text fields and are used as a convenient way to hide program state data (remember that the nature of the Web is that it is stateless) in a manner in which it will not be overly noticeable by the browser user (unless they use the "view source" capability of their browser).

```
<input name=nnn type=hidden value=text>
```

name—the name of this button

type—must be hidden

value—the text to be sent to the server as the value of the name/value pair when the form is submitted

As a File Name Field. This field is a text-input field with an associated Browse button. Clicking on the Browse button causes the system File Dialog to be displayed. You can then select a file on your file system by double-clicking on the file or selecting it and clicking on the Open button. This will close the dialog box and place the name of the selected file in the text input portion of the control. This widget is not supported on all browsers.

```
<input name=nnn type=file value=text size-s maxlength=m accept=a,b,c>
```

name—the name of this button

type—must be file

value—the text to be displayed on the button face when a file is selected from the file dialog and sent to the server as the value of the name/value pair when clicked on

size—same as for text input field

maxlength—same as for text-input field

accept—a comma separated list of MIME file types to be used by the file dialog to determine which file typed to display

Select Tag. The <select><option></select> allows us to present selection lists as a drop-down list, a one-of-n scrollable selection box, or an m-of-n scrollable selection box.

```
<select name=nnn size=n multiple>
<option value=v selected>text</option>
</select>
```

name—the name of this list

size—number of visible options, if omitted default is one

multiple—if present, the list will be m of n; otherwise, one of n

value—the value submitted for the name/value pair for one of n; multiple name value pairs will be submitted for m-of-n lists

selected—if present, indicates preselected value(s)

See Figure 7-7 for an example of the <select> tag.

Textarea Tag. The <textarea></textarea> tag set is used to give our form a multiline text-input area. Initial text data can be supplied to the field by placing it between the opening <textarea> and closing tags </textarea>.

```
<textarea name=nnn cols=m rows=n wrap=virtual>
</textarea>
```

name—the name of this list

cols—width, in characters, of the input area

rows—height, in characters, of the input area

wrap = virtual—if present, will enable text wrapping at the right border; if absent, a return key is required to move the cursor to the next line

The following HTML produces the textarea in Figure 7-8:

```
<html><head><title>Cars</title></head>
<body><form><center>
<p>Textarea:<br>
<textarea name=tarea rows=4 cols=25 wrap=virtual>
Now is the time for all good students to come to come to the aid of
their teachers
</textarea></center></form></body></html>
```

That pretty much takes care of our 5-minute HTML refresher course. All we have left to understand is how the information is read from the screen and something called URL-encoding.

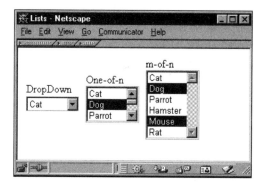

Figure 7-7 Sample drop-down list.

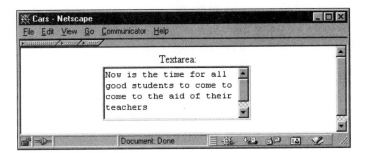

Figure 7-8 A sample textarea.

Reading the Form Screen. When a user clicks on a submit button the browser builds a list of name/value pairs, the ordering of which is determined by the placement of the fields on the screen. Scanning is done left-to-right and top-to-bottom; whatever is found in that path is placed in the list in the order it is found.

URL-encoding is a scheme devised for attaching parameter lists to URLs. The last character of a URL is the first blank character encountered after the beginning of the URL. To ensure that all forms data is sent to the Web server, we must make sure that there are no blank (space) characters in the data. To do this, the browser does some character substitutions as it builds the list of name/value pairs. Spaces are replaced with '+' characters, and any special characters like punctuation are replaced by a '%' character followed by the hexadecimal value of the character in the ASCII code set. Finally the ampersand character ('&') is used to separate name value pairs.

A Servlet Version of the Featured App

As we have done in previous chapters, we will re-examine our featured Appointment Calendar application. In doing so, we will borrow a few programming techniques from CGI programming and apply what we've already learned about servlet programming.

Because our Appointment Calendar will now have a very thin client presented to the end user that will be purely HTML, there is little that we can reuse from the client interface that we developed for the other chapters. We have done pretty well on reuse so far; in each implementation, we have only had to modify the *NetworkModule.java* file and write a new server (except in the case of the JDBC implementation). In looking at what we might consider reusing, we can easily reuse the AppointmentType class because it is pretty straightforward. In examining the NetworkModule for the JDBC version, we notice that we can use it as our server-side interface to the access database we created.

Figure 7-9 shows the user interface for the Calendar and the appointment forms we have decided to use. Notice that we have made the time more granular so as to be more realistic.

Before we go too much farther, let's look at what the overall architecture of our servlet will be. Our servlet will be made up of four methods: doGet, getAppointments, newAppointmentForm, and insertNewAppointment. doGet is our required overload of the doGet method of the HttpServlet base class. We chose GET instead of POST as our forms submission method so that you could see the URL-encoding of the forms data in the location box of your browser. Normally we would use a POST so that the user couldn't see the submitted URL.

The function of doGet is to act like a traffic cop and analyze the input from the submitted URL and decide if it is to:

1.   Display the appointment list by invoking getAppointments, which in turn uses the getAppointments method of our previously written NetworkModule. (That's a nice little bit of reuse.)

2.   Display the add an empty appointment form by invoking the newAppointmentForm method.

3.   Insert a new appointment into the database by invoking insertNewAppointment method, which in turn uses the scheduleAppointment method of a NetworkModule object.

It looks like Figure 7-10.

Figure 7-9   Appointment calendar user interfaces.

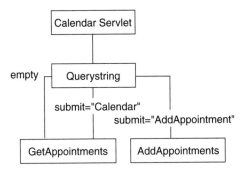

Figure 7-10 Calendar Servlet.

We'll start out with a skeleton view of our application's architecture:

```
Public class CalendarServlet extend HttpServlet
{
    Public void doGet(HttpServletRequest req,
                      HttpServletResponse resp)
                      Throws ServletException, IOException
    {
    }
    public void getAppointments() throws IOException
    {
    }
    public void newAppointmentForm() throws IOException
    {
    }
    public void insertNewAppointment() throws IOException
    {
    }
}
```

Looking at each of the methods individually, we can analyze what is taking place one thing at a time. The entire listing for the servlet will appear at the end of this section.

doGet( )

```
public void doGet (HttpServletRequest req,
                   HttpServletResponse resp)
                          throws ServletException, IOException
{
    String values[];
    out = resp.getOutputStream();

    // add standard HTML header
    resp.setContentType("text/html");
```

```
      out.println("<html><head><Title>Calendar</title></head>");
      out.println("<body><form method=GET
                      action=/servlet/CalendarServlet>");
   // if querystring is null this is the initial call
   String s = req.getQueryString();
   if (s == null)
   {
      this.getAppointments();
   }
   else
   {
      // not initial call decode the submit button value
      String submit = "";
      values = req.getParameterValues("submit");
      if (values != null) submit = values[0];
      // check for add an appointment
      if (submit.equals("Add Appointment"))
         this.newAppointmentForm();
      // check for display appointment form request
      else if (submit.equals("Calendar"))
         this.getAppointments();
      // check for insert a new appointment
      else if (submit.equals("Insert"))
      {
         // get the appt data and add it to the database
         String reason = "";
         int   time = 0;
         values = req.getParameterValues("reason");
         if (values != null) reason = values[0];
             values = req.getParameterValues("time");
         if (values != null)
             time=Integer.parseInt(values[0]);
         // go insert the data
         this.insertNewAppointment(reason, time);
      }
   }
   // standard trailer
   out.println("</body></html>");
}
```

The first few lines of code just reserve a string array for parameter handling, attach an OutputStream to our globally defined ServletOutputStream, and use the stream to write a standard HTML prolog to the client.

The outermost if statement checks the QueryString for null; this is an old CGI trick used to determine if this is the initial invocation of a script. If we invoked our servlet from an anchor tag on another HTML page like:

```
<a href="/servlet/CalendarServlet">Appointment Calendar</a>
```

The submitted URL, when clicked on, would be:

```
http://someserver.com/servlet/CalendatServlet
```

Submitting this URL will invoke the servlet, but the QueryString will be empty because there is no parametric data attached to the URL.

In this case doGet passes control to the getAppointments method to finish building the form. At this point the servlet is done.

If this isn't the first invocation, then there must have been some parametric information (name/value pairs). Because all our forms have at least one submit key, all we have to do to decide what to do next is decode the value of the submit key. If the key was the submit key for inserting a new appointment into the database, there will be additional parametric information in the QueryString so we retrieve it and pass it to the insertNewAppointment method.

getAppointments( )

```
public void getAppointments() throws IOException
{
    try
    {
        AppointmentType appt = new AppointmentType();
        Vector v = new Vector();
        out.println("<h3>Appointment<br>Calendar</h3>");
        out.println("<p><select name=item size=10 >");

        // create a NetworkModule object to talk to database
        NetworkModule nm = new NetworkModule();
        v = nm.getAppointments();
        int temp = 0 ; String ampm = "";
        for (int i = 0 ; i < v.size() ; i++)
        {
            appt = (AppointmentType) v.elementAt(i);
            if (appt.time > 12)
                { temp = appt.time - 12 ; ampm = "PM ";}
            else
                { temp = appt.time ; ampm = "AM ";}
            out.println("<option>" + temp + ":00 "+ ampm +
                        appt.reason );
        }

        // close the selection list & add a submit button
        out.println("</select>");
        out.println("<p><input type=submit name=submit
                    value='Add Appointment'>");
    }
    catch (IOException e)
```

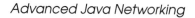

```
    {
        System.out.println("IOException: " + e.toString());
    }
}
```

The getAppointments method first creates an AppointmentType object (reuse here . . .) to hold the appointments retrieved from the database and a vector to hold the AppointmentType objects returned from the database by the Network-Module. We then create a NetworkModule object and invoke its getAppointments method; this places the appointments into the vector we created previously. The for loop iterates through the vector and formats each AppointmentType object into the <option> part of an HTML selection list. Notice in Figure 7-9 that the appointments are sorted by time; this is done by the NetworkModule's select statement (sort by clause).

newAppointmentForm( )

```
public void newAppointmentForm() throws IOException
{
    out.println("<h3>Add an Appointment</h3>");
    out.println("<table><tr>");
    out.println("<td align=center>
                <input type=text   name=reason
                maxlength=20 >");
    out.println("<tr><td>");
    out.println("<input type=radio name=time
                value=8 selected>08:00 AM");
    out.println("<br><input type=radio name=time
                value=9>09:00 AM");
    out.println("<br><input type=radio name=time
                value=10>10:00 AM");
    out.println("<br><input type=radio name=time
                value=11>11:00 AM");
    out.println("<br><input type=radio name=time
                value=12>12:00 Noon");
    out.println("</td><td>");
    out.println("<input type=radio name=time
                value=13>01:00 PM");
    out.println("<br><input type=radio name=time
                value=14>02:00 PM");
    out.println("<br><input type=radio name=time
                value=15>03:00 PM");
    out.println("<br><input type=radio name=time
                value=16>04:00 PM");
    out.println("<br><input type=radio name=time
                value=17>05:00 PM");
    out.println("</td><tr>");
    out.println("<td align=center>"
```

```
        + "<input type=submit name=submit
          value='Calendar'>");
   out.println("<td align=center>"
        + "<input type=submit name=submit
          value='Insert'>");
   out.println("</td></tr></table>");
}
```

This method is pretty straightforward and just uses the ServletOutputStream to build the empty "add a new appointment" page. If we were to add a Modify Existing Appointment button to the Appointments main screen, we could modify this method either to display an empty screen for adding a new appointment or to display the field, filled in with the parsed information from the main appointment selection list.

insertNewAppointment( )

```
public void insertNewAppointment(String reason, int time)
                  throws IOException
{
   // create a NetworkModule object to talk to the database
   NetworkModule nm = new NetworkModule();
   //add the appointment
   nm.scheduleAppointment(reason,time);
   redisplay the Appointment list
   this.getAppointments();
}
```

Finally the insertNewAppoinment method creates a NetworkModule object to talk to the database and invokes the NetworkModule's scheduleAppointment method to place the appointment information into the database; once safe in the database, the getAppointments method is invoked to redisplay the main form. You can now see the appointment that was just added.

Java Server Pages

A recent addition to our toolbox of Web application development tools are Java Server Pages. To explain what a JSP is, think about what it was that we actually did with servlets; simply put, we wrote a Java application that, as its output, created (on the fly) HTML with embedded data that were returned to the requesting browser. This is very CGI-like and, as natural as this felt 10 years ago, is not a very natural way to create dynamic Web pages. Our other server-side technologies like Microsoft's ASP, Allaire's Cold Fusion, and PHP take the approach of developing an HTML page and then adding scripting instructions to the HTML to give the page a dynamic nature. Let's examine, very briefly, these technologies and then look at JSP. Now, remember that these are all server-side technologies.

Microsoft Active Server Pages (ASP)

In the case of ASP, you include a very Visual Basic–like scripting language that allows database interaction via ODBC and interaction with other Windows APIs, in line with your HTML code. The files are typed as *.asp* files rather than *.html*. The Web server is set up to automatically process *.asp* files differently than *.html* files; the *.asp* file type causes the IIS Web Server to process (resolve) the embedded scripting to static HTML with embedded data. This capability is built into the IIS Web Server and comes with NT Server.

PHP

PHP takes the same approach (i.e., an embedded [unique to PHP] scripting language that is resolved by a Web server plug-in that is installed separately from the Web server itself). PHP is freely downloadable from the PHP Web site and, due to its price, is very popular with many smaller ISPs; it is also popular with many ISPs as it runs on LINUX, which is also popular with ISPs.

Allaire Cold Fusion

Cold Fusion takes a slightly different approach in that it has created a set of what looks like additional HTML tags and uses a Web server plug-in to resolve the *.cfm* files into plain old HTML to be delivered to the browser. The plug-in is not a CGI but an actual server that runs alongside of your Web server. Cold Fusion is currently available for both NT and Solaris (code portability is pretty good, although there are some problems, which we won't elaborate on here). To allow the user to extend the tag set, Cold Fusion supports a "custom" tag extensibility that allows new tags to be created in Cold Fusion, C/C++, or Java.

Allaire recently purchased Live Software, which sells a server-side product called Jrun. Jrun is a server-side plug-in that lets you add a servlet compliant JVM to Web servers that either don't implement the servlet API or don't implement it completely or correctly. The JRun server is also compliant with the JSP specification. One last thing about Jrun is that it supports a technology called <CF_Anywhere>, which will run Cold Fusion applications anywhere that Jrun will run—almost every major platform.

On to JSP

Java Server Pages is a technology that is still in active development. The current version of the reference release by Sun is version 1.0 and can be downloaded from the Sun Java developer's site.

Java Server Pages starts out as an HTML page. This lets us start out a project with a set of prototypes that are made entirely using a high-productivity HTML GUI interface tool like Macro Media's Dreamweaver. Once we've used the prototypes to sell management or a customer on the project, we can go and turn those static pages into active pages using JSP.

JSP is currently in its initial release from Sun Microsystems. The JSP 1.0 approach is similar to Cold Fusion's approach of using special tags, but that is where the similarity ends. To the standard HTML tag set, JSP adds a handful of JSP Action tags (six tags) including:

- Directives for the JSP engine

- In-line expression evaluation

- Scriptlets (small in-line scripts for gluing things together or supplying functionality not included in base tags).

This make a JSP page a combination of HTML and JSP directives, scriptlets, and expressions.

Java Server Pages must be run on a Web server that is compliant with the servlet specification. The JSP engine is similar in function to the Cold Fusion server in that it is a server running alongside your Web server. When the Web server gets a request for a URL for a JSP (file type *.jsp*), the request gets handed off to the JSP engine, which now resolves, on the fly, all the JSP tags and information into a Java servlet and then runs the servlet. Remember that once a servlet-compliant Web server runs a servlet, the servlet is maintained in cache for subsequent use.

Sounds pretty neat; it is. Let's go a little farther and look at the JSP components.

JSP Directives. Directives are used to pass information on processing the page to the JSP engine; this includes things like "included" files, custom tag libraries available, language for scripting (currently v1.0 supports only a Java-like scripting language but I would expect Javascript as an option in future releases).

JSP Tags. JSP tags will do the majority of your JSP processing. The base tag set is made up of five tags, as shown in Table 7-2.

Scriptlets and Expression Evaluation

Scriptlets are snippets of Java code that you use to "glue" the parts of your JSP together.

Table 7–2 JSP Tags

Tag	Use
jsp:useBean	Declares the usage of a JavaBean component
jsp:setProperty	Sets a property of a Bean
jsp:getProperty	Retrieves a Bean property
jsp:include	Replaces this tag with the contents of the specified file
jsp:forward	Forwards a client request to another jsp, an HTML page, or a servlet

To include a scriptlet in your JSP, place the Java code inside a set of scriptlet delimiters. Use <% . . . %> to identify the beginning and end of your scriptlet.

To evaluate an in-line expression and have its result placed in line with your HTML, place the expression inside <%= . . . %>. Essentially the result replaces the <%= *exp* %>.

NOTE: Expression evaluation tags (<%= ...%>) cannot be nested inside a script-let (<% ...%>). The scriptlet must be terminated (as shown). In a like manner, HTML tags cannot be nested inside a scriptlet; the scriptlet must be terminated (as shown).

The following excerpt from the featured Appointment Calendar illustrates the use of both of these. This section of code includes two scriptlets, an HTML <option> tag, and two expression evaluations. The top cell in the following box is the first scriptlet and is not a complete piece of code; it is only a fragment, but it contains the code to retrieve the list of appointments from the database via the Appointments bean.

The second box contains the HTML <option> tag and two expression evaluators to get the time and appointment text from the list of appointment objects retrieved in the top box. The third box contains the code needed to complete (syntactically) the Java code in the top box.

```
<%
    try
    { // build the options tags for the select
        Vector v = new Vector();
        v = appt.getAppointments();
        for (int i = 0 ; i < v.size() ; i++)
        {
            Appointment a = (Appointment) v.elementAt(i);
    %>
```
```
            <option><%= a.getTime() %> <%= a.getReason() %>
```
```
        <%
        }
    }
    catch(Exception e)
    {
        System.out.println(e.toString());
    }
%>
```

The Featured Application as a JSP

To give you a better idea of the power of Java Server Pages, we have made a JSP version of the Internet Appointment Calendar, our featured application. To do this, we have simply made two Java Server Pages, one for the Appointment List, which will be retrieved from the Access Database (using JDBC) when the application is started. The second JSP is for the data entry screen for the Add A New Appointment function. To take the place of the NetworkModule from the previous versions of the application, we have rewritten the NetworkModule as a server-side Java Bean to take advantage of the JSP facilities for defining and using Java Beans. The workings of the Appointments Bean will be explained in the component models chapter (Chapter 8) where the topic of Java Beans is addressed. Figure 7-11 shows the architecture of our application.

Keep in mind as we go through this that the first time a browser requests the Calendara.jsp or the Appointments.jsp page that they will be linked to the Appointments Bean by the JSP engine and turned into a servlet that will be immediately compiled and run (and cached on the Web server) and returned to the client browser as an HTML forms page. If the user clicks on the AddAppointment button, the server will run the cached servlet, which will decode the button click and chain (forward) to the AddAppointment.jsp. The AddAppointment.jsp will now go through the same process and end up as a cached servlet and returned to the client browser as an HTML version of the Add Appointment Page. When a user clicks on the Add button, the cached Add Appointment will use the Bean to insert the appointment into the database using JDBC. Now that both of the JSPs are cached as servlets, any other users requesting the JSPs will get the compiled versions.

The Calendara.jsp. The following HTML page is the basis for the main page of our appointment calendar application; it is completely static and ready to be made dynamic by adding JSP tags to it.

```
<html>
<head><title>Appointment Calendar</title></head>
<body bgcolor="white">
```

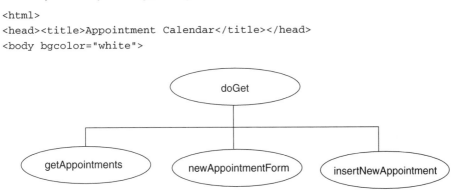

Figure 7-11 Architecture of JSP version of the featured app.

```
<form name="myappt" method="get" action="Calendara.jsp">
<h3>Appointment<br>Calendar<br>JSP Version</h3>
<select name="appts" size="10">
      <option>
</select>
<br><input type="submit" name="submit"
      value="Add Appointment">
</form>
</body>
</html>
```

The first thing we add is a JSP page directive. This is an instruction to the JSP engine that identifies the scripting language to be used (currently only Java is supported) and any packages that need to be imported. This belongs right at the beginning of the page. In general, the JSP engine parses through all the code that gets collected together, resolves all the JSP tags, and converts HTML tags to Java stream output statements. When everything has been parsed and converted, the entire collection becomes the source code for a Java servlet, which is finally compiled and run by the server.

The JSP tag is the next line we add to identify a Java Bean class that we wish to use. This tag assigns an identifier to the instantiated Bean and generates the Java code that will actually instantiate the Bean.

The next code to be added is between the <body> tag and the <form> tag; this scriptlet retrieves the value of the submit parameter from the request header. By testing the value of submit, we can determine whether this is the first time into the JSP. A value of null indicates that submit is not defined; the only time submit is undefined is on the initial entry to the page.

The next scriptlet to be added is after the <select> tag, and it is used to build the <option> tags for the <select> statement. To do this, we create a vector to hold the list of Appointment objects returned from the database by our Java Bean. Once they are retrieved, we iterate through the vector retrieving each Appointment object, using its getter methods to obtain the time and Appointment text for each appointment.

The scriptlet following the creation of the <option> tags is required to syntactically complete the code from the first scriptlet.

Following the last of the HTML (</html> is a short scriptlet with just an "else" statement). This is for further decoding of the submit parameter; in this case, it allows us to forward control to the AddAppointment.jsp page. It also gives us an if/then/else structure that we could use for decoding other requests. For example, were we to add Modify and Delete buttons to the main form, we could decode them here and pass control to the appropriate JSP Page.

```
<!-- Calendara.jsp -->
<%@ page language="java" import="Calendar.* " %>
<jsp:useBean id="appt" scope="session" class="Calendar.Appointments" />
<html>
<head><title>Appointment Calendar</title></head>
<body bgcolor="white">
<%
    String submit = request.getParameter("submit");
    if (submit==null)
    {
        %>
          <form name="myappt" method="get" action="Calendara.jsp">
          <h3>Appointment<br>Calendar<br>JSP Version</h3>
          <select name="appts" size="10">
        <%
        try
        {  // build the options tags for the select
           Vector v = new Vector();
           v = appt.getAppointments();
           for (int i = 0 ; i < v.size() ; i++)
           {
              Appointment a = (Appointment) v.elementAt(i);
              %>
                  <option><%= a.getTime() %> <%= a.getReason() %>
              <%
           }
        }
        catch(Exception e)
        {
            System.out.println(e.toString());
        }
        %>
          </select>
          <br><input type="submit" name="submit"
              value="Add Appointment">
          </form>
          </body>
          </html>
        <%
    }
    else
    {
        %>
          <jsp:forward
              page="AddAppointment.html?submit=Add+Appointment" />
        <%
    }
%>
```

The AddAppointment.jsp. The AddAppointment page is very similar to the Calendar page functionally because they both use the Appointments Bean to accomplish their database interactivity. They start off with the same page directive and useBean tag. Upon entry to the page from the Calendar page, the empty data entry form for adding an appointment is displayed. The user action of clicking on the Add New Appointment button causes the JSP (now a servlet) to be re-entered with the submit parameter now set to Add New Appointment. This will cause the decoding structure to follow the lone "else" statement and the scriptlet to retrieve the time and reason parameters from the request header and then pass them to the Appointments Bean, which will pass them to the setAppointment method of the Bean. Pretty simple, huh?

```
<!-- AddAppointment.jsp -->
<%@ page language="java" import="Calendar.*" %>
<jsp:useBean id="appt" scope="session"
            class="Calendar.Appointments" />
<%
    // decode the submit parameter to know what to do
    String submit = request.getParameter("submit");
    if (submit.equals("Add Appointment"))
    {   // make the data entry form
        %>
        <body>
        <form name="add" method="GET" action="AddAppointment.jsp">
        <h3>Add An Appointment<br>JSP Version</h3>
        <table><tr>
        <td align="center">
        <input type="text"  name="reason" maxlength="20" >
        <tr><td>
        <input type="radio" name="time" value="8" selected>08:00 AM
        <br><input type="radio" name="time" value="9">09:00 AM
        <br><input type="radio" name="time" value="10">10:00 AM
        <br><input type="radio" name="time" value="11">11:00 AM
        <br><input type="radio" name="time" value="12">12:00 Noon
        </td>
        <td>
        <input type="radio" name="time" value="13">01:00 PM
        <br><input type="radio" name="time" value="14">02:00 PM
        <br><input type="radio" name="time" value="15">03:00 PM
        <br><input type="radio" name="time" value="16">04:00 PM
        <br><input type="radio" name="time" value="17">05:00 PM
        </td></tr>
        </table>
        <input type="submit" name="submit"
               value="Add New Appointment">
        </form>
```

```
        </body>
        </html>
    <%
    }
    else // submit must = "Add New Appointment"
    {
        // get the forms data and add to the database
        String reason = request.getParameter("reason");
        int time = Integer.parseInt(request.getParameter("time"));
        appt.setAppointment(reason,time);
    %>
        <h1>Appointment added</h1>
    <%
    }
%>
```

Dynamic Documents Overview

We've shown how servlets and Java Server Pages can be made to create documents dynamically and supplant the universal acceptance of a Web browser. What if we were able to take the power of IDL or RMI solutions and bring them to the Web as well? Servlets and JSPs allow us to merge the server-side programming ability of Web servers with the widespread acceptance of tools such as CORBA or Java RMI.

Multipurpose Servers

What we've created so far is the Java code to allow our HTTP server to be able to serve dynamic data. As we've seen, the server routes requests from normal HTTP clients to Java servlets that return HTTP-conformant requests. We've also created several Java servers that promote the distributed object paradigm. What if we were able to create a Java server that was a servlet at the same time that it was a CORBA server?

What servlets give you is the ability to access your servers in many different ways. Today, if a business is a CORBA shop and chooses to implement all their distributed processing using an ORB, they will often have to create another component altogether to allow Web-based clients to access their data. In the three-tier model, this means that the middle tier has several objects, all handling multiple types of requests and translating them into data storage and retrieval actions.

By incorporating a servlet alongside a CORBA or RMI server, the server can accept Web requests directly. Once again, the determination of which approach you may wish to take could end up being a philosophical one. By splitting the Web server component from the distributed object server as shown in Figure 7-12, you can achieve a highly modular middle tier. If the Web server has a bug, you

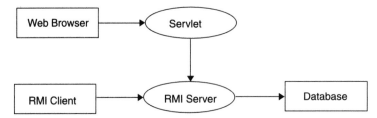

Figure 7-12 Servlet calling RMI objects directly.

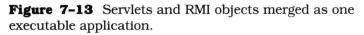

Figure 7-13 Servlets and RMI objects merged as one executable application.

can swap in a new servlet without affecting the rest of the system. However, if performance and a fast development cycle are at a premium, combining the servlet with the object server (see Figure 7-13) may be an excellent solution. By keeping redundancy to a limit you can speed up the time it takes to deploy a new server. Administration of your combined object system may be easier simply because there are fewer parts that can go wrong.

Summary

Servlets are a great way to bring the ease of use and power of the Java language to Web servers. Rather than creating a hacked solution that adds complexity to your existing software development process, why not merge the Web server with Java? Most major Web servers today accommodate the Java servlet API. With all major application platforms having Java support (including mainframes), we are able to serve up Web pages containing interfaces to our large legacy corporate databases with little to no trouble at all. If we have Java and TCP/IP support on a platform, we can run a Java-based Web server to allow access to data sources like DB2, Oracle, IMS, and VSAM. The Java Web Server is a Web server in its own right, meaning that the ability to access static documents is definitely not lost. However, with a little additional work, you can create executable content for your Web pages and begin to truly harness the power of the Internet by making it a place where applications are run, not simply downloaded.

Chapter 8

Java Beans

▼ COMPONENT MODELS

▼ OVERVIEW OF THE JAVA BEANS COMPONENT MODEL

▼ JAVA BEANS

▼ MAKING A BEAN

▼ USING JAVA BEANS

▼ SERVER-SIDE JAVA BEANS

▼ ENTERPRISE JAVA BEANS

▼ COM/DCOM AND ACTIVEX

Java Beans, Microsoft COM/ActiveX, and the newly announced CORBA Component Model support the notion of an application component model. A component model enables software parts from several different programmers to work together. In the Internet world, we refer to everything from Java applets to parts that directly interface to databases or desktop applications as components that we can reuse. By developing reusable components, you can preserve the effort you place into software development by packaging them in modules that you can publish to others.

A Bean is a class that follows a specific naming convention for its methods, can handle its own persistence, and is packaged in a way that makes it easy to distribute and use. By placing our componentized Beans in one place, with a well-defined interface, we can easily assemble applications by picking our components and wiring (connecting) them together using events and some additional Java code as glue. This is the same way that digital engineers build hardware systems; logic chips are componentized into families by technology type (TTL, CMOS, ECL, . . .). As long as we stay within a logic family, assembling a system is like programming in hardware. If we understand the function(s) to be provided and understand the functions provided by our components, designing and building a system is reduced (maybe simplistically) to plugging everything together in the right order. Of course, we have to worry about "timing" and "leading and trailing edge triggers," but it's not much different than worrying about things like "pass by value," "pass by reference," and "side effects."

Java Beans technology is currently in wide use both in client- and server-side applications. Whether you realize it or not the Abstract Windowing Toolkit (AWT) and Swing components (a la JDK 1.2) we use for building user interfaces for our applications are implemented as Beans. A Java component industry, like the after market VBX/OCX component industry created by the popularity of Microsoft's Visual Basic, has begun to spring up and, while slow in coming, will blossom as more and more enterprise business moves to the Enterprise Java Beans component model.

Component Models

As an example of a component-based system, think of your home entertainment center. It consists of a number of components (pieces) each having a well-published interface that has been agreed upon by the manufacturers in the home entertainment industry. Each component has a set of properties and controls that govern the way each operates. In much the same manner, Beans are software components with properties and methods (controls) that govern the way they work. Beans also have a well-published interface for interaction by means of the Java event model (see Figure 8-1).

Component models are not necessarily examples of network programming. Instead, component models provide a means to assemble several networked components under one umbrella. One of the components in a large application may be a network component in charge of talking to remote objects. When you group it with other non-networked objects, that one component makes all of the components networked.

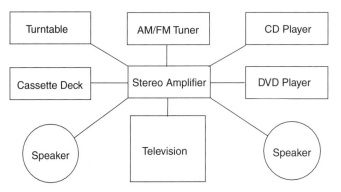

Figure 8-1 Your home entertainment center is composed of several different components.

The Competition

Sun's Java Beans and Microsoft's Component Object Model and Distributed Component Object Model (COM/DCOM) are component models competing for what they feel is their fair share of the Internet. Today, the Abstract Window Toolkit and Swing classes provide a static component model that promotes interaction between components within the same applet or application. It does not address the issue of many kinds of Internet parts within the same page. Instead, it defines interaction between components within an applet or application.

In this chapter, we focus on the Java Beans component model and will spend a little time looking at COM/DCOM. As the owner and progenitor of the Java language, Sun Microsystems has a competitive edge over Microsoft in the Internet arena. Even though Microsoft will continue to dominate the desktop, new Java technology will emerge the fastest and the most reliably from Sun and its partners.

Overview of the Java Beans Component Model

In conceptual terms, a component model is a definition of how different parts interact with one another within one granular space. Translating the big picture definition into Java APIs is a more difficult task. A component model becomes both an overall architectural plan as well as a set of individual APIs that enable programmers to realize the vision.

Every component, referred to as a Bean, should provide each of five services designed to promote interaction between Beans:

1. Interface Publishing
2. Event Handling
3. Persistence
4. Layout
5. Builder Support

At its simplest, Java Beans is a set of naming conventions, a method for packaging a Bean and the simple requirement that a Bean handle its own persistence.

Interface Publishing

In order to enable one Bean to make another Bean do something, the Beans must have a published set of methods that follow a simple naming convention and a published set of events that are generated. The naming convention is straightforward; if a method is to allow the setting of an attribute, then it must start with the characters "set"; if it is to be used to retrieve the value of an attribute, it should start with the characters "get". For example:

```
class  SimpleBean implements Serializable {
   private String myName;   //attribute
   public String getName(){
      return myName; }
   public void setName(String n) {
      myName = n; }
}
```

When several Beans join together, they form a Java Beans application. In order for a Bean application to function properly, its constituent Beans must be able to communicate with one another.

The component Beans must publish their interfaces to the container Bean application so that any Bean within the application can acquire a reference to a component. Other components may then invoke the Bean and use it as it was intended. For example, if we were to create a Java Beans application to catalog all our toys, we would create several individual Beans and then link them together. One of the Beans may talk to a database that keeps track of our toys; another Bean may display and handle a user interface. In order for the user interface Bean to get to the database, it must use the database Bean. The database Bean must publish an interface to itself in order for it to be used.

Event Handling

In the AWT, you can create a user interface with a button and a text area. When the button generates an event, it can trigger a event in the text area. The end result is that the event is handled and passed on to another object.

Similarly, Beans must be able to pass events to one another. Java Beans applications need not be unified under one user interface. In fact, a Java Beans application may have several different applets contained within it, all of which have their own user interface. When something happens in one applet, the other applets may want to know. In our toy catalog example, we want to have two different applets. One applet lists every toy; the other displays a picture of each toy. If you select "Buzz Lightyear Action Figure" from the list, the list sends a message to the display Bean to show a picture of the toy. We can model our Java Beans application to use each applet and unify them.

In much the same way, Bean components can be made to talk to one another and trigger events in each other. The powerful component model on top of which Java Beans was developed promotes the idea of object separation. Remember that you are really creating separate objects that could exist in their own right without a Beans container. The fact that you are combining each of these separate components under one roof says a great deal about the highly object-oriented nature of the Java language.

Persistence

As we discussed in the Chapter 1 section on object serialization, persistence of objects is a very important topic. Persistence moves us from a session-based paradigm in which objects are started, exist for a little while, and then disappear, to a lifecycle-based paradigm in which objects are started and exist for a little while. This time, however, instead of the object disappearing off the face of the earth, it is saved, restored, and allowed to exist again. Java Beans supports persistence primarily through object serialization. You may, however, attach a JDBC or JNDI application to your Bean and store your Bean in a relational database or directory server. Java Beans will let you handle your own persistence if you choose not to take advantage of its own brand of object storage. Even if you choose to do this, it is still an interface and you need to follow the get/set naming convention for methods.

Layout

Earlier we spoke of Java Beans applications whose components each have their own distinct user interfaces. The Beans framework provides a set of routines to lay out the various parts effectively so that they don't step on one another. The layout mechanisms also allow the sharing of resources. Let's say your two different user interfaces both used a fancy picture button. You could share the picture button class across each component, saving download time and improving the efficiency of your application. Java Beans applications assist a great deal in improving the performance of large applications.

The Java Beans layout mechanisms allow you to position your Beans in rectangular areas. The programmer is left to decide whether the regions overlap or maintain a discrete layout space. Beans makes no effort to provide a complex layout manager, choosing instead to implement the standard Java managers.

Builder Support

One other area in which you might want to invest significant design time is builder support. Builders are applications that allow the creation of user applications by selecting various Beans and graphically connecting them together by their events. Most notably, builders take the form of GUI builders such as Visual Cafe, JBuilder, J++, and Visual Age for Java. Chances are that other programmers who desire to take advantage of your hard work could reuse your Bean. Packaging your Beans in such a way that GUI builder applications can access them may be beneficial to you.

A GUI builder could obtain a catalog of methods used by your Bean application, as well as the proper means to access each individual Bean. That way, the builder can graphically represent the Beans application and provide connections into the application from outside. The end result is that your Bean application could be used by another application.

Distributed Beans

Because Beans are written in Java, they are fully portable and can take complete advantage of the write-once-run-anywhere principle. Furthermore, Java Beans ensures that no matter how small your constituent components, it will not in any way overburden them. This allows full distribution of applets and applications wrapped in Java Beans containers. You will not have to make trade-off decisions on whether or not to use Beans, and you will have complete freedom to use Java Beans.

Java Beans also does not interfere with the communication mechanisms we described earlier in this book. It exists peacefully alongside both Java IDL and Java RMI. Just because your applications want to communicate with the network does not mean that Java Beans is off limits to you.

Why Use Beans?

If you've ever tried to create a series of applications on a single Web page, no doubt you've discovered the limitations of the applets themselves. Your applets cannot communicate with one another, and an event in one cannot trigger an event in another. Java Beans proposes a solution to that limitation. Beans, at its essence, is nothing more than a giant Tupperware container for applets and applications. By sticking all your applets within the same container, you can effectively have them communicate freely, so long as they do not leave the container.

But, Beans adds several more capabilities than does a simple container class, many of which we've discussed in this section. Java Beans is Java; Java Beans is easy; Java Beans is fun. Most importantly, however, Java Beans is a flexible way to group Java applets and applications under a unified umbrella.

Java Beans

Java Beans provides a lot of functionality for a low price. When you use the Java-endorsed component model, you are ensured a language-compliant implementation that does nothing to violate the spirit of the Java language. The same security model, application interaction model, and event model are used throughout Java Beans.

In fact, the creators of Beans intended their component model to be an extension to the process of learning the language itself. They didn't want anything to be too hard, or too ineffective. Often, sacrificing ease of use for functionality leads projects to failure. However, the opposite is also true. Making a project so easy to use will often leave it devoid of any usefulness. Java Beans avoids both pitfalls and provides a more than adequate middle ground.

Component Interaction

As you can see in Figure 8-2, a given Java Bean supports three levels of interaction. Each Bean exhibits certain properties, can be invoked by several methods, and can, in turn, trigger events in other Beans. This component interaction model lends Beans its great flexibility. Simply by publishing the APIs for itself, a given Bean can tell every other Bean about its properties and methods and trigger events based on other published APIs and invocations on its own method library.

Properties are discussed in detail a bit later, but they are essentially the internal representation of a Bean. Imagine that you have a vase filled with an assortment of flowers. In this instance, the vase is the Bean; it can hold a certain amount of water based on its size, but it can also hold a maximum number of flowers, based on the size of the throat of the vase. Properties are the basic things about an object that describe it at some point in time, its state variables.

Methods are those things that can be done to a Bean. Can you add flowers or remove flowers from a vase? Can your vase also be filled with water? In that case, water is a property, and filling with water is a method, or something that is done to one of the properties.

Let's say your flowers give off a wonderful scent that everyone appreciates. These are events triggered by the vase and pushed out to the rest of the Beans within the same component model.

Network Communication

A key element of effective distributed design is deciding where to split the local computation and the remote computation. When we created the Internet Calendar Manager discussed in the previous chapters, we had to determine where we were going to split the local processing of appointments from the remote storage of the appointments. We decided to create the Network module that would handle that

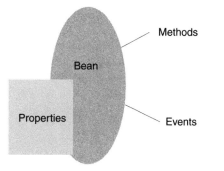

Figure 8-2 Each Java Bean supports three interaction levels: properties, methods, and events.

situation for us. The module receives raw data from the network and translates it into usable data structures for the rest of the application (see Figure 8-3).

We recommend that Java Beans be used in much the same way for networked communication. Create a Bean whose sole purpose is to funnel information to and from remote processes. With this kind of modular design, your Bean can act as a go-between to network resources, saving precious computation cycles.

As of now, the Java Bean product road map calls for Java IDL, Java RMI, and JDBC support. Further revisions of the Beans specification will implement other network mechanisms as they are created.

User Interface Issues

Java Beans was designed with the idea that Beans can be integrated very easily into GUI builders. GUI builders need access to each component that they play with, so the Beans APIs were designed accordingly. Every standard Bean supports the notion of introspection. Each Bean can be looked into, in much the same way we could look into a window (see Figure 8-4). We don't see the whole picture, and we certainly don't see what exactly is going on, but we can see a snapshot of what is possible. Introspection enables us to see the APIs for a given Bean, and more importantly, for an application builder of some kind to plug into the Bean and hook other components to it.

Introspection services come in two types: low level and high level. Low-level introspection allows trusted applications, like GUI builder programs, a very low level of access to a Bean's internals because that is what is needed to be able to hook Beans up to one another. The higher level introspection is provided for application interfacing and only provides information about public properties, methods, and events.

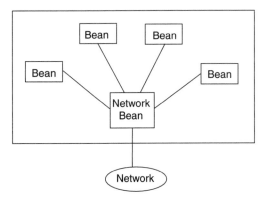

Figure 8-3 A set of Beans can use a network Bean to connect to the network.

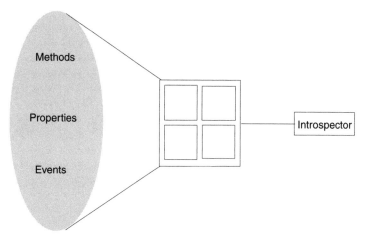

Figure 8-4 The notion of introspection supported by each standard Bean enables GUI builders to see inside the Bean and access components needed.

TIP: Java Beans also supports Uniform Data Transfer (UDT) between components. The UDT mechanism alluded to in the Beans specification declares that data can be transferred between Beans in a variety of easy-to-implement ways. Choosing between drag-and-drop, cut-and-paste, keyboard, and other methods is a matter of Bean implementation.

Java Beans also supports the notion of GUI merging. In GUI merging, child Beans can pass their user interface properties up the hierarchy tree to their parent. In so doing, the parent Bean can set up a consistent look and feel for a GUI, and child Beans can add components to the GUI. The classic example is a menu bar. The parent Bean provides the general appearance of the bar. Child Beans then add entries to the bar (File, Edit, View, and so forth). This way, the child Bean has total and complete control over what a GUI is, whereas the parent sets a general policy for what it will look like.

Persistence

Beans should also be able to save their internal properties between invocations. For example, if we were to instantiate a Bean, change its state, and then shut the Bean down, in some instances we'd want the data we changed to return when the Bean is started up again. This is referred to as a persistent state; in other words, the values are not reinitialized every time.

> **TIP:** Persistence can be implemented in several ways, but in the end you have the choice between automatic, Bean-provided persistence and self-managed persistence. When you manage your own persistence, more than likely you will want to do so using the network. Your Bean can store its internal properties on a remote database, and you can access and store the changes using JDBC. Or you may want to use RMI or IDL to handle your storage techniques.

Events

Java Beans provides an AWT-friendly event notification mechanism. If an event is triggered in your Bean, you should be able to pass that event on to other Beans in your component model. Sometimes events will come in over a network. In these cases, you should handle them as if they were coming from a local Bean.

Properties

Because Beans are nothing more than Java classes, you can create whatever member variables you desire. Furthermore, Beans can contain other Beans within them. In our earlier vase of flowers example, our vase Bean could very easily be contained within a "living room" Bean, which could be contained within a "house" Bean, which could be contained within . . . , well, you get the picture.

Beans in a Nutshell

Beans enable you to harness the power of object-oriented programming and take it to a new level. Instead of publishing libraries of classes, you can now publish entire objects that can be used, abused, imported, delegated, or whatever else you choose to do with them. Beans could just as easily be applications in their own right, but instead are there to help you.

This book only glosses the surface of what Beans can do for you. Trust us, there will be much, much more written on this fascinating and exciting topic. To whet your appetite, however, let's create a simple Bean that models our National Pastime.

Making a Bean

Making a Bean is relatively straightforward. We need to make sure that the Bean implements the serializable interface and that we follow the Java Beans naming convention for the Bean's getter and setter methods. Getters and setters are the Bean methods that are provided to get and set the values of the Bean's properties. The naming convention is simple and requires that setter methods are named starting with the characters "set" (e.g., setVolume, setHeight) and that getter methods start off with the characters "get" (e.g., getVolume, getHeight). By using these prefixs for our getter and setter functions, the introspection facilities can easily identify the methods that can set and retrieve property values.

The following example illustrates the creation of a simple Bean that contains no GUI components.

```
class GasTank implements Serializable{
    private double  capacity;
    private int  percent_full;
    public void setCapacity(double pounds){
        capacity = pounds; }
    public double getCapacity(){
        return capacity;}
    public void setPercent_full(int p){
        percent_full = p; }
    public int getPercent_full(){
        return percent_full;}
}
```

We've fulfilled our minimum requirements for the Bean (i.e., it implements Serializable) and we've followed the getter/setter naming convention. By implementing Serializable, we've enabled our Bean to be a serializable object that our application can make persistent by writing and later reading to/from a file using an ObjectOutputStream. This allows us to create an object as a matter of the operation of an application and to save a "state" object just before we shut down our workstation for the day. When we come in the next morning, the application loads the state object as part of startup and we're right where we left off, as if we never shut down the workstation. The following code snippet illustrates this:

```
import java.io.*;

public MyApp
{
    public static void main (String[] args)
    {
        // as the app runs the State object gets modified
        State currentState = new State();
        loadState();
            .
            .
            .
        saveState();
    }
    public void loadState()
    {
        FileInputStream fis = null;
        ObjectInputStream ois = null;
        try
        {
            fis = new FileInputStream(State.ser);
            ois = new ObjectInputStream(fis);
```

```
            State currentState = (State)ois.readObject();
        }
        catch(ClassNotFoundException e)
        {
            System.out.println(e.toString);
        }
    }
    public void SaveState()
    {
        FileOutputStream fos = null;
        ObjectOutputStream oos = null;
        try
        {
            fos = new FileOutputStream(State.ser);
            oos = new ObjectOutputStream(fos);
            oos.writeObject(currentState);
        }
        catch(IOException e)
        {
            System.out.println(e.toString;
        }
    }
}
```

This illustrates the "almost" creation of a Bean. To complete the process, we must package the Bean in an appropriate manner. Beans are packaged in Java Archive files or JARs for short. The JAR utility comes with the latest version of the JDK and also with the latest download of the Beans Development Kit from Sun (BDK1_1).

Using Java Beans

The basic principle underlying Bean development is that you create the constituent parts just as you normally would. Every applet, every document, every component in the Beans application should be developed, tested, and ready by the time you get to the Beans stage. Once the components are available, you can use one of two methods to bring them together. As we mentioned earlier in this chapter, the Beans specification calls for easy manipulation of a Bean by a GUI builder. GUI builders like IBM's VisualAge for Java or the BeanBox that comes with Sun's BDK can be used to connect Beans together using a simple drag-and-drop type interface. We will discuss that scenario in a moment.

Creating a Java Beans Application

Before a Java Beans application can be developed and deployed, you must first understand the underlying principles of the Beans. Every application consists of the various components as well as two critical base objects that handle the flow and storage of information.

Events are exchanged among Beans through the EventListener and EventSource objects. The EventListener object is created to look for certain kinds of events within the application. Each Bean creates a listener for itself if it wants to receive events. In essence, it subscribes to a list of specific events. A Bean may also create for itself an EventSource to create and publish events for other Beans within the application. Figure 8-5 shows how events can be triggered between Beans.

A Simple Example

If we were going to model a baseball game, we would first need to create a container for the whole game to fit inside. For simplicity's sake, we will include only a pitcher and a catcher. Our pitcher object will throw an event, similar to a baseball, and the catcher object will catch the event later on.

Our baseball game must be configured to listen for events fired by the pitcher. We will have to create an interface called PitchListener for the pitches to be sent to. The PitchListener object is a user-created extension to the AWT standard EventListener object. We simply add a method called throwPitch to the Pitch-Listener. Our BaseballGame object will implement throwPitch, but we will define the PitchListener interface here and implement the throwPitch method when we are ready to connect all our Beans.

```
public interface PitchListener extends EventListener
{
    public void throwPitch(
        String pitch);
}
```

We must then create a BaseballGame object that will listen to all of the other objects and fire the events that it catches to each of its constituent components. In

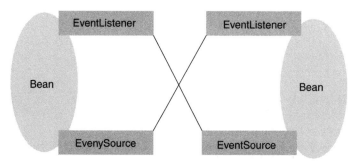
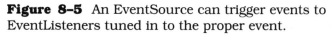

Figure 8–5 An EventSource can trigger events to EventListeners tuned in to the proper event.

order for it to listen in on the other objects, it must implement the PitchListener base class.

```
public class BaseballGame extends Applet implements PitchListener
{
    Pitcher pitcher;
    Catcher catcher;
}
```

Now, the Pitcher and Catcher must be created within the BaseballGame applet. We will do this as we normally would for any other Java object.

```
public class BaseballGame extends Applet implements PitchListener
{
    Pitcher pitcher;
    Catcher catcher;

    BaseballGame()
    {
        // set our layout
        setLayout(new GridLayout(2, 1));

        // create the pitcher
        pitcher = new Pitcher();
        add(pitcher);

        // create the catcher
        catcher = new Catcher();
        add(catcher);
    }
}
```

Finally, we must add the BaseballGame object as a listener of the Pitcher object. Remember that in our simple game of catch, the pitcher is going to fire events and the catcher is going to do nothing but receive them.

```
public class BaseballGame extends Applet implements PitchListener
{
    Pitcher pitcher;
    Catcher catcher;

    BaseballGame()
    {
        // set our layout
        setLayout(new GridLayout(2, 1));

        // create the pitcher
        pitcher = new Pitcher();
        add(pitcher);

        // create the catcher
        catcher = new Catcher();
        add(catcher);
```

```
        // add the game as a listener to the pitcher
        pitcher.addListener(this);
    }
}
```

Instantiating Components

You create the EventSource and EventListener objects within a component object
much as you would a String or Hash Table. They are merely member variables
within the object. The difference is that they are fully capable of talking outside
the component to the Java Beans container application. So, our constructor for the
Pitcher object will initialize the data as well as create the event objects:

```
public class Pitcher implements Serializable
{
    private Vector myListeners;

    private Button fastball;
    private Button curveball;
    private Button slider;

    Pitcher()
    {
        // set our layout
        setLayout(new GridLayout(1, 3));

        // initialize the buttons
        fastball = new Button("fastball");
        add(fastball);
        curveball = new Button("curveball");
        add(curveball);
        slider = new Button("slider");
        add(slider);

        // create the listener vector
        myListeners = new Vector();
    }
}
```

The pitcher must implement methods to add and remove listeners.

```
public class Pitcher implements Serializable
{
    private Vector myListeners;
    private Button fastball;
    private Button curveball;
    private Button slider;

    Pitcher()
    {
        // set our layout
        setLayout(new GridLayout(1, 3));
```

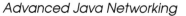
```
            // initialize the buttons
            fastball = new Button("fastball");
            add(fastball);
            curveball = new Button("curveball");
            add(curveball);
            slider = new Button("slider");
            add(slider);

            // create the listener vector
            myListeners = new Vector();
        }
    public void addListener(
        PitchListener listener
    )
    {
        myListeners.addElement(listeners);
    }
    public void removeListener(
        PitchListener listener
    )
    {
        myListeners.removeElement(listeners);
    }
}
```

And finally, we must add code from within our event handler to pass the event back up to all our listener objects. Remember that our listener is a PitchListener object and that we need to cast our vector result to it.

```
public class Pitcher implements Serializable
{
    private Vector myListeners;

    private Button fastball;
    private Button curveball;
    private Button slider;

    Pitcher()
    {
        // set our layout
        setLayout(new GridLayout(1, 3));

        // initialize the buttons
        fastball = new Button("fastball");
        add(fastball);
        curveball = new Button("curveball");
        add(curveball);
        slider = new Button("slider");
        add(slider);

        // create the listener vector
```

```
        myListeners = new Vector();
    }
    public void addListener(
        PitchListener listener
    )
    {
        myListeners.addElement(listeners);
    }
    public void removeListener(
        PitchListener listener
    )
    {
        myListeners.removeElement(listeners);
    }
    public boolean action(
        Event evt,
        Object obj
    )
    {
        // do this only for button events
        if(evt.target instanceof Button)
        {
            // create a pitch to throw based on the button pressed
            String p = new String((String) obj);
            // go through each vector and push the event up
            for(int x = 0; x < myListeners.size(); x++)
            {
                PitchListener listener =
                    (PitchListener) myListeners.elementAt(x);
                listener.throwPitch(p);
            }
        }
    }
}
```

The catcher object is nothing more than a normal Java object. It need not implement any special Java Beans code. Rather, the listener will push events onto the catcher as if they were normal button events. The catcher will then respond to them accordingly.

```
public class Catcher extends Panel
{
    TextArea pitchArea;

    Catcher()
    {
        // set our layout
```

```
        setLayout(new GridLayout(1, 1));

        // create the area where the catcher tells us what he got
        pitchArea = new TextArea();
        add(pitchArea);
    }

    public void catchPitch(
        String pitch
    )
    {

        pitchArea.addText("And the pitch is a ... " + pitch);
    }
}
```

When the listener calls the catcher's catchPitch method, the catcher can then do something with it. Our hierarchical structure could very easily be implemented without the Beans infrastructure. But, once again, this is the beauty of Beans as opposed to ActiveX or OpenDoc. Java Beans is Java.

Connecting Beans Events

Now that we've created a BaseballGame container, Catcher Bean, and Pitcher Bean, we need to connect them so that events fired by the Pitcher are caught by the BaseballGame and passed down to the Catcher. In fact, we need only call catchPitch on our Catcher instance within the BaseballGame object:

```
public class BaseballGame extends Applet implements PitchListener
{
    Pitcher pitcher;
    Catcher catcher;

    BaseballGame()
    {
        // set our layout
        setLayout(new GridLayout(2, 1));

        // create the pitcher
        pitcher = new Pitcher();
        add(pitcher);

        // create the catcher
        catcher = new Catcher();
        add(catcher);

        // add the game as a listener to the pitcher
        pitcher.addListener(this);
    }

    public void throwPitch(
        String newPitch
    )
    {
```

```
        // tell the catcher to catch my pitch
        catcher.catchPitch(newPitch);
    }
}
```

So, in the end, we have three networked components talking to one another using the Java Beans infrastructure, as shown in Figure 8-6.

Bean Introspection

As we have mentioned, introspection is the ability of your Bean to be probed from another outside, or introspecting, class. The introspecting class surveys the contents of your Bean and keeps track of what services are available within it. After introspecting a Bean, the outside class can then go about creating its own methods to interface with your Bean. Typically, introspection will occur on behalf of object builders that will know nothing about the implementation of a Bean, only being able to survey its internals.

These GUI builders could have a suite of Beans already existing locally. It can then allow you to create your own Bean by tying in the functionality of other Beans. This can be displayed graphically. GUI builders that take full advantage of Beans introspection will soon be available. In addition, the Bean Developer's Kit will include all the tools and Java classes necessary to develop your own Beans and Beans-based applications.

Server-Side Java Beans

Server-side Java Beans are Beans that, rather than being part of the client, live out their lifecycle on the server. Newer server-side technologies like Servlets and Java Server Pages are users of server-side Java Beans. On the server side, Beans can be simpler than on the client side because they typically don't have a visual component nor must they be placed in a JAR file. They can just be used as a compiled Java class, which in itself makes them simpler to use than the client-side Beans.

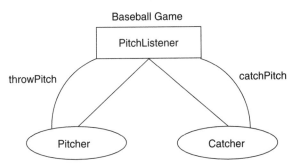

Figure 8–6 Component interaction is simple using the Java Beans infrastructure.

As promised in the section on JSP in the Web server chapter, the following is the Appointments Bean developed for the featured Internet calendar application. As you look over the code, you'll notice that it looks more than vaguely familiar. It is essentially the same code from the code used previously for the JDBC, RMI, and servlet implementations of the calendar application; it is just packaged a little differently.

```java
//-------------------------------------------------------------------
// File:     Appointments.java
// What:     A Server-side bean that will handle all interaction
//           with the database.
// Who:      Dick Steflik (steflik@binghamton.edu)
//
//-------------------------------------------------------------------
package Calendar;

import java.beans.*;
import javax.servlet.http.*;
import javax.servlet.*;
import java.util.Hashtable;

import java.awt.*;
import java.util.*;
import java.net.*;
import java.io.*;
import java.sql.*;

public class Appointments
{
    // create the database connection object
    Connection dbConnection;
    // constructor to make network connection
    public Appointments()
    {
        initNetwork();
    }

    // empty method for getting a single appointment
    public void getAppointment()
    {
    }

    // method to add an appointment to the database
    public void setAppointment( String appointmentReason,
                                int appointmentTime )
    {
        try
        {
            Statement insertStatement =
                            dbConnection.createStatement();
```

```java
            String insert = "INSERT INTO SCHEDULE " +
                            "VALUES('" + appointmentTime + "','"
                                + appointmentReason
                                + "')";

        System.out.println(insert);

        insertStatement.executeUpdate(insert);
    }
    catch(Exception e)
    {
        System.out.println("NetworkModule 3  Error: " +
                            e.toString());
    }
}
// methods to get list of appointments
public Vector getAppointments()
{
    // the variable to store all of our appointments in
    Vector appointmentVector = new Vector();
    try
    {
        Statement statement = dbConnection.createStatement();
        String s = "SELECT TIME, REASON " +
                   "FROM SCHEDULE " +
                   "ORDER BY TIME";
        ResultSet result = statement.executeQuery(s);
        while(result.next())
        {
        // create a variable to stick the appointment in
            Appointment appointment = new Appointment();

        // now get the next appointment from the string
            appointment.time = result.getInt("TIME");
            appointment.reason = result.getString("REASON");
            appointmentVector.addElement(appointment);
        }
    }
    catch(SQLException exc)
    {
        System.out.println("NetworkModule Error 4: " +
                            exc.toString());
    }
    // return the Vector
    shutdownNetwork();
    return appointmentVector;
}
// empty method to set multiple appointments
```

```
public void setAppointments()
{
   shutdownNetwork();
}

private void initNetwork()
{
   try
   {
      // load the database driver
      Class.forName("sun.jdbc.odbc.JdbcOdbcDriver");
      //create a URL object for the database
      String url = "jdbc:odbc:Calendar";
      // connect to the database
      dbConnection = DriverManager.getConnection(url,"","");
   }
   catch (ClassNotFoundException e)
   {
      System.out.println("NetworkModule 1 Error: " +
                          e.toString());
   }
   catch (SQLException se)
   {
      System.out.println("NetworkModule 2 SQL Error: " +
                          se.toString());
   }
}

private void shutdownNetwork()
{
   try
   {
       dbConnection.close();
   }
   catch(Exception e)
   {
     System.out.println(e.toString());
   }
}
}
```

Enterprise Java Beans

The Enterprise Java Beans component model is the next logical extension of the
Java Beans component model. Enterprise Java Beans is a server-side technology
that allows the creation and deployment of Java components that are designed
to run in an EJB-compliant application server environment. It is important to
note that Enterprise Java Beans is a specification and not a product. Many application server providers recognize the importance of the specification and are in

the process of making their application servers and associated development frameworks compliant with the specification.

Application servers will be covered separately in Chapter 9. Suffice it to say that application servers are entire server environments designed to provide high performance, massively scaleable, and highly reliable application deployment environments.

Application server products typically provide their own tools for the assembly of applications from components at deployment time and also provide the tools necessary for building the components. EJB provides a framework for developing enterprise-class applications that allow the developer to focus on the business logic of the problem rather than the environmental issues.

EJB Goal. A primary goal of Enterprise Java Beans is to take the concept of "Write Once Run Anywhere" (WORA) to the level of Enterprise class applications. This means that not only can a component run on any platform, but it will interface with any vendor's EJB-compliant application server. Portability is the order of the day and is made possible by the Enterprise Java platform and its standard infrastructure APIs like JDBC, JNDI, RMI, Java IDL, Servlets and Java Server Pages, JMS (Java Messaging Service), and JTS (Java Transaction Service); most of these have been covered in previous chapters of this book. These APIs attempt to make applications vendor neutral and, therefore, very portable.

EJB Services. The Enterprise Java Beans framework relieves the application programmer of the tedium of having to manage a number of programming issues that are really environmental in nature rather than business logic related. These include:

1. **Lifecycle** The EJB container manages process allocation, thread management, object activation, and object destruction and cleanup.

2. **State Management** The EJB container automatically maintains state persistence for contained Beans.

3. **Security** Enterprise Java Beans do not have to worry about authenticating users or validating the level of access; the EJB container performs all security checking on behalf of the component Beans.

4. **Transactions** The EJB container has the ability to "start," "commit," and "roll back" transactions submitted to transaction-oriented systems on behalf of member Beans.

5. **Persistence** The EJB container can manage the storage and restoration of persistent state data for member Beans, thereby relieving the Beans of having to manage their own persistence.

The EJB server must provide containers for the Enterprise Java Beans that are to be deployed. The EJB container provides all the environmental services described earlier for the enterprise Beans that it holds.

Session and Entity Beans. The EJB specification make provisions for two types of Beans: persistent and nonpersistent (transient). Persistent beans are called **entity Beans**, and transient Beans are called **session Beans** because they are usually associated with only the current client/server session.

Entity Beans are maintained in permanent data storage such as a relational database, an object store, or a directory server. Entity Beans are fully recoverable after a system crash due to their persistence.

A session Bean performs operations for the client such as database access or calculations. Session Beans can be stateless or stateful for the session but will not be persistent across sessions like an entity Bean. Because they are only stateful for the current client/server session, session Beans are not recoverable in the event of a system crash.

In the EJB 1.0 specification, the implementation (by OEMs) of entity Beans is optional, and the implementation of session Beans is required.

The EJB Container. Just as when we used our client-side Java Beans to build an application, we need a container in which we can build our EJB applications. The EJB container is provided by an application server and provides all the environmental services mentioned earlier. Application servers can take many forms (TP Monitors, Web servers, and database management systems to name a few).

Summary

The magical world of Java Beans is only the beginning of the "component race." As corporations look to streamline the all-important software development process, they will look more and more to the theories of object-oriented programming and component models. Java Beans is but one of the many component models seeking the hearts and minds of software engineers and their bosses. Not to be left out of the software development race, Microsoft has its own answer, which is highlighted in the next section.

COM/DCOM and ActiveX

Let's say you want to create a Web page with your company's sales figures on it. Your sales department maintains all its information in a Microsoft Excel spreadsheet. Rather than creating a graph in some kind of paint program and putting a GIF on your Web page, you want to do something dynamic, something that requires no additional effort on your part. If you remember anything from this book, remember that anything and everything is possible in the Internet.

What Is ActiveX?

ActiveX isn't exactly a new product from Microsoft. In fact, it's been around for several years under different monikers and within different parts of the Microsoft Corporation's organizational structure. ActiveX controls, for example, are nothing more than Visual Basic's OCX controls. Nevertheless, the hype and hoopla surrounding ActiveX's "introduction" caused quite a stir within the Internet community.

Today, you more than likely fiddle with your Microsoft Word documents, saving them on your local disk. You create and link in some Excel spreadsheets to illustrate points within your Word documents. You might even link the whole she-bang into a PowerPoint presentation. This is called Object Linking and Embedding, or OLE. The object part refers to each component of your presentation, everything from the Word document to the Excel spreadsheet. Objects are linked into other Microsoft products and embedded within the documents, presentations, spreadsheets, or databases that you create. This model is illustrated in Figure 8-7.

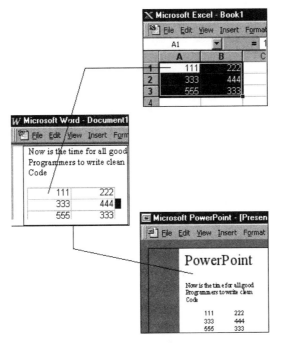

Figure 8-7 Today, you can link various Microsoft components into one "package" using Object Linking and Embedding, or OLE.

ActiveX takes everything one step farther. Let's get back to our original proposal. Our fictitious company wants to stick the data within the spreadsheet onto the Web without any effort. ActiveX lets you link and embed objects into Web pages. Wait just a darned minute! As shown in Figure 8-8, your Web page will now display spreadsheets, graphs, and data created within Excel. The actual living, breathing spreadsheet is inside your Web browser! Pretty cool, huh?

Well, there's one catch. This only works on Microsoft Windows machines. Yes, for better or worse, the operating system from Redmond is required to view ActiveX documents. Moreover, ActiveX works only within Microsoft's own proprietary browser, Internet Explorer. Granted, Microsoft provides an ActiveX plug-in for its archrival, Netscape Navigator, but you can't really expect them to put the same effort and functionality into a Netscape version, can you?

To make things even more Microsoft-centric, ActiveX documents that embed Microsoft objects do so in a pretty clever manner. The object that is inside the Web page is quite literally an Excel spreadsheet. It's just a tad bit smaller than a usual Excel spreadsheet. Because that Excel object is a real Excel spreadsheet, it actually uses the Microsoft Excel executable program to drive it. This means that in order

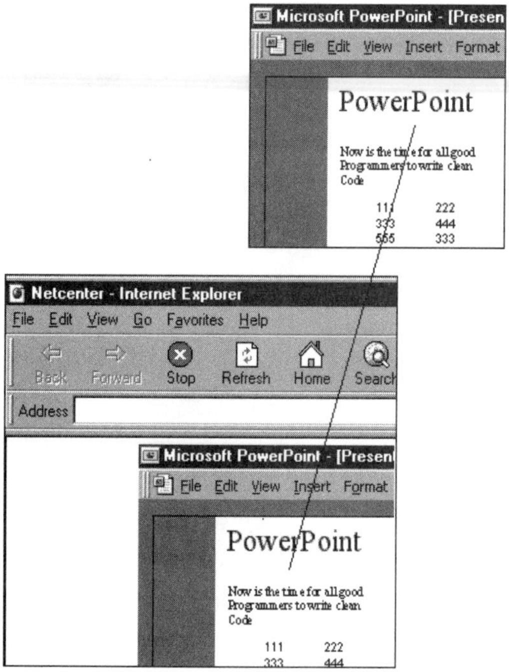

Figure 8-8 ActiveX does for Web pages what OLE did for desktop applications.

to see the object, you must have Microsoft Excel installed on your system so that the Web browser can use the Excel executable. That's right, go out and buy some more Microsoft software. The real problem here is that the "thin client" Web interface that we originally started out with has gotten a little fatter by using Java applets but now has become a full-fledged "fat client" by requiring users to install native applications just to be able to view things that have been embedded in a Web page.

ActiveX Controls

An ActiveX control is a component in the same sense that a Java Bean is. Where we created Java Beans to enable different parts of a dynamic document to talk and work with one another seamlessly, we can use ActiveX controls. Both Beans and ActiveX communicate with OLE, enabling Java Beans to do the same fancy document editing that ActiveX allows. Nevertheless, with Java Beans six months behind ActiveX, Microsoft finally has what it has wanted: the chance to be ahead in the Internet race.

With ActiveX, your controls are free to make several computations so long as they reside within an ActiveX container. A container is the boundary of the ActiveX control. Each control needs a parent OLE component. Microsoft's Internet Explorer serves as an ActiveX container. With Microsoft's plug-in, Netscape Navigator also acts as an ActiveX container.

Once the ActiveX control is contained, it can begin to go about its work in the same way that a Java Bean does. For example, I could have several ActiveX controls embedded within the same Web page. One could be a Java applet, one could be a spreadsheet, and another could be an ActiveX button. The spreadsheet and button could be made to talk the OLE protocol, enabling each of them to compute and exchange data as they wish. The Java applet could gather the information and, because it is fully capable of talking TCP/IP, send the information across the Internet.

ActiveX controls can also start the applications that created them. For example, we created a spreadsheet using OLE and then stuck it inside an ActiveX control. When you view the ActiveX control inside your Web page, or directly on your ActiveX-enabled desktop, the native application will literally be running within the confines of the control.

ActiveX and Java

Part of the hype surrounding ActiveX concerns the future of Java. Anyone who has ever used the language (and we assume that because you are reading this book, you fall in that category) will agree that it is easy, fun, and exciting to finally enjoy programming again. The alternatives of the past (namely C++ and C) were frustrating, difficult, and involved a very steep learning curve. When Java came around with its promise to make computers fun and easy again, most people jumped on the bandwagon instantly.

Sun, in a rare stroke of marketing brilliance, made Java freely available to anyone who wanted it. As a result, in the course of the past few years, Java has become the de facto Internet programming language. ActiveX is not a programming language; it is a component model. Therefore, ActiveX does not threaten Java; it actually improves it! Even though it may seem illogical that Microsoft may improve a Sun product, it brings credibility to a language perceived by some intellectuals as a "toy language."

ActiveX and Java form a very unusual partnership. Nevertheless, ActiveX and Java are complementary technologies. There is nothing wrong with mixing ActiveX and Java especially when the "shop" you a working in is a Microsoft only shop, meaning that you are going to deploy to Microsoft desktops and browsers (such as on an intranet). In cases like this, you might want to use the Microsoft Java Virtual Machine implementation to best take advantage of the special hooks built in the JVM for Windows. To use the underpinnings of the Windows environment using the Standard Java Virtual Machine, one should use the Java Native Interface (JNI, not to be confused with Jini).

Of course, the problem with all of this is that we are using a "closed," not an "open," technology. If we ever plan on deploying our applications on the Internet or on an intranet with a mixture of Mac, UNIX, Linux, and Windows desktops, we will have a problem.

Java Native Interface (JNI)

Including the keyword "native" in the Java Language Specification and subsequent development of the Java Native Interface is an admission on the part of Sun Microsystems that the goal of "100% Pure Java" is not always possible or necessarily desirable. When you write applications, there will always be times when you must determine the requirements for a set of users who will, for one reason or another, be forever working on Windows-based machines. For these users and for situations wherein performance-oriented requirements exist (that just can't be met by Java), we need to have another option.

There are four options for getting at Windows native code. The JDK 1.0 interface that would let a Java application (no applets) access DLL functions, Netscape's Java Runtime Interface (JRI), Microsoft's Raw Native Interface (RNI), and Sun's Java Native Interface. Of these options the JNI is the only one that provides binary compatibility across multiple versions of the JVM.

If you find yourself in a situation that requires access to Windows binaries, refer to Rob Gordon's excellent book *Essential JNI* from Prentice Hall PTR.

Summary

ActiveX and Java Beans will compete toe to toe for a place on every Windows developer's platform. Even though Microsoft locks you into the Windows environment, Beans is an open, more flexible Java-based alternative. While the component models from the "big two"—Microsoft and Sun Microsystems—contend for being the components model of choice for the Internet, the Object Management Group (OMG) has announced its own component model for CORBA. The plot thickens.

Summary

The software war among Apple, Sun, and Microsoft, which was alluded to in the first edition of this book, is all but over, OpenDoc all but disappeared after the alliance of companies at its core fell apart a couple of years ago. With the demise of OpenDoc the "CyberDog," these efforts never came to fruition. What led to this? One of the big factors is the growing popularity of the eXtended Markup Language (XML). XML is the heir-apparent to HTML and will bring a level of functionality to browser-based GUIs that will be unparalleled. Because XML is based on Standard General Markup Language (SGML), it would not surprise me in the least to see a flavor of XML that will parallel the Dialog Tag Language (DTL) that IBM had originally embedded in OS/2. One of my favorite parts of OS/2 was DTL because it was way ahead of its time; it allowed the definition of user interfaces for desktop applications via a tag language. When the Web and HTML became popular, the vision of DTL appeared in the form of the HTML form tags. It will only be a matter of time before we will use XML to define our Java Beans and to compile the XML into the Beans byte codes.

It is interesting to note that in the current JDK 1.2 release all the AWT and Swing components are implemented as Java Beans.

Chapter 9

Application Servers

▼ HOW DID WE GET TO HERE?

▼ WHAT IS AN APPLICATION SERVER?

▼ SOME EXPLANATIONS

Examining what is happening in the information systems (IS) shops of corporate America, we see a move away from the deployment of traditional client/ server applications and a large shift towards multitier, Web based computing. Delivery of application functionality in the form of desktop-based, fat client tools is being dumped in favor of server-generated, lightweight HTML-based user interfaces that derive their presentation layer from the lowly Web browser (that is already installed on almost every desktop in corporate America). The browser used as an application presentation engine and user input collection device (rather than a processing engine) coupled to a powerful server architecture that provides processing power and a multitier approach to data connectivity provides a very powerful and versatile application delivery vehicle.

How did we arrive at this point? The answer is through the evolution of Web-based computing. In the early days of the Web (i.e., the not too distant past) we started to develop applications that used the Web browser as the application presentation layer speaking via the HyperText Transfer Protocol and the Common Gateway Interface to programs being run on the Web server at the request of a browser page. Voilà! Our Web server had become an application server; now instead of delivering content to a Web browser, the Web server was delivering an application.

Many of the early Web-based applications were pretty simple, consisting usually of an HTML form and a script run by the Web server (these came to be known as CGI scripts) to read data returned to the Web server and act on it. As time progressed and applications became more sophisticated, we became quickly aware of the limitations of using the stateless HTTP and came up with a number of mechanisms (hidden variables, cookies, . . .) that allowed us to make our applications more stateful and take on the guise of traditional client/server applications without having to resort to the heavyweight client model.

Ahhh, life was good and computing was even better. As the Web became more popular and we (corporate America) decided that we needed to take commercial advantage of the new application deployment platform, we began to notice that there were some flaws in our new paradigm. First, applications that operated well for a few users didn't do so well when we tried to scale them to thousands and tens of thousands of users. Second, there was this ever-present pain-in-the-neck of state preservation problem. Determined not to let happen to Web computing what happened in client/server computing, we started to examine our new environment and make improvements where needed.

One of the first things that we noticed was that the CGI scripts that we were using to add the processing power to our Web pages was a pretty bad way to do it. There were a number of options to increasing the throughput. We could get rid of those shell and Perl scripts and move that processing to a compiled language (C or C++) that would run faster and free up processor horsepower; or we could take the tried-and-true approach to automotive repair philosophy and "jack up the radiator cap and drop in a new car" (i.e., if our current machine is too slow, save the software and buy a bigger, more powerful machine).

Both of these approaches have severe flaws. Replacing the scripts with compiled versions only masked or postponed the real problem and actually introduced a few problems of its own. The real problem was in the way that the scripts were being run (i.e., every time a script was called for, the Web server started up a new process to run the CGI program on, and we quickly ran out of system resources). Another problem was that, if we weren't religious about memory management and I/O programming, it was relatively easy for a hacker to figure out how to overload an I/O buffer and get the process to crash hard enough to bring down the entire site or accidentally give over control of the machine to the hacker.

Along comes Java and server-side programming, and developers recognize that, because of the Java security model and its lightweight nature, it would be an ideal tool for doing server-side programming.

Servlets are born. The first servlets showed up as *.BAT* files and scripts that loaded the Java Virtual Machine and ran the Java code as a CGI program would be run. The performance and scalability of these servlets is pretty bad due to having to load so many copies of the JVM, but the stage was set for the servlet API. It was only a matter of time until the release of the all-Java Web server and the integration of the JVM into OEM Web server products like Netscape's Enterprise Server that true server-side servlet computing came on the scene.

As we looked more seriously at the Web as an application deployment platform, a new type of program called an application server started to appear. The application server started out as an application that could be run in conjunction with our Web server and would do things like state management and legacy system access. Little by little, the application server architecture took on the general functionality shown in Figure 9-1. Currently there are more than 40 products on the market that all claim to be application servers.

The following common threads run through all the application servers currently on the market and should be a help when comparing marketing information from the various vendors:

1. Inclusion of a high-performance Web server or the ability to integrate any of the popular currently available commercial Web servers easily.

2. Integrated development environment or the ability to integrate any of the commercially available development IDEs.

3. The ability to interface with Enterprise Resource Planning (ERP) systems especially SAP, BAAN, or PeopleSoft.

4. The ability to interface with Transaction Processing (TP) monitors.

5. Support for stateless and stateful database connections.

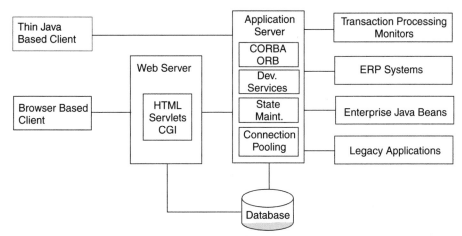

Figure 9-1 General application server architecture.

6. Connection pooling of database connections.

7. Access to legacy applications and legacy databases.

8. Massive scalability through hardware replication and load balancing.

9. Automatic fail-over capability in the case of a processor failure.

10. Support of the Enterprise Java Beans Specification.

This is shown in Figure 9-1.

High-Performance Web Servers

Web servers have always played a central role in Web-based computing. In the past they were used to serve content to users and provide the capability to run CGI scripts to create dynamic Web pages with database connectivity. Newer Web servers have integrated JVMs and support the full servlet API, making the use of CGI programming unnecessary. This new breed of Web servers also support remote administration via a Web-based GUI interface and even the administration of multiple servers through the same GUI.

Integrated Development Environment

Because the environment provided by application servers is so rich and supports so many APIs, OEMs all provide Integrated Development Environments to help the end user create applications that are timely and supportable. Included with the tools are source control and configuration management systems.

Interfacing to Enterprise Resource Planning Systems

Today the darling application of the corporate IS shop is the ERP system. One of the things that was painfully (and expensively) pointed out to IS Managers over the last 3 years (Y2K preparation) was how terribly dependent corporations were on old legacy systems written 20 and 30 years ago in COBOL and PL/1. One of the options to becoming Y2K compliant was to move the corporate computing model away from the hodge-podge of legacy applications and databases that had grown up with the corporations that fostered them and toward a relatively standardized model that had been developed relatively recently under the guise of ERP systems.

ERP systems, like SAP, BAAN, and PeopleSoft, are based on a large database model of the entire corporation. After all, most corporations have a similar make-up (i.e., an accounting organization, accounts payable, accounts receivable, payroll, personnel, manufacturing, planning, etc.). If all these functions could share a common database and a common set of processes and procedures, the corporation could run more effectively and efficiently.

Since one system can never meet all possible needs, application servers provide certified tools that allow interfacing with ERP systems in such a way that application server–based programs will be well behaved and supported even through new releases of the ERP system software.

Ability to Interface with Transaction Processing Monitors

One of the applications that was developed during the client/server paradigm of application development was a program called a Transaction Processing (TP) Monitor (BEA Tuxedo is the most notable of these). TP Monitors are systems that handle high transaction-rate-based jobs like airline reservation systems, banking systems, and such. To be able to interface with these systems from the Web is crucial to e-Commerce.

Support Stateful Applications

One of the hardest things about programming the Web has always been how to make stateful applications. In our attempt to do this, we have tried every trick we could come up with from cookies to hidden variables. Application servers take a more rigorous approach by actually maintaining state databases of our applications. In most cases, databases are maintained in two forms: a state that can be recovered after a reboot (persistent via a DBMS) and a state that cannot be recovered after a reboot (in memory data caching).

Connection Pooling of Database Connections

One of the lessons we learned from the two-tier client/server model of database programming is that databases are not good connection managers and that making the initial connection to the database in many cases takes longer than the actual database activities we are trying to perform. To help improve overall database performance, the application server will open a number of database connections at startup and then manage those connections for the various applications that are using the database(s). This way the cost (time) of establishing the database connections is only incurred once (at startup). Once opened, the connections are never shut down; instead, they are shared by the applications. After all, a connection is a connection is a connection . . . and Web-based applications do not usually need a connection for more than the current query.

Access to Legacy Applications and Legacy Databases

There are a number of ways to provide access to legacy system applications.

- One is to incorporate a terminal emulator in the form of a Java applet as one of the client interfaces provided by the application server and actually allow the end user to interact with the legacy system.

- Another is to provide a screen scraper that allows the data portion of a legacy screen to be scraped out and placed in a dynamic HTML form or a Java applet.

- A more common way is to place a CORBA wrapper around the legacy system and provide a new CORBA (Java or C++) client for the user to interface with the application through.

For access to a legacy database, the approach is somewhat dependent on the database and the hosting operating system. In many cases, we are looking at IBM mainframes and DB2, VSAM, and IMS databases. Because these databases are based on IBM's proprietary SNA (System Network Architecture) connectivity scheme rather than TCP/IP, one requirement is the installation of a gateway between the two systems (TCP/IP and SNA) that is responsible for the protocol conversion between the two systems. Because DB2 is a relational database, JDBC drivers can be installed on client workstations; they will allow normal JDBC access to DB2. VSAM (Virtual Sequential Access Method) is an older, flat file data structure in which many legacy databases are maintained. In many cases, these databases should have been moved to DB2 years ago, but the "if it isn't broken don't fix it" mentality prevailed. IMS is a database model from the 1970s that viewed a database as a hierarchical structure and provided its own database programming language to support it. For VSAM and IMS databases there are tools from IBM and companies like Intersolv and Cross Access that allow these databases to be treated as relational tables. Because of the number of gyrations that these have to go through to make everything look like a table, the performance is limited.

Scalability Through Load Balancing

Scalability is the ability of a system to meet the performance demands of an increasingly larger user community. A single processor, no matter how fast, can only service a finite number of user requests with some degree of performance. Adding multiple processors to a box can buy some additional performance but not really increase the overall scalability of the overall system. To increase the scalability of the system in a meaningful way requires the introduction of additional processing units (boxes), one of which is to be used as an HTTP dispatcher. All requests will come in to the dispatcher, and the dispatcher will direct the request to the least busy box in the cluster of processing units. Many Web sites today handle more than a million requests a day using old hardware (66-MHz 486s and 100-MHz Pentiums) and by running large clusters of them (20–25).

Automatic Fail-Over

To add some redundancy to the system and eliminate a single point of failure, dispatchers can be set up on multiple machines and deployed so that if one dispatcher dies the other dispatcher will take over the load of both until the failed processing unit can be put back in service.

Support of the Enterprise Java Beans Specification

The latest set of acronyms added to the list of things that application servers do and/or comply with are Java 2 Enterprise Edition and Enterprise Java Beans. Java 2 Enterprise Edition is the latest release of the Java Platform from Sun Microsystems and contains all the previously missing pieces of Java to make it a serious contender for Enterprise-class applications. Things like the new security model, JNDI (Java Naming and Directory Interface), JDBC 2.0, and RMI-IIOP to name a few, complete the suite of tools that make Java capable of fulfilling the goals of Enterprise applications development.

Summary

Although not strictly a Java topic, application servers are playing and will continue to play a large part in the development and deployment of large, scalable applications for the enterprise. Many of the application server vendors are taking the all-Java route and are doing well (the Silverstream Application Server and the BEA Weblogic Application Server are examples of all-Java application servers). As more and more functionality has been built into the application server, it is no longer something to add to a Web server but something that has had a Web server added to it and taken on an identity of its own.

Jini: Sun's Technology of Impromptu Networks

The introduction of the iMac was no small factor in Apple's rejuvenation. It was also a revolutionary computer. The iMac's success came from its appeal to regular folk, those ordinary people who cared less about the size of its hard drive and more about the color of the case. In short, the iMac was marketed (and purchased) as an appliance. People could buy it, bring it home, plug it in, and it just worked. It worked right out of the box, no hassles, and no complicated instructions. That concept is what Jini is all about.

Jini is Sun's solution for creating common, everyday, networking appliances that just "plug and work." I use the word "appliances" instead of "application" because an appliance is a simple piece of technology that everyone can use. An application, on the other hand, is a technology that often requires development of a skill set in order to use it productively. Few people would consider the ability to start a dishwasher a skill set.

Examples of Jini

So what is Jini? Jini is a paradigm for how the service providers and service consumers should interact on a network. It is a layer of architecture that is dependent on a variety of other pieces of architecture as described in Figure 10-1. Sun's current implementation of Jini, Jini 1.0, is written completely in Java, but not all pieces of the Jini architecture must be. The best way to introduce Jini is to describe the technology in use. Sun's promotional literature is full of interesting examples, and examples of the technology aren't hard to dream up. The most common example is that of a printer.

ABC Industries recently doubled the size of its office staff from 12 people, to 24. Laura Cogswell, ABC Industries office manager, noticed a situation brewing over the limited printing resource of their single laser printer. The lines were long, and the printer never seemed to stop spitting out paper. It was obvious that ABC Industries simply needed an additional printer.

Laura took a trip down to the local office supply depot where she casually purchased an additional name brand laser printer. Getting it back to the office, Laura took it out of the box, plugged in the power chord, plugged in the networking cable, and switched it on. Within moments, the printer came to life and began printing out reports. The two printers continued to work side by side satisfying the printing needs of ABC Industries. Several members of the office staff were impressed to find the new printer, which they hadn't even known existed there when they clicked the print icon, had automatically printed their reports. How was this possible? Both the printers, and the PCs of ABC Industries, were "Jini Enabled."

What's important about the last example? Well, the first and foremost thing is that Laura is not an IT specialist. She's an office manager. The same person who might

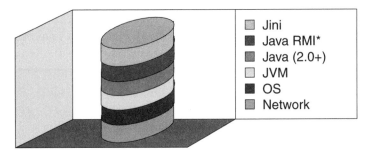

*The Jini specification does not require RMI; Sun's implementation of Jini does. Technically, Jini is a specification and doesn't require Java at all. The only available implementations of Jini use Java, however.

Figure 10-1 The layers of architecture needed by Jini.

arrange to purchase copier paper, a fax machine, or even break-room supplies. She treated the printer problem the same way she might have treated a problem with a refrigerator that was too small, or a coffee machine that didn't make enough coffee. She went out and got another one, plugged it in, and went about her business. She did not have to deploy a set of drivers across the company's computer system (incidentally consisting of UNIX boxen, Macintoshes, and Windows machines), nor did anyone have to set up the new printer on his or her PC.

The rest of the chapter is dedicated to explaining the basics of Jini and a little about how Jini can make this possible. This chapter is, by no means, meant to be an in-depth study of Jini, but it is intended to provide an introduction to the technology and a glimpse at how to get started with it.

Where Did Jini Come From?

Jini is Sun's continued dedication to the founding principles of a language called Oak. Oak was intended as a platform-independent, simple, object-oriented approach to working with "smart appliances," like set top boxes, clocks, microwaves, cell phones, you name it. The problem was that companies in the smart appliance market found themselves spending lots of time and money supporting a myriad of software environments. It seemed that each appliance they developed used different hardware that either had its own software environment or was different enough from the "standard" programming environments to require individual attention.

Oak was intended to help companies deploying different smart appliances concentrate on the appliance itself and not on the overhead of the software environment. Oak was supposed to be write once, run anywhere. Sound familiar? It should because out of Oak came Java. Java gained its popularity because it offered platform independence for application developers on personal computers. You can write an application on a Mac and have the exact same code run on a Windows machine, or a UNIX box. Over time, Java technology has become more robust and mature. Sun never abandoned its roots in the smart appliance market. Instead, they are redefining what people think an appliance is, and bringing the full weight of Java (both its strengths and weaknesses) to bear on the genre. Sun's reference implementation of Jini is a software architecture layer that makes extensive use of Java RMI, which makes possible the concept of a "plug and work" network appliance.

Our Working Jini Example

For the rest of this chapter, we will discuss Jini in terms of a single example, that of a Morse code printer. The Morse code printer itself is a small black box out of which come two cables, one for the Ethernet network, and one for power (some networking solutions use standard 60-Hz ac power lines as their medium rather than Ethernet cables. In that instance, we would only need one cable, the power cord!). Also affixed to the box are two large LEDs, one red and one green. Inside our little network printer is a complete JVM with all of the appropriate Java 2.0 and Jini 1.0 libraries. The printer works by translating messages sent to it into "dashes" and "dots" flashed out by the green LED according to the standard Morse code protocol. In this way, a message consisting of "SOS" would cause the green light to pulse three times quickly, three times slowly, and then three times quickly again.

Morse code was invented over a century ago and wasn't originally conceived of for use as a Jini-based print server (although it does work surprisingly well for this). During the course of a message translation, it is possible that a situation could arise that Morse code is unable to account for. In this case, the red LED will flash, indicating that an error has occurred, and the printer will skip the untranslatable characters and continue on.

In our example we will assume that a standards organization has blessed a particular Java interface to network printers and that this interface is well known. Any entity wishing to use the services of the network printer can do so by utilizing this well-known interface. In our example, an ambitious Java programmer has created a simple client utilizing this interface in the hopes of communicating with our network printer.

The idea, of course, is that someone can walk into a room, plug the "Jini'fied Morse code printer" into the network, go over to a computer that was already running and on the network, activate the client application, and be able to immediately print to the new printer. How could this happen? Let's look at Jini's basic infrastructure.

Basic Jini Concepts: "Discovery, Join, and Lookup Oh My!"

In any Jini community, sometimes called a Djinn, federation, or collectives, there exist three main elements: a service, in our example the Jini'fied Morse code printer; a client that consumes the desired service, like our Java PrintClient application; and a Jini Look Up Service (JLUS) that acts as a coordinator to help the Jini client find the Jini service it is looking for. To see how these three Jini elements interact with each other, let's look to our example.

Server

In the beginning, we plug our patented "Jini'fied Morse code printer" into the network and switch it on. At first, it is unaware that anything else on the network exists. Luckily, Jini has a protocol for getting in touch with other Djinn; it's called

Discovery. In our example, Discovery takes the form of a message broadcast to our entire local network asking for any available JLUSs to identify themselves. Each JLUS that hears this broadcast responds by giving our network printer a representative of the JLUS. This representative takes the form of a ServiceRegistrar object. The ServiceRegistrar object works as a proxy to the JLUS. Any work that we want to do with the JLUS we can do by invoking methods on the registrar object.

Figure 10-2 illustrates the concept of Jini Discovery. Here the service finds the local JLUS and obtains an object that functions as an interface.

To simplify things, only one JLUS responds to our printer's discovery effort. In reality there could be multiple JLUSs out there, or none at all! (In the last case, we could include in our service implementation code that would create its own JLUS. For now, we just assume that there will be at least one.)

Next we want to tell JLUS all about the great service our Jini'fied Morse code printer offers so that others can take advantage of our printer's availability. This process is referred to as the Join protocol.

In order to join a Djinn, our service has to do two things. First, it must create and provide a proxy object. A proxy, in general, is an agent through which someone or something interacts with another, a go-between. Here, the proxy object is exactly its namesake. It provides the mechanism through which an interested client will communicate with our printer.

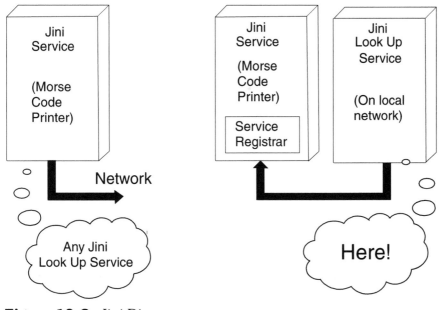

Figure 10–2 Jini Discovery.

The proxy can be any Java object! It could be a full-blown Java GUI application using TCP/IP sockets to "talk" to its server, or it could be an object implementing a simple Java RMI interface. The actual protocol used between the service and the client depends upon the particular implementation of Jini. The interface is defined by whatever the proxy object is. In our example, our printer will use Java RMI to communicate with any interested clients, so the proxy object will be something that implements PrintServiceInterface.

The second thing we should do as part of the Join process is define the set of attributes that our service possesses. These could be anything from defining the name of the printer, or the location of the printer, to expressing all the classes that our proxy implements. Why do this? Well, by providing more information about our service, prospective clients have more information from which to say why our service may or may not be the best for them.

Both pieces of information are packaged up and sent to the JLUS by providing them as arguments in one of the ServiceRegistrar's methods. The JLUS receives these items and stores them for later. This is shown in Figure 10-3.

In Jini Join, as shown in Figure 10-3, our service first constructs a service item describing itself as JLUS and then gives that service item to the JLUS, thus officially joining the local DJinn.

This is all well and good, but what happens if our Jini'fied Morse code printer gets "accidentally" kicked across the room by a frustrated red–green color-blind

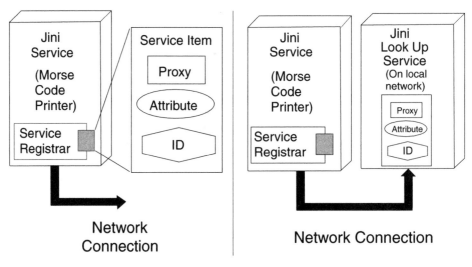

Figure 10–3 Jini Join.

user? Well, in its battered, disconnected state it certainly isn't available to print messages anymore. How does the JLUS know that our printer isn't available?

One possible methodology would be for the JLUS to continuously poll the service to see if it's still alive. The greater the frequency of polling, the smaller the period of uncertainty about the status of a service and the quicker the response of the Djinn as a whole in dealing with the loss of a service. This approach, however, puts a great deal of burden on the JLUS and also creates quite a lot of network traffic.

As Figure 10-4 shows, the Jini Service continually tracks time elapsed on its lease and renews each lease cycle before the expiration of the lease.

Jini actually deals with this by assigning a "lease time" to a service. In an abstract sense, a Jini lease is an agreement between the JLUS and the Jini Service that guarantees that the Jini Service will be up and available throughout the duration of the lease. Jini puts the burden of renewing the lease squarely on the Jini Service, not on the central JLUS. When the lease time period expires, the JLUS will simply remove the information it has about the subject service from availability to the Djinn. It will not, of its own accord, inform the subject Jini Service that the lease has expired. It is up to the Jini Service to enquire about the lease time granted to it by the JLUS. It is also the responsibility of the Jini Service to track the amount of

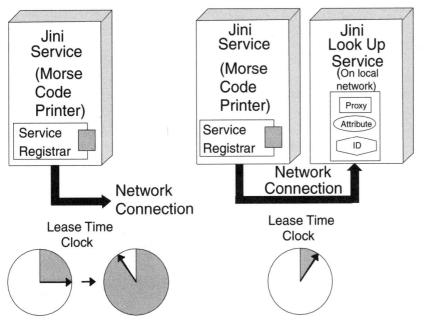

Figure 10–4 Jini Lease Renewal.

time transpired and to renew its lease when appropriate.. This is sort of a feed forward system. The Jini Server pushes the lease renewal effort. This is illustrated in
Figure 10-4.

Client

Now that our printer is plugged in and participating in the Djinn, let's look at Jini
from a service consumer's perspective. Remember that right now, in our example,
a service item describing our Jini'fied Morse code printer exists on the JLUS. Also
remember that the service item contains a proxy object for our Jini-enabled printer.

For the purposes of demonstrating Jini, we have a client whose only job is to find
the Jini'fied Morse code printer and send messages to it. The client doesn't have to
be a stand-alone Java program, however. It could just as easily be part of an operating system. Such integration would provide our plug-and-work Jini printing
capabilities to every application running on that operating system. For the purposes of our example, we will just consider the stand-alone application case.

When the client is run, it has to find the JLUS, just like the service did. It goes
through exactly the same Discovery process the service did, eventually obtaining
a ServiceRegistrar object for each JLUS that responds. Again, in our example, only
one JLUS exists and responds.

Next, the client has the task of using the JLUS to find the desired service. To do
this, the client describes the desired service in any one of several ways. The general method is shown in Figure 10-5. The client provides a template against which
the JLUS can stack up potential services and find the one that's a match. This template describes desired server characteristics including attributes that services
may have defined, such as their name or location, and interfaces that services
must match. Our client could try to look up the service by the "well-understood"
PrintServiceInterface it should implement. In our example, however, the client
actually looks for a match by name. It fills out the appropriate attribute in the template, and gives it to the JLUS by invoking a method on the ServiceRegistrar
object. Again, the service registrar is the interface to the JLUS for the client as well
as the service.

The JLUS then uses the template to find potential matches, which it does in our
example. It then takes the proxy object from the matching service item and
returns that as the search result to the client. Had the search been unsuccessful, it
would have returned a null instead.

The client receives the proxy and then uses it to communicate directly with the
service, leaving the JLUS entirely out of the picture at this point. All future communication between the client and service can now happen directly. In our example, the proxy object given to the client simply uses Java RMI to remotely invoke

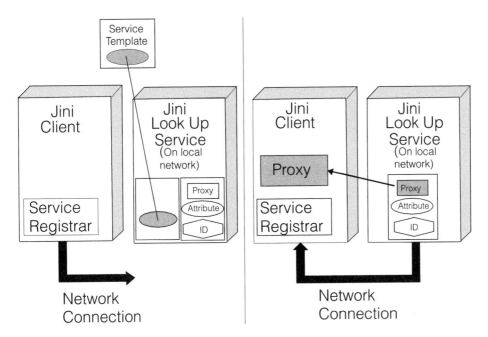

Figure 10–5 The Jini Client constructs a template identifying the desired service, and the JLUS matches this template against all registered service items and returns the proxy object from the matching service item.

the print method on our service. We could have chosen as our proxy to have a little program that would simply have streamed data to our print service through a TCP/IP socket.

The user makes the client send the message "SOS" and watches as the dots and dashes get flashed out on the Jini'fied Morse code printer.

It is interesting to note, however, that the JLUS itself follows a similar protocol. Both the client and the service received a ServiceRegistrar object through which they communicated with the JLUS. The ServiceRegistrar object is the JLUS's proxy!

Getting Started with Jini

Before you can delve into making your own Jini services, clients, or even look-up services, you must overcome a few preliminary hurdles before you set up your development environment. These hurdles are neither overwhelming nor are they trivial, however. They often represent an initial challenge to getting started with Jini.

- Obtain the latest Java SDK for your OS (should be 2.0 or higher).
- Install the Java SDK.
- Set up your Java environment as appropriate.
- Test your Java environment to make sure it works.
- Obtain the latest Jini SDK (should be 1.0 or higher).
- Install the Jini SDK.
- Adjust your classpath as appropriate.
- Test the Jini installation to make sure it works.
- Keep the Jini Service and Jini Client environments independent from each other during development. This avoids accidental and invalid dependencies on resources that otherwise wouldn't be shared.

The Java and Jini SDK are available by download directly from Sun (*http://java.sun.com*). These both include some setup instructions and example applications, which you can run to make sure everything is working. It's just good common sense to make sure you have a working initial setup *before* you start writing and trying to debug your Jini code.

The last point is not so much a setup step as a development consideration. Keep in mind that, when you develop for Jini, you're developing for a distributed computing environment. When the Jini Service is first brought online, it will be completely unaware of the client. Likewise when the client is first brought up, it is unaware of the service. These two entities make initial contact through a JLUS and, before this, can have no shared resources (data files, code snippits, whatever) that aren't supposed to be explicitly built into both.

The resources mentioned at the end of this chapter can lend considerably more help in dealing with these issues than any discussion possible in the space allotted here. I encourage you to peruse them.

Let's Get to the Code!

The following code only looks at the Jini portions of our examples. The Java code comprising the LED device driver and Morse code translation system are not central to understanding how Jini works and aren't presented here. Those interested in further exploring these pieces of software can obtain the original source online at *http://watson2.cs.binghamton.edu/~steflik/jini* or on the accompanying CD-ROM.

Implementing the Jini Server

One of the first stipulations we made about our Jini'fied Morse code printer was that it implemented an agreed-upon well-known interface. In practice, this is currently the most difficult part of Jini's promise. There have been ads showing Jini-enabling digital watches to communicate with toasters and other currently brainless home appliances. The problem here (besides understanding why you would want to do such a thing in the first place) is that this means all the people who make digital watches and all the people who make toasters have all agreed on what their equipment's interface will be. At the time of this writing, there are efforts underway to define such well-known interfaces for printers and what not, but they have not come to a conclusion, so for our purposes, we will assert that such a well-known interface already exists and looks like this:

```
import java.rmi.*;
import java.io.*;

public interface PrintServiceInterface extends Remote  {
    public boolean print(String printString) throws RemoteException;
}
```

This code is standard Java RMI. It defines an interface called PrintServiceInterface that defines the relationship between the client and the service. The client can invoke the method print on any object implementing this interface and pass to that object a string. The object is allowed to pass back to it a boolean or throw a remote exception, that is, the whole interface. The idea, of course, behind this interface is that the object implementing this interface will be the proxy from our printer and that it will take the string passed to it and flash it out in Morse code. If it is unable to do so, for some reason, our printer should inform the client that there was an error by passing a false back as the return value from the method. Hopefully, however, it will be successful and pass a true value as the return value from the method call.

Let's look at the Service code:

```
/*-------------------- Imports -------------------------------------*/
import java.io.*;
import java.rmi.*;
import java.rmi.server.*;
import com.sun.jini.lookup.*;
import net.jini.core.entry.*;
import net.jini.core.lookup.*;
import net.jini.core.discovery.*;
import net.jini.lookup.entry.*;
import com.sun.jini.lease.*;
/*-----------------------------------------------------------------*/

public class PrintService extends UnicastRemoteObject
    implements PrintServiceInterface, ServiceIDListener, Serializable
{
    LightDriver      ld;
    MorseTranslator  mp;
```

```java
// Print Service Constructor
public PrintService() throws RemoteException
{
    super();
    try
    {
        ld = new LightDriver();          // create light driver
        mp = new MorseTranslator(ld); // connect translator to driver
    }
    catch (Exception pse) { pse.printStackTrace();
        System.exit(0);
    }
}
// This method is what satisfies the PrintServiceInterface ,
// requirement it is through RMI that the client remotely calls
// this method to deliver a string to the server.
public boolean print(String printString) throws RemoteException
{
    try
    {
        System.out.print("PRINT SERVICE, Printing: " +
                    printString + " Length= " + printString.length());
        mp.doTranslation(printString);   // morse print message
        return true;                     // return success
    }
    catch (Exception pe) {pe.printStackTrace();
            return false;                // return failure
    }
}
// This satisfies the ServiceIDListner interface
public void serviceIDNotify (ServiceID id)
{
}

public static void main(String[] args)
{
    // this will define our service to the JLUS
    Entry[] serviceAttributes;
    // this object handles discovery & join
    JoinManager joinManager;
    // this becomes our server proxy
    PrintService printService;
    // holds the ID given to us by an JLUS
    ServiceID myID;
    try
    {
        // This creates a security manager, allowing our service to go
        // to tp remote sources for code.  This is the same as in Java
```

```
        // RMI. We need this to download the JLUS ServiceRegistrar
        // Object.
        System.setSecurityManager(new RMISecurityManager());

        //Setup to perform the Jini Discovery and Join Process
        printService = new PrintService();
        serviceAttributes = new Entry[1];
        serviceAttributes[0] = new Name("Jinified Morse Code Printer");

        //Create the JoinManager object, which automatically Discovers
        // and Joins Jini Look Up Services.
        joinManager = new JoinManager(
            printService,               // proxy object
            serviceAttributes,
            printService,               // ServiceIDListner
            new LeaseRenewalManager()   // auto-renews leases
            );
    }
    catch (Exception me)
    {
        System.out.println("PrintService main(): Exception ");
        me.printStackTrace();
    }
  }             // End Main Method
}             // End PrintService Class
```

A Walk Through the PrintService Code. So what's happening here?

Well, what do we know about a Jini Service so far? We know that a Jini Service must go through the Discovery process to find a JLUS. We know that once it's found the JLUS it must go through the Join process to make its services available to the Djinn. We also know that as part of the Join process the service has to provide a proxy object and somehow describe itself to the JLUS so that it can be found by interested clients. Does all this happen here? Yes, let's dissect the code a little.

After the initial includes, we can see that our constructor instantiates a Light-Driver and a MorseTranslator object. These two objects simply provide the mechanics of making a message flash out in Morse code; as mentioned before, we won't discuss them in detail here. What's important is that our service constructor initialize the mechanics necessary to implement the service. No big deal yet.

The next thing we stumble upon as we traverse the code is the Print method. Aha! This is the method that our well-known interface said we had to have; indeed, if we jump back a couple of lines, we see that our class does in fact implement that interface. Examining the message reveals that basically all our service does is pass the string argument to a method on our MorseTranslator object and then pass back a true. Ideally, we should have some way to determine whether our message was printed or not and pass back a true or false accordingly; nonetheless, we satisfied the requirements of the interface. OK, but that's only useful once you are actively participating in the Djinn. We haven't gotten to that code yet, so now what?

Continuing through the code we bump into an empty little method entitled service-IDNotify. It doesn't do anything, so we must need it to satisfy an interface, and sure enough we see that our class also implements the ServiceIDListener interface. What's that for? This is a piece of the Discovery process as we'll see in a moment.

Next we hit the main of our PrintService class. The next significant thing we do here is instantiate an RMI security manager. This is done so that we will be able to download remote code and use it locally. Why would we do that? We need to do that in order to obtain the ServiceRegistrar object from the JLUS.

Next we have to do a few things to explicitly set up for Join the discovery process. We create our proxy object, an instantiation of our PrintService class, and we create an array of Entry objects, although we only hold a single element. These entry objects are used to describe our service. In the very next line we define a name object, which we set equal to what we're calling our service. In our example, this is what is going to be used to identify our service by the client. We'll talk more about that later. For now we have proxy object, and we have our service description.

Finally, we instantiate a JoinManager. What is this guy? Well for us, it's the lazy coder's (and simplest) way to handle all the service's basic Jini responsibilities. Let's look at this.

It takes four arguments in its constructor: a proxy object, the Service Item, a Service-IDListener, and a LeaseManager. There's a lot of powerful stuff all packed into one class! We pass it our brand-new PrintService object as the proxy, which makes sense. We then hand it our attributes, which we knew we had to do, but for the third object we pass our PrintService again. What is a ServiceIDListener anyway?

Well, in Jini, all services are assigned an ID when they first register with a JLUS. The ID that is given to your service is guaranteed to be completely unique. There shouldn't be another service in the whole world that has that same ID. The idea is that your service is supposed to remember this ID and pass it as all the other JLUSs that it may register with as time goes by. In that way, there is a single common way to recognize a specific service regardless of what JLUS a client finds it on. The method for passing this ID back to a service is through a ServiceIDListener. Each ServiceIDListener has to implement the ServiceIDNotify method, which ours does. In reality, this is simply an RMI callback from the JLUS saying, "This is your serviceID." For our example, we don't do anything with this ID. In general, you will.

That leaves only the final argument. Here we create something called a Lease-RenewalManager. As you can guess by the name, that class is all we need to keep our lease fresh and our service part of Djinn. You can see that in one single object we've delegated Discovery (it downloads and utilizes the ServiceRegistrar object), Join, and lease renewal all away! This works great in our simple case, but there are many other circumstances when you will want a more fine-grain control over how your service participates in a Djinn. For that to happen, you won't be able to just use a JoinManager. You will have to do a little more work. Because this chapter is just intended to get you introduced to Jini, we don't cover that here, but all the references mentioned at the end of this chapter can assist with that.

What's after that? Nothing, our main ends, and our service exits. Right? Almost; it turns out that the Join manager creates some threads to handle all the activities that we've just delegated to it. As long as it's alive and active (which is until the power is pulled), our service will continue to run. If you wind up implementing Discovery, Join, and lease managing yourself, you will also have to include a way to keep your service from just exiting. A simple while(true) {} works pretty well.

Implementing the Jini Client

Our Jini Client is a simple stand-alone Java application that finds our Jini'fied Morse code printer service and prints out "Hello World." Somewhere in this code, we will have to create a template to identify the service we're looking for, perform Discovery to find a JLUS, do a lookup on that JLUS to actually find our service, and finally use that service through its proxy.

```
/*------------------------ PrintClient Imports ----------------*/
import java.io.*;
import java.net.*;
import java.rmi.*;
import com.sun.jini.lookup.*;
import net.jini.core.entry.*;
import net.jini.core.lookup.*;
import net.jini.core.discovery.*;
import net.jini.lookup.entry.*;
import net.jini.discovery.*;
/*-----------------------------------------------------------*/

public class PrintClient implements DiscoveryListener
{
    public ServiceRegistrar[] registrars; // holds list of JLUSs'
                                           // registrars
    public boolean JLUSfound = false;      // will trigger lookup
                                           // process

    // This method is required to implement DiscoveryListener.
    // This is how our client will be notified when a
    //    ServiceRegistrar object is received from a JLUS
    public void discovered(DiscoveryEvent ev)
    {
        // Obtain the array of registrar objects from all available
        // LUSs'
```

```
            registrars   = ev.getRegistrars();
            JLUSfound = true;
        }

        // Used to deal with the situation when a JLUS is discarded by
        // our discovery object.  We don't use it here, but more
        // robust code would.
        public void discarded(DiscoveryEvent ev)
        {
            //just satisfying DiscoveryListener interface
        }

        public static void main(String[] args)
        {
            LookupDiscovery discovery;     // discovers available LUS
            ServiceRegistrar ourreg;       // holds the test registrar
            LookupLocator lookup;          // used to lookup service
            Entry[] desiredattribs;        // attributes desired in service
            // a template the service must fill
            ServiceTemplate desiredtemplate;

            Object serviceobject;              // result of the search
            PrintServiceInterface printer;     // handle to hold found service
            PrintClient     printclient;       // This holds the instantiation
                                               // of our client

            try
            {
                // Set the security manager for handling downloaded code:
                // needed to obtain the ServiceRegistrars and the servers
                // proxy object
                System.setSecurityManager( new RMISecurityManager() );

                // Perform Discovery Process for all JLUS containing the
                // public group
                discovery = new LookupDiscovery(new String[] {""});

                // add a DiscoveryListener to recieve the ServiceRegistrar
                // objects our LookupDiscovery finds.
                printclient = new PrintClient();
                discovery.addDiscoveryListener(printclient);

                // create a description for the service we are looking for
                // must have the name PrintService...
                desiredattribs = new Entry[1];
                desiredattribs[0] = new Name("Jini'fied Morse Code
                                  Printer");
                Class[] clArray = new Class {PrintServiceInterface};
                desiredtemplate = new ServiceTemplate(null, clArray,
                                  desiredattribs);
                while (true)
                {                                          // begin while
                    if (printclient.JLUSfound)
```

```
{                                               // begin if found
    printclient.JLUSfound = false;        // reset flag
    System.out.println("PrintClient: " +
                    printclient.registrars.length +
                    "Jini Lookup Service(s) Found.");

    // Go through the complete array of registrar objects
    // lookup on each one to find the PrintService
    // if found print out "Hello World!"
    for (int i=0; i<printclient.registrars.length; i++)
    {  //begin for
        lookup = printclient.registrars[i].getLocator();
        System.out.println(
        "PrintClient: LUS found at " +
        lookup.getHost() + " on port " +
        lookup.getPort());

        // perform the actual Jini lookup
        serviceobject = printclient.registrars[i].lookup
                        (desiredtemplate);

        if (serviceobject instanceof PrintServiceInterface)
        {
            System.out.println("Found a match!\n" +
            "Calling print method: Hello World!\n");
            printer = (PrintServiceInterface) serviceobject;
            if (!printer.print("Hello World!\n"))
            {
                System.out.println("PrintClient: Print Failed!");
            }
            else System.out.println("PrintClient: Print
                Successful!");
        }
        else System.out.println("No match Found. :-<");
    }  //end for
    }   //end if
    }  //end while
}
catch (Exception me)
{
    me.printStackTrace();
}
}  // end main
}  // end client
```

A Walk Through the PrintClient Code. Unlike our PrintServer class, we won't use a single class to handle all our responsibilities. Therefore, it will be the responsibility of our PrintClient class to handle the Discovery and Lookup process directly as well as have the main method. The first hint at how we are going to do this occurs as we see our PrintClient implementing the DiscoveryListener interface. Much as in AWT programming, by implementing this interface, we can use an instance of our PrintClient class to register itself as an event handler. The events we will handle are the two methods of the DiscoveryListener interface, Discovered and Discarded. Discovered is called when a JLUS is found and its ServiceRegistrar object is obtained. Discarded is called when a JLUS we had been aware of, becomes unavailable to us. Since we don't care too terribly much about the second situation in this example, we don't do anything in the Discarded method. On the other hand, the Discovered method is going to be the way our PrintClient will get its hands on the ServiceRegistrar object, so we will want to do something here, and we do.

We obtain the array of ServiceRegistrar objects from the method's only parameter and store it for later use. The next, and last, thing we do here is to set a flag. As you might guess, this will signal other mechanics to do the bulk of the work later.

In our PrintClients main method, we start off by creating placeholders to handle the other things we're going to need to get through the Discovery and Lookup process. Just like the service, we have to extend the security model in order to run remote code in our local VM. Unlike the service, however, we will not just be obtaining the ServiceRegistrar object, but also the print service's proxy object.

Next, we actually go through and perform Jini Discovery. This is done by simply creating a LookupDiscovery object. Just creating it will send it off to find all the JLUSs it can. We don't have to tell it any more information. During the instantiation of this object, however, a new Jini concept called groups comes into play.

Basically, groups are a way to logically organize services together in a Djinn. Without going into great detail, a company may be a single large Djinn but may also decide to define different groups within that Djinn, like the "Engineering Services" group or the "Cafeteria Services" group. Groups are just a way for Jini Services to further differentiate and organize themselves within a Djinn. For our Discovery, we pass an empty string as the argument. This says that we want to look in the public group, which is the default group all services join.

Since we sent the LookupDiscovery object to go out and discover the available JLUSs, we must have a way for it to give us all the ServiceRegistrars it discovers. This is where our PrintClients DiscoveryListener interface comes in handy. We create an instance of our PrintClient and pass it to our LookupDiscovery object as the event handler for Discovered and Discarded events. Now whenever our LookupDiscovery object finds new JLUSs, it will notify us by calling our Discovered method.

Next, we define the service we want to look for. Here again, we create an array of Entry objects with only 1 element. We make this element a Name and initialize it to our "Jini'fied Morse Code Printer."

Finally we get to the driving while loop of our PrintClient class. Here we will loop forever. Each time we loop, we will check the JLUSfound flag kept by our Print-Client to see if there are any targets to perform Lookup on. While there aren't any, we'll loop forever. When we get one, we fall through the if statement and begin to process it.

Now, in a real Jini environment, there just may be multiple lookup services. That's why, when we ask the DiscoveryEvent object back in the Discovered method for a ServiceRegistrar, it actually hands us an array of them. We can query this array, just like any other in Java, and find out exactly how many registrars we found. The answer we get here will depend on how many JLUSs you started up when you went to run our little example, probably one. Our client is a little robust at least and will handle the case of N JLUSs.

We index through the array, just as you would any other. On each element (JLUS ServiceRegistrar object), we perform Jini Lookup. To do this, we pass the Service-Template we made to identify our service by its name as the argument in the reg-istrar's aptly named lookup method. The result will either be NULL, meaning no match, or the proxy object of the first service that matched the template.

We check to make sure that the proxy object implements our well-known PrintSer-viceInterface by using a bit of RTTI, and if it does, we send "Hello World!" out to the printer. If the proxy object doesn't implement that interface (who knows why you would have a service out there calling itself Jini'fied Morse code printer that didn't implement our interface, but you may), we say that we couldn't find a match.

After we have exhausted all the ServiceRegistrar possibilities, we fall out of the four loop and eventually out of the if where we check the JLUSfound flag. Since we reset that flag, we will loop forever until the user kills the process, or our LookupDiscovery Object finds a new JLUS.

Running the Jini Server

Because standard RMI stubs and skeletons are being utilized, this service requires a Web server running to distribute the stub file to anyone who needs it. Don't for-get to set the RMI codebase parameter to point to the URL where the stubs are served from. If this is confusing, it may be helpful to go back and refresh your knowledge of Java RMI. In effect, the PrintService_Stub.class file *is* the PrintSer-vices proxy object.

As an additional note, we will need a security policy file that allows the service enough privilege to be able to download and run code given to it by the JLUS.

Required Files in Service Directory for running:

- LightDriver.class—Light Driver for Linux System
- MorseTranslator.class—Actual Morse code translator
- MorseTable.dat—Table used by MorseTranslator
- PrintService.class—The Jini PrintService
- PrintServiceInterface.class—The well-known interface
- PrintService_Skel.class—The server-side part of the RMI stubs
- policy.all—The Java RMI security policy

Required Files to be served by the service's webserver:

- PrintService_Stub.class—The client-side part of the RMI stubs

To run the server, you must have at least one JLUS running already on your local network, such as Reggie the JLUS that comes with the Jini SDK.

The following commands will start up the Web server to serve the Stub file and run the service.

In a UNIX environment:

```
echo Starting Server Codebase Webserver
java -jar /path_to_Jini/jini1_0/lib/tools.jar -dir
/path_to_service_codebase_directory/service-codebase -verbose
-port 8001 &

echo Starting Service
java -Djava.security.policy=policy.all
-Djava.rmi.server.codebase=http://192.168.1.4:8001/ PrintService
```

You would replace the text in italics with the appropriate path for your system.

In a Windows environment:

```
echo Starting Server Codebase Webserver
java -jar Drive:\path_to_Jini\jini1_0\lib\tools.jar -dir
\path_to_server_codebase_directory\service-codebase -verbose
-port 8001 &

echo Starting Service
java -Djava.security.policy=policy.all
-Djava.rmi.server.codebase=http://192.168.1.4:8001/ PrintService
```

You would replace the text in italics with the appropriate path for your system.

Assuming the appropriate classpath setup, the server should then run. As it is written, the server will execute and remain silent. It would be an easy task to include some code to inform the user that it is up and running. Because the serviceIDNotify method gets called when the JLUS first assigns an ID to the service, a statement could be placed here indicating to the user that a successful join had occurred.

Running the Jini Client

Running the client is a little simpler. Again, we assume that there is a JLUS already running on our local network. Here also, a policy file that allows the client enough privilege to download and execute code from both the service and the JLUS is needed.

Required Files in Service Directory for running:

* PrintClient.class—Our PrintClient class

* PrintServiceInterface.class—The well-known interface

* policy.all—The Java RMI security policy

The following commands will run the client.

In a UNIX or Windows environment:

```
echo Starting the Client
java -Djava.security.policy=policy.all  PrintClient
```

Again, this assumes that your classpaths are set up properly for your Java and Jini installations.

Good References to Get You Started

As mentioned earlier, this chapter is really only an introduction to Jini. I highly recommend purchasing *Core Jini* by W. Keith Edwards, as both an excellent introduction *and* a comprehensive text on this technology. In addition, several kind individuals have made tutorials and examples of their Jini efforts available online. Much of this is equally helpful in getting your own Jini projects up and running. Because the Web is ever changing, I don't include the URLs, but I do encourage people to use their favorite search engine to find and visit these resources:

* Noel Enete's Jini and Java Nuggets

* Jan Newmarch's Guide to JINI Technologies

* Bill Venner's Jini resources at Artima

* All the material available through Sun on Jini, from the FAQ to the specifications.

Concerning the actual Jini'fied Morse code printer, an actual Morse code printer was built at Binghamton University in 1999. The prototype system utilized a simple plastic box containing two LEDs wired to a parallel cable. This parallel cable was connected to a Red Hat Linux box running on an old 486 class PC. The PC acted as the "embedded smarts" of the Jini device, implementing the full Java 2.0 SDK and Jini 1.0 SDK. Though the prototype system was quite large, and thus not "embedded" by any standard, its use as a model was still valid. The operating system, Java and Jini Runtimes, Ethernet, and parallel ports all could have easily been implemented on one of several credit-card-sized PC systems commonly available from embedded systems manufacturers.

It is worth mentioning that Linux was the operating system of choice for this application for a couple of reasons. Linux is a freely available, full-fledged UNIX clone. Linux has been used in a variety of embedded applications. Also, because of the security restraints and cross platform features of Java, it wasn't possible to access the printer hardware directly as an address in memory, as you might in C or C++. However, in Linux, as in other UNIX systems, hardware is accessible as simple files in the */dev* file structure. In this way, Java code could easily be written to twiddle the output bits on the parallel port (/dev/lp1) in exactly the same manner as writing to a file! This made the entire task of writing a "device driver" in Java trivial.

Summary

In summary, most basic Djinn consist of a JLUS, a service provider, and a service consumer. Both the service provider and consumer must use the JLUS as a middleman to coordinate initial contact between them. Once contact has been made, however, they do not need to use the JLUS to communicate with each other. Direct service to client communication is handled through the services proxy object, which is given to the JLUS by the service, and obtained by the client from the JLUS. This client can be anything from a full-fledged, stand-alone Java GUI to a simple RMI client that implements a "well-known interface." Jini's mechanism for removing services that fail is through leasing. It is the responsibility of the service provider to maintain its lease with the JLUS. The JLUS will not usually inform the service that its lease has expired. These are the basic concepts of Jini.

Chapter 11

JMX/JMAPI: Java Management API

▼ WHAT IS NETWORK MANAGEMENT?

▼ MODIFYING CLIENTS FOR JMAPI

▼ MODIFYING SERVERS FOR JMAPI

Since the original publication of this book the Java Management API has been renamed Management Extensions and placed under the Java Community Process. In June 1999 at SuperComm '99 Sun Microsystems announced the availability of the Public Draft of the Java Management Extensions (JMX) specification. Sun and a number of leaders in the field of enterprise management—Powerware, IBM, Computer Associates, BullSoft, TIBCO, and Xylan—jointly developed the specification.

JMX is built on the JMAPI foundation and draws on Sun's experience with the Java Dynamic Management Toolkit (JDMT). The JDMT has been out and in the hands of developers for the last 2 years and has been proven to provide the tools for building distributed, Web-based modular and dynamic solutions for managing devices, applications, and service-driven networks.

The JMX Draft Specification can be downloaded from *http://java.sun.com/ aboutJava/communityprocess/first/jsr003/index.html*. What follows is the original book's discussion of the JMAPI, which, for the purposes of this book, should still be appropriate and informative.

The Java Management API as originally released was a heavy-duty implementation of the Solstice suite of network management tools that come bundled with Sun Microsystems' Solaris operating system. Even though JMAPI does not require Solaris, it can help you to bring the power of Solstice to your operating environment. Your Java objects can be ensured of some semblance of stability if you provide a means by which your applications can be monitored by a "neutral third party." If your applications go down, JMAPI can help you bring them back up. At the heart of networked communication is the need for the reliability that JMAPI can help provide.

In this chapter, we cover network management and show you how to introduce a management scheme for your clients and servers. Also, we touch briefly on how and when to manage your objects. The concept of network management is discussed in short, with emphasis on the needs of a management API and how those needs are met by JMAPI.

What Is Network Management?

At first glance, a book about Java networking does not appear to need a chapter on network administration. After all, system administrators are hired by most organizations to ensure that a network stays up and running. Most of the time, however, system administrators are presented with a horrendous number of different tools with which to do their job.

To make matters worse, these tools generally have no relationship to one another and have vastly different user interfaces. For the system administrator, this amounts to a significant amount of frustration. For the organization for which they work, this amounts to a significant amount of money spent on training.

What is needed is a simple set of tools that can be used to build a homogeneous environment for the administrator. If the tools have a common interface, then the system administrator needs to learn only the basics of one tool to understand the others. The Java Management API, or JMAPI, provides a robust environment in which you can create administrative tools, provide administrative functionality, and modify your regular Java objects so that they can be administered by the JMAPI.

As the Internet grows, and as programming the Internet becomes more and more accessible, the need for complex network management will be apparent. If you create your Java applications with management in mind, you can prepare for the eventual arrival of Internet system administrators.

Network Management at a Glance

A long time ago, the notion of a network did not exist. In fact, computers were connectionless entities that resided in a room and did not in any way talk to one another. Soon, the Local Area Network emerged and computers in the same physical location could be connected to one another. It enabled information to flow from computer to computer, and even for data to be centrally located on another computer. Then, these little networks began to merge with larger networks and, eventually, the Internet developed and connected them all together (see Figure 11-1).

Some day, our children will hear the tale of the birth of the network as they bounce on our knees, but today we are presented with a very adult problem: how to make sure each one of those computers stays up and running and how to fix them when they do break. This is the high-pressure world of network administration.

To complicate the matter further, network administrators often are asked to handle software concerns as well. To facilitate this, several protocols that hook into applications and determine and/or fix their health were developed. Once again, network administrators are called on to fix ailing applications and bring them back to a usable state.

As Java applications become more and more popular, and JavaStations and the Java operating system gain greater acceptance, a burden will be placed on network administrators to ensure the reliability of applications and the hardware on which those applications run. To assist with this matter, Sun's Solstice network administration group put forth the Java Management API. The JMAPI will be discussed in detail in the next section, but for now we concentrate on traditional network administration problems and how they relate to Java.

Simple Network Management Protocol

One of the protocols created by the Internet Engineering Task Force to assist with local and wide area network administration is the Simple Network Management

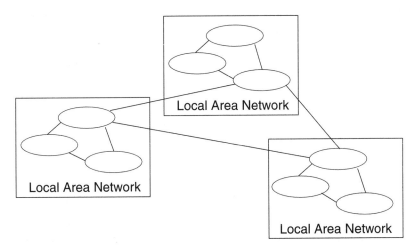

Figure 11-1 The growth of connectivity among small networks eventually gave rise to the Internet.

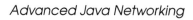

Protocol. SNMP has several advantages over its competitors; chief among them is its ease of use. By setting up something called an SNMP trap, network administrators are able to identify crucial components, protect them, and give themselves a means by which to be notified when the component fails.

SNMP exchanges information between the manager application and the managed component through something called a Protocol Data Unit (PDU). A PDU contains information about a component and is sent over a network connection to the manager application. The application can read the PDU and determine the health of the component. PDUs usually contain information about an application's name, type, and current state. The SNMP trap we referred to is actually a form of a PDU.

SNMP is in wide use today. Chances are high that your network connection to the Internet uses SNMP in one form or another to maintain its integrity. SNMP manager applications are monitored by network administrators who can determine if and when a component fails and from there arrive at a solution to the failure fairly quickly.

It is important to understand that we refer to SNMP in "application" space. The truth is that SNMP can be incorporated within applications themselves. In so doing, a network administrator can pinpoint the exact causes of failures because he or she has a direct hook into the code that failed. In a moment, we will see how Java programmers can create similar applications by using JMAPI rather than SNMP.

The Unique Management Problems of Java

One of the biggest problems encountered with incorporating SNMP into Java is that SNMP is not Java. Java is a wonderful language, with great ease-of-use features. We want to be able to deploy large-scale Java applications both over the Internet and within our corporate intranets. In order to do so, and still have control over network administration, we must have a way to hook into Java code and obtain information about it.

In the next few sections, we will examine the JMAPI closely and learn where it can be used appropriately when deployed Java applications are created. As the language gains more acceptance, as Java hardware becomes more and more prevalent, and as applications that are written in Java exclusively are shipped, some form of Java management mechanism must be developed and used if our networks are to maintain a semblance of integrity.

Network Administration Overview

Network administration is often the underemphasized aspect of the Internet revolution. Without a coherent network administration strategy, all networked applications will fall apart, and the network backbone will break. It is because of the importance of this that we will undertake a discussion of its relevance to Java network programming.

Modifying Clients for JMAPI

The client code that is included as part of the Java Management API consists of a series of RMI clients that interact with managed object servers. These RMI objects enable you to communicate seamlessly with the object your client is designed to manage. Your client should be able to affect the performance and activity of the server, provided the managed object follows the JMAPI architecture and implements its core objects.

The JMAPI client architecture also consists of what can only be called a user interface bonanza. From pie charts to line graphs, lists to graphical lists, icons to animation, the JMAPI's Admin View Model (AVM) is nothing more than a layer on top of the Abstract Window Toolkit. In so doing, the AVM is, like the AWT, completely platform independent and AVM does not rely on any windowing system to function.

AVM Base Classes

The AVM base classes are, as we discussed, an extension of the AWT. They implement several components, including image buttons, scrolling windows and panels, toolbar, image canvases, dialog boxes, and things you can do while your application is busy. There are also several generic tables, HTML browsers, and chart objects for you to use as you see fit. We will not show you how to use each of these individually because they are used the same way the normal AWT classes are used.

AVM Help Classes

The AVM help classes provide a general-purpose help utility for application programmers. By using the AVM Help functions, your application's help documentation could be used just as easily by other, non-JMAPI, applications and vice versa. Why duplicate documentation efforts when the JMAPI can assist you in creating a uniform documentation structure? AVM help documentation is nothing more than HTML with a few JMAPI authoring tags sprinkled within it. The JMAPI tags are contained in comments within the HTML documentation, so the HTML documentation can be used elsewhere without giving away the fact that the same text is also used by the JMAPI.

The help classes consist of four modules. The first of these modules is the UI-based Table of Contents and Navigator. The TOC/Navigator allows you to survey your documentation and build a hierarchical list of the topics contained therein. It uses the authoring tags within the documentation set to determine the arrangement of the contents list.

A documentation generator also is included to assist you in creating indices, glossaries, and even table of contents files. The documentation generator (jmapidoc) acts on the HTML file, parses the authoring tags within it, and spits out a series of HTML files that can be used by the Help Navigator.

The third module is a series of help files built by the JMAPI documentation generator and referring to the JMAPI itself. This way you can pass on information about how JMAPI operates as part of the documentation for the ManagedObjects you create. A set of help templates that you can fill in yourself is included along with the standard JMAPI help files. They will help you get started with building documentation for your objects.

Last, a search engine is included with the AVM help utilities so that end users can find the information you have created for them quickly.

Managed Object Interfaces

Let's say we have a series of objects that model each individual employee in our large, monolithic corporation. Traditionally, the solution to poor employee morale is more management. Therefore, to improve our employee's morale, we will add a manager.

Our EmployeeManager is based on RMI, so we must include the RMI classes in our file. Furthermore, we must create a StatusObservable object to oversee the object. The StatusObservable object will link our ManagedObject to an event notification mechanism. If we so desire, we can set up a notification link within our client. If any other client fiddles with our employee, we would know about it instantly.

```
public class EmployeeManager
{
    public static void main(
        String args[]
    )
    {
        // our employee
        EmployeeInterface employee;

        // our observable class
        StatusObservable statusObserver =
            new StatusObservable();
    }
}
```

Once we have set up our EmployeeManager, we must go to the ManagedObject-Factory to get an EmployeeInterface object. The first argument to the newObj call is the name of the object, including any Java package containers that are associated with it. The second argument is the name of the object in the name space (in our case "EMPLOYEE").

```
public class EmployeeManager
{
    public static void main(
        String args[]
    )
    {
        // our employee
        EmployeeInterface employee;

        // our observable class
        StatusObservable statusObserver =
            new StatusObservable();

        // create the employee object
        try
        {
            employee = (EmployeeInterface)MOFactoryObj.newObj(
                "sunw.jmapi.EmployeeInterface",
                "EMPLOYEE");
        }
        catch(Exception exc)
        {
            System.out.println("Error in create: " +
                exc.toString());
        }
    }
}
```

Now we must set our employee's attributes. We will create a setTask method and a setName method here and implement them in a few moments. We will then go about adding the object to the management system (in other words, we'll place the employee in our org chart).

```
public class EmployeeManager
{
    public static void main(
        String args[]
    )
    {
        // our employee
        EmployeeInterface employee;
        // our observable class
        StatusObservable statusObserver = new
            StatusObservable();

        // create the employee object
        try
```

```
{
    employee = (EmployeeInterface)MOFactoryObj.newObj(
        "sunw.jmapi.EmployeeInterface",
        "EMPLOYEE");
}
catch(Exception exc)
{
    System.out.println("Error in create: " +
        exc.toString());
}
// assign a task
try
{
    employee.setName("Heath");
    employee.setTask("Throw a touchdown");
}
catch(RemoteException exc)
{
    System.out.println("Error in setup: " +
        exc.toString());
}
// add this client to the list of objects listening
// in on this employee
try
{
    employee.addObject(statusObserver);
}
catch(Exception exc)
{
    System.out.println("Error in addObject: " +
        exc.toString());
}
    }
}
```

There are two operations analogous to the addObject method we just employed. We just as easily could have modified the object and then notified any other observers of this change by invoking modifyObject on the employee. If we wanted to remove the object from the management system, we could invoke deleteObject on the employee. Remember that the clients can set and modify attributes, the servers can use those settings to do their business, and the clients can notify other clients that a change has been made.

Setting Up Notifications

In order to create the notification mechanism in our client, we must implement the MOObserver and create an ObserverProxy within the employee object. We must also implement the update function as required by the MOObserver. The update function will be the callback function. As we have discussed in Chapter 6 on IDL and Chapter 5 on RMI, simply setting up a callback is not enough. We also must create a place for the server to invoke that callback.

```java
public class EmployeeManager implements MOObserver
{
    public static void main(
        String args[]
    )
    {
        // our employee
        EmployeeInterface employee;

        // our observable class
        StatusObservable statusObserver =
            new StatusObservable();

        // create the observer proxy
        ObserverProxyImpl observerProxy =
            new ObserverProxyImpl(this);

        // create the employee object
        try
        {
            employee = (EmployeeInterface)MOFactoryObj.newObj(
                "sunw.jmapi.EmployeeInterface",
                "EMPLOYEE");
        }
        catch(Exception exc)
        {
            System.out.println("Error in create: " +
                exc.toString());
        }

        // add the observer proxy to the managed object and
        // tell it to notify on modifications only
        employee.addObserver(observerProxy,
            ManagedObject.OBSERVE_MODIFY);

        // assign a task
        try
        {
            employee.setName("Heath");
            employee.setTask("Throw a touchdown");
        }
        catch(RemoteException exc)
        {
            System.out.println("Error in setup: " +
                exc.toString());
        }
```

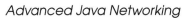

```
        // add this client to the list of objects listening
        // in on this employee
        try
        {
            employee.addObject(statusObserver);
        }
        catch(Exception exc)
        {
            System.out.println("Error in addObject: " +
                exc.toString());
        }
    }

    public void update(
        ManagedObject mo,
        Observation observation
    )
    {
        if(observation instanceof ModifyObservation)
        {
            . . . do our modification stuff here . . .
        }
    }
}
```

When any other manager client invokes modifyObject on the ManagedObject, we get a notification in the Update method. This enables us always to stay in synch with the managed object, even if there are many other clients modifying it at the same time. Now we must set up our servers so that the clients we just created can manage them.

Modifying Servers for JMAPI

The Java Management API includes a set of objects to be used on the server side of a Java networked system. These objects are known collectively as the Administration Runtime Module (ARM). The ARM is the focal point of all management associated with Java applications. Once Java applications include the ARM, they are essentially instantiated objects that can be readily administered.

The various components of the ARM are discussed in the next sections. Each component contributes a specialized function to the overall goal of administering your clients fully. Your Java applications can be plugged into existing system management protocols and software including SNMP, Solstice, and others using the ARM. Once your Java applications can be administered, you can rest easy in the knowledge that your object system can handle network situations beyond your control.

The Admin Runtime Module. The diagram in Figure 9-2 outlines the various components of the ARM that we will soon discuss. All of the components are interchangeable. For example, your application may need to use the Managed-Object routines, but you can omit the Notification module easily should you so desire. Furthermore, your managed applications remain fully scalable and the performance of your system should not be degraded. Figure 11-2 illustrates the modular design of JMAPI applications.

When a JMAPI client is used to communicate with your server, it can inquire as to its status and overall health. This information may take the form of a notification, essentially a callback set up by the client using the JMAPI server, or the client may inquire of its own volition. This kind of communication and data exchange is the heart of networked computing and is required in order to administer the network with which you communicate.

ManagedObject Classes. The ManagedObject class implements a distributed management architecture. It enables multiple clients to obtain links to the same managed server and affect changes on them simultaneously. Its underlying communication mechanism is Java RMI (see Figure 11-3). Using remote method invocations, the ManagedObjects residing on the client side can talk to the RMI ManagedObject server running within the managed server.

In order for a ManagedObject to begin communication with the object it wishes to manage, the management server must be configured. This is done using the RMI paradigm of creating a public interface for the ManagedObject clients to talk to first. Here we are going to create an employee object and attempt to manage it:

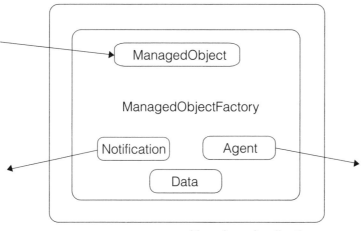

Your Java Application

Figure 11–2 Modular design of JMAPI applications.

Figure 11–3 RMI is the underlying communication mechanism of JMAPI.

```
public interface EmployeeInterface extends ManagedObject
{
    // set and get a task
    public void setTask(
        String newTask);
    public String getTask();

    // set and get the employee's name
    public void setName(
        String newName);
    public String getName();
}
```

As you can see, this public interface inherits from ManagedObject and, therefore, gets all the RMI functionality it needs. In so doing, we need not mention RMI throughout the server explicitly. Indeed, the RMI network code is part of ManagedObject.

Implementing the ManagedObject. Once we have created the interface, we must create the implementation of the ManagedObject class. This adds the functionality to the interface so that we have much more than a skeleton. We will add a constructor and implement the functions prescribed in the EmployeeInterface object.

```
public class EmployeeImpl extends ManagedObjectImpl
                          implements EmployeeInterface
{
    public EmployeeImpl() throws RemoteException
    {
        super();
    }

    public void setTask(
        String newTask
    )
    {
    }

    public String getTask()
```

```
    {
    }
    public void setName(
        String newName
    )
    {
    }
    public String getName()
    {
    }
}
```

In addition, we must implement the performAction methods that map the creation of ManagedObjects using the ManagedObjectFactory of our implementation. Whenever this ManagedObject is created, deleted, or modified using the factory, one of the performAction methods will be called.

```
public class EmployeeImpl extends ManagedObjectImpl
                          implements EmployeeInterface
{
    public EmployeeImpl() throws RemoteException
    {
        super();
    }
    public void setTask(
        String newTask
    )
    {
    }
    public String getTask()
    {
    }
    public void setName(
        String newName
    )
    {
    }
    public String getName()
    {
    }
    public void performAddActions(
        StatusObservable observable,
        CommitAndRollback commitObj
    )
    {
    }
```

```
public void performModifyActions(
    StatusObservable observable,
    CommitAndRollback commitObj
)
{
}

public void performDeleteActions(
    StatusObservable observable,
    CommitAndRollback commitObj
)
{
}
}
```

The perform methods accept an observable parameter. This facilitates notifications, which we will discuss shortly. Perform methods also take a CommitAndRollback object to keep track of all the operations on the ManagedObject. If we encounter any kind of error during the Perform method, the CommitAndRollback object will allow the ManagedObject to backtrack and resume its previous unaltered state. This ensures that the perform methods are always atomic in nature, meaning that either the whole thing is complete or none of it is. In keeping with their implementation, the perform methods are intended for atomic operations (database access, file manipulation, or the like). We have not implemented anything in them here, but they are still required as part of the ManagedObject implementation.

Managed Attributes. The name and task attributes of our employee need not be created in the EmployeeImpl object itself. Instead, we can take advantage of the ManagedObject's attribute mechanism. We can enable the ManagedObject to handle persistence and network-related tasks associated with the attribute for us by storing our attributes within the ManagedObject's infrastructure.

```
public class EmployeeImpl extends ManagedObjectImpl
                          implements EmployeeInterface
{
    public EmployeeImpl() throws RemoteException
    {
        super();
    }

    public void setTask(
        String newTask
    )
    {

        setKnownAttributes("employee-task", newTask);
    }
```

```
public String getTask()
{
    return (String) getAttribute("employee-task");
}
public void setName(
    String newName
)
{
    setKnownAttributes("employee-name", newName);
}
public String getName()
{
    return (String) getAttribute("employee-name");
}
public void performAddActions(
    StatusObservable observable,
    CommitAndRollback commitObj
)
{
}
public void performModifyActions(
    StatusObservable observable,
    CommitAndRollback commitObj
)
{
}
public void performDeleteActions(
    StatusObservable observable,
    CommitAndRollback commitObj
)
{
}
}
```

ManagedObjectFactory Classes. In the previous section, we saw how a
ManagedObjectFactory enables a client to obtain a handle to the server with
which it wishes to speak. The ManagedObjectFactory is no different from the
BMW auto factory in Spartanburg, South Carolina. In Spartanburg, BMWs flow
off the assembly line one by one. Here, our ManagedObjectFactory enables us to
serve up ManagedObjects on demand, creating them on the fly, initializing them,
and readying them for use. As long as our objects implement the ManagedObject
interfaces, they can be created and obtained through a factory.

Notifications. We discussed how notifications are based on the Java Observer
and Observable classes in the client section. Unlike in Chapter 5, "Java RMI:

Remote Method Invocation," supporting notification callbacks in JMAPI involve virtually no effort on our server's behalf. The ManagedObject implementation takes care of tracking the individual subscribing clients and publishing information when necessary. By using attributes as we did earlier, the ManagedObject is able to intercept changes made to the server without the programmer having to supply it with any additional information.

Managed Data. JMAPI also enables you to set up your data structures and member variables so that they can be managed from clients as well. You can allow clients to check on the integrity of the data contained within your remote Java servers by registering your data with the ManagedObject class. The client then could execute a series of steps if it finds something to act on.

Server Agents. Leigh Steinberg is the sports world's greatest agent. He is able to obtain lucrative contracts and signing bonuses for his numerous clients. Similarly, software agents act on behalf of parent applications and obtain information or make invocations when triggered by certain events. The agents are remote objects, so they run in their own process, perhaps on their own machine, perhaps even on a remote network. In so doing, they do not affect the performance of the calling object.

Setting up an agent is similar to setting up an RMI object, but again you must handle much of the RMI overhead.

Summary

Managing your networked applications is a complex and difficult task. The more objects you introduce into your system, the greater your chances are of things going wrong. JMAPI enables you to plug your applications into a predefined management scheme easily. In so doing, you can start your object system and watch from afar how it behaves. By setting up alerts and "traps," you can make sure that your object system alerts a global manager when a problem arises. Together with JMAPI, your applications can be reliable systems of objects.

Now that we've spent a few chapters discussing how to develop systems of objects using software, let's take a moment to examine how Java-based hardware can change your professional and personal worlds. Someday soon, every computer-based appliance will be Java-powered, fulfilling Java's original intention as a language for embedded systems.

Chapter 12

What Are Directory Services?

▼ SOME BACKGROUND

▼ INTRODUCING JAVA NAMING DIRECTORY INTERFACE

▼ USING THE JNDI TO ACCESS LDAP-BASED DATA

Directory services are the services provided by special network databases that are used, much as paper phone books are (i.e., to map names to addresses, phone numbers, and services). The directory is really a distributed hierarchically arranged database made up of keys and associated attribute name/value pairs.

Whether or not you realize it, you use directory services whenever you use the Internet. The Domain Name System is a form of directory, although not as general purpose as the directories we will be discussing in this chapter. DNS provides a UDP-based naming lookup service, namely that of mapping IP addresses to host names and vice versa. Whenever we use our Web browser to retrieve a Web page, IP must use DNS to look up and retrieve the IP address of the host computer that has the page we wish to view. The same is true for FTP: whenever we want to retrieve a file from an FTP server, IP uses DNS to look up the IP address of the host running the FTP server.

Whenever we use our e-mail client, whether it be Netscape Messenger, Outlook, or any number of other e-mail clients (SMTP/POP3/MAPI), the e-mail address books provided are usually based on Directory Services and the Lightweight Directory Access Protocol (LDAP). If you are a Netscape Messenger user and check out directories under your browser preferences (for newer browser users Directory definition is right with the Address Book), you will be able to see the hostnames of a number of commercial directories that allow general access to the public. If you then select your personal address book, export (under the file drop-down menu) it to a file, and then use Notepad or Wordpad to view it, you will notice that each entry is keyed by a set of tags. You should see the dn: tag followed by a set of name/value attributes. Files in this form are in a format known as LDAP Data Interchange Format (LDIF). This file format is used for the batch process loading (and backing up) of Directory Servers. The LDIF file itself is usually populated with information from other data sources (possibly your company's Human Resources Database, the Userid/password database for your Local Area Network, or data extracted from a relational database that keeps track of the hardware configuration of all the workstations in your site and is used via Directory Services by your local helpdesk).

Currently the two most popular uses of directory servers are for user authentication (by userid and password) for accessing limited access Web pages/sites and as e-mail address books for intranet-based address books (for a corporation) and by the large ISPs as address books for their users. In the near future, a big user of directory servers will be e-Commerce applications using the Enterprise Java Beans framework because directory servers are extremely fast. As a special-purpose database, they provide an ideal mechanism for giving persistence to Java objects.

Some Background

The concept and architecture of modern directory services comes to us from the ISO X.500 specification for directory services.

A directory is intended to be a hierarchically arranged database; arrangement of the database is left up to the designer of the Directory Information Tree (DIT). The DIT of a multinational corporation could be arranged a number of ways. It could be arranged hierarchically by geographic location as in Figure 12-1 or by organizational function as in Figure 12-2.

Every directory entry is uniquely identified by an ordered sequence of name/value attributes. The ordering of the attributes is such that it reflects the hierarchical relationship that exists between the attributes. Assume the following naming attributes:

Attr. Name	Meaning
c	Country
o	Organization
ou	Organizational Unit
cn	Common Name

If we use the concatenation of these attributes and their values to identify an entry in the directory, we have defined the entry's distinguished name. Distinguished names are unique, much like the primary key in a relational database table. My distinguished name using the preceding schema would be

`{C=US, O=SUNY, OU=Binghamton, CN=Dick Steflik}`

Figure 12-1 shows this pictorially.

Each node in the tree structure has a distinguished name made up of the list of attributes up to and including that node. The distinguished name for Binghamton University would be

`{ dn: ou=binghamton, o=suny, c=us}`

X.500 defines the directory service as an object (see Figure 12-2), accessed through a set of service ports. Each port is intended to provide access to a specific set of services. Three of the primary service ports defined early in the X.500 development are:

1. **Read Port** provides the ability to read information from a directory.

2. **Search Port** provides the ability to search and list directory information.

3. **Modify Port** provides the ability to add, modify, and delete directory entries.

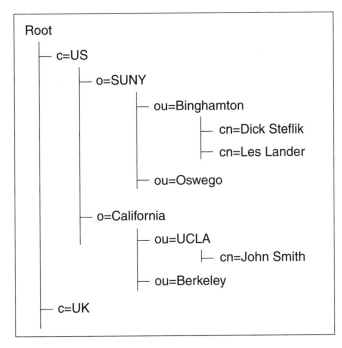

Figure 12-1 Distinguished name structure by geographic location.

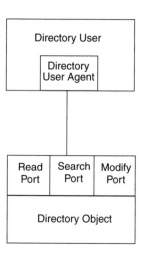

Figure 12–2 Distinguished name structure by organizational function.

To support these service ports, the DAP has a very comprehensive set of protocol-based operations that address all the facilities needed to create and maintain a large distributed directory.

For applications that are directory-oriented but of a scale smaller than what X.500 and DAP were designed for, applications like address books for Web browsers, authentication for Web pages, a lighterweight version of the DAP has been developed. This slimmed down version of DAP is named Lightweight Directory Access Protocol or LDAP for short. LDAP is described in RFC 2251 as an access mechanism to X.500 directories. It is a language-independent description of the protocol operations required to interact with an X.500 directory.

Introducing Java Naming Directory Interface

The architecture of Java Naming and Directory Interface (JNDI) is a Java-specific architecture for accessing a number of directory-based data repositories including LDAP. The Java Interface to LDAP is only one of a number of services provided through the JNDI architectural model shown in Figure 12-3.

If we re-examine the architectural picture of JDBC in Chapter 4, we can see some very real similarities. In Figure 12-3, if we replace "JNDI" with "JDBC," "Service Provider Interface" with "Driver Manager," and "CORBA, NDS, NIS, LDAP, DNS, RMI" with words like "DB2, Oracle, Access, Sybase," we essentially have

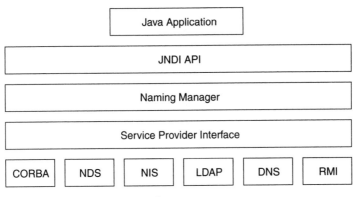

Figure 12–3 JNDI architecture.

the same picture. The architecture is essentially the same after all; directories are really just special-purpose databases, and for each database (datasource) there is a driver or service provider.

The main difference between directories and relational databases is that the directory information model is hierarchical, whereas, the model for relational databases is a set of tables. Relational databases are much more general purpose than directories; because directories are special-purpose, their data model can be tailored to their special-purpose uses. This can make them extremely fast for the types of queries done against them, much faster than the equivalent query using a relational database.

Using the JNDI to Access LDAP-Based Data

The Netscape Directory server comes with a sample LDIF file for the Airius Corporation that can be imported to set a reasonably sized and typically set up database. We'll use this directory to demonstrate the major LDAP features.

Setting up the Airius Directory

To start this exercise, go to the Netscape download site for server software and download a trial copy of the Directory Server. This will get you a 30–60 day copy of the world's best Directory Server (yes, I am a little biased). This won't run on W95/W98 so make sure to download a copy for the appropriate platform you want to run the service on.

Using the Netscape Admin Interface, turn off the instance of the Directory Server that you wish to install Airius on. (In Netscape Suite Spot there is a separate Admin server through which you do all Suite Spot server administration.) Click on the button with the name of the instance you want to administer. When the page for the Netscape Directory Server administration is displayed, click the Database Management button and then click on the Import choice in the left-hand frame. On the Import panel, select the radio button for Airius.ldif and then click the OK button. Once imported, remember to turn the Directory Server back on before exiting the Admin Server.

To test your installation, enter the directory setup screen for your browser (and add the server by, assign it a name, enter the IP Address/Hostname or Localhost (if you are using it locally), enter port 389 as the LDAP port, and enter "o=airius.com" as the search root. Save this and try to query *; you should get an address book filled with the people of the Airius Corp.

The Airius Schema

The following is the first part of the Airius LDIF file. If we examine it a little bit, we can determine the schema of the Airius directory and will start to see the power of the LDIF import/export file format. We will also see that some of the information in the LDIF file can be added/updated through the Administration Interface to the Directory Server and that some of the data is best put in via the LDIF file, even though some of the data is directly put in by the people in the directory.

NOTE: When examining the LDIF file, keep in the back of your mind the fact that lines that are indented by a single space are continuation lines for the preceding line.

```
dn: o=airius.com
objectclass: top
objectclass: organization
o: airius.com
aci: (target ="ldap:///o=airius.com")
 (targetattr !="userPassword")
 (version 3.0;acl "Anonymous read-search access";allow
 (read, search, compare)(userdn = "ldap:///anyone");)
aci: (target="ldap:///o=airius.com")
 (targetattr = "*")
 (version   3.0; acl "allow all Admin group"; allow(all)
 groupdn = "ldap:///cn=Directory Administrator
 s, ou=Groups, o=airius.com";)

dn: ou=Groups, o=airius.com
objectclass: top
objectclass: organizationalunit
ou: Groups
```

```
dn: cn=Directory Administrators, ou=Groups, o=airius.com
cn: Directory Administrators
objectclass: top
objectclass: groupofuniquenames
ou: Groups
uniquemember: uid=kvaughan, ou=People, o=airius.com
uniquemember: uid=rdaugherty, ou=People, o=airius.com
uniquemember: uid=hmiller, ou=People, o=airius.com
```

The line `dn: o=Arius.com` identifies this as the distinguished name for the root of the directory tree and is also a member of the "top" and "organization" object classes; the only information stored in this node is "o: airius.com," which identifies the organization as airius.com.

```
dn: o=airius.com
objectclass: top
objectclass: organization
o: airius.com
```

The next group of lines is really a single line (notice the indention) that identifies the aci (access control information) for the current node (root)

```
aci: (target ="ldap:///o=airius.com")
 (targetattr !="userPassword")
 (version 3.0;acl "Anonymous read-search access";allow
 (read, search, compare)(userdn = "ldap:///anyone");)
```

Letting our imagination run a little bit wild, we can surmise that anyone in the directory has authority to read, search, and compare the userPassword. The second aci:

```
aci: (target="ldap:///o=airius.com")
 (targetattr = "*")
 (version  3.0; acl "allow all Admin group"; allow(all)
 groupdn = "ldap:///cn=Directory Administrator
 s, ou=Groups, o=airius.com";)
```

authorizes anyone in the group with the common name "Directory Administrators" full authority for the tree rooted at "o=airius.com" (target attribute). The next distinguished name:

```
dn: ou=Groups, o=airius.com
objectclass: top
objectclass: organizationalunit
ou: Groups
```

identifies at the next level in the tree an organizational unit called Groups. The addition of the next `dn: ou=Directory Administrators` structures our tree as shown in Figure 12-4. This dn: has additional information in it in the form of the "uniquemenbers," which stores each dn: of the unique members as part of the data for that node.

Examining the node

```
dn: cn=Directory Administrators, ou=Groups, o=airius.com
cn: Directory Administrators
objectclass: top
objectclass: groupofuniquenames
ou: Groups
uniquemember: uid=kvaughan, ou=People, o=airius.com
uniquemember: uid=rdaugherty, ou=People, o=airius.com
uniquemember: uid=hmiller, ou=People, o=airius.com
```

we notice that the uniquemembers tag identifies a dn: that is in another branch of the tree. The unique members are in the ou=People branch of the tree—which implies that the tree actually looks like Figure 12-5.

Notice that to reference information in another branch of the tree all that needs to be done is to identify its dn:.

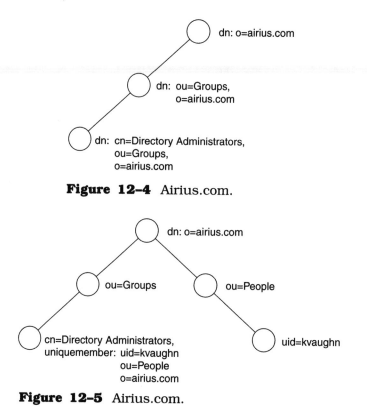

Figure 12–4 Airius.com.

Figure 12–5 Airius.com.

If we examine more of the LDIF, we quickly come to the realization that the majority of the file is taken up with the definitions of the individual people in the company. Let's look more closely at a single entry because it is the meat of the schema and identifies the attributes that we can query against:

```
dn: uid=kvaughan, ou=People, o=airius.com
cn: Kirsten Vaughan
sn: Vaughan
givenname: Kirsten
objectclass: top
objectclass: person
objectclass: organizationalPerson
objectclass: inetOrgPerson
ou: Human Resources
ou: People
l: Sunnyvale
uid: kvaughan
mail: kvaughan@airius.com
telephonenumber: +1 408 555 5625
facsimiletelephonenumber: +1 408 555 3372
roomnumber: 2871
userpassword: bribery
```

Most of the attribute entries are self-explanatory. Now that we understand the schema, let's get on to the business of using the JNDI to access information in our directory.

Connecting

Recall from JDBC that, before we can query, add to, update, or delete anything from a database we must make a connection to it. To do this we need to create a reference to an object that implements the DirContext interface. This is usually done by creating an InitialDirContext object and assigning it to a DirContext variable. To make the connection, we need to pass some environmental information to the InitDirContext object; this is done by loading a Hashtable with a minimum of two pieces of information:

1. The fully qualified name of the service provider to be used

2. The URL (including port number) of the directory server we want to access.

We do this using predefined keys set up in the Context interface.

```
// create a hash table for passing environment info
Hashtable  environment = new Hashtable( );
// identify the service provider
environment.put(Context.INITIAL_CONTEXT_FACTORY,
                "com.sun.jndi.ldap.LdapCtxFactory");
// identify the directory to be accessed
```

```
environment.put(Context.PROVIDER_URL,
                "ldap://mydirectory.com:389");
// get a reference to the directory context
DirContext context = new InitialDirContext(environment);
```

Searching

This gets us a connection to the directory we wish to use, but to do a search we must supply some additional information. A useful search would be to search the directory for uid=kvaughan and display her attribute information.

When searching, we must set up a SearchControls object to tell the search engine the scope of our search. The SearchControls class has three scopes, identified as constants, that we can use depending on what it is we want to search for:

1. OBJECT_SCOPE—Limits the search to the names object.

2. ONE_LEVEL_SCOPE—Limits the search to all of the objects at the same level in the named context.

3. SUBTREE_SCOPE—Limits the search to the named subtree.

```
//set the search scope
SearchControls scope = new SearchControl;
Scope.setSearchScope(SearchControls.SUBTREE_SCOPE)
```

To do the actual search, we invoke the Search method on the DirContext object we created a little while ago. The Search method has a number of overloads; make sure that you read the API carefully, or you may not get the results you are after. For our example, we will need to identify the base of our search, a search filter (similar in purpose to the "where" clause of an SQL select statement), and any constraints we set (SUBTREE_SCOPE). The results from a directory search come back in a data structure called a NamingEnumeration. NamingEnumeration is a JNDI-specific extension of the Enumeration class that allows exceptions to be thrown during enumeration (this implies that it needs to be in a try/catch statement).

```
public static String BASE = "0=airius.com";
public static String FILTER = "uid=kvaughan";
NamingEnumeration result = context.search(BASE, FILTER, scope);
```

If we have done everything right to this point, the search results are waiting for us in the NamingEnumeration. Each entry in NamingEnumeration is a SearchResults object; remember that NamingEnumeration holds objects and that as we take objects out of it we must cast them to the appropriate type.

```
SearchResult  srchresult = (SearchResult) result.next();
```

At this point, we can retrieve the distinguished name from the SearchResult object by using its getName method;

```
String dn = srchresult.getName();
```

This will give us the distinguished name relative to where we rooted our search. To get the entire distinguished name, we must concatenate the variable we used to base our search on

```
String temp = "dn= " + dn + BASE;
```

The attributes are still in the SearchResults object and can be retrieved into an Attributes object using the SearchResults getAttributes method

```
Attributes attrs = srchresults.getAttributes();
```

Recall from our brief introduction to LDIF that any attribute may have multiple values (e.g., a person may have multiple e-mail addresses). What we need to do now is iterate through the returned attributes and, for each attribute found, iterate through the list of returned values for that attribute.

```
NamingEnumeration ne = attrs.getAll();
While (ne.hasMoreElements)
{
    Attribute attr = (Attribute) ne.next();
    System.out.println(attr.getID());
    Enumeration values = attr.getAll();
    while ( values.hasMoreElements())
        System.out.println("    " + values.nextElement());
}
```

The whole example follows:

```
import java.util.Hashtable;
import java.util.Enumeration;
import javax.naming.*;
import javax.naming.directory.*;

public class DirectorySearch
{
    public static String BASE = "o=airius.com";
    public static String FILTER = "uid=kvaughan";

    public static void main (String args[])
    {
        try
        {
            // create a hash table for passing environment info
            Hashtable  environment = new Hashtable( );
            // identify the service provider
            environment.put(Context.INITIAL_CONTEXT_FACTORY,
                        "com.sun.jndi.ldap.LdapCtxFactory");
            // identify the directory to be accessed
            environment.put(Context.PROVIDER_URL,
                        "ldap://mydirectory.com:389");
```

```
                // get a reference to the directory context
                DirContext context = new InitialDirContext(environment);
                //set the search scope
                SearchControls scope = new SearchControls();
                scope.setSearchScope(SearchControls.SUBTREE_SCOPE);
                NamingEnumeration result = context.search(BASE, FILTER,
                                            scope);
                SearchResult  srchresult = (SearchResult) result.next();
                String dn = srchresult.getName();
                String temp = "dn= " + dn + BASE;
                Attributes attrs = srchresult.getAttributes();
                NamingEnumeration ne = attrs.getAll();
                while (ne.hasMoreElements())
                {
                    Attribute attr = (Attribute) ne.next();
                    String attrname = attr.getID() + ": ";
                    Enumeration values = attr.getAll();
                    while ( values.hasMoreElements())
                        System.out.println(attrname + values.nextElement());
                }
            }
            catch (Exception e)
            {
                System.out.println("Exception: " + e.toString());
            }
        }
    }
```

After compiling and running the program, we get Figure 12-6.

This just happens to be what we were looking for. Neat stuff.

So far we've covered most of the basics that we need to be able to start thinking about adding, modifying, and deleting entries to/from the directory. We'll address these topics using code snippets and some associated commentary.

Adding Persons to the Directory

The hardest part about adding a person to the directory, besides creating the data input panel, is creating a class that defines all the attributes that identify the person. This is necessary because, to add the person to the directory, we must bind the person object to their distinguished name.

```
String dn = "uid=mtoad, ou=People, o=airius.com";
Person newperson = new Person("mtoad","Mark","Toad",
                            "ou=Engineering",
                            "mtoad@airius.com");
context.bind(dn, newperson);
```

```
MS-DOS Prompt - EDIT

  7 x 12

dn: uid=kvaughan,ou=People,o=airius.com
givenname: Kirsten
telephonenumber: +1 408 555 5625
sn: Vaughan
ou: Human Resources
ou: People
l: Sunnyvale
roomnumber: 2871
mail: kvaughan@airius.com
facsimiletelephonenumber: +1 408 555 3372
objectclass: top
objectclass: person
objectclass: organizationalPerson
objectclass: inetOrgPerson
uid: kvaughan
cn: Kirsten Vaughan
```

Figure 12–6 Output from the DirectorySearch program.

Modifying Information Already in the Directory

To modify attributes of an existing entry, we first set up our environment and get
a reference to a directory context as we have in the previous examples. After we
have the reference, we create a ModificationItem array to hold the modifications
we wish performed on the item. Finally, we use the modifyAttributes method of
the DirContext object to update the data.

```
ModificationItem[] updates = new ModificationItem[3];
Attribute update0 = new BasicAttribute("roomnumber", "1234");
Attribute update1 = new BasicAttribute("l", "Chicago");
Updates[0] = new
        ModificationItem(DirContext.REPLACE_ATTRIBUTE,update0);

Updates[1] = new
        ModificationItem(DirContext.REPLACE_ATTRIBUTE,update1);
context.modifyAttributes(dn,updates);
```

The DirContext interface also provides the tagged constants ADD_ATTRIBUTE and
DELETE_ATTRIBUTE for effecting the adding and deleting of attribute information.

Removing Entries from the Directory

To delete an item from the directory, we start out as we have previously, by
obtaining a reference to a directory context; then all we do is use the destroySub-
context method of the DirContext interface.

```
context.destroySubcontext(dn);
```

Authentication

One additional thing we must remember for any of the directory modification operations is that, according to our directory ACI (refer to the section on LDIF), only people belonging to the Directory Administrator group had all authority and would be allowed to write into the directory. To do this, the application must authenticate with the uid and password of one of the Directory Administrators. This is done by adding three additional tagged values to the context environment Hashtable.

```
public static String ADMIN = "uid=kvaughan, ou=People,
                                o=airius.com";
public static String ADMIN_PW = "bribery";
   .
   .
   .
env.put(Context.SECURITY_AUTHENTICATION,"simple");
env.put(Context.SECURITY_PRINCIPAL,ADMIN);
env.put(Context.SECURITY_CREDENTIALS,ADMIN_PW);
```

Summary

There you have the five-penny tour of Directory Services, LDAP, and JNDI. As the industry progresses in its quest for ultimately scalable applications that are robust and secure, we will see the Directory Server, LDAP, and JNDI take on larger roles. One of the most exciting of which is the storage of Java objects. This is exciting because Directory Servers are so darned fast that they make an ideal place to store serialized objects produced as part of an application's shutdown process; as part of the application's startup process, it retrieves the object from the server and picks up where it left off. The best part is that this is just the normal way that Directory Servers do business (i.e., binding names to objects).

Chapter 13

Java and Security

▼ SAFETY IN JAVA

▼ THE JAVA SECURITY MODEL

▼ JAVA CLASS SECURITY

▼ ENCRYPTION

▼ AUTHENTICATION

▼ SECURE SOCKETS LAYER

▼ THE GOVERNMENT AND SECURITY

We have all heard that Java is a "secure" programming language. What exactly does that mean? In this chapter, we discuss the unique features of Java that make it the ideal choice for distributed network programming. Furthermore, we will discuss the nuances of the applet host security model, as well as how security is handled from within your Java applications.

We will also touch very briefly on Internet security and some of the alternatives you may want to explore in your own networked applications to make them safe for cross-network transmission. We begin our examination with the topic of cryptography. The primary goal of cryptography is to provide data privacy, but, as we will see, cryptography can be used to provide other essential security principles including nonrepudiation, data integrity, and access-controlled authentication. We will then look at the issues surrounding authentication, a security process that attempts to identify a participant (user, server, and applet) transaction.

Safety in Java

When we refer to Java as a safe language, we are referring to the fact that you cannot "shoot yourself in the foot." There are no memory leaks, out of control threads, or chance of ending up in the dark spiral of C++ debugging. Make no mistake—Java is a powerful language, and you will always end up with the possibility of sitting in an infinite loop. You can still freeze your Java code with thread deadlocks, and you can certainly end up accessing parts of an array that aren't really there. In short, Java is safe, but it isn't idiot-proof. The fact remains that, in order to screw up your Java programs, you still have to make a major effort.

Most Java programmers are pleased that Java has no pointers to memory locations. This makes program debugging much easier, and it also makes security verification possible. It cannot be verified at compile time that a pointer will do no harm. It can be loaded at runtime with a naughty address to poke a hole in the password file or branch to some code that sprinkles at-signs all over a disk. Without pointers, Java ensures that all mischief is done within the downloaded applet running inside a Java Virtual Machine. Moreover, memory is not allocated until runtime, and this prevents hackers from studying source code to take advantage of memory layout because it is not known at compile-time. Attempts to write beyond the end of an array, for example, raise an ArrayIndexOutOfBoundsException. Had the C language had this feature (array bounds checking), the infamous Morris Internet worm would not have been able to trick the sendmail daemon (running with root privileges) into giving root access to the worm.

Garbage collection, exceptions, and thread controls are part of Java no matter how you try to use it. But, security and safety are two entirely different things. Safety refers to protecting ourselves from our own misadventures. Security refers to protecting ourselves from other people's devices. Because Java objects are loaded dynamically, Java ensures that the objects are "trusted." Java's class security mechanism makes sure that your applications are using the proper objects and not an object that someone has slipped into the download stream to wreak havoc on your machine.

The Java Security Model

The Java security model has been a constantly evolving part of Java. In the JDK 1.0 model, the "sandbox" concept was introduced. In the sandbox model, all local code (JDK-provided code) was run as part of the Java Virtual Machine, and all code retrieved from remote servers (applets) was run in a "sandbox" area of the JVM that provided only a limited set of services. The reason for doing this was based on the fact that any remotely retrieved code could be hostile. To protect the local machine the sandbox provided only minimal access to the machine resources (Figure 13-1).

The JDK 1.1 added to the JDL 1.0 security model the concept of "trusted applets" that could run with the same privileges with respect to the local hosts system

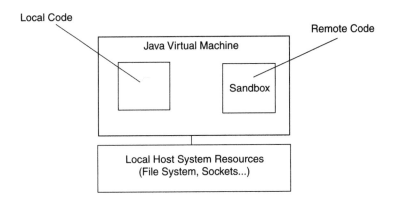

Figure 13-1 JDK 1.0 sandbox model.

resources as local code. This was done through the advent of the Java Archive file format and the inclusion of a correctly signed digital signature in the JAR file. Unsigned applets in JDK 1.1 sill run in the sandbox (Figure 13-2).

The JDK 1.2 evolves the security model by changing the goals to make it:

1. Easy to use fine-grained access control
2. Easy to configure security policy
3. Easy to extend the access control structure
4. Easy to extend security checks to Java applications as well as applets (Figure 13-3).

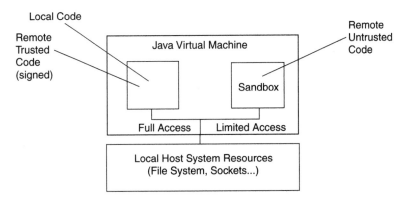

Figure 13-2 JDK 1.1 security model.

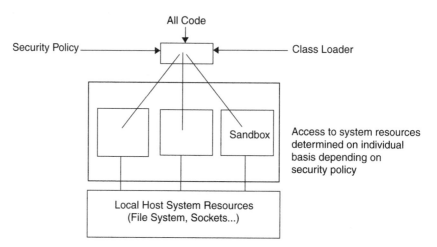

Figure 13-3 JDK 1.2 security model.

Easy to Use Fine-Grained Access Control

Fine-grained security has always been a part of Java; the main problem was that the JDK 1.0 and 1.1 models made it extremely hard to use. To get the degree of control required, subclassing and customizing of the SecurityManager and Class-Loader classes is required (not a task for the uninitiated or the faint of heart). This required quite a bit of programming and an in-depth knowledge of computer and Internet security.

Easy to Configure Security Policy

Because of the amount of code required to configure security policy with the earlier JDKs, it would be more user friendly if the software developers and users could easily configure the security policy via an external policy file built with either a text editor or a GUI tool.

Easy to Extend Access Control Structure

To extend the access control structure in JDK 1.1 required adding additional "check" methods to the SecurityManager class. The new model does not require the addition of new "check" methods to the SecurityManager; the new architecture is based on permissions in the policy file. Each permission defines access to a system resource.

Easy to Extend Security Checks to Applications

In an effort to simplify things and have all code treated equally, the JDK 1.1 concept of "trusted" code was dumped in favor of a model where all code (local or remote) is treated equally, including JDK 1.1 trusted applets. It is for this reason that some JDK 1.1 applications and trusted applets will fail with security exceptions when run under the JDK 1.2 virtual machine.

Java Class Security

Java's security model is made up of three major pieces:

- The Bytecode Verifier
- The Class Loader
- The Security Manager

The Bytecode Verifier

The designers of Java knew that applets could be downloaded over unsecured networks, so they included a bytecode verifier in the Java Virtual Machine's interpreter. It checks to make sure that memory addresses are not forged to access objects outside of the virtual machine, that applet objects are accessed according to their scope (public, private, and protected), and that strict runtime type enforcement is done both for object types and parameters passed with method invocations. The bytecode verifier does these checks after the bytecodes are downloaded but before they are executed. This means that only verified code is run on your machine; verified code runs faster because it does not need to perform these security checks during execution.

The Class Loader

Each imported class executes within its own name space. There is a single name space for built-in classes loaded from the local file system. Built-in classes can be trusted, and the class loader searches the local name space first. This prevents a downloaded class from being substituted for a built-in class. Also, the name space of the same server is searched before the class loader searches other name spaces. This prevents one server from spoofing a class from a different server. Note that this search order ensures that a built-in class will find another built-in class before it searches an imported name space. So, when classes are downloaded, the client's built-in classes are used because they are trusted (see Figure 13-4).

The Security Manager

New to Java in the JDK 1.2 is the ability to define a security policy that can be defined for each application separately from the Java code in a policy file. The policy defined in this external file is enforced at runtime by the Java security manager class. Java classes that have the possibility of doing things that might violate the security policy have been rewritten to include checks of the defined policy so as to verify that the application writer really wants to allow certain operations.

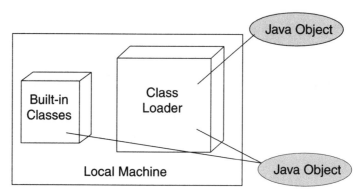

Figure 13–4 Downloaded Java objects use the local built-in classes rather than their own.

Java 1.2 Security Policies. New to Java with the release of Java 1.2 is a methodology that provides a much finer-grained approach to the security of important system resources like the file system, sockets access, system properties, runtime facilities, and security facilities themselves. This is done by establishing security policies; when an application/applet/servlet is loaded, it is assigned a set of permissions that specify the level of access (read, write, connect, . . .) that the code has to specific resources. If code isn't specifically given permission to access something, it won't be able to. These sets of permissions are specified in an external text file called a policy file. Policy files can be created with a text editor or by using the policy tool that comes with the JDK.

For the sample code in this book, a policy file called "policy.all" is provided on the CD. This file will grant all permissions to everything (which is good for the purposes of this book but bad from the standpoint of production code deployment; code placed into a production environment should define only the permissions that it needs to run).

Policy Files. Policy files are made up of a set of "grant" statements that have the general form of:

```
Grant [SignedBy "signer names"] [, CodeBase "URL"]
{
    permission "permission_class_name" ["target name"]
        [, "action"] [, SignedBy, "signer names"];
    permission. . ..
}
```

where

- SignedBy—Indicates that this is signed code (as in a signed JAR file) and that signatures should be checked. This is used to verify that downloaded code is from a trusted source. This is an optional attribute; if it is absent, signature checking is skipped.

- CodeBase—A URL (usually either http:// or file://) of either a file or a directory to which the grant applies.

- permission—The class that enforces the policy; the most commonly used are:

  - java.io.FilePermission—access to files

  - java.io.SocketPermission—access to sockets

  - java.lang.RunTimePermission—access to threads and system resources

  - java.util.PropertyPermission—access to properties

- target—A path to the resource. This is optional and, if absent, refers to the current directory.

- action—Operations allowed (read, write, execute, delete).

- SignedBy—Signers of the permission classes; if signers can't be verified, the permission is ignored.

There are, by default, two policy files that establish the permissions that an application runs under—a system-wide policy file and an optional user (application) specific policy file. The system-wide policy file is kept in *java.home/lib/security/java.policy* (*java.home* is a system property that contains the name of the directory that the JDK is installed in).

The default policy java.policy follows. It grants all permissions to standard extensions, allows anyone to listen in on ports above 1024, and allows any code to read standard system properties that aren't considered sensitive.

```
grant codeBase "file:${java.home}/lib/ext/*" {
    permission java.security.AllPermission;};

// default permissions granted to all domains

grant
{
    // Allows any thread to stop itself using the
    // java.lang.Thread.stop() method that takes no argument.
    // Note that this permission is granted by default only to remain
    // backwards compatible.
    // It is strongly recommended that you either remove this
    // permission from this policy file or further restrict it to code
    // sources that you specify, because Thread.stop() is potentially
    // unsafe. See "http://java.sun.com/notes" for more information.
    // permission java.lang.RuntimePermission "stopThread";
```

```
    // allows anyone to listen on un-privileged ports
    // permission java.net.SocketPermission "localhost:1024-", "listen";
    // "standard" properties that can be read by anyone
    permission java.util.PropertyPermission "java.version", "read";
    permission java.util.PropertyPermission "java.vendor", "read";
    permission java.util.PropertyPermission "java.vendor.url", "read";
    permission java.util.PropertyPermission "java.class.version", "read";
    permission java.util.PropertyPermission "os.name", "read";
    permission java.util.PropertyPermission "os.version", "read";
    permission java.util.PropertyPermission "os.arch", "read";
    permission java.util.PropertyPermission "file.separator", "read";
    permission java.util.PropertyPermission "path.separator", "read";
    permission java.util.PropertyPermission "line.separator", "read";
    permission java.util.PropertyPermission "java.specification.version","read";
    permission java.util.PropertyPermission "java.specification.vendor", "read";
    permission java.util.PropertyPermission "java.specification.name", "read";
    permission java.util.PropertyPermission "java.vm.specification.version", "read";
    permission java.util.PropertyPermission "java.vm.specification.vendor", "read";
    permission java.util.PropertyPermission "java.vm.specification.name", "read";
    permission java.util.PropertyPermission "java.vm.version", "read";
    permission java.util.PropertyPermission "java.vm.vendor", "read";
    permission java.util.PropertyPermission "java.vm.name", "read";
};
```

User- or application-specific policy files are kept by default in *user.home/.java. policy* (*user.home* is the system property that specifies the user's home directory.

Your overall security policy is created at runtime by first setting up permissions in the *java.policy* file and then setting the permissions found in the user policy file. To set up the system policy to your own policy just set the java.security.policy property to the URL of the policy file to be used. The URL can be specified as:

1. A fully qualified path to the file (including the file name).

```
java -Djava.security.policy=c:\advjavacd\rmi\stats1\policy.all
        rmi.Stats1.StatsServerImpl
```

2. Any regular URL.

```
java -Djava.security.policy=http://policy.all StatsServerImpl
```

3. The name of a file in the current directory.

```
java -Djava.security.policy=policy.all rmi.Stats1.StatsServerImpl
```

The *policy.all* file we have been referring to follows:

```
// this policy file should only be used for testing and not deployed
grant
{
    permission java.security.AllPermission;
};
```

Security Tools. The JDK comes with several tools to help you manage the security of code that you write and wish to deploy:

1. policytool—A Java application that comes with the JDK and that provides you with a GUI tool for creating and maintaining policy files.

2. keytool—Used to create digital signatures and key pairs and to manage the keystore database.

3. jarsigner—Allows the attaching of a digital signature to a JAR file.

For detailed instructions on using these tools, refer to the JDK documentation and the security path of the online Java Turorial at *http://java.sun.com/docs/books/ tutorial/security1.2/index.html.*

Security Problems and Java Security Testing

Finally, the Java language has been thoroughly field-tested by high school and university students, college dropouts, and professional hackers lurking in the dark alleys of the World Wide Web. Each and every one of their creative minds was confident it could find a flaw in such a seemingly wide-open door to any system in the world! The most publicized security breaches happened early in Java's distribution, and all have been corrected in the current releases. It has been very quiet ever since. The flaws that were uncovered were implementation errors, not design problems. One group was able to insert its own class loader instead of the one loaded from a secure local file system. Clearly all bets are off if an untrusted class loader that doesn't enforce the class search order we described earlier is used. Another implementation bug was exploited by using a bogus Domain Name Server in cahoots with an evil applet. Java 1.0.2 uses IP addresses instead of hostnames to enforce the network access security levels described earlier.

Details about these early security flaws and their corrections can be found at *http://java.sun.com/sfaq.*

Encryption

In this section, we describe some of the techniques commonly used to provide privacy during data exchanges between two parties. Data traveling through the Internet can be captured (and possibly modified) by a third party. Certainly, you do not want your credit card number to be revealed to a third party and you probably also want the merchandise you purchased to be delivered to your address and not to a different address inserted by a third party. Data encryption ensures that a third party will not be able to decipher any message sent between a client and a server.

A very simple algorithm used to scramble "sensitive" jokes on the Internet is called "rot13" because it rotates each character by 13 positions in the alphabet. That is, "a" is mapped to "n," "b" is mapped to "o," and so on. This algorithm also decrypts a message that was scrambled by it. This is adequate for its purpose: to protect people from reading a joke that they might feel is offensive. This is an example of symmetric key encryption, where both sides use the same key (13) to encrypt and decrypt a scrambled message (see Figure 13-5).

In its most commonly used mode, data encryption standard (DES) uses a 56-bit key to scramble message blocks of 64 bits; in this form DES encrypts large amounts of data relatively fast. DES is currently one of the encryption algorithms used by Secure Sockets Layer (SSL). Recent research has shown that 56-bit DES is becoming insufficient for providing robust encryption for security-sensitive applications. Many companies now use "triple DES," which encrypts each block of data three times with three different keys.

One problem with symmetric key algorithms such as DES is key distribution (i.e., how do I share the private key securely among the participants?).

Public key, or asymmetric cryptography, uses a pair of mathematically related keys for each user. Everyone can know a user's public key, but the private key must be kept secret. To send data to another user, the sender encrypts the data using the recipient's public key and sends the encrypted message to the recipient. The recipient decrypts the message using his or her private key. Because only the recipient knows the private key, data privacy is ensured. Asymmetric algorithms are inherently slower than their symmetric counterparts. The key distribution problem of symmetric algorithms is overcome through the use of the public/private key pairs because the public key can be widely distributed without fear of compromise. There is still one problem with key management in public key encryption schemes. Namely, how do I know that the key I am using for Joe is really Joe's public key? It could be possible for a network interloper to substitute his or her public key for Joe's public key. A variety of trust models have risen to combat this problem. For corporations, the most prevalent model is the hierarchical trust model, which relies on the use of digital certificates and certificate authorities to validate users' public keys.

Real-world cryptographic implementations utilize a combination of public and private key encryption to provide not only data privacy but also nonrepudiation

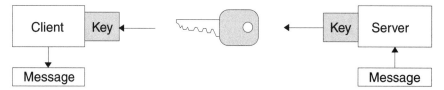

Figure 13-5 Symmetric key encryption decodes messages with a key on both the sending and receiving ends.

(via digital signatures), access control, and authentication. These solutions use the strengths of both public key (key distribution) and private key cryptography (speed); an example follows.

John creates a document and wants to send it to Mary. John first encrypts the document using a symmetric algorithm (like DES) and a randomly selected key. The randomly selected key is then encrypted using an asymmetric algorithm (like RSA) and Mary's public key. A message digest function (one-way mathematical function (like MD5) is performed on the original document producing a fixed-length message digest. This message digest is encrypted using an asymmetric encryption algorithm using John's public key. These three elements are then sent to Mary over some unsecured communications link. This is shown in Figure 13-6.

The process of decrypting and verifying the encrypted document is shown in Figure 13-7 and goes something like this: Mary uses her private key to retrieve the random symmetric key used to encrypt the document. Because Mary is the only one who knows her private key, she is the only one who can open the "digital envelope," thus ensuring data privacy. The retrieved symmetric key is used to decrypt the document. Using the same message digest function as John, Mary produces a message digest for comparison to the one sent by John. Mary now uses John's public key and the asymmetric encryption (RSA) to retrieve the message digest sent with the document. By using John's public key to retrieve the message digest, Mary has also verified that the message was sent

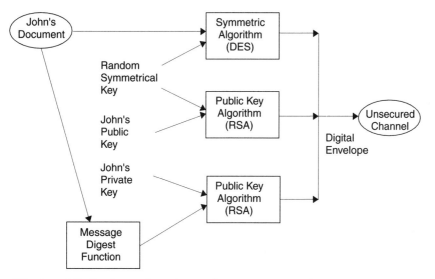

Figure 13-6 A combination of symmetric and asymmetric encryption.

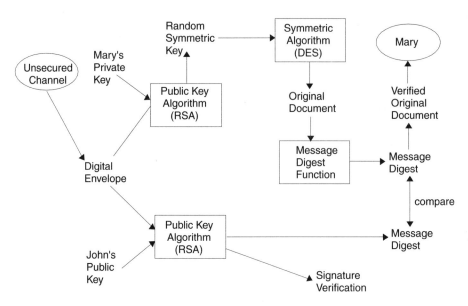

Figure 13-7 Decryption of example.

by John (i.e., retrieved his digital signature) because only John's private key could have been used to encrypt the message digest. The message digest sent with the document is compared with the one computed by Mary. This comparison ensures the data integrity. If the digests match, the document was unaltered during transmission.

Java Cryptography Extension (JCE)

The JCE provides a set of APIs that allow you to encrypt, decrypt, and password-protect information.

Authentication

In many applications, it is important to authenticate the identity of a client making a request for a service. Examples include banking, financial, real estate, medical records, and ISP (Internet Service Provider) applications. An ISP, for example, wants to ensure that Internet access is being provided to a paying customer and not the customer's housekeeper. The online stock trading application wants to make sure that it is the portfolio owner who is making trades.

The usual way to do this is to require an account number or customer name and a password. This is adequate for workstations and time-sharing systems and client/server sessions such as calling Charles Schwab to manage your stock portfolio. In a distributed system, many different servers provide services. Instead of a single authentication to a single server or application, that server must authenticate each service request sent over the network.

One obvious requirement of such an authentication system is that it be transparent to the user. The user does not want to type in a password for each service each time it is requested. Another requirement is that it be available at all times because, if a server cannot authenticate a request, it will not provide the service. When the authentication service is unavailable so are all the services that use it. A less obvious requirement is that authentication must be protected against capture and playback by another user on the network. Capture cannot be prevented on broadcast media such as an Ethernet cable, so the authentication procedure must be able to prevent a playback by an impostor.

Kerberos

One popular authentication system is Kerberos, which is named after a three-headed guard dog in Greek mythology. It depends on a third party that is trusted by both client and server (see Figure 13-8). Clients request a ticket from the third party. The ticket is encrypted using the server's secret password, so the server trusts the client when it can decrypt the ticket. The server's password is known only to itself and the third party. The third party knows everyone's password! This means that all systems are vulnerable if the trusted third party is compromised.

A well-known bank has two major data centers, one in San Francisco and the other in Los Angeles. Each center backs up its data at the other site. In this way, the bank can resume operation soon after serious damage to either data center. The Kerberos servers are replicated at both sites and kept behind "the glass wall." In fact, there is a sealed walkway with locked doors at both ends and a badge reader with a video camera in the middle. If your face doesn't resemble the one on the badge, you are not allowed into the room that houses the Kerberos servers. In fact, two or more very large people will promptly escort you out of the building.

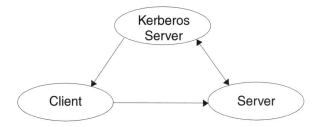

Figure 13–8 Servers can trust clients only if they can decrypt the ticket from the Kerberos server.

Including a timestamp in the ticket thwarts playback. That is, the Kerberos server encrypts the client's IP address, a session key, and a timestamp using the server's key. The client encrypts its service request message with the session key and sends it, along with the ticket, to the server. The server uses its key to decrypt the ticket. If the IP address in the ticket matches the IP address in the IP packet header and the timestamp is within a few milliseconds of the current time, then the server accepts the client's request. It uses the session key to unscramble the request and perform the service. It's as simple as that. Playback is impossible because the encrypted timestamp will have "timed out" before an impostor can capture and try to replay the request. Also, the IP address of the impostor will not match the IP address encrypted in the ticket.

Digital Signatures and Public Key Encryption

The theory behind digital signatures and public key encryption is that in a given system every user has a pair of digital keys. In the case of the Web, the mere act of installing a browser on your system will generate the private and public keys to be used with that browser. If you have two browsers installed (e.g., Netscape and IE4), then you will have two sets of private and public keys, one set for each browser. The basic premise behind public key encryption is that using some algorithm you can use your private key to generate a permutation (encrypt) of a message that can only be decrypted using your public key. If you carefully distribute your public key to the people you normally deal with, anytime you send them a message they will be able to read it using your public key.

Secure Sockets Layer

By far the most widely used authentication and encryption on the Internet in general and on the Web specifically is Secure Sockets Layer. SSL can be used with any connection-based protocol. It's called a layer because we essentially insert an additional protocol layer between TCP and the Application layer of the TCP/IP stack (see Figure 13-9).

SSL adds the following features to the reliable stream provided by TCP/IP:

1. Authentication and nonrepudiation of the server via digital signatures.

2. Authentication and nonrepudiation of the client via digital signatures.

3. An encrypted stream to provide privacy.

4. Data integrity through message authentication codes.

Netscape Corporation designed SSL as a way of ensuring secure communications between its browser and server products. SSL has become the de facto standard for secure communications between Internet clients and servers.

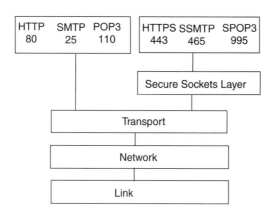

Figure 13–9 Secure Sockets Layer.

For a look at the SSL v3.0 specification, see *http://home.netscape.com/eng/ssl3/ ssl-toc.html*. To use SSL requires cooperation between the client browser and the server. At the server, a secure instance of the Web server must be running on the well-known port 443. (Some Web sites run both an unsecure and a secure instance of the Web server on the same machine. The unsecure instance is listening on port 80, while the secure instance is running on port 443. Some sites run the unsecure and secure instances on completely separate hosts.)

At the browser end, all references to the URLs of documents or applications must be preceded with the protocol https rather than http. As long as the protocol notation is https, the port is defaulted to 443 (the secure server port).

The attachment of an SSL client to an SSL server starts off with what is known as an SSL handshake. During the handshake, the client and server agree on the protocol version to be used, select the cryptographic algorithm they will use to protect data transmission, optionally authenticate one another, and use public-key encryption to generate shared secrets. After this has been done, the rest of the transmission takes place in an encrypted manner using the parameters selected during the handshake.

The Government and Security

The issue of security on our computers is greatly affected by the restrictions on security technology placed on a company by its home government. Because this is not by any stretch of the imagination a comprehensive text on security, we instead outline the two major controversies concerning government intervention in computer security. We attempt not to pass judgment on either the government or the security community; you can make that determination for yourself. Instead, in this section, we simply point out the two sides to the arguments of governmental control of security export and the government's right to possess keys to domestic security apparatuses.

Export Control

The United States government is extremely adamant about protecting against U.S. technology falling into nondomestic hands. Two of the more important regulations that are in place are the DoD International Traffic in Arms Regulation (ITAR) and the U.S. Department of Commerce Export Administration Regulations (EAR). Both sets of regulations concern the export of technology to foreign governments; ITAR primarily concerns U.S.-based defense contractors, and EAR applies to all commercial ventures that involve the sale and export of technology-related items to non-U.S. persons.

Because the Internet is a worldwide medium and social phenomenon, without boundaries and governments to hinder it, the government realizes that some form of security technology must be used to transmit information across national boundaries. Therefore, the U.S. government restricts the level of security found in certain products that are international in nature. For example, the Netscape browser has two versions. One is a U.S. domestic version with full browser security features. The other is an international version that implements the Secure Socket Layer with less security. The international version may be exported outside the United States, whereas the domestic version may be used only within the United States.

Never mind the inability to actually protect against the dissemination of the more powerful security technology to international audiences, the United States simply makes the distinction. If Netscape were to blindly distribute the domestic version without making a statement such as "Domestic Use Only," they would be breaking the law. Is the law enforceable to end users? Probably not, but the law is there, written as plain as day, and should be followed by "morally upstanding citizens." For you, as application programmers, secure networked applications should follow the same kind of export controls if they are applicable.

The "Clipper" Controversy

Historically, the U.S. government has always known that there are ways for its citizens to keep information hidden from the government. In fact, the Fourth Amendment to the Constitution of the United States of America specifically outlines this right that all American citizens possess:

> The right of the people to be secure in their persons, houses, papers, and effects, against unreasonable searches and seizures, shall not be violated, and no Warrants shall issue, but upon probable cause, supported by Oath or affirmation, and particularly describing the place to be searched, and the persons or things to be seized.

But, over the years, a distinction has been made as to what is "unreasonable." The government, in interests of "national security," may, with permission from the Judicial branch, execute a search of one's property and possessions. How does this apply to the digital age?

The entire "Clipper chip" controversy centers around the government's willingness to publish an encryption algorithm for telephones, computer files, and any other form of communication. The transmissions would be encrypted and mathematically impossible to break. However, the government would always be able to have a "back door" to the encryption with its own special key. As outlined in the Fourth Amendment, the government may use the key only with a written warrant; nevertheless, the idea that "Big Brother" may be watching is enough to bring chills down the spines of some people.

Lost in the argument is the fact that there are several other encryption methods that could be used instead of Clipper (e.g., PGP) and that are just as good and do not encourage governmental interference. Clipper represents the entire belief that, in the end, the U.S. government, as well as the other governments of the entire world, has no idea how to protect itself in the digital age without sacrificing intellectual freedom.

Summary

Secure, networked transmissions are of the utmost importance to many people. If the Internet is truly to become the focus of all our communication in the next century, then we must all have confidence that no one can intercept and decode our innermost thoughts. Although we have very briefly outlined the concerns of the U.S. government, we hesitate to endorse or criticize any one position. In the end, the debate over the involvement of government authorities will be settled in another, more appropriate, forum. For now, as application programmers, you should be keenly aware of the position of your government, whatever it may be, on how you can send secure transmissions.

With this solid base of network programming underneath us, we must now make a decision about which alternative to choose. Each has its advantages and disadvantages, and we will discuss them in detail in the next chapter.

Chapter **14**

Making an Architectural Decision

▼ JAVA SOCKETS

▼ JAVA RMI DECISIONS

▼ JAVA IDL

▼ JDBC

▼ OTHER JAVA TECHNOLOGIES

▼ APPLICATION SERVERS

Making a decision is difficult, particularly when the fate of your company's entire vision may be at stake. Although we make no attempt to salvage the many *Titanic*s of free enterprise, we do offer our thoughts on what the world of Java networking can mean to you. In this chapter, we candidly browse the advantages and disadvantages of each communication alternative. Do you want the heavy-duty power of CORBA or the lightweight simplicity of RMI? Are databases vital to your business process, or do you require customizable protocols?

As we have seen, Java networking is a vast and expansive subject. This book is the tip of the iceberg, and as the industry begins to shake out, more and more information will be brought forward. This chapter will help you separate fact from fiction, reality from hype, and engineering from marketeering.

Java Sockets

Many of the alternatives we have discussed in this book involve sockets in one way or another. To recommend that you not use sockets essentially would be to say that you should not use any of the technologies we talk about. Sockets by themselves are useful for quite a few different things. Remember that, when you

367

send an RMI or IDL message, you are essentially sending a big chunk of data and the headers to that data. When we discussed our own message format in Chapter 3, "Java Sockets and URLs," we were able to put together a small, lightweight messaging system. If speed and efficiency are of the utmost importance to you, then certainly you would be interested in using Java sockets alone.

Flexibility

Remember that we created our own message format and transmitted it with great speed. Our message format was not inadequate as it transmitted all the information we required. Notice too that we did not have to learn anything new. As long as we know what a socket is and how to use it, we can easily transmit a message to our server.

Servers are equally easy to create. With Java IDL and Java RMI, we needed to create an entire infrastructure for our server. With sockets, converting an application to a server application was not only easy but also extremely powerful. Once again, we lost no functionality by using sockets instead of some other communication alternative.

Furthermore, we could simply convert our connection-oriented socket to a broadcast socket. Then we could use the broadcast socket to send information to a port while allowing anyone else to listen in on that port. Because of this ability to switch between paradigms easily and quickly, sockets can be an excellent choice for both the beginner and the advanced networking programmer who wants to build his or her own infrastructure.

Simplicity

As we saw, using sockets is extremely simple. Once you get the concepts down, actually changing your applications to use sockets is quite an easy task. Using the ServerSocket, you can build a simple server. By integrating threads, you can make sure that your server handles data efficiently. In addition, there is no confusing IDL to learn and no RMI API to understand. By using only sockets, you sacrifice the functionality of RMI and IDL for speed and ease of use.

Because the networking world understands and knows sockets so well, having built and deployed applications that use sockets for years, you will also have a ready supply of applications to use from within Java. Because sockets do not actually send data "over the wire" and instead send strings of information, you can seamlessly plug your Java applications into new or existing applications written in other languages. Just as with Java IDL, sockets give you the promise of being able to easily integrate legacy applications.

Again, there are several tradeoffs between sockets and the other alternatives we discuss in this book. Java IDL also integrates legacy applications well, but the plug-and-play ability of Java IDL gives it a distinct advantage over using sockets alone. With sockets, you have to make sure that everyone is speaking the same protocol. With Java IDL, there is no message format or protocol to worry about. Simply invoke remote objects as if they were already on your machine.

Java RMI Decisions

After surveying the entire spectrum of Java solutions we offer in this book, it is time to make a decision. Perhaps Java RMI has piqued your interest. The promise of never having to see C++ again seems like a good thing. Using the fun and robust networking ability inherent in Java may be an even better reason to turn to a Java-only alternative. Whatever the reason, this is the place to get an honest account of what RMI can and cannot do for you.

RMI Advantages

One of the absolute best things about JavaRMI is that you never ever have to see C++ again. C++ is arcane, difficult, and frustrating. Meanwhile, Java is fun, easy, and exciting. Because Java offers the strongest alternative yet to a series of frustrations wrought upon the computer science population, Java RMI has garnered significant attention from the masses. It follows a simple notion of abstracting distributed implementations by publishing interfaces and linking in implementations of those interfaces later on.

Because we invested a significant amount of time, money, and effort in the Java revolution by learning and promoting the language, we may be tempted to jump directly into an all-Java solution to the communication quandary. Because invocations on Java objects are simple to begin with, Java RMI makes sure that it is equally simple to make the same kinds of invocations across different virtual machines. It is precisely this simplicity that makes Java RMI appealing.

Riding on the coattails of Java 1.2, the long awaited RMI-IIOP connection is now in place. This technology allows RMI's ease of use with CORBA's cross-language interoperability. By following a few rules, we can now mix-'n-match RMI and CORBA clients and servers.

Another new feature of RMI is Remote Object Activation. This feature allows an RMI server to be shut down once it has been registered with the registry and then be restarted remotely (functionally the same way a CORBA server can be remotely started).

RMI Disadvantages

With the introduction of RMI-IIOP one of Java's main drawbacks has been eliminated (i.e., the Java 1.1 restriction that RMI was a "Java Only" solution). Because we can now mix-'n-match RMI and CORBA clients, we can still put a CORBA wrapper around a legacy application and access it with a Java client application.

This leaves the old "Java is not fast" argument. Indeed, it is an interpreted language and, therefore, is subjected to a layer of processing that C++ and C are not. However, the introduction of JIT compilers and other performance enhancements (like Sun's HotSpot technology and IBM's current JVM technology) help negate the issue. Still, it is important to realize that if performance is of the utmost importance, Java may not be the language for you.

Three-Tier Applications in RMI

As we discussed in previous chapters, the notion of three-tier and n-tiered client/server computing will not go away. It is the foundation for most of today's distributed systems. MIS managers love it because it enables them to funnel access to data sources through a central repository. Programmers love it because they can revise and update the various components of their applications without massive overhauls. After all, the business logic contained in servers defines how and when databases are accessed. Client-side GUIs are concerned only with getting and displaying information. If a programmer makes a change in the business logic, there is no need to push the change to the client as well.

JavaRMI does not readily facilitate the notion of three-tier client/server computing any more than JavaIDL does. Both are, in fact, middle-tier technologies. Java RMI can easily use JDBC to connect to a relational database and JNDI to connect to Directory Services just as CORBA can do with ODBC and LDAP. The real functionality, brains, and resource management take place on the server end. The data source is nothing but a repository of information.

Once again, the performance problem rears its ugly head. Because the middle tier is intended to be home to all the business logic in an object system, JavaRMI servers may have to process data extremely efficiently, perhaps more efficiently than possible.

Java RMI Is Not Robust. Perhaps the most important aspect of RMI is its lack of support for true distributed computing. When invoking across machines and networks, the fact is that a client generally has no control over how processes are executed on the remote end. Indeed, the remote end can very well be an entirely different hardware architecture than expected. Java RMI offers no ability to allow a client to invoke without knowing the destination of the request. The lack of location independence should be quite a significant factor in making an architectural decision toward RMI.

Even though Java RMI is easy to understand, get started with, and design frameworks around, it does not address some of the fundamental network concerns of distributed-object programmers. Location independence is one of these concerns. Another concern is automatic startup. With the recent introduction of Remotely Activatable Objects, when a client invokes a server for the first time, as long as the server has been registered, an attempt to restart the server will be done.

> One thing we shouldn't lose sight of regarding RMI registry is that it is only one possible implementation (Sun's implementation) of what is really RMI's naming service. It could be implemented a number of other ways that would allow for automatic load balancing, fail-over, and all those things CORBA is famous for.

This requires the server programmer not only to have the server available but also to provide for fault tolerance. What if the server goes down unexpectedly? Part of the software design specification should provide an automatic fail-over to a backup server or automatically restart the server itself. Needless to say, these are difficult tasks to program and may be more trouble than they are worth.

Java IDL

Every year for the past 3 years was touted as "the year CORBA will break out." Every January a flood of articles in trade rags and industry newsletters trumpets the arrival of the Common Object Request Broker Architecture. Although it is anyone's guess as to what the future will be, it is a relatively safe assumption that CORBA, or a derivative thereof, will power the forces of the Internet for quite some time. The reasons are numerous, but the fact remains that CORBA technology, although not devoid of major shortcomings, is the most robust, mature, and powerful alternative presented in this book. Any investigation into an Internet communication strategy should place CORBA at the top of the list of technologies to investigate.

Advantages of Java IDL

Java IDL is a well-thought-out, coherent set of base objects that can be used to create a tightly woven distributed-object system. Because of the maturity of CORBA, many of the questions about Java RMI and sockets have been addressed in the specification and in the products currently available. In a moment, we will discuss the advantages and disadvantages of the various implementations of the specification that are on the market today. Yet, regardless of the great number of ORBs, Java IDL is a solidly engineered set of core components that facilitate Java to ORB programming.

As we have discussed, the ORB isolates an object from the underlying mechanisms that ensure that a client does not need to know the physical location of a server, how to start the server, or even if it should shut the server down. When you walk into a supermarket, the doors are automatic. You don't have to open them automatically, and you don't have to close them behind you. Similarly, an ORB handles a lot of the internal machinations of networked communication for you.

Beyond its maturity and the fact that it handles much of the boredom of working with networked objects, Java IDL is also Java. It uses the same memory handling, parameter passing, serialization, and so on, that Java does and, therefore, helps to alleviate the learning curve of CORBA itself.

Disadvantages of Java IDL

Java IDL's biggest disadvantage is also one of its strong advantages: Java IDL is CORBA. CORBA is a complex series of rules and regulations (in the software sense) governing how distributed objects should behave. Java IDL is completely CORBA compatible and is, therefore, an extension of CORBA itself. It plugs into CORBA very easily and without much hassle, but at a pretty steep price. In order to use Java IDL effectively, you must understand CORBA and truly understand the principles of distributed objects. Even though this book attempts to outline what CORBA is and why you would want to use it, it is not the ultimate resource.

Yet, because of Java, much of the memory management morass and the differences between varied ORBs is rendered moot because the nature of Java removes it. Java is platform independent and requires no memory management on the programmer's part. Even though CORBA programming is hard, thank your lucky stars for Java. Just taking a look at a C++ CORBA program compared to a Java CORBA program will make a Java believer out of you.

Java IDL Implementations

Sun Microsystems is a major proponent of CORBA but has announced that it is getting out of the business of providing full-featured ORBs (NEO/JOE) as a product, and it is deferring to such companies as IONA (Orbix), BEA, and Borland/ Inprise (Visibroker). Inprise's Visibroker is a smart, easy-to-use CORBA option that offers strong three-tier client/server capabilities. If talking to a database is of the utmost priority for your software architecture, Visibroker for Java might be your best option.

The current industry leader is Orbix. Orbix is available on every platform and is a reliable, easy-to-use object broker. Many customers find getting started with Orbix to be a relatively easy task and discover soon thereafter that CORBA isn't as bad as it was cracked up to be.

One of the biggest problems with the various CORBA implementations is that the code is not portable from one ORB to another. Although they all comply with the CORBA specification, the specification is general enough for each implementor to do it its own way. APIs from one ORB to another are quite different.

Java IDL Is Robust

Imagine creating a client application that can invoke a server, get information, and report results without even once having to worry about network code, server-side behavior, or slow system resources. CORBA, and the ORB specifically, handle all those tasks for you. So long as an ORB is on both the client and the server platforms, the request can get through to the server, the server can be started up if necessary, and the server can process information for the client.

The notion of an ORB on every platform is not as far-fetched as you might expect. Sun's Solaris operating system is incorporating Sun's own NEO family of CORBA products directly. When you get Solaris, you will also get the plumbing necessary to create CORBA fixtures. Similarly, OLE and COM have always been present on the Microsoft Windows operating environment, and with CORBA offering a strong OLE/COM to CORBA connectivity solution as part of its specification, the client side on Windows platforms will soon be a reality.

Furthermore, a Java IDL application also includes its own "mini-ORB" that provides limited functionality so that an ORB need not be present within the Web browser itself. Netscape, however, as part of its ONE technology includes a version of the Visibroker ORB with every 4.0 or newer browser. In this way, the Web browser can act as a communication mediator between clients and CORBA servers.

Java IDL Is Difficult

One of the big gripes we have heard and emphasized in this book is that CORBA is difficult. Well, there's no getting around the fact that in the past you had to be a true C++ expert to understand CORBA itself. You could allocate a chunk of memory on the client side, pass it to the server, where it got deallocated, and still have a memory leak on your client side. That was just one of the many, many, many problems with C++ and CORBA.

Yet, that is much more of a C++ problem than a CORBA problem. True, you still need to know much more than the basics of object-oriented programming to use CORBA, but with Java things become much easier. Memory management, for one, is no longer even an issue.

The Interface Definition Language is blasted by critics as just one more thing you need to know in order to use the CORBA architecture. True, the IDL is a layer on top of your normal application, but it serves a very important purpose. It prevents your applications from being locked into one language. Who knows? Tomorrow, a new programming language may emerge with its own cool name, its own cult following, and its own list of strengths. The entire world may jump on that bandwagon much as it has with Java. But CORBA applications still will be important and will not be rendered obsolete because they can be phased into the new language in a short time without affecting the rest of the system.

Language independence, while not of real importance to the subject of this book, is the single most interesting thing about CORBA. It enables you to migrate applications to new platforms, new languages, and even new algorithms without having to adjust the entire object system. Remember that, with JavaRMI, you are locked into Java until you have a reason to change. That kind of thinking is why many people are trying today to figure out how to migrate from COBOL.

Java IDL Is Powerful

Java IDL is a flexible, distributed-object environment. With it, you can invoke C++ objects half a world away as if they were both local and written in Java. To you, the application programmer, the Java to CORBA to C++ is hidden. You simply instantiate Java objects and talk to C++ servers on the other end without even knowing. Of course, if you prefer to write Java servers, more power to you.

Remember that language independence is a very good thing for large-scale object systems. You can swap components in and out using the language most appropriate for the task. If you happen to have a CORBA to LISP language mapping (don't panic, there isn't one), you could write all your artificial intelligence components in LISP, while saving UI or computation components for an object-oriented language like Java or C++. Java IDL is the only alternative we present that can possibly integrate such disparate object components.

But, for many people, the simplicity and elegance of Java RMI may be all that is needed. Maybe you don't have any legacy systems to be integrated. Maybe language independence is of no use to you. Maybe all you want is a simple remote object invocation system. In that case, Java RMI is definitely your cup of tea.

JDBC

Java Database Connectivity is an enabling technology, not necessarily a communication framework in and of itself. By "enabling technology," we mean that it enables you to link other communication strategies with repositories of information and data to form a cohesive network of objects that can communicate vast quantities of information. JDBC is not the answer in itself, but in combination with Java IDL, Java RMI, or even Java Sockets, it can be a heck of a powerful answer to the Internet question for the next decade.

Why JDBC Is Not Enough

JDBC alone limits you in what you can accomplish with advanced networking. Every client that talks to a database connects directly with the database. There can be no additional intelligence added in the business logic to assist with routing messages. Basically, your applications are connected to the database, and if that causes some kind of sluggishness between the database and the client, then so be it. In the end, the decision to use JDBC alone or with another technology amounts to a decision between the two-tier and three-tier architectural models.

The two-tier architecture links clients directly with the data repository as shown in Figure 14-1. This means that any kind of processing for the access and any further processing for the data retrieved from the repository is left to the client. Splitting the business logic out of the client is the driving force behind the three-tier model. However, in some cases that trait is not a necessary qualification. If your applications are deployed often, or maybe even deployed over the Web, then updating a client is not a major factor because it will be done no matter what architecture you choose. If you are deploying shrink-wrapped applications written in Java—as will be common in just a few years—then updating applications constantly will be a major pain, and you may want to revert to a three-tier model.

The biggest drawback to the two-tier model is the sheer number of clients that may attach themselves to a data repository. Typically, data repositories are not set up to handle the intelligent management of resources required to process multiple simultaneous invocations. If your applications ping the database only rarely, then this is not a factor for you. However, if there are to be many instances of your client application, you will want to go to a three-tier model.

A three-tier model is predicated on the belief that business logic should not exist in either a client or a database. It dictates that the client should be a pretty application the sole purpose of which is to funnel information back to the user. The client is typically a rich GUI with simple execution steps that relies completely on the information given to it by the middle tier (see Figure 14-2).

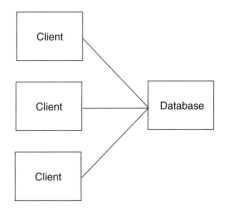

Figure 14-1 Two-tier client to database architecture.

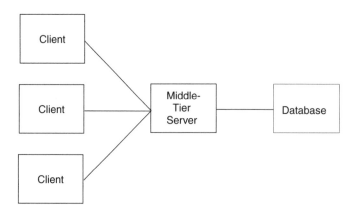

Figure 14-2 Three-tier application architecture with server middleware.

The middle-tier is a server that talks to a data repository. The server is written using Java IDL, Sockets, or Java RMI and can talk to the database using JDBC. JDBC acts, as it always does, as the interface from a client (in this case the middle-tier server) to a database. It just so happens that the server is fully capable of handling multiple invocations and requests and houses all the business logic. The business logic could range from simply adding a number of results from a database query and passing it back to the client, to invoking other servers using the same data. Whatever it does with the data it retrieves, the server can manipulate the information as it sees fit and then pass it back to the client.

JDBC and Java IDL or Java RMI

As we discussed, the middle tier in the three-tier architecture could easily be Java IDL or Java RMI. Indeed, IDL and RMI are complementary technologies to JDBC. JDBC is not their competition because the vast majority of people using JDBC use it within a middle-tier paradigm. This is why Java IDL and Java RMI are vital to JDBC's success. Moreover, JDBC lends credibility to Java IDL and Java RMI. Without a simple technology to enable database access, Java IDL and Java RMI would be largely useless in the business community.

The largest investments made by most companies in their computing infrastructure is contained within their databases. Databases often are used to maintain important records ranging from medical history to employment records and to keep track of business processes from supply purchases to stock maintenance. Most of the time, changing the database to a Java-only application is not only difficult and expensive but also completely unreasonable and unfeasible. For this reason, JDBC can be used to communicate and update the database, while the middle-tier server can be quickly migrated to Java using the techniques in this book.

Client applications can be generated quite easily using the many visual Java builders on the market today. Often, client applications are not only simpler to create, test, and deploy but are also less vital and less error prone than the rest of the architectural model.

JDBC Alone

While using JDBC alone is certainly not out of the question, it is highly discouraged for mission-critical applications. However, for proof of concept applications, applications requiring limited data access, and even for heavy-duty applications with large chunks of data transfer, JDBC may be an excellent option.

What JDBC gives you is a simple, clean interface to a database that requires no additional knowledge of network programming, distributed design, or remote procedure calls. For database programmers, JDBC is a welcome arrival for Java because it means that they need not build special server programs whose sole purpose is to funnel information back to the client. In other words, for those programmers who desire not to use three-tier computing, JDBC is the perfect answer.

Because of its simplicity, you will find that, for major application development efforts, JDBC is all you need to affect some kind of persistence for your client applications. Clients can do their heavy computation, cool graphics, or whatever and store their state in a database using JDBC. The next time the client is executed, it can retrieve its previous state from the database and start again where it left off.

JDBC Overview

JDBC is a fantastic set of APIs to connect Java applications and applets directly to databases. With its simplicity, robustness, and ability to bring together the disparate worlds of databases and the Internet, JDBC will be a successful venture for Java. By modifying your existing database clients for Java, you can capture all the usefulness of the Java Revolution without sacrificing the power required to manipulate your data stores.

Other Java Technologies

In addition to the four major Java communication technologies, we have shown you three other mechanisms that you can use to plug your Java applications into the Internet. Beans, servlets, and JMAPI give you the means necessary to package, publish, and administer the applications you have written in RMI, IDL, JDBC, or Sockets. Even though the "big four" are fascinating and powerful in their own right, they need the additional functionality provided by the other Java APIs that have been or will be published in the future.

When to Use Beans

Let's say that you've created a bunch of gee-whiz Java applications to interface with your hand-held Personal Information Manager. These applications have several modules that translate the data on the device to a format that is readable by your on-disk schedule manager. These modules are for your address book, to-do list, and schedule. By dividing your Java applications into separate, self-contained Beans, you can publish the components. Moreover, if you were to split out the network component that interfaces the device with your computer, then others could write their own customizable applications that use your network module (see Figure 14-3).

This is precisely what we intended to do with our featured application. Although we didn't exactly use Beans, we could have done so easily and allowed others to pick out the Beans they wanted and interface with our calendar manager. Currently, the network module talks to a server on a remote machine. The server stores the information on the disk on which it resides.

What if we were to modify our calendar manager to use Beans? It would simply be a matter of encapsulating our various Java objects in Java Beans containers. Then we could allow anyone who wanted to interface to the rest of our calendar manager to do so using the Network module. Remember that Java Beans supports the notion of introspection, which enables people to take our Network module, browse it from within a GUI builder, and then generate their own objects that interface directly to it. Even if they do not like our user interfaces, people still can use the Network module rather than invest their own time and effort into learning the RMI, IDL, or JDBC APIs.

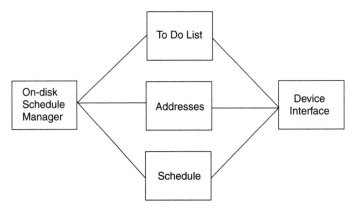

Figure 14–3 Beans enable you to build components such as the Schedule component that can be used by other applications.

When to Use Servlets and Java Server Pages

Servlets and Java Server Pages are information publishing tools. If we wanted the people in our department to know what our schedule is simply by browsing our personal Web page, we could allow them to do so by sticking the server portion of our calendar manager inside a servlet. The servlet then could be queried via an HTTP request, and the information contained within the server could be displayed on the Web page. Then, when we modify our server, people talking to our servlet would get the latest and greatest list of what we are doing that day (see Figure 14-4).

The alternative to servlets is to create a Web page by hand and stick it on a Web server. But, if we were to change the times of our appointment, we would have to generate a new Web page. By incorporating the servlet technology within our server, we do not have to regenerate a Web page every time. Remember that the entire Internet game is about information—how to get, disseminate, and update information constantly. Servlets enable you to publish information contained within servers that get and update that information constantly.

Java Server Pages are an extension of servlet technology and allow the initial creation of server-side Web pages to be done using traditional GUI-based html editors. After we get the page to look the way we want, we attach it with a text editor or our favorite Java IDE and add Java functionality via the JSP API. Once we rename it from *.html* to *.jsp* we have our JSP, and it can be pretty much managed and served as a plain old html page.

Application Servers

At last we come to application servers. The application server seems to have overcome all the problems we have pointed out with other technologies. Important issues like state management, scalability, fault tolerance, and fail-over have been addressed and taken care of. Enterprise Java Beans is on track, and in general the application server really seems to be the way to go.

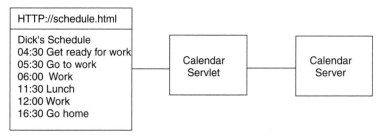

Figure 14–4 Servlets provide dynamic documents via Web servers.

When things sound too good to be true they usually are. Application servers are a relatively big-ticket item and may not be affordable for many medium- and small-size organizations. Technology comes at a price, and in the case of application servers the price is dollars. In the case of the stand-alone technologies we've looked at, they are relatively inexpensive to implement and deploy. The big application servers are pretty much priced for large enterprises where significant amounts of cash are transacted via the Internet, require architectures that guarantee zero downtime sites, and are massively scalable.

Summary

Whew! There you have it! There are several different alternatives, all of which accomplish different things and, in many cases, the same things. We hope that this book has been of some help to you as you sort out your information strategy for the next decade. The Internet is a fabulous phenomenon and, as you know, much more than a collection of Web sites, e-mail accounts, and chat rooms. Using the technologies we presented to you in this book, you can begin to harness the power of the Internet to publish and receive information right from within your Java applications.

After all, we firmly believe that Java is the Internet Programming Language, and, after reading this book, we hope you will agree.

Glossary

ActiveWeb   Active Software's publish/subscribe system for corporate intranet information publishing.

ActiveX   Proprietary Microsoft component model for the Internet.

AWT   Abstract Window Toolkit. One of the windowing environments supplied as part of the core Java classes, uses peer components of the OS.

Bytecode   The binary language produced by the Java compiler and used as the native binary language for the Java Virtual Machine.

C++   Compiled, object-oriented programming language.

Callback   Saving a method with an object in the hopes that the function will be invoked, or "called back," at a later time.

CGI   Common Gateway Interface. The original way of creating executable content on the server side of an HTTP connection. *See* servlet.

Client   Program that invokes another object from a remote location.

COM   Common Object Model. Proprietary Microsoft protocol for platform-independent interobject communication.

Component   A separate object that can be reused, modified, and redeployed without requiring access to its source code.

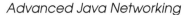

Component Model   Next wave in object-oriented programming that promotes the reuse of objects without exposing any source code whatsoever to the end user or programmer.

Concurrent Access   Occurs when multiple threads get the same piece of data. *See* mutual exclusion.

Constructor   The function of an object that initializes the object and readies it for invocation.

CORBA   Common Object Request Broker Architecture. Industry standard for Distributed Object programming.

Deadlock   Occurs when a thread grabs a mutual exclusion lock and hangs on to it indefinitely, thereby preventing other threads from getting the same lock.

EJB   Enterprise Java Beans. A specification from Sun Microsystems whose goal is to provide corporate America with the ultimate in reusable, scalable, and robust application.

Encapsulation   Object Oriented programming practice of packaging data and behavior together as a single entity.

Encryption   The translation of data into unreadable sequences of characters so that "untranslation" back into its original state is impossible without a "key."

Firewall   Protective barrier between the internal information of a business and the external information it makes available to the world.

HTTP   HyperText Transfer Protocol. The de facto standard for Web communication. Specifies the format of transmissions between Web clients and Web servers.

IDL   Interface Definition Language. The part of the CORBA language that enables objects and their interfaces to be specified easily.

IIOP   Internet Inter-Orb Protocol. New standard for object communication over the Internet. Enables objects to invoke one another over the Internet regardless of the communication mechanism that was used to create them.

Information Hiding   Creating objects that provide one set of user interfaces to data while keeping the plumbing of the data hidden.

Inheritance   The derivation of an object's interfaces or implementations from another object.

IPC   Interprocess Communication. Act of programs talking to one another through a link of some kind, usually a socket.

Java   A platform-independent and architecture-neutral programming language from Sun Microsystems, Inc. Also, slang for coffee.

Java Beans   Component model for Java. *See* component model.

Java IDL   The Java binding to CORBA and IDL.

Java RMI   Remote Method Invocation. A means by which to invoke methods on objects that are not necessarily on the same virtual machine.

Java Web Server   The name for the set of components that includes servlets and the written-in-Java HTTP server that allows connections to them.

JDBC   Java Database Connectivity. A set of simple APIs used to connect Java objects directly into databases.

JINI   Sun Microsystem's technology for impromptu networking.

JIT   Just In Time. A kind of compiler that, as part of a Virtual Machine's bytecode interpreter, can take bytecodes and optimize them for a machine's native language.

JNDI   Java Naming and Directory Interface. The set of APIs that allows consistent use of Internet Naming services (like DNS) and LDAP-based access to Directory Services.

JNI   Java Native Interface. APIs used for interfacing with native windows code.

JSP   Java Server Pages. An all-Java solution to producing active server pages; part of servlet technology.

Kerberos   A secure network authentication system based on private key encryption.

Key   The special code that allows the decryption of encrypted data.

Language Mapping   The means necessary to take one language and convert its syntax and semantics to another language.

Layout   Graphical construct in Java's Abstract Window Toolkit that allows components to be placed on the screen.

LDAP   Lightweight Directory Access Protocol. A TCP/IP-based interface to Directory Services (ISO X.500).

Location Independent   CORBA-added functionality that enables a client to invoke a server without having to know where it is or how to start it.

Method   An operation on an object. *See also* Marlon Brando.

Mutual Exclusion   A method used to prevent multiple threads from affecting the same chunk of data.

Naming Service   Any of a number of services that map names to values (DNS, CORBA Naming Service, RMI Registry).

Object Reference   A pointer to an object.

ODBC   Open Database Connectivity. Microsoft-created paradigm and API for communicating with databases. JDBC uses it as a base for interacting with databases from Java applications.

OLE   Object Linking and Embedding. A proprietary Microsoft protocol for interobject communication.

ORB   Object Request Broker. Component of the CORBA environment that routes requests from the client to the server.

OSI   Open Systems Interconnection. A reference model for a layered approach to networking.

Orbix   Iona Technologies' industry-leading entry in the CORBA market.

RSA   RSA Data Security, Inc. One of the patent holders for public key encryption algorithms. RSA usually refers to the specific algorithm.

Serialization   The act of transforming a Java object into a string representation.

Server   Program that accepts invocations from objects at a remote location.

Servlet   A component of the Java Web Server that allows you to create executable programs on the server side of an HTTP connection.

SET   Secure Electronic Transaction. Major credit card vendors' proposal for secure electronic commerce.

Socket   Fundamental tool for network communication. Defines endpoints of communication, the origin of the message, and the destination of the message.

SQL   Structured Query Language. The language most commonly used to construct database queries.

SSL   Secure Socket Layer. Web browser functionality that provides encryption of data across a network.

Streams   A flow of data from which you can get information or to which you can add information.

String Tokenizer   A construct that allows you to search through a string, extracting parts delimited by a token or set of tokens.

Sun   Cool company responsible for the Java programming language.

Swing   The other windowing toolkit supplied with the JDK. It uses 100% Java components to produce user interfaces that are OS independent.

Synchronized   Java's version of a mutual exclusion lock.

TCP   Transmission Control Protocol. Socket protocol for point-to-point communication.

Thread   A series of executable steps that are executed along with other steps.

Three-Tier Computing   The philosophy of splitting the client application from the data, using a middle tier called a server. The server routes requests from one or more clients to the data source and sends information back to it.

UDP   User Datagram Protocol (sometimes called Unreliable Datagram Protocol). Socket for broadcast communication.

Vector   Complex Java data type that allows you to store and retrieve information easily in an arraylike construct.

Virtual Machine   Software component of Java that translates Java bytecode into native code that can then be executed on a machine.

VisiBroker   Imprise's CORBA ORB product. Bundled as part of the Netscape Communicator.

Index

A

abstract base class, 8
abstract keyword, 8
Abstract Window Toolkit (AWT), 9,
    15–16, 260, 261, 323
    event handling, 262
Access control structure, extending,
    352
Access database, 99, 104, 109
    creating, 105, 117–18
access errors, 18
activatable objects, 167–68
ActiveX, 283–85
    controls, 285
    and Java, 285–86
addObject method, 326
Address Resolution Protocol (ARP),
    47–48
Administration Runtime Module
    (ARM), 328, 329

Admin View Model (AVM), 323
    base classes, 323
    help classes, 323–24
Allaire Cold Fusion, 250
AlreadyBoundException, 136
Any type, 182
applets
    versus application, 132
    download performance of,
        31–32
application programming interfaces
    (APIs), 1
    JDBC, 101
    servlet, 230–32
application servers, 289–95, 379–80
    automatic fail-over, 294
    scalability through load balancing,
        294
    support of Enterprise Java Beans
        specification, 295

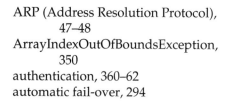

LICENSE AGREEMENT AND LIMITED WARRANTY

READ THE FOLLOWING TERMS AND CONDITIONS CAREFULLY BEFORE OPENING THIS SOFTWARE PACKAGE. THIS LEGAL DOCUMENT IS AN AGREEMENT BETWEEN YOU AND PRENTICE-HALL, INC. (THE "COMPANY"). BY OPENING THIS SEALED SOFTWARE PACKAGE, YOU ARE AGREEING TO BE BOUND BY THESE TERMS AND CONDITIONS. IF YOU DO NOT AGREE WITH THESE TERMS AND CONDITIONS, DO NOT OPEN THE SOFT-WARE PACKAGE. PROMPTLY RETURN THE UNOPENED SOFTWARE PACKAGE AND ALL ACCOMPANYING ITEMS TO THE PLACE YOU OBTAINED THEM FOR A FULL REFUND OF ANY SUMS YOU HAVE PAID.

1. **GRANT OF LICENSE:** In consideration of your payment of the license fee, which is part of the price you paid for this product, and your agreement to abide by the terms and conditions of this Agreement, the Company grants to you a nonexclusive right to use and display the copy of the enclosed software program (hereinafter the "SOFTWARE") on a single computer (i.e., with a single CPU) at a single location so long as you comply with the terms of this Agreement. The Company reserves all rights not expressly granted to you under this Agreement.

2. **OWNERSHIP OF SOFTWARE:** You own only the magnetic or physical media (the enclosed disks) on which the SOFTWARE is recorded or fixed, but the Company retains all the rights, title, and ownership to the SOFTWARE recorded on the original disk copy(ies) and all subsequent copies of the SOFTWARE, regardless of the form or media on which the original or other copies may exist. This license is not a sale of the original SOFTWARE or any copy to you.

3. **COPY RESTRICTIONS:** This SOFTWARE and the accompanying printed materials and user manual (the "Documentation") are the subject of copyright. You may not copy the Documentation or the SOFTWARE, except that you may make a single copy of the SOFTWARE for backup or archival purposes only. You may be held legally responsible for any copying or copyright infringement which is caused or encouraged by your failure to abide by the terms of this restriction.

4. **USE RESTRICTIONS:** You may not network the SOFTWARE or otherwise use it on more than one computer or computer terminal at the same time. You may physically transfer the SOFTWARE from one computer to another provided that the SOFTWARE is used on only one computer at a time. You may not distribute copies of the SOFTWARE or Documentation to others. You may not reverse engineer, disassemble, decompile, modify, adapt, translate, or create derivative works based on the SOFTWARE or the Documentation without the prior written consent of the Company.

5. **TRANSFER RESTRICTIONS:** The enclosed SOFTWARE is licensed only to you and may not be transferred to any one else without the prior written consent of the Company. Any unauthorized transfer of the SOFTWARE shall result in the immediate termination of this Agreement.

6. **TERMINATION:** This license is effective until terminated. This license will terminate automatically without notice from the Company and become null and void if you fail to comply with any provisions or limitations of this license. Upon termination, you shall destroy the Documentation and all copies of the SOFTWARE. All provisions of this Agreement as to warranties, limitation of liability, remedies or damages, and our ownership rights shall survive termination.

7. **MISCELLANEOUS:** This Agreement shall be construed in accordance with the laws of the United States of America and the State of New York and shall benefit the Company, its affiliates, and assignees.

8. **LIMITED WARRANTY AND DISCLAIMER OF WARRANTY:** The Company warrants that the SOFTWARE, when properly used in accordance with the Documentation, will operate in

substantial conformity with the description of the SOFTWARE set forth in the Documentation. The Company does not warrant that the SOFTWARE will meet your requirements or that the operation of the SOFTWARE will be uninterrupted or error-free. The Company warrants that the media on which the SOFTWARE is delivered shall be free from defects in materials and workmanship under normal use for a period of thirty (30) days from the date of your purchase. Your only remedy and the Company's only obligation under these limited warranties is, at the Company's option, return of the warranted item for a refund of any amounts paid by you or replacement of the item. Any replacement of SOFTWARE or media under the warranties shall not extend the original warranty period. The limited warranty set forth above shall not apply to any SOFTWARE which the Company determines in good faith has been subject to misuse, neglect, improper installation, repair, alteration, or damage by you. EXCEPT FOR THE EXPRESSED WARRANTIES SET FORTH ABOVE, THE COMPANY DISCLAIMS ALL WARRANTIES, EXPRESS OR IMPLIED, INCLUDING WITHOUT LIMITATION, THE IMPLIED WARRANTIES OF MERCHANTABILITY AND FITNESS FOR A PARTICULAR PURPOSE. EXCEPT FOR THE EXPRESS WARRANTY SET FORTH ABOVE, THE COMPANY DOES NOT WARRANT, GUARANTEE, OR MAKE ANY REPRESENTATION REGARDING THE USE OR THE RESULTS OF THE USE OF THE SOFTWARE IN TERMS OF ITS CORRECTNESS, ACCURACY, RELIABILITY, CURRENTNESS, OR OTHERWISE.

IN NO EVENT, SHALL THE COMPANY OR ITS EMPLOYEES, AGENTS, SUPPLIERS, OR CONTRACTORS BE LIABLE FOR ANY INCIDENTAL, INDIRECT, SPECIAL, OR CONSEQUENTIAL DAMAGES ARISING OUT OF OR IN CONNECTION WITH THE LICENSE GRANTED UNDER THIS AGREEMENT, OR FOR LOSS OF USE, LOSS OF DATA, LOSS OF INCOME OR PROFIT, OR OTHER LOSSES, SUSTAINED AS A RESULT OF INJURY TO ANY PERSON, OR LOSS OF OR DAMAGE TO PROPERTY, OR CLAIMS OF THIRD PARTIES, EVEN IF THE COMPANY OR AN AUTHORIZED REPRESENTATIVE OF THE COMPANY HAS BEEN ADVISED OF THE POSSIBILITY OF SUCH DAMAGES. IN NO EVENT SHALL LIABILITY OF THE COMPANY FOR DAMAGES WITH RESPECT TO THE SOFTWARE EXCEED THE AMOUNTS ACTUALLY PAID BY YOU, IF ANY, FOR THE SOFTWARE.

SOME JURISDICTIONS DO NOT ALLOW THE LIMITATION OF IMPLIED WARRANTIES OR LIABILITY FOR INCIDENTAL, INDIRECT, SPECIAL, OR CONSEQUENTIAL DAMAGES, SO THE ABOVE LIMITATIONS MAY NOT ALWAYS APPLY. THE WARRANTIES IN THIS AGREEMENT GIVE YOU SPECIFIC LEGAL RIGHTS AND YOU MAY ALSO HAVE OTHER RIGHTS WHICH VARY IN ACCORDANCE WITH LOCAL LAW.

ACKNOWLEDGMENT

YOU ACKNOWLEDGE THAT YOU HAVE READ THIS AGREEMENT, UNDERSTAND IT, AND AGREE TO BE BOUND BY ITS TERMS AND CONDITIONS. YOU ALSO AGREE THAT THIS AGREEMENT IS THE COMPLETE AND EXCLUSIVE STATEMENT OF THE AGREEMENT BETWEEN YOU AND THE COMPANY AND SUPERSEDES ALL PROPOSALS OR PRIOR AGREEMENTS, ORAL, OR WRITTEN, AND ANY OTHER COMMUNICATIONS BETWEEN YOU AND THE COMPANY OR ANY REPRESENTATIVE OF THE COMPANY RELATING TO THE SUBJECT MATTER OF THIS AGREEMENT.

Should you have any questions concerning this Agreement or if you wish to contact the Company for any reason, please contact in writing at the address below.

Robin Short
Prentice Hall PTR
One Lake Street
Upper Saddle River, New Jersey 07458

About the CD-ROM

The CD-ROM included with *Advanced Java Networking, 2nd Edition*, contains the source code for example programs in the book.

The CD-ROM can be used with Linux , Sun Solaris, Microsoft Windows® 95/98/NT.

License Agreement

Use of the software accompanying *Advanced Java Networking* is subject to the terms of the License Agreement and Limited Warranty, found on the previous two pages.

Technical Support

Prentice Hall does not offer technical support for any of the programs on the CD-ROM. However, if the CD-ROM is damaged, you may obtain a replacement copy by sending an email that describes the problem to: disc_exchange@prenhall.com.